ORIGINAL NARRATIVES
OF EARLY AMERICAN HISTORY

REPRODUCED UNDER THE AUSPICES OF THE
AMERICAN HISTORICAL ASSOCIATION

GENERAL EDITOR, J. FRANKLIN JAMESON, PH.D., LL.D.

DIRECTOR OF THE DEPARTMENT OF HISTORICAL RESEARCH IN THE
CARNEGIE INSTITUTION OF WASHINGTON

JOURNAL OF JASPER DANCKAERTS

1679—1680

ORIGINAL NARRATIVES
OF EARLY AMERICAN HISTORY

———

JOURNAL OF
JASPER DANCKAERTS

1679—1680

EDITED BY

BARTLETT BURLEIGH JAMES, B.D., Ph.D.
OF THE MARYLAND HISTORICAL SOCIETY

AND

J. FRANKLIN JAMESON, Ph.D., LL.D.
DIRECTOR OF THE DEPARTMENT OF HISTORICAL RESEARCH IN THE
CARNEGIE INSTITUTION OF WASHINGTON

WITH A FACSIMILE AND TWO MAPS

CHARLES SCRIBNER'S SONS
NEW YORK

CONTENTS

JOURNAL OF JASPER DANCKAERTS

Edited by Bartlett Burleigh James and J. Franklin Jameson

v

34914

CONTENTS

MAPS AND FACSIMILE REPRODUCTION

NOTE A

THE present translation is substantially that of Mr. Henry C. Murphy, as presented in his edition of 1867 (see the Introduction, *post*). Mr. Murphy was an excellent Dutch scholar. Careful comparisons have been made, at various points, between his translation and the original manuscript, of which the Long Island Historical Society, its present possessor, kindly permitted an examination to be made. These comparisons, made partly by the general editor of the series and partly by Mr. S. G. Nissensen of New York (to whom cordial thanks are rendered), showed that Mr. Murphy's translation was in the main excellent. Some revision and correction of it has been effected by Mr. Nissensen and by the general editor. In particular the spelling of the proper names has been brought into accord with that of the original manuscript, except that certain familiar names, after being once given in the original spelling, have thereafter been put into their modern forms.

Danckaerts's descriptions of his Atlantic voyages to America and back, especially the former, are excessively long, and at times tedious. It has been found possible to omit some portions of these without impairing the interest or value of the narrative or excluding any useful information.

Of the three illustrations, the frontispiece is a photographic reproduction of one of Danckaerts's pen-and-ink sketches accompanying the diary. It has never before been photographically reproduced, though lithographed in Mr. Murphy's book. It represents New York from the southeast, as seen in 1680 from Brooklyn Heights, and is obviously of great interest, being topographically accurate, and drawn with no slight degree of skill. Thanks are due to the Long Island Historical Society for permission to reproduce it, and to the society's secretary, Miss Emma J. Toedteberg.

That portion of the journal which relates to the Delaware River and northeastern Maryland is illustrated by a photographic reproduction of the northeast corner of the celebrated map of Maryland which Augustine Herrman made for Lord Baltimore, and which was published in 1673 (see *infra*, p. 114 and p. 297, note 2). The portion reproduced extends from the falls of the Delaware as far down the eastern shore of Chesapeake Bay as our travellers went. It is photographed from the photolithographic copy made from the unique original in the British Museum by Mr. P. Lee Phillips, and published by him in 1912, but is reduced to dimensions about two-thirds of those of the original.

To illustrate the North River journey of the diarist, and the other parts of his narrative centring around New York, a section is presented of the map of 1671 entitled "Novi Belgii, quod nunc Novi Jorck vocatur, Novaeque Angliae et Partis Virginiae Accuratissima et Novissima Delineatio" (Most Accurate and Newest Delineation of New Belgium, now called New York, of New England, and of Part of Virginia). This map appeared both in Montanus's *Nieuwe en Onbekende Weereld* (Amsterdam, 1671) and in Ogilby's *America* (London, 1671). It is N. J. Visscher's map of 1655 or 1656 (for which see the volume in this series entitled *Narratives of Early Pennsylvania*, etc., introductory note, and map opposite p. 170), with slight alterations made in order to adapt it more closely to the date 1671.

For the names of the two Labadist agents, Mr. Murphy adopted the forms Dankers and Sluyter. These he apparently took from references to them by others, for the journal, except once in the case of Sluyter, gives only the assumed names, Schilders and Vorstman, by which alone they were at first known in America. Domine Selyns of New York, in his letter to Willem à Brakel,[1] gives their true names. For the proper spelling of the diarist's name, it should seem that we should rely on his own signature to his note prefixed to his copy of Eliot's Indian Old Testament.[2] There the spelling is Danckaerts, and such is the form used by the family, still or till lately extant in Zeeland. But the form Dankers occurs often in contemporary references.

The case of his companion presents no difficulty. The register of students at the University of Leyden, *Album Studiosorum Academiae*

[1] Murphy, *Anthology of New Netherland*, p. 95.
[2] See *infra*, p. 264, note 2.

Lugduno-Batavae (Hague, 1875), gives, under date of 1666, "Petrus Sluyter Vesaliensis, 21, T," *i. e.*, Peter Sluyter of Wesel, 21 years old, student of theology, which no doubt is our traveller, known to have studied theology and, from Labadist sources relating to Herford, to have come originally from Wesel. Our traveller's will, dated January 20, 1722, the original of which is preserved in the court house of Cecil County at Elkton, Maryland, is signed in autograph, "Petrus Sluyter alias Vorsman," and it seems that this must be regarded as authoritative. The Maryland family descended from the Labadist leader's brother used the same spelling. Schluter is found in some contemporary sources, Schluyter and Sluter in others,[1] while on the title-page of a book translated by our traveller from French into Dutch, and printed at Herford in 1672,[2] presumably under his eye, the spelling is Sluiter. But his signature should be conclusive.

The annotations in this volume are by the general editor of the series.

J. F. J.

[1] *a.* Paul Hackenberg's letter, see p. 291, note 2, *post;* Willem à Brakel, *Trouwhertige Waerschouwinge* (Leeuwarden, 1683), p. 63; *Album Acad. Lugd.-Bat.*, 1650, "Henricus Schluterus," the brother. *b.* Brakel in Murphy's *Anthology*, p. 95. *c.* Letter from Herford in Schotel, *Anna Maria van Schurman* (Hertogenbosch, 1853), app., p. 40.

[2] *Verklaringe van de Suiverheid des Geloofs en der Leere van Jean de Labadie.*

INTRODUCTION

In the year 1864 Mr. Henry C. Murphy, then corresponding secretary of the Long Island Historical Society, had the good fortune to find in an old book-store in Amsterdam a manuscript whose bearings upon the history of the middle group of American colonies made it, when translated and made accessible as a publication in the Memoirs of the Long Island Historical Society,[1] an historical document of much interest and value. The Journal of two members of the Labadist sect who came over to this country in order to find a location for the establishment of a community has served to throw a flood of light upon what otherwise might have been a lost chapter in the history of Maryland. For so meagre are the sources of ready availability for a knowledge of the Labadist colony which was effected in Maryland that without this account the story of the first communal sect in America might have failed of adequate recording.

But while the Journal of Jasper Danckaerts and Peter Sluyter, the two envoys—or of Jasper Danckaerts, who did the actual writing —is of especial interest in relation to an incident in the early settlement of Maryland, the gauge of its value may be applied as well in other directions. This extended narrative, often discursive and circumstantial, contains much that is suggestive upon the beginnings of the middle group of states, and, indeed, the narrative bears upon facts of importance in connection with Massachusetts as well.

The original manuscript of the Labadist narrators is now in the possession of the Long Island Historical Society. It was bought by the Society at the Murphy sale in 1884. It is written in a fine, good hand on paper of about 8½ by 6½ inches. The pages are numbered with three successive numberings: (A) 1–72, (B) 1–16, 25–192, 217–231, (C) 1–47, the first section corresponding to the voyage to

[1] Volume I. *Journal of a Voyage to New York and a Tour in Several of the American Colonies in 1679–80, by Jasper Dankers and Peter Sluyter of Wiewerd in Friesland* (Brooklyn, 1867).

America; the second, to the travels in the middle colonies; the third, to the experiences of the journalist and his companion in New England and on the voyage home. In the second division there is no gap between pages 16 and 25, but after page 192 there is a considerable hiatus. In narrative, this extends over a few days only, June 13–19, but the omitted portion probably also contained a description of the city of New York and the beginning of an account of the Indians. The remaining pages of this section, pages 216–231, proceed with this account, treating of the weapons of the Indians, their treaties with the whites, their intelligence, their burial customs, their virtues and vices, their knowledge of God and their worship, and finally of the beaver and his habits. As the journalist could have had no original contributions to make with regard to the American aborigines, his observations upon this subject have no especial value, and have been omitted.

The manuscript when found was accompanied with six sheets of pen-and-ink drawings. The text appears to be a carefully transcribed copy, plainly written in a different handwriting from that of the drawings. The latter, as the marks upon them show, are the original sketches made upon the spot. All are reproduced in Mr. Murphy's edition of the journal. The first shows the figure of an Indian woman and four fishes, two of them rare and two common. The second drawing shows the entrance to New York Bay at Sandy Hook as seen from the house of Jacques Cortelyou at Nayack (Fort Hamilton). The third is a detailed and exceedingly interesting view of New York as it was in 1679, taken from Brooklyn Heights; it is reproduced in the present volume. The fourth and fifth give views of New York from the east and from the north, while the sixth plate presents a map of the Delaware River from the Falls at the present site of Trenton down to Burlington.

The manuscript of the narrative reproduced in this volume is accompanied by a similar manuscript for a second voyage made in 1683, April 12–July 27, entered upon 16 pages of foolscap, and then copied upon 48 pages of quarto size, the former in a different and much more difficult hand than the journal of 1679–1680, the copy in a handwriting similar to that of the latter. Twelve pages of the 48 are verses, and the remainder do not carry the traveller beyond the completion of his voyage. As this second narrative includes nothing bearing directly upon the experiences of the chronicler after his arrival upon the shores of the New World, it has not seemed worth while to translate it and bring it into the present volume. It is much to be regretted that the continuation was never written, or has not been preserved, since it would record the actual settlement of the Labadist community in northeastern Maryland. With the fragment was found an interesting manuscript map of the Delaware River, which gives Philadelphia as in existence, and therefore belongs to the period of the second voyage.

Prior to the discovery of the Journal of Danckaerts it was indeed traditionally known that a sect of Labadists in the first half of the seventeenth century had located a colony on the estates of Augustine Herrman in Maryland. There were fragmentary references to these people in the early records of the state and in historical manuscripts, with isolated notices in contemporary writers. Yet this information would of itself have been too meagre for a critical valuation of the Labadists in the early history of Maryland. The publication of the manuscript secured by Mr. Murphy stimulated interest in the subject, and at various times monographic contributions appeared upon one or another phase of the Labadist settlement. Notable were those of General James Grant Wilson, whose paper on "An Old Maryland Manor" was published by the Maryland Historical Society in 1890, and his paper on "Augustine Herrman, Bohemian," by the New Jersey Historical Society in the same year, and of Reverend Charles Payson Mallary, whose monograph on the *Ancient Families of Bohemia Manor*, a publication of the Delaware Historical Society in 1888, disclosed the wide genealogical interest pertaining to the Labadist settlement. Thus there was built up a body of substantial information with regard to the environment and the relations of the Labadist colony in the New World. In 1899 was published, in the Johns Hopkins University Studies in Historical and Political Science, *The Labadist Colony in Maryland*, by the writer of the present introduction. This monograph was largely based upon fresh sources obtained from Europe, including contemporary works by Labadie, his associates and his antagonists, as well as studies of the subject by Dutch and German scholars. The literature of Labadism in the New World, which, in a manner, has been an outgrowth from the journal of the Labadist envoys, is now ample for all serviceable purposes.

The journal of the Labadists, while primarily of value as elucidating an obscure episode in the religious history of the New World, has worth as a human narrative bearing upon incidents and personages and social conditions in New York, New Jersey, Delaware, Maryland, and Boston. Thus the student of social, economic, institutional, or geographical conditions in the early period of the settlements upon the Atlantic seaboard will find in this journal much of suggestive and pertinent contribution. Danckaerts viewed his surroundings through the eyes of a fanatical self-satisfaction. For this reason his criticisms or strictures upon persons and conditions are to be received with much discount. But he was an intelligent man, and a keen-eyed and assiduous note-taker; and the variety and fecundity of his material is not a little due to the trivial and relatively unimportant details which are embodied in the narrative.

The two agents came to North America in search of a suitable place to establish a colony of their sect. Two distinct sets of forces drew them toward Maryland. One of these was the religious toleration which, from the beginning, was established in that province. There is no warrant in the journal for a presumption that this was an inducing cause for their location within the domain of Lord Baltimore. There is much, however, in their antecedent history, and the pressure of persecution to which the Labadists were subjected, to make it exceedingly probable that this policy in the government of Maryland formed a circumstance in the selection that was made. The journalists, who travelled under pseudonyms for the express purpose of keeping their mission secret, might have established their colony in New York had it not been under the rule of Governor Andros, a Catholic, and therefore a subject of particular antipathy to the Labadists.

But the practical weave of circumstance that tended to attract the Labadists to Maryland centred in the fact that, as stated in their narrative, they met in New York one Ephraim Herrman, a young trader from Maryland and Delaware, then recently married. This was the son of Augustine Herrman, "first founder and seater of

Bohemia Manor." Augustine Herrman was a Bohemian adventurer, born in Prague, who, after a career of much vicissitude, made his way to New Netherland. He became a force at New Amsterdam, and was an original member of the council of nine men instituted by Governor Stuyvesant in 1647. His connection with Maryland matters dates from his appointment by Governor Stuyvesant as a special commissioner, along with Resolved Waldron, to negotiate with Governor Fendall of Maryland concerning the eastern boundary of Lord Baltimore's province.[1] This mission effected, Herrman entered into negotiations with Lord Baltimore for the drafting of a map of Maryland and Virginia, which would be valuable to his lordship in bringing to a settlement the boundary dispute pending between the two colonies, and in other ways.[2] In this manner Herrman became invested with not less than 24,000 acres of the most desirable lands of what is now Cecil County, Maryland, and Newcastle County, Delaware, which he divided into several tracts under the names Bohemia Manor, St. Augustine Manor, Little Bohemia, and the Three Bohemia Sisters. It is of interest to note that among the acts passed by the Maryland Assembly is one dated 1666, which provides for the naturalization of "Augustine Herman of Prague, in the Kingdom of Bohemia, Ephraim Georgius and Casparus, Sonns to the said Augustine, Anna Margarita, Judith and Francina, his daughters," this being the first act of naturalization passed by any of the colonies.[3]

It was upon Bohemia Manor that the Labadists located their colony. Danckaerts and Sluyter, under the guidance of Ephraim Herrman, made their way to Delaware and Maryland. Upon meeting them the elder Herrman was at first so favorably impressed that he consented to deed to them a considerable tract, in pursuance of his ambition to colonize and develop his estates. On June 19, 1680, the Labadists, having accomplished their mission, set sail for Boston, to which fact are due such interesting recitals as that of their visit to John Eliot, the so-called apostle to the Indians, and their visit to

---

[1] Journal of the Dutch Embassy to Maryland, 1659, by Augustine Herrman, in *Narratives of Early Maryland*, in this series, pp. 309–333.

[2] A copy of this map is in the British Museum. No other is known.

[3] *Maryland Archives*, II. 144.

and description of Harvard College. On the 23d day of July the
Labadists set sail for Europe.

In 1683 the two Labadists returned again to Maryland, bringing
with them the nucleus of a colony. In the meanwhile Augustine
Herrman had repented of his bargain, and it was only by recourse
to law that the Labadists compelled him to live up to its terms. The
deed he executed, dated August 11, 1684, was to Peter Sluyter (alias
Vorstman), Jasper Dankers (alias Schilders), of Friesland, Petrus
Bayard, of New York, and John Moll and Arnold de la Grange.[1]
The tract conveyed embraced four necks of land eastwardly from the
first creek that empties into Bohemia River, and extended at the
north or northeast to near the old St. Augustine or Manor Church.
It contained 3,750 acres. Those engaging with Sluyter and Danckaerts in the transaction were all professed converts to the Labadist
faith. It may be noted in passing that the Petrus Bayard named in
the conveyance, and who for some time was an active member of the
Labadist community, was an ancestor of the late Thomas F. Bayard,
ambassador at the Court of St. James.

When fairly settled upon Bohemia Manor, the Labadists undertook communal modes of life and industry, such as characterized
them at the European centre of the church, which was Wieuwerd, in
Friesland. They cultivated tobacco extensively, and engaged in the
culture of corn, flax, and hemp, and in cattle-raising. Their expressed zeal for the conversion of the Indians did not take any practical form. At its most flourishing period the colony did not number
as many as a hundred persons, and in the year 1698 a division of the
tract occurred. Sluyter, who was the active head of the colony,
reserved for himself one of the necks of land and became wealthy.
He died in 1722. Some form of organization had been maintained
among the Labadists even after the division of the land, but five
years after the death of Sluyter the Labadists had ceased to exist as
a community. The division in 1698 which marked the disintegration
of the community occurred at about the same time as a similar division of the estates of the mother church at Wieuwerd. There the
disintegration came about through consultative action; in Maryland, by the logic of events.

[1] Baltimore County Land Records.

The founder of the system of religion which came to be known as Labadism, Jean de Labadie, was born in France, at Bourg near Bordeaux, on February 13, 1610. His father was a French noble and a soldier of fortune, who rose to be governor of Guienne. His parents entered him at the Jesuit College, where he completed his novitiate and took the first vows, and in 1635 he was ordained as a priest. Early manifestations of an erratic temperament, a mystical habit of mind, and physical frailty, led to his severance from the Society of Jesus. He entered upon a preaching mission, and, coming under the attention of Père Gondran, second general of the Congregation of the Oratory at Paris, he received a call to that city, and, according to his own statement, the entire body of the Sorbonne united in the call.

Labadie soon acquired a fame that went beyond the borders of France, for oratorical ability and theological precision. His former associates, the Jesuits, originated stories against his morality and sought to bring him into trouble with the authorities. The attacks to which he was subjected led him to adopt a broad though wholly fanatical scheme of reforms for the Church.[1] During the lifetime of Cardinal Richelieu, who befriended him, he was safe from attack, but upon the succession of Cardinal Mazarin the Jesuits obtained an order of the court for his arrest, the execution of which was prevented by the death of the king. In the year 1645 he was cited to appear at court along with his friend, the Bishop of Amiens, and was sentenced to perpetual imprisonment, which sentence was modified on an appeal made by the assembly of the clergy of France then in session. He was, however, ordered to renounce his opinions and to refrain from preaching for a period of years. In one of his treatises he states that during a second forced retirement he obtained and read a copy of Calvin's *Institutes*. This had a determining influence upon his after career.[2] He summed up the result of his solitary reflections in the words, "This is the last time that Rome shall persecute me in her communion. Up to the present I have endeavored to help and to heal her, remaining within her jurisdiction; but now it is full time for me to denounce her and to testify against her."

[1] *Déclaration de la Foi*, pp. 84, 122, 123.
[2] *Traité de la Solitude Chrétienne.*

At Montauban in 1650 Labadie abjured his former faith and was later ordained a Protestant minister. According to Mollerus[1] the acquisition of the widely famous preacher was heralded as the greatest Protestant triumph since the days of Calvin. Banished from France in 1657, Labadie preached for two years at Orange (then independent) and for seven years at Geneva, whence he was called to the pastorate of the Walloon Reformed Church in Middelburg, Zeeland. At Middelburg he became embroiled with the ecclesiastical and civil authorities, because of controversial writings and because, filled with zeal to reform the Reformed Church in the Netherlands and to awaken it from its formalism, he carried his own congregation into positions and practices manifestly tending toward schism. Driven out of Middelburg, he established a church at Veere, which he styled the Evangelical. The States of Zeeland kept the troublesome preacher on the move, and Labadie journeyed to Amsterdam, where he had an opportunity to establish a communal society, of which the chief ornament was Anna Maria van Schurman of Utrecht, famed as the most learned woman of her day.[2]

The church at Amsterdam grew and prospered, and overtures were received from many sectaries, including the Society of Friends, all of which Labadie declined to consider. It may here be remarked that similar overtures made by representatives of the Society of Friends to the colony later established in Maryland were likewise unfruitful. Certain disorders arising, the civil authorities placed such restrictions upon the church at Amsterdam that another removal became expedient. At this juncture, in 1670, an invitation was received from the Princess Elizabeth, eldest daughter of Frederick V., Elector Palatine and King of Bohemia, and granddaughter of King James I. of England. Elizabeth[3] was Protestant abbess of Herford in Westphalia, and placed quarters in that town at the disposal of the Labadists, but on account of certain religious excesses and the suspicions aroused in the minds of townspeople and neighbors, the Imperial Diet caused the Labadists to remove. Some of

---

[1] *Cimbria Litterata*, III. 37.

[2] Her *Eukleria seu Melioris Partis Electio* (Altona, 1673) is perhaps the chief authority for the history of the Labadists from this point on.

[3] For this princess, see Guhrauer's article in the *Historisches Taschenbuch* for 1850, and Miss Elizabeth Godfrey's *A Sister of Prince Rupert*.

them tarried for a while at Bremen but the majority sought refuge immediately at Altona, then under the King of Denmark, in 1672. At this place, in February, 1674, Labadie died. His death evoked estimates of his work and worth from high ecclesiastical sources, and much of this was of a laudatory nature. The Dutch historians are disposed to regard Labadie's chief work the leavening of the old lump by the many hundreds of his converts inspired with his evangelical zeal, who remained in connection with the Reformed Church.[1]

The next removal of the Labadists was to Wieuwerd in Friesland, the northernmost of the Dutch provinces, where they were established under the lead of Pierre Yvon on an estate called Thetinga or Waltha House, which was tendered to them by three ladies devotedly attached to their teachings, the three youngest daughters of the great diplomatist Francis Aarsen, Lord of Sommelsdyk. Here the communal sect attained its full measure of strength, declined, and died. For more than half a century Wieuwerd was the seat of the new church and from it feeble colonies were established at various centres. From Wieuwerd proceeded the colonists who settled in Maryland, and from Wieuwerd proceeded the voice of authority that controlled these colonists. The final disruption of the Labadists at Wieuwerd was due largely to the inevitable difficulties that have beset and destroyed almost every experiment in the establishment of an industrial community upon a footing of religion.

The system of faith and practice which came to fruition at Wieuwerd and was transplanted to the New World, did not have the catholicity necessary for adaptation to the conditions of an undeveloped country. Labadism, theologically, belonged to the school of Calvin; in its spirit it was in line with the vein of mysticism which is met throughout the history of the Christian Church. In general respects the theology of Labadism was that of the Reformed Church of the Netherlands. Like so many other adventitious but zealous movements, Labadism centred in its millennial hopes. These, however, were rather an expression of the spirit of pietism which pervaded

[1] H. van Berkum, *De Labadie en de Labadisten* (Sneek, 1851), II. 170 *et seq.* The history of the sect can be followed in Van Berkum, in the first volume of Ritschl's *Geschichte des Pietismus* (Bonn, 1880), and in Ypeij and Dermout, *Geschiedenis der Nederlandsche Hervormde Kerk* (Breda, 1827), vol. III.

the doctrines of the church than a fundamental positive proposition. Labadism, theologically, recognized a scheme of covenants
extending from Adam to Christ. The symbols of the last covenant
were baptism and the Lord's Supper. The church was to be a community of the elect kept separate from the world by its pure teachings.

The Labadists taught rigidly the doctrine of the separation of
the believer from the unbeliever, and to this is attributable the communal mode of life they adopted. The rule of the sect made it necessary for a husband and wife to separate if either were not of the
elect church, which came to be synonymous with the church of the
Labadists. In compliance with this rule, a number of the converts
to the faith in Maryland separated from wives or husbands. This
was the case with Petrus Bayard, who later returned to his wife, and
with Ephraim Herrman.

The Labadists came close to the Friends in their doctrine of the
law of the spirit as being the only law to which they were to yield
final subjection. They conceived this law to nullify the ceremonial
system of the Old Testament, and even to reduce to a place of inci-
dental importance specific moral injunctions. Sabbath observance
was not fundamental, and while the reading of the Bible was a medium
of communication by God's spirit, its importance was secondary to
the immediate movements of the spirit. The works of the Labadists
disclose a high form of faith and aspiration, but vitiated by many
visionary and impracticable features, in Maryland by the mercenary
instincts of their leader, Sluyter. Nor was the general state of religion in Maryland at the time of their experiment such as to foster
a profoundly pietistical community. Some of the members of the
Labadist community acquired prominence in Maryland affairs, and
their company of thrifty and industrious persons, bent upon illus-
trating the virtues of religion, must have done good, however far
they may have fallen short of their ideals; but of the personality of
most of them we know little or nothing.[1]

While the Journal of the Labadists has particular bearing upon
Maryland by reason of the location within its bounds of the colony

---

[1] An interesting description of the life of the community on Bohemia Manor
is given in *An Account of the Life, Travels, and Christian Experiences in the Work
of the Ministry by Samuel Bownas* (London, 1756).

of the sectaries, the recital brings into the range of vivid and intimate knowledge some of the leading characters in the contemporary life of several of the sister colonies, and it has been recognized as a valuable aid to students of the early period of New York.

There are no material remains of the Labadists in this country. They did not affect either the institutions or the spirit of their times, nor leave memorials behind them. That Augustine Herrman's sentiments towards the strange visitants and settlers upon his estate became radically altered, before his death in 1686, is indicated by a codicil in his will in which he directs that certain of his neighbors administer his estate in the place of his son Ephraim, giving as his reason his son's alliance with the Labadists.

The Labadists abroad exerted an appreciable influence upon the life of their times, and did much to infuse a spirit of evangelical earnestness into the Reformed Church of the Netherlands, which, at the rise of Labadism, was formal and pedantic in its modes of worship and given to theological disputation. Labadie has importance in the history of that church, and is accorded honor in its records. The futility of the sect in the New World was due not wholly to its communal form of organization, but is to be attributed as well to the fact that the Labadists migrated in obedience to no high and lofty impulse, but because in their nomadic passage from place to place, under the pressure of religious and civil proscription, due in most cases to acts of insubordination, there seemed no place remaining for them except the shores of the New World. No history of communism can be complete that does not include the experiment entered upon by Jean de Labadie and his followers in the Old World, and by the Labadist colonists in America. It is unfortunate that more complete information with regard to the actual economic value of the Labadist community cannot be had, but such information could not greatly differ from the facts that are well known as to the economic and industrial character of the Maryland population in general.

BARTLETT B. JAMES.

NOTE B

Since Dr. James's introduction was written, I have come upon some facts of interest respecting the two Labadist travellers which were not known to Mr. Murphy, who indeed had practically nothing to say regarding their previous life.

Jasper Danckaerts was born at Flushing in Zeeland May 7, 1639, the son of Pieter Danckaerts and Janneke Schilders—which explains his using Schilders as a pseudonym during his American expedition. He became a cooper in the service of the East India Company at Middelburg.[1] A curious book in which Pierre Yvon, pastor of the Labadist church after Labadie's death, describes the death-bed conduct and speeches of members of the sect, gives us glimpses of the diarist's family life.[2] They may enable us to look more kindly upon that censorious writer. Under date of May, 1676, the pastor commemorates the death of "our sister Susanna Spykershof, wife of our brother Dankers. She came to us at Zonderen" (Sonderen, a temporary stopping-place near Herford) "with her husband, leaving without difficulty her birth-place and dwelling-place Middelburg and all her acquaintances. . . . The trials and dangers they underwent were common to the two. . . . Both were at the same time, at Altona, accepted as members of the body of Christ [the Labadist church]. . . . She loved her husband tenderly, but when God called him elsewhere, to the service of His work and children, she embraced His will therein with much love; which was especially edifying in her, since before this, when she was living in the world, she was wont to

[1] F. Nagtglas, *Levensberichten van Zeeuwen* (Middelburg, 1890), I. 146.
[2] *Getrouw Verhael van den Staet en de laetste Woorden en Dispositien sommiger Personen die God tot sich genomen heeft, uyt de Gereformeerde en van de Werelt afgesonderde Gemeynte, voor desen gegadert tot Herfort en Altena, en tegenwoordig tot Wiewert in Vrieslant* (second ed., in New York Public Library, Amsterdam, 1683), pp. 30–32. The original French, *Fidelle Narré des États et des Dernières Paroles* (Amsterdam, 1681), and an English version (*ibid.*, 1685), are in the British Museum.

be in great anxiety whenever he was away from home on their own concerns. At Bremen, when a portion of our community was there, then at Altona, and here in Friesland, God visited her with great sufferings," and she died at the age of thirty-three, soon after the death of their youngest child.[1]

When Cornelis van Sommelsdyk went out to Surinam as governor in 1683, a body of Labadists sought an asylum there. A little later Danckaerts, after his second voyage to New York, went out with reinforcements to their settlement of La Providence in Dutch Guiana, which soon proved a failure.[2] In 1684 he was naturalized by a Maryland act,[3] but this does not prove that he was then in the province or long remained there. Thereafter he seems to have lived mostly at Wieuwerd, but he died at Middelburg between 1702 and 1704. He left behind him an elaborate manuscript, which he was just about to publish at the time of his death, entitled "Triumf des Hebreeuwsche Bibels" (triumph of the Hebrew Bible over secular chronology) in which he styles himself "Jasper Danckaerts, lover of wisdom, of sacred emblems, history, and theology, at Middelburg in Zeeland." The antiquary from whose book this fact is derived says also, "In 1874 I bought at a book-stall in Middelburg a very neatly written translation of the Psalms, with musical notes, prepared by Danckaerts mostly during his American journey, dated at Wieuwerd, and perhaps revised by Anna Maria van Schurman."[4] This manuscript is now in the library of the Zeeland Academy of Sciences at Middelburg. I am greatly indebted to Mr. W. O. Swaving, librarian of that society, who has kindly furnished me with a copy of the preface

---

[1] See p. 130, note 1, *infra.*

[2] Some writers put the Surinam venture before the voyage of 1679, and it is noticeable that Danckaerts says he has been in the West Indies; p. 61, *infra.* But the little "book of saints" which has just been mentioned says, of a Juffrouw Huyghens, who died in January, 1680, a lady very zealous for the conversion of the Indians, that she said that "if any of us went out thither, she would wish to be one of the first." Evidently no such expedition or migration had yet taken place in 1680; van Sommelsdyk's going out as governor gave the opportunity, he being a brother of their patronesses.

[3] *Maryland Archives,* XIII. 126, also naturalizing Sluyter, Bayard, and de la Grange.

[4] F. Nagtglas, *Levensberichten van Zeeuwen,* I. 146; J. Kok, *Vaderlandsche Woordenboek,* XI. (1708) 41.

to this manuscript, as also of Danckaerts's note on his Indian Bible.[1]

The manuscript is entitled "De CL Psalmen Davids op Nieus volgens de Nederduitschen Text in Nederduits Sangh-Rym gebracht door J. D., Liefhebber der Poësie tot Wiwert in Vrieslant," *i. e.*, "The 150 Psalms of David, translated afresh into Dutch verse in accordance with the Dutch text, by J. D., lover of poetry, at Wieuwerd in Friesland." Explaining the deficiencies of the metrical version by Petrus Dathenus, the writer sets forth his wish to make a better translation (from French into Dutch), and narrates how the opportunity at last arrived "when I found myself called upon for the second time to make a journey to New Netherland in the year 1682–1683. And although such journeys by water and land seem to offer little good opportunity for composition, beyond the keeping of a good journal, yet I began with a good will, and by God's grace pursued and happily finished it. . . . After returning home and revising and correcting it, it was thought advisable to submit it for further revision to the Juffrouw N. N.,[2] which was done, and after two years I received it back with corrections," copied it again, kept it still longer, but then in view of the publication of Hendrick Ghysen's version (1690) found it useless to publish. In the next winter, however, he put it into its present form, for his own use and that of any who might be edified by it. The preface is dated at Wieuwerd, January 8, 1691, and signed Jasper Danckaerts.

With Sluiter we are perhaps somewhat less concerned, but he was a more important figure in the Labadist church. We have seen (Note A) that he came originally from Wesel, was born in 1645, and was studying theology at Leyden in 1666. With his brother Hendrik, who was also educated in theology and had preached at Wesel, he had joined the sect at Herford. His sister Elizabeth had already joined them at Amsterdam. The brother withdrew, the sister remained, and figures in Yvon's hagiology, having died at Altona in 1674, *aet.* 23.[3] Hendrik and Peter were "speaking brothers" in the

---

[1] See p. 264, note 2, *infra*.   [2] Meaning Anna Maria van Schurman.
[3] Schotel, *Anna Maria van Schurman*, app., p. 40; Schurman, *Eukleria*, II. 38; *Getrouw Verhael*, pp. 16–24.

church. Some editions of the Declaration issued at Herford [1] bear
on the title-page, along with the names of Labadie, Yvon, and Du-
lignon as pastors, those of Hendrik and Peter Sluyter as preachers.
Paul Hackenberg found him one of the chief disputants at the time
of his visit.[2]

It seems almost certain that it was Sluyter of whom William Penn
speaks, in his account of his visit to Wieuwerd in 1677, when he had
conferences with the Labadists marked on his part by appreciation
of the affinity between them and the Friends. "With these two," he
says, meaning Anna Maria van Schurman and one of the three ladies
van Sommelsdyk, to whom the estate of Wieuwerd had belonged,
"we had the Company of the Two Pastors [Yvon and Dulignon]
and a Doctor of Physick. . . . After him the Doctor of Physick,
that had been bred for a Priest [Quaker dialect for any minister], but
voluntarily refused that Calling, exprest himself after this Manner:
I can also bear my Testimony in the Presence of God, that tho' I
lived in as much Reputation at the University, as any of my Col-
leagues or Companions, and was well reputed for Sobriety and
Honesty, yet I never felt such a Living Sense of God, as when I heard
the Servant of the Lord J. de Labadie: Adding, The first Day I
heard him, . . . it was to me as the Day of my Salvation; . . . Upon
which I forsook the University, and resolved to be one of this Family."[3]
This corresponds with what we know of "Dr. Vorstman."

Sluyter's later life, to his death in 1722, is sufficiently set forth by
Dr. James. It need only be added that in 1692 Lord Nottingham,
then Secretary of State, writes from Whitehall to Governor Copley
of Maryland that "the King being informed that Mr. Vorsman, Moll,
Danckers, De la Grange, Bayert, and some others . . . do live
peaceably and religiously together upon a plantation on Bohemia
River, and the said persons being in some Respect strangers may at
one time or other stand in need of your particular protection and
favour," His Majesty directs that such protection and favor be ac-

---

[1] See p. 265, note 1, *infra*.   [2] See pp. 168, note 1, and 291, note 2, *infra*.
[3] *Works of William Penn* (London, 1726), I. 90, 91. See also p. 202, note 1,
post. Sluyter is also mentioned as a leading disputant and exhorter by the neighboring minister, Willem à Brakel, in his *Trouwhertige Waerschouwinge voor de
Labadisten* (Leeuwarden, 1683), p. 63.

corded;[1] also that in 1693 and 1695 governors Copley and Nicholson give "Peter Sluyter *alias* Vorsman" license to marry persons, as he "hath made it appear to me that he is an Orthodox Protestant Minister, ordained according to the Maxims of the Reformed Churches in Holland." [2]

J. F. J.

[1] *Maryland Archives*, XX. 163.   [2] *Ibid.*, pp. 398, 399.

JOURNAL OF JASPER DANCKAERTS,
1679-1680

JOURNAL OF JASPER DANCKAERTS,
1679–1680

JOURNAL OF OUR VOYAGE TO NEW NETHERLAND

Begun in the Name of the Lord and for his Glory, the 8th of June, 1679, and undertaken in the small Flute-ship, the Charles of New York, of which Thomas Singelton was Master; but the superior Authority over both Ship and Cargo was in Margriete Flips,[1] who was the Owner of both, and with whom we agreed for our Passage from Amsterdam to New York, in New Netherland, at seventy-five Guilders for each Person, payable in Holland. We had ourselves registered, to wit: I, J. Schilders, and my good friend, P. Vorstman.

ON the eighth of June, 1679, we left home [2] at four o'clock in the morning, taking leave of those with whom God had joined us fast in spirit, they committing us, and we them, with tenderness of heart, unto the gracious protection of the Highest. Although for a time separated in body, we remained most closely united in soul, which is, always and everywhere, but one and the same. We went on foot to Oost[erend], expecting there to take the canal boat, which we did, at six or half past six o'clock, after waiting an hour. We took leave finally of those of our beloved and very worthy friends who had accompanied us, and thus far made it a pleasant journey for us. Our hearts had been strengthened in discoursing, on the road, of God and his will concerning us, and of the disposition and readiness of our hearts, as we then felt, to bear it whatever it might be, although we foresaw that it would be

---

[1] Margaret Filipse. See *post*, p. 5, note 1.

[2] The manor-house of Thetinga, at Wieuwerd in Friesland, about seven miles southwest of Leeuwarden. By walking to Oosterend and a little beyond one found, as the canals then lay, a canal route to the Zuider Zee. The diarist, it will be observed, refrains from naming the place, and gives only the beginnings of the place-names mentioned just below.

3

mortifying enough for us. We arrived at B[olsward] about eight o'clock, where we discovered the reason why there were so few people in the boat and tavern, for by the ringing of the bells we understood that it was a holiday, namely, Ascension Day,[1] which suited us very well, as we thus had an opportunity of being alone in the tavern, and eating out of our knapsack a little breakfast, while waiting for the canal boat to leave. We were greatly pleased, while we were in the tavern, to see several persons there, representatives of the schout,[2] who were going the rounds in all the taverns of the city, to see whether there were any drunkards or whether any other disorderly conduct subject to the penalty of any fine was being practised. When the time arrived, we stepped on board the canal boat, where we found few people: but these passed the whole way in tattling, principally about a certain miser who had died and cheated his friends, leaving them more than they themselves had hoped to find. As our own thoughts were otherwise employed, this talk was very annoying to us. We reached W[orkum][3] before the hour fixed for departure from there, so we went to the Amsterdam packet, on board of which there were different kinds of people, but all wicked. Among them was a family consisting of father, mother and children, who even after the manner of the world were not spoken of much better. They had two daughters of a very easy disposition. We had the good fortune to have the cabin to ourselves, where we could be perfectly accommodated. We left Workum at twelve o'clock with a strong head wind, but it soon became calm, so that it was six o'clock before we passed Enckhuysen.[4]

[1] The chronology needs explanation. Thursday, June 8, 1679, new style (which was the style our travellers observed), was May 29, old style, and May 29, old style, was Ascension Day, the keepers of old style observing Easter this year on (their) April 20, though the keepers of new style observed it on (their) April 2. The new style had been adopted by the province of Holland in 1582, immediately upon its promulgation by Pope Gregory XIII., but in Friesland and the other provinces of the Dutch Republic the old style continued to prevail until 1700.

[2] The chief executive officer of a Dutch town.

[3] A port on the west coast of Friesland, where they took the packet to cross the Zuider Zee to Amsterdam.

[4] An important commercial town in North Holland, on the chief point they would pass on the west side of the Zuider Zee.

We came to anchor before Amsterdam about eleven o'clock at night.

9th, *Friday*. We stepped ashore early and went first to look after our ship, the *Charles*, which we found lying in the stream. When we went aboard, we found some passengers already on the ship. We inquired when they intended to sail. The mate, who like the captain was a Quaker, answered, "to-morrow," that is, Saturday. We went immediately to the house to which our chest had been directed, taking another with us. We lodged there as long as we were at Amsterdam. The proprietor made no objection to deliver us the chest which had arrived before us, upon our receipts which we had brought. This done, we went to Margaret's,[1] to whom we spoke of ourselves, voyage, and purpose, and who showed us some attention. All this was accomplished before noon-time, when we went to our lodgings to brace ourselves up. The house being full of people the whole time, it was very difficult for us, though we obtained a room, to be tolerably alone during the day; but as the people who carry on this business desire to have much money spent, and as it was not for us to do so, we went out a great deal into different parts of the city, and returned there in the evening, where we slept together.

10th, *Saturday*. We performed some errands, and also spoke again to Margaret, inquiring of her when the ship would leave. She answered she had given orders to have everything in readiness to sail to-day, but she herself was of opinion it would not be before Monday. We offered her the money to pay for our passage, but she refused to receive it at that time, saying she was tired and could not be troubled with it that day, about which we passed a little joke with her, and she asked us if we were not of such and such people, who lived at such a place, to which we most of the time answered, yes.[2]

In the afternoon we took on board our chest and what we

---

[1] Margaret Philipse. Frederick Philipse (1626–1702), who in 1674 was listed as the richest man in New York, and later owned the great Philipse manor and was for twenty years a member of the governor's council, had in 1662 married Margaret, widow of Pieter Rudolph de Vries, herself a well-to-do and enterprising merchant. She was the daughter of Adolf Hardenbroek of Bergen, and died before 1692. It is not necessary to accept *in toto* the diarist's estimate of her.

[2] *I. e.*, if they were not Labadists of Wieuwerd.

deemed necessary for the voyage, by means of an ordinary row-boat. We reached the boom without the least questioning, as the officers of the customs were employed with a lighter inspecting some wine of which they needs must taste. Coming on board, we selected our berth, put our bed-clothes in it, and requested the mate to keep the berth for us, which was next to the large hatchway, according to Margaret's orders. We then returned to our lodgings.

11*th, Sunday.* Not being able to do anything in the city, we determined to cross over the Y [1] to Buiksloot, where we went to hear the preaching, which was wretched. It was by an old minister and according to the doctrines of Voetius. His text was of the seed sown among thorns. We had hitherto eaten out of our provision basket without refreshment, and we therefore took the opportunity now to refresh ourselves a little. We went at noon to Niewendam and heard a sermon by a person who had recently come there. He gave a short exposition of his opinions, from which we clearly saw that he was a Cocceian; [2] and he seemed zealous, but not serious or earnest enough. We recrossed the river in the evening and went to our lodgings.

12*th, Monday.* This whole day we were in expectation of the ship's leaving, and therefore went out continually to see about it; but it was to no purpose. I went again to inquire at the house of Margaret, but could obtain no assurance. Our lodging house was the while constantly full of drunkards, and we did all that we could to avoid them.

13*th, Tuesday.* The ship still lying in the stream: we expected she would sail; but at the appointed time, nothing coming of it, we went on board and found there more passen-

---

[1] The Y (now spelled Ij) is the river or inlet on which Amsterdam is situated. Buiksloot and Nieuwendam are suburban places on its north side.

[2] The Voetians and the Cocceians were at this time the leading theological parties in the Reformed Church of the Netherlands. Gysbertus Voetius (1589–1676), professor of theology at Utrecht, was the pietistic, rigidly orthodox Calvinist; at first favorable to Labadie as to a man of earnest zeal to increase piety in the church, he turned against him as Labadie developed into separatism. Johannes Cocceius (1603–1669), professor at Leiden and one of the chief exponents of the "federal" theology (theology of covenants), represented a school more liberal in tendency and freer in exegesis, though still closely Biblical. Our travellers approved neither group.

gers than before. We inquired again of the new mate when
they had determined to leave, but we could obtain no information. The mates advised us to go to the Texel [1] and wait
there for the ship, and this, for other reasons, we concluded to
do. I saw to-day a certain cooper who had visited us several
times at A[ltona] [2] and who conducted himself very commonly
chez la famme reformé,[3] and I believe comes also to the assembly of Mr. B. He looked at me, but made no recognition,
and passed along. This is the only one of my acquaintance
whom I have seen at Amsterdam.

14th, *Wednesday*. Having resolved to go to Texel to-day,
whether the ship left or not, we prepared ourselves for the
journey. We took dinner with our host and paid him for our
lodging there. About seven o'clock we went in the Texel
barge, where we found many passengers, but it was ten o'clock
at night before we got off. After leaving the piles we had a
strong head wind, which gradually increased to blow so hard
that we could scarcely keep before it, fearing to sail into
others.

15th, *Thursday*. We passed Enckuisen early in the morning, and had then to proceed against the wind with hard
weather. We kept tacking with great assiduity till about
midday, when the tide compelled us to stop, and we came to

[1] A large island at the mouth of the Zuider Zee. Ships outgoing to America
would pass between it and the Helder, or extreme north point of North Holland.

[2] The Labadists had dwelt at Altona, in Holstein, then Danish, from 1672
to their removal to Wieuwerd in 1675. Labadie died there.

[3] No doubt the allusion is to Antoinette Bourignon and her conventicles.
Mlle. Bourignon (1616–1680), born in Lille, France, was a mystical enthusiast of
tendencies not dissimilar from those of Labadie. Like him she wrote much,
had temporarily a great vogue, and removed with her followers from place to
place—Amsterdam, Schleswig, Holstein, Hamburg, East Friesland, Friesland.
Their congregation was at Hamburg when the Labadists were at Altona, close
by, and was now at Franeker, not far from Wieuwerd. Efforts had at first been
made toward union, but by this time there was open opposition between the two
sects. The "assembly of Mr. B." means the conventicle maintained at Amsterdam by a merchant named Bardowitz or Bardewisch. He had been one of the
foremost followers of Labadie, had interpreted his discourses into Dutch for those
who did not understand French, and when Labadie retired to Herford in 1670
had been left in charge of that portion of the congregation which remained in
Amsterdam. There he for many years, without pretending to be a minister,
held a conventicle of separatists in his own house.

anchor under the Vlieter.[1] The boat being full of drinking
people, there had been no rest the whole night. My good
friend [2] was sea-sick, and particularly suffered from the tooth-
ache, but felt better after taking a little of his usual medicine.
The wind subsiding somewhat, and the tide having fallen, some
of our passengers were put on board a ship-of-war, which was
riding at anchor under the Vlieter, and then we proceeded on
our course to Texel. Tacking until in the evening, as far as
the Oude Schilt,[3] we came near being run down, which happened
in this way. There came a small English ship in from sea,
when an English galiot, lying close in shore, weighed anchor
and set sail in order to speak to her. Coming down close before the wind, they were just going to speak to the ship, when
we lay on their bow in order to wear about. They were all
taken up therewith and took no notice of us, whereupon we
began to shout and scream very hard, but they did not hear
us; we not being able to avoid them, redoubled our cries, every
man of us, but they, coming close by, heard us and hauled off.
It was a narrow escape, as they were within two inches of
being right upon us; but as there was a ship-of-war's boat on
our vessel, we were probably in no great danger of losing our
lives, since by means of that we could have saved ourselves,
or they could have caught us up. We landed at the Oude
Schilt about half past nine in the evening, and took lodgings
at the Court of Friesland, one of the principal inns, although
we had been recommended to the Moor's Head, but that did
not suit us, because it was mostly frequented by tipplers.
Having taken something to eat, we retired together to rest in
a quiet little chamber which they prepared for us.

16th, Friday. My companion still suffering from the tooth-
ache and also a pain in the stomach, remained in bed till noon,
when he found himself better. We dined with our landlord
and then wrote a letter home, which we posted. We were in
momentary expectation of the arrival of our ship, for which
we were constantly on the look out; but as it continued
blowing hard with a contrary wind, we did not discover

---

[1] The southern extremity of a great shoal near the mouth of the Zuider Zee,
northeast of the island of Wieringen. "Under the Vlieter" would mean at the
east side of this shoal, in the Tesselstroom or channel to the Texel.

[2] Sluyter.   [3] A village on the east side of the Texel.

anything of her, and, by force, took this time to recruit ourselves a little.

17th, *Saturday*.   Waited for our ship as before, but saw
nothing of her.

18th, *Sunday*.   Went to hear preaching this morning at
Oude Schilt by a very poor man, both in body and mind, for
he was all awry from top to bottom, without and within, his
face as well as his feet, but displeasing as he was to look at,
he endeavored to please everybody.   His text was, "humble
yourselves under the mighty hand of God." [1]   We went in the
afternoon through Burght,[2] the principal village on the island,
walking along the dunes and sea-shore, where we were amused
by the running about of an incalculable number of rabbits.
Being upon the outside of the strand, we watched for a while
the breakers of the North Sea, which were being driven against
the shore by a northwest wind; then we turned back to Burght
and came to a brewer, the only one, not only in that place, but
on the whole island.   We drank of his beer, which in our opinion was better than any we had found on our journey.   Being
a Mennonist [3] he would gladly have entertained us with pleasant conversation, but admonished of the time, we returned to
our lodgings at Oude Schilt.

19th, *Monday*.   We looked out again for our ship, going
along the dyke to Oostereindt,[4] a considerable village, but we
saw no signs of her.   We therefore left the shore and returned
home inland, passing through another small village, called
Seelt.

20th, *Tuesday*.   Perceiving nothing of our ship we began to
feel very anxious, for besides being at much expense for our
lodgings, we were sometimes compelled to eat with very godless men.   Our lodging house was the one most frequented by
the superior officers of the ships-of-war, of which there were
seven or eight lying there ready to convoy different fleets to
various parts.

---

[1] I Peter v. 6.   [2] Near the middle of the island.

[3] Or Mennonite.   Their sect, largely Dutch, were followers of Menno Simons
(1492-1559), refraining from military service, oaths, and public office.   It sprang
from among the Baptists of the Reformation period, and had much in common
with the Society of Friends in the period of the present book.

[4] Still another Oosterend, at the east point of the Texel.

We went in the afternoon to the Hoorn, quite a large village west of the Oude Schilt.   When we had passed through it, we found ourselves near the dunes, over which we crossed to the beacon, walking upon the shore to the extreme point of the island, from whence we saw the Helder before us on the other side, and between, the two mouths of Texelsdiep,[1] observing how the lines agreed with the beacons.   Time running on, we returned to the Hoorn, where we were compelled to drink once.   The landlord of the house was a Papist, who quickly took us to be Roman ecclesiastics, at which we laughed between us for his so deceiving himself.   He began to open his heart very freely, and would have told us all his secrets if we had asked him; but we cut off the conversation, and answered his questions with civility.   When we reached home in the evening, we saw some ships had arrived, and supposed certainly one of them was ours; but, as it was dark, we were compelled to wait till next morning.

21st, *Wednesday*.   As soon as we had taken a little breakfast we went along the dyke to Oosterent, near which the ships had come to anchor.   As we approached the place, we could no longer doubt ours was there, which we were the first to discover.   We therefore hired a boat immediately and went on board, when we not only found it was our ship, but that she was full and overladen.   She was so full of passengers of all kinds, and so stowed, that we saw no chance of finding a place in which to sleep, and there were scarcely any of our goods to be found.   The berth, which we had selected, had been taken by others, which there was no use of resisting; but it caused us no regret, as we thereby secured another near the cables, almost entirely out of the way, and always removed from the greatest noise.   We determined to go ashore and come back the next day; but after taking our dinner there and paying our landlord, we returned on board.   When we came on the ship, they began immediately to inquire of us about everything, and we answered them discreetly and civilly.   Among others who thus made themselves conspicuous, was Jan, whom we did not know, and whose deportment did not accord with what we had imagined of him; but we supposed he was one of the passengers, and one of the best, and most

---

[1] The main channel past the Texel.

slovenly. He asked my comrade if we were not of such a people, expressly naming them, who answered him according to his and our condition.[1] After we had been on board some time, seeing we obtained no place, I went myself to look after one and observed where we could make a berth. I spoke to the captain, who had the chests removed and a berth arranged for us on the larboard side near the forehatch; but as the cable was lying there so that it could not be stretched out as long as it ought, and as there was room enough, I took a little old rope and set to work to lengthen it out, which I accomplished before evening, so that we could sleep there that night. Certainly we had reason to thank the Lord that He had given us a berth in a more quiet place than we ourselves had chosen, which He had of His will allowed to be taken from us. His providence truly extends over all things and His foolishness is wiser than the wisdom of men, and sometimes even of His children.

22d, Thursday. We slept little during the night in consequence of the clatter of so many godless and detestable men, and the noise of children and others. We had, however, to content ourselves. I went in search of our chest, which was stowed away in the bow, but to no purpose, as it was necessary to creep on hands and knees to get in there. We remained in the hope it would come to light at Faelmuyen.[2] The ship was so low between decks, that sitting on the chest we could not sit upright even between the beams, for it was only about three feet high. But we were here in the forecastle well content.

23d, Friday. My comrade wrote a letter home. Our captain having caused the boat to be made ready in order to go with his wife to another English ship, we requested permission to accompany him ashore. He roundly refused us; and we had to wait for a boat to pass and hail it, which we did. Having posted the letter on shore, and refreshed ourselves somewhat, we started to go on board again. We found our boat, when our captain and the captain of the English ship came up. Our skipper asked us if we would accompany them, to whom we

---

[1] Jan is not otherwise known to us, though apparently he had, or had had, some connection with the Labadist community which made his name familiar to their agents.

[2] Falmouth, England.

civilly replied, and so went on board with them in the evening. The sailors had caught some plaice which were for the guests in the cabin. I assisted in cleaning them.

24th, Saturday. The wind was southeast, the same as yesterday, which made us all very anxious for Margaret to arrive, so that we might not miss a good wind. Jan and some others of the passengers were much dissatisfied, and said: "We know very well where she is. She is in Friesland." Upon this Jan declared, "if this wind blows over our heads, I will write her a letter which will make her ears tingle," and used many other rude expressions. He was one of the greatest of grumblers, and even against her. He revealed himself more freely in a conversation with my companion, from which we could clearly discover that he was of the feelings of Bohéém,[1] though he denied he had ever read his books. He also expressed himself profanely and in very foul language, worse than the foulest sailor or dock-loper would have done. The wind changed towards evening, and thus this day passed with murmuring, and we doubted no longer that this was Master John.

25th, Sunday. It blew very hard from the west so that we had to lower the topmasts and let drop the sheet anchor. We saw at daylight a yacht coming down to us before the wind and were rejoiced to find that Margaret was on board, with some other females. The yacht not coming well up, our captain sent a boat to her, but they could not reach her on account of the current. However, the yacht succeeded in coming along side of us, and Margaret came on board with her little daughter, and a Westphalian woman, who was a widow, and a girl, both of whom were in her service, and to go as passengers. They were welcomed by all, and all of them came and shook us by the hand. Some said they thought she had been to Friesland. Whereupon she answered: "How do you know where I have been?"[2] We had nothing to detain us now, except the wind.

---

[1] Jacob Boehme (1575–1624), a pious German shoemaker, author of many noted mystical writings.

[2] We are left to infer that Margaret Philipse also, like Jan, had some relation to the Labadists, and perhaps that she had just visited them. But her husband, Frederick Philipse, was a native of the town of Bolsward, mentioned above, and she may therefore have gone there.

26th, *Monday.* The wind began to blow a little from the south, but calmly. It veered round more and more to the southeast so that we determined to get under sail. We therefore took a pilot, weighed anchor, and set sail about ten or eleven o'clock. We sailed smoothly onward to the Helder. The pilot had a brother who was older, and had been a pilot longer than he had, and who sailed ahead of us in the pilot boat, continually sounding the depth of water with the deep lead. When we were going by the Oude Schilt there came a barge off with two more women who desired to go with us; but as they could not reach the ship, the pilot boat went after them and took them on board of her, where they had to remain until the ship arrived outside. It was about two o'clock when we came in the channel of the Lant's-diep or Nieuwe Diep.[1] You run from Oude Schilt strait to the Helder, and so close to the shore that you can throw a stone upon it, until you have the capes on this point opposite each other, namely, the two small ones; for to the westward of these there is a large one which is not to be regarded. Having the capes thus opposite each other, you are in the middle of the channel and by the first buoy. The current runs outside along the shore, east and west, to wit: the ebb tide westerly, and the flood easterly, and also very strong. The ebb runs until it is half flood. There are still two other channels, the old one which is the middle one, and the Spanish Channel stretching to the east. We had reached the middlemost buoy when it became entirely calm, for which reason we could hardly steer the ship, and, in the meanwhile, the current was steadily setting us over to the west bank. Hereupon a dispute arose between the pilot in our ship and those in the pilot boat going ahead of us. The one in the ship on throwing the lead and finding it begin to be shallow, and seeing, moreover, that the current was driving us more upon the shoal, was of opinion that we should wear ship, which his brother was not willing to do, saying that she should stand over further. This continued so long that at last it became entirely dry, when he wished to tack about; but it could not then be done in consequence of the current

[1] These are channels leading out around the Helder, the Nieuwe Diep close to that cape on the inside, the Lands Diep close to it on the outside. Farther out lay the old channel and the Spaniard's Channel.

running with so much force upon shallow ground, and carrying the ship violently against the shoal, where the current ran obliquely. They got out the boat at the bow of the ship to row, which would not yield in consequence of the strong current which also drove the boat as well as the ship; so that, in a word, we were aground on the west bank of the channel, and although the water was nearly at its lowest there was still a strong ebb tide. Immediately there was great clamor and running to and fro both of seamen and those not acquainted with navigation. Every one was alarmed, and every one did his best in that respect, the more so, because there was not far from us the wreck of a ship with her masts sticking out of water, though it was on the east side of the channel. Nevertheless, we remained fast, and the ship began to thump hard and fall entirely on one side. They ran straightway to the pumps, but found no leak. The pilot remained in good spirits, though put out and angry with his brother, who had misled us, and who, in consequence of the strength of the current, and the lightness of the wind, could not come on board of us. They said we were in no danger, although it looked very strange, as the current had washed the sand very much from under the lee of the ship whereby she had fallen much on her side. But we hoped with the flood tide she would come off again.

There were several passengers, not only women, but men, and some of the bravest, who began to secure the best they had, and were ready and looking out how they might safely reach the land. But the Lord possessed us with His grace. Though seeing all this and knowing the danger, I was not disturbed by it. Margaret proposed throwing some of the cargo overboard, but the pilot and I dissuaded her from it. The captain wished to start the tanks of fresh water, but we hindered him. Of all the men in the ship I saw no one who was so frightened as Jan. He ran backwards and forwards and hardly knew what he said or did. This happened about half past three o'clock in the afternoon, and as we had not yet taken any dinner, and could effect nothing as long as the ship was fast, the victuals were brought out to be eaten. We sat before the hut and ate; but we had not finished when I perceived the ship dragging, as had been predicted. I sprang up

quickly and cried out: "We are afloat; the ship's afloat."
Immediately thereupon the whole ship was in commotion.
The victuals were removed, the boat put to the bow, and every
one did his best, rowing as well as he could.   The ship, floating more and more, gave some good pushes and was brought
into four fathoms of water, in the middle of the channel, and
there anchored.   My companion and myself thanked God in
our hearts, and all were very much rejoiced.   But no sooner
was the danger over, which had somewhat bridled the godlessness of these bad men, than they returned to their old courses,
with cursing and foul language.   They were not affected in
the least by what had happened, nor by God's gracious preservation of us.   Truly was His hand visible, for it remained perfectly calm, so the ship labored very little.   It would otherwise have been all over with us, for our ship not being the
strongest, and being moreover very heavily laden, if the wind
had changed to the east and forced us on a lee shore, she would
have soon gone to pieces; or if we had grounded on the opposite side, which might easily have happened, there would have
been little probability of her getting off, because the flood tide
would have driven us higher up, especially if it had blown
somewhat hard.   The flood having run in and a light breeze
springing out of the S. E. and S. S. E., the anchor was raised
and in a short time we came outside, having been there about
six hours.   The pilot was paid, and he left the ship; the women
whom he had taken in his boat were put on board and we bade
him adieu, and set our course.

Before we proceed further we will say a word concerning
the island of Texel, where we were about eight days, although
the island is well known.   It is said to be twenty-eight miles[1]
in circumference, and is nearly oval in form.   The shore, inside
along the Texelsdiep, is dyked; on the outside, along the
North Sea, it is beset with dunes.   There are six villages,
namely Oosterend, Seelt, the Hoogh, the Burgh, which is the
principal one, and has privileges like a city, such as that of
inflicting capital punishment and others; the Oude Schilt,
which is mostly resorted to by ships, the Hoorn, and also the
West End, which has now fallen into decay.   We saw four of
them but not the Hoogh which lay out of the way, and the

[1] In this translation distances are stated in English miles.

West End which had fallen into decay. Inland the country is rough, and some of it high, so that there are few ditches, except in the low lands for the most part on the side of Texelsdiep. Otherwise they protect their land with small dykes of earth. The soil is sandy, which affords very good water in the high places. The meadow lands are somewhat dry, but yield a fine grass. The inhabitants gain their livelihood, for the most part, by raising sheep and making Texel cheese. The sheep are smaller, but fatter and more hardy than they are in Friesland. They seldom bring forth two young at a birth, and when they do, one usually is killed in order that the other may be better nourished. The inhabitants have cows for their own use. The dyke is not high or thick, but is lined with *wier*, a kind of sea grass, which they put together and lay against the dyke somewhat higher than the earth work. Piles are driven outside to hold this wier against it, and prevent the sea from washing it away. This dyke is repaired every year by contract. Many fishermen and pilots live along it, both qualifications generally being in the same person, as well as the other pursuits pertaining to navigation. There are about five hundred pilots in all living on the island of Texel, as can be seen by the numbers which they carry on their sails or wings.

The law is that no ship can go in or out without a pilot; and in case any captain will not take a pilot, he is nevertheless bound to pay the fees of one, and in case the captain will not pay them, the pilots can go to Amsterdam and there obtain it at the expense of the captain. And if the captain take no pilot and an accident happen, the consequences fall upon him; but I believe this first rule only applies to ships belonging to Amsterdam or other ports in Holland; and that foreign ships are more free in that respect, but cannot relieve themselves from the second. The pilots who bring in ships from the outside bring them to the Texel roadstead or the Helder, and others take them to Amsterdam or elsewhere; and those who take them from Amsterdam, go no further than the Texel road or the Vlie,[1] and other pilots carry them out to sea.

[1] The Texel channel being the great western passage out from the Zuider Zee, the other or eastern passage was the Vlie, lying on the other side of the great shoal known as the Bree Sand, and leading out between the islands of Vlieland and Schelling.

The fee of the pilots is a guilder[1] a foot for every foot the ship draws, though any sum may be fixed by agreement.

During the whole time we were there we saw few or no fish, though we supposed this was the place for fish. We remarked further that the inhabitants of Texel were more polite than the boors of Friesland. A large portion of them are Romanists. There was no home-brewed beer tapped in the taverns, but it was all foreign beer, and this I suppose was for the purpose of saving the excise. They are under the jurisdiction of West Friesland and the particular government of the city of Alckmaer,[2] whose weights and measures they use. West of the Oude Schilt there is a small fortification with four points and two redoubts on the dyke, and some small batteries; but they afford little protection to the place, and still less to the harbor. It was closed and without men, when we were there. When we first came there, the people, unaccustomed to see such persons, regarded us as some individuals in particular. The innkeepers took us to be farmers of the revenue, especially of brandies, and supposed our presence there was to prevent their smuggling, as they themselves told us. The Roman Catholics, as they declared, looked upon us as priests; the Mennonists, as a class of their exhorters; and the ordinary Reformed, as preachers; whereby they all showed they did not know us in truth, according to the word in Christ Jesus.

Leaving Texel and the land we came outside the coast, laying our course S. W. with a S. E. wind, with which we sailed some distance from the shore. Towards evening the wind began to blow from the S. and S. S. W. quite hard, and so we stood off through the whole night. I do not know that I ever had in my life so severe a pain in the breast as I had this evening, whether it was from hard work or change of our condition.

27th, Tuesday. The wind from the same quarter as before, but blowing harder, for which reason we reefed our topsails. We had twenty-six and twenty-eight fathoms of water. By evening it was somewhat calmer; but as the wind was not steady we stood off from the shore.

---

[1] A guilder or florin was equivalent to about 40 cents.

[2] West Friesland was the ancient name for the northern part of the province of Holland, Alkmaar one of its chief towns.

28*th*, *Wednesday*. Finding ourselves in twenty-five and twenty-six fathoms of water and the wind still south and southwest we sailed over by the wind. It continued to blow hard, and we sailed for the most part N. by E. and N. N. E. It annoyed me that I could not get at our chest, in order to obtain my charts and books of navigation. Our mate and others observed the latitude, and found it to be 52° 16′; and we tacked about. The wind continued in the same quarter, sometimes a little lighter, sometimes sharper. We kept mostly a S. S. E. course, with hard weather the first part of the night.

29*th*, *Thursday*. Having twenty-six and twenty-seven fathoms of water we lay over again. Every day there were many mackerel caught, which for several days were for the cabin only, whatever number were caught, because they were taken with the captain's hooks; but the passengers and sailors began to get their hooks ready also and thus every one began to catch and eat. The weather was delightful. I had obtained my things out of the chest, and found the latitude 52° 18′ [?]. We stood over to the Flemish or Zeelandish coast, calculating we were not far from Sluis and Bruges. I therefore went aloft frequently to look out for land. We saw several fishing boats, one of which we hailed toward evening. He was from Zierickzee, and told us Walcheren[1] was about twenty-eight miles E. S. E. of us, and we could see it from the mast head, as was the fact. We laid over again immediately. It now began to blow more from the S. W. and S. W. by W. We had sailed the last night west by north, according to reckoning, twenty-eight miles. This result agreed with my observation within less than four miles, and that of our mate, named Evert. But the captain's and the English mate's calculation brought us before the Maes, as Evert[2] told me.

We sailed now for a day or two among great quantities of June-bugs or cock-chafers, which had been driven off from the land and drowned,[3] which caused us to reflect upon what God did formerly in Egypt and elsewhere, and still often does, for

[1] The westernmost island of the province of Zeeland.

[2] Evert Duyckinck; see *post*, p. 28, note 2.

[3] In the fragmentary manuscript journal of the voyage of 1683, Danckaerts notices, on land, between Canterbury and Dover, the same great abundance of beetles, which every evening fly out to sea from Dover in great numbers.

His power is always the same, although it is not always understood.

30th, Friday. We tacked over to the Flemish coast this morning in twenty-five fathoms of water; but it was so calm that we made little progress. It was too cloudy to take the latitude. The wind was very variable, and we could not keep on S. W., or even south, and so drifted for the most part with the tide.

JULY 1*st, Saturday.* We had drifted the whole night in the calm, and had gone backwards instead of forwards; but in the morning the wind began to blow out of the N. W. and N. N. W. with a stiff breeze. We therefore set all sail, and went ahead tolerably well on a straight course W. by S. and W. S. W. against the current. We saw land many times about two hours' distance, both on the starboard and larboard, that on the starboard being the cape of Dover, and on the larboard, the cape of Calais. There was a free wind and fine weather, though a little haze on the horizon. The land began to loom up more distinctly, and I sketched it twice with crayon. We continued to catch plenty of mackerel, and also weevers and whitings. We arrived before Dover at sunset, when we fired a gun, and a boat came off to us immediately, by which the captain sent some letters ashore. We inquired of them the news, and they answered us all was well; but they told the captain privately that 30,000 Scottish Papists had taken up arms for the conspirators.[1]

It is proper that I should say something here of the North Sea. In case you are driven about by strong contrary winds and cannot obtain the latitude, and, indeed, under any circumstances, you should use the deep lead frequently, for the depth is well shown on the chart, and often you cannot get sight of the land. The Flemish coast is the least dangerous, although the English is the most surveyed, because the water becomes shoal gradually. You may get into thirteen and fourteen fathoms of water. In the true channel it is twenty and twenty-two fathoms, and in the middle it is deeper, namely, twenty-six and twenty-eight and over, but it is somewhat more uneven. In approaching the English coast the shoals are more

[1] A distorted rumor of the rising of the Covenanters in June, 1679; but everything was now seen in the light of the Popish Plot.

even, as twenty-six, eighteen, seventeen fathoms.   To navigate
the channel it is best to keep nearest the Flemish coast, because
it affords a better course, and the current makes it easy to go
north, and the sandbars such as the Galper, Wytingh, and
Goyn,[1] are more to be avoided than the Flemish banks; and,
moreover, close by the shore it is very deep, yet by the setting
of the current to the north you may soon be upon them, that
is, with an ebb tide.

2d, Sunday.   Made fair progress during the night.   We
found ourselves in the morning before the point of Bevesier,[2]
which I sketched.   The wind was northerly with a cool air.
About breakfast time a large English ship came up behind us,
which we hailed.   She was from London and bound for the
Straits.[3]   She had much sail on, and after passing us, set all
she had; but not long afterwards a small breeze blowing off
shore, she was compelled to begin to take in her topgallant-
sails and upperstay-sails.   This was scarcely half done when
her maintop-mast and mizzentop-mast went by the board, and
remained hanging on the side of the ship.   The man who was
taking in the topgallant-sail fell overboard.   When this accident happened she was only a short distance ahead of us; and
we, therefore, all ran forward to the forecastle to see whether
there were any pieces of wood at our bow to damage us.   We
sailed by her, close under her lee, and saw somewhat of a crowd
running about the ship.   Finally they launched their jolly-
boat for the purpose of looking after the man who had fallen
overboard with the top-mast.   Whether there were any more
we did not know, and as we sailed ahead of them with considerable speed, we could not see whether they fished any one up
or not; but the ship sailed before the wind the best she could,
when her top-mast went overboard; we took in very quickly
our own topgallant-sail, which we had set, but more from pre-
caution than necessity.   Shortly afterwards it was so calm
that we merely drifted along; and being nearly midway between Bevesier and the Isle of Wight, and the ebb tide running
out, we were compelled by the current to anchor about a mile
from the shore.

[1] Sandbanks off the southeast coast of England, called by the English the
Galloper, the Whiting, and the Goodwin Sands.

[2] Beachy Head.   [3] Of Gibraltar.

About four o'clock in the afternoon Margaret came to me while I was engaged in sketching the Isle of Wight. We talked over various matters which were almost the same as those about which she had conversed with my companion the day before, and I therefore met her with the same objections.

3d, Monday. We did not advance any during the night, and had drifted along; but a breeze springing up we went ahead a little. It was very foggy, so that we could not see the land. It cleared up in the afternoon, when we found ourselves off against the Isle of Wight; but the wind subsiding, and the tide being spent, we ran for the point of the island, and came to anchor in ten or eleven fathoms near some other ships which were waiting there for a good wind and tide. The jolly-boat was launched and our Dutch mate and two other persons went ashore in order to see if they could obtain some fresh provisions. The tide having passed, and the wind shifting, we signalled to them to come on board again, which they did in the evening, when we were already almost under sail. They brought nothing with them, except a little milk which served us as a good refreshment for this evening. Sailing ahead, we steered above the point with the wind W. S. W., and so gained the open sea. There is a very strong current here, and hard beating along the shore and around the point. The current sent us ahead more than the wind. The coast is quite good and it is deep enough close up to the shore.

4th, Tuesday. We found ourselves in the morning opposite Wight with the wind S. S. E., and quite still. After a while there came up a breeze. We passed Peveril Point,[1] however, with the ebb. About noon a flute-ship[2] came near us which we hailed. She was from Amsterdam, bound to Cadiz. It was so calm in the evening that we drifted, and turned round several times. We perceived fifteen or eighteen large ships on the French coast, which saluted each other with many heavy guns. The ebb being spent, we came to anchor again in twenty-one fathoms of water, about two miles from the shore. The flood having run out by evening, we weighed anchor, and before we were under sail had a fresh wind astern. We therefore set all the sail we could, having a favorable wind and tide, by which means we came before Portland.

[1] Durlston Head.   [2] A small long three-masted trading-ship.

5th, Wednesday. We still had a fair wind and kept our course W. by S. We passed Portland, and came in sight of Goutstar,[1] and arrived off against it about noon. Our mate was of opinion that we had run by the rock of Meeusteen or Jetston,[2] and should have it on the larboard; but on looking out afterwards we found it right before us, about four miles off. We had therefore to hold up and leave it on the starboard. It is a large rock having its head just above the water. It rises up straight, but is very much hacked, which makes it look like a reef. Whenever the sea is rough it is under water. It is dangerous enough, and lies far out in the channel, farther than it is marked down on my chart. We certainly had reason here again to observe the care of the Lord, and His protection through His good providence, which always watches paternally over His children, shown in our becoming aware of this rock before the evening, and just before the evening, for we had not well gone by it before it was dark. If we had been sailing so at night, or if we had not now discovered it, the mate's calculation being as it was, we certainly should not have missed sailing upon it; for when we first saw it, it was straight before us, and we were sailing with a fair wind and tide up to it. We were therefore touched, and thankful to the Lord. This passed, we still, while the sun was going down clear, made Deadman's Head,[3] a point jutting out from England, so that we reckoned we were still twenty-eight or thirty-two miles from Falmouth Bay; but the wind had fallen off somewhat. My calculation was, that we were about twelve or sixteen miles from Falmouth.

6th, Thursday. During the night I heard the ship tack close about, and therefore supposed that the wind had changed, or that the ship had run too far, or, what was more probable, I was afraid, the wind being about S. E., we had fallen more to the shore. Our mate Evert and I thought we should stand off a little till daylight; but the captain tacked about again, so that we then sailed N. E., intending thus to enter the harbor

---

[1] Start Point.

[2] This dangerous reef was called by the Dutch Meeuwsteen (Sea-mews' Rock), by the English Eddystone. Of the lighthouses for which it has been celebrated, the first was begun in 1695.

[3] Dodman Point.

of Falmouth, but we found no opening, and when the day broke, discovered that they had made a mistake, and had taken the point of Deadman's Head for the point of Falmouth Bay. When the sun rose, they saw they were deep in the bay, on a lee shore, where it all looked strange, and they had a tolerably hard wind. When they saw they were wrong it continued so some time before they became informed. They then wore ship, and sailed with quite easy sheets out of the bay.

This mishap was mainly caused by Master Jan, who wishing to play the part of a wise man, though truly it was from fear, had been on deck several times during the night in order to look out, afraid, as he said himself, that we might sail upon the point of the Lizard.[1] Coming up at this time with drowsy eyes, and catching a glimpse of the land, through the mist, he began to call out, that we had passed by Falmouth, and would certainly sail upon the Lizard. It was the English mate's watch, who was not very well acquainted with him, and could not keep him still. The captain was therefore called, who also came up rubbing his eyes, and unable to see the land well in the mist. He agreed with Jan, being apprehensive that the ship had sailed more than they thought, and as I myself considered might well be the case, and so let the ship tack about. I deemed it better, however, to keep off from the shore till daylight, when they could see where they were; but the captain relying more upon Jan's opinion, and wishing to accomplish half a masterpiece, by going into Falmouth in the dark, and surprising the people there to whom the ship was consigned, and so to pass hereafter as a good and skillful captain, insisted upon sailing in, and so they went in, as has been mentioned. It is no part of the business of a good seaman to run into a place by night, or when it is dark, where he is not well acquainted; but in such case he should work off shore slowly, waiting until day and light, and know where he is, and then see what can be done. Thus the fear of one danger, and the rashness accompanying it, brought us into another, greater than the first.

Sailing then out of this bay, around the west point, we saw

[1] The southernmost point of Cornwall. Falmouth is about midway between it and Dodman Point.

at once the neck from which this point of land takes its name of Deadman's Head. It is shaped like a coffin or the mound of earth which peasants form over a grave, one end a little higher than the other, and going up sharp on either side; but it is on the top somewhat jagged. It is on the east side of the point, three or four cable lengths from the main land. We had a third mate (Titus), on board the ship who was to go on the other ship at Falmouth, and who was well acquainted here. He said he had passed through the opening between the rock and the main land, and that it was a mile wide and tolerably clear and deep enough. After having passed Deadman's Head and this rock, we came to a small pretty sand-bay, but it lies open. From Deadman's Head you can see, on the point of Falmouth Bay, a church with a small spire, and near it a stone wind-mill, which forms a good land-mark, for along the whole coast there are few or no steeples. As you sail along this point the castle comes into view standing upon the west point of the harbor of Falmouth, where also there is a stone wind-mill.[1] The easterly point should be avoided, for it runs out considerably. It is hard bottom, and at low tide there is three fathoms water always; and we sailed in with that depth. As soon as you perceive it is deeper, you have passed the east point. Then keep along this shore if the wind be fair, for there is a rock almost directly in the channel. You can go around it close enough, but this should not be done. As it was low water when we entered, it stuck up out of the water. At high tide it is covered. There is a spar or pole upon it, which cannot be seen far, but the breakers are sufficiently visible. When you sail in, in this manner, you see the other castle also, lying on the east side, on a point inside. After having passed the rock, keep a little again on the inside, and then to the west, so as to avoid the second point, upon which the east castle is situated. As soon as you have passed that, you have deeper water and softer bottom; and you must then look out that you do no damage to the shipping, for the roadstead commences there,

---

[1] Falmouth, which had come into existence in 1613, numbered in 1679 some two hundred and fifty houses. The two castles alluded to as commanding the harbor were Pendennis castle on the west (southeast of the town), famous for its obstinate defence in 1646 by the royalists under Lord Arundell, and St. Mawes on the east.

and you can see the town or village of Falmouth lying upon the west side of the bay, and appearing somewhat prettier than it is in fact.   When we arrived, we found a large number of vessels lying there; but being desirous of sailing high up, several ships received good thumps from us, in passing by them, and our endeavoring to keep off the shoals.   It would have resulted much worse, if our sheet anchor, which was lying up forward, had not caught between the rails of a small vessel, whose mizzenmast we also came foul of, whereby our ship turned round, and at the same time our anchor fell, and we touched bottom in the mud, with fine weather and still water. We thanked our God again, with our whole hearts, for the double mercy shown us this morning, having not only in a fatherly manner preserved us from an apprehended danger, but delivered us from this one into which we had truly fallen, and had then caused us to arrive so well.   To Him belongs all praise and glory, from all His children, and especially from us, to all eternity.   Amen.

Our anchor had not yet touched bottom when the inspectors or tide-waiters all came on board to examine.   Our captain and Margaret went immediately ashore; and after the cook had served the breakfast, almost all the passengers, both old and young, putting on their best clothes, did the same.   My comrade also went to see if any letters had arrived for us, whilst I remained on board to look after things a little; for all our goods were in the berth, and otherwise within reach, and the ship was constantly full of strange people.   My comrade soon returned, but brought no letters.   This morning while we were launching the boat, I hurt myself in the loins, on my left side; the pain extended through the whole of that side of my body, to my left breast, and across the middle to the right breast.   I was all bent up while standing, and had to sit down.   I could scarcely draw a breath or move myself; but I felt it was my old complaint, forced upon me anew when I hurt myself.   This pain continued for some days, when it gradually passed over.   At high water we towed the ship higher up, to the warehouse, where we had to unload.   The custom house officers, and Mr. Roggers,[1] came on board with

---

[1] The custom house had lately been transferred to Falmouth from Penryn. Bryan Rogers was one of the chief merchants of the former.

some other persons, and when they left, they promised us the ship should be unladen by Tuesday, for which we were glad.

7th, *Friday.* They began early to break open the hatches and discharge the ship. My comrade and I went ashore to a place called Pe[n]ryn, a little further up the bay, where it ends and as far as they can go with any vessels. We went walking thence into the country, over and among the hills, for the purpose of recreating and recruiting ourselves, which refreshed us very much, after having been so long in an over-burdened ship and with such wicked men.

We returned to Pe[n]ryn at noon in order to see if we could obtain some place or other to lodge and rest ourselves for a time. By chance we came to an inn in that place, called The English Ship, the landlord of which was named Maitre Jean, who spoke a little Dutch, but, as we afterwards discovered, better French, so well indeed that we could converse with him. We took dinner there, and agreed with him to lodge there for several days, with the privilege of a chamber to ourselves.

8th, *Saturday.* Having slept on board the ship we went in the morning to our new lodgings, where we breakfasted, and then rambled into the country to divert ourselves, and thence to Falmouth, and so returned by evening to our lodgings.

9th, *Sunday.* My companion being disposed to write, I went to their church, to wit the Episcopal,[1] where I was surprised to find in the church yard a great crowd of people sitting together, smoking tobacco and waiting for the last toll of the bell. On entering the church I was still more astonished at the ceremonies which indeed did not differ much from those of popery, and continued quite long enough. Then followed a sermon, if it may be called such, delivered in a white gown, as were the first services and other ceremonies in like vestments. The sermon was read out of a little book, without the addition of a single word. It began about ten o'clock, and was not very edifying. The text was from II Cor. xiii. 11; and all this continued till about half-past eleven, when church was over, and the burgomasters or mayors,[2] with two golden royal sceptres, were escorted home. In the afternoon I went out

---

[1] The new church at Falmouth, built by Sir Robert Killigrew. The sermon was probably from the *Two Books of Homilies* authorized by the Church.

[2] There was but one mayor.

for a walk to the ship, which lay about a half-hour from here toward Falmouth, and nearly midway between the two places for the purpose of being unladen.

10th, Monday. We remained at our lodgings almost the whole day writing letters. Our ship was nearly discharged, which I went in the evening to ascertain.

11th, Tuesday. We continued still at our lodgings, but in the afternoon visited the ship in consequence of their telling us that our chest would be examined, as indeed took place. There were some passengers on shore whose chests were broken open, because they did not attend to them, and the inspectors would not wait. They cut to pieces the cords of their berth under which they found some things; but although there were more berths so arranged, and still better furnished than this one, they did nothing to them, as they well knew beforehand whose they were, and why they did what was done. When they examined our chest, they took almost all our goods out of it. However, they did not see our little box, or perhaps they thought it contained medicines, as they found in the other one. The two small pieces of linen were entered, and registered against my name. They went to our berth, but did nothing; nor was anything there.

12th, Wednesday. This whole day was a writing day, for the post would leave to-morrow. They began to reload the ship in the afternoon. I went on board once, and also went with another to see if there were any letters for us, which turned out to be the fact; for, on finding the captain, he gave me a letter for which I paid twenty-two pence postage. This was the first letter we had received from home. It is unnecessary for me to say that I was rejoiced, or that we thanked the Lord that He still thought of us. I went immediately with it to my companion, who was as glad as I was, and also because the letter came just in time to be answered, as we did with joy and tenderness of heart.

13th, Thursday. As the post was soon to leave, we took our letters to the post office at Penryn, next to The White Dolphin. The package was weighed, and was one ounce and a quarter in weight, for which we paid fifteen pence postage to London; and they informed us it would reach London on Monday. Our ship being almost laden again, we paid our land-

lord and returned on board ship. We could have easily remained a day or two longer at our lodgings, but our landlord
had given us reasons for leaving. Coming on board the ship,
we began to arrange our place a little for keeping house again.
Meanwhile I helped fill the water casks. There was also some
beef to be salted in barrels.

14th, *Friday*. Our ship was entirely laden, that is, with the
goods she had to take, for there was a large quantity of them
which had come out of her, remaining for the other ship which
Margaret had bought there, and which was to be made ready
there to go to the Isle of May,[1] and thence to Barbados. She
was a large but very weak ship, short and high, small and
meagre as regards bulk, not altogether old, but misbuilt.
She sailed tolerably well, but was very lank. Two of our
crew went with her, namely, Titus, who was to be boatswain,
and one of our carpenters, named Herman, who was the best
one we had. They went, from the first, to work upon her, for
she was lying in winter quarters. Our ship being laden, our
captain went on board the large one with an English lad, the
cabin boy, and his, the captain's wife. This captain had obtained a Quaker for his mate, a young man and a very poor
seaman, as I have been able to observe. Hereupon our English mate, named Robert, who also was a Quaker, became
captain in the place of the other, and our Dutch mate, or
rather New Netherland mate, named Evert van Duike—for
he was a New Netherlander born, and his parents and relations
were still there, though he had married at Amsterdam and
had lived there a long time, but was now taking his wife and
children with him to New Netherland—became mate in place
of the other.[2] In return for the three persons and the boy
who had gone from our crew, we obtained only one in their
place, a poor creature, called Jan, the doctor, of Boston, who
seemed more a charlatan in his behavior and gestures than a
good seaman. Meanwhile we went walking, to see the country, and in the afternoon came to the east castle, where a soldier conducted us from the gate and took us before the gov-

---

[1] One of the Cape Verde islands.

[2] Evert Duyckinck was the son of a Westphalian painter and glazier of the
same name who had come out to New Netherland early, in the service of the
Dutch West India Company.

ernor,[1] who asked us who we were, where we came from, what flag our ship bore, when and with whom we had arrived, and for what purpose we had come to the castle. We answered him politely; but we could not make ourselves well understood by him, for he spoke nothing but English, which we could not do, or very little, though we could understand it pretty well. He finally ordered the soldier to conduct us around the castle, in order that we might look at it. Having satisfied the soldier, we left, and went down the hill. The beer brewed at the castle is very poor; there is little or no fresh water up there, and what there is, does not amount to much. The castle is otherwise strong and well provided, having over an hundred guns in different batteries, which command the harbor and the entire roadstead. When we reached the ship she was laden.

15th, *Saturday.* As our ship was now full, and orders had come to haul the ship at high water from before the warehouse and off from the ground, they did so this morning. We went to Penryn to buy some butter, and when we returned the boat was sent for fresh water, which was brought on board, and the ship then towed to the roadstead below, where she arrived in the evening, somewhat late, and was moored at once.

16th, *Sunday.* The weather was misty and rainy. We went ashore with one of the passengers and one of the sailors, a young fellow, a Scotchman, by birth, from the Orkneys, and a Presbyterian by profession, named Robert,[2] who took us, at our request, to the Presbyterian meeting, which we left quite satisfied with the zeal of the preacher. Their mode of service is not different from that of the Reformed in Holland, but the common people sat there with very little reverence. At noon we went to dine at a very good inn, called The Golden Fleece, and in the afternoon we attended the meeting of the Episcopalians, of whose church service we have before spoken, and so in the evening returned on board the ship.

---

[1] Pendennis castle is meant. The governor was Richard, Lord Arundell of Trerice, son of the old governor who had commanded during the siege of 1646.

[2] Robert Sinclair. Though he returned on the *Charles,* he came back to New York in 1682, married the sister of Evert Duyckinck, became a sea-captain, and died in 1704.

17*th, Monday*. We went this morning again with some passengers to Penryn, where the yearly market day was held, with the intention of laying out a little money in some purchases, having rid ourselves of Mr. Jan, who had sought to get it out of our hands, and would by that means have cheated us. He promised us, if we would let him have the money, thirty per cent. interest payable in New York, or ducats[1] there at twelve guilders of *zeewan* each; but the Lord, who has care over the least of His children, saved us from this fox, and excited the attention of another passenger, namely, Jan Theuniesen, who lived on Long Island, and who advised us what to do.[2]

We bought several things on which we thought we could make a profit, because the peril of the sea was to be encountered. The Lord, who, as I have said, takes care of the least of His children, so ordered it that we not only did not lose any thing by our Dutch money, which commonly brings not more than five shillings for a ducat; but we received for almost all that we used, five shillings and six pence, that is 67 stivers.[3] The reason of this was, that the man who took our money was about going to Norway, for timber, where he could pay it out at a higher rate than English money. Having made our purchases, we went to Falmouth, but as we could not take our goods on board the ship without first declaring them, we had to take them to Mr. Roggers's, where one Mr. Jacobs lived, who had assisted in inspecting the ship's lading, and who would do the same with these. Thinking over the purchases we had made at Penryn, we discovered there was a mistake in the payment of a bill, arising from the counting of the money by our Dutch mate and Jan Theunissen. The difference amounted to one pound sterling. We, or our friends on our account, had paid the bill. We discovered the mistake at Falmouth, and immediately went back to Penryn, informed the merchant of the mistake, which he did not have much trouble in comprehending. He gave us back the money, for

---

[1] A gold coin of Holland, worth originally about two dollars and a half, but at this time less. It would apparently have been worth fifteen guilders of *zeewan* (wampum) in New Netherland.

[2] Jan Teunissen van Dykhuis, of Brooklyn.

[3] Twenty stivers made one florin or guilder, and three guilders one ducat.

which we were glad, and returning, arrived by evening on
board the ship.

18th, *Tuesday*. One Mr. Lucas, the most rigid of the inspectors and custom house officers, came on board this morning. We spoke to him, told him what we had bought, and
requested him to examine them. We said we might buy something more and he could assess them all together. He replied
he did not wish to examine our chest, or what we might have
bought previously; but would go ashore with us and look at
what we had there. He told us also that he had a small piece
or two of stuffs, which, if we would buy, he would let us have
at a bargain. We went to Mr. Jacobs's where he looked over
what we had bought. He told us we had paid dear for them,
although we thought we had bought them cheap. Mr. Jacobs
said he had a remnant of tin which he would sell us for ten
stivers a foot, and we had paid twelve for ours. We were
directed to pay Mr. Jacobs three shillings English for duties
upon the goods we had there, whenever we should have all our
merchandise together. Mr. Lucas went with us to a shop
over the door of Mr. Roggers, where he bought several things
for us at a low price; he even compelled the merchant almost
to give us the goods for what he chose, for the merchant did
not dare to refuse or disoblige him. They were always good
purchases. He also brought us something of his own which
he sold us on favorable terms. I supposed these were con-
fiscated goods, which they wanted to get rid of, and that this
was the reason they were so accommodating to us.[1] Our
purchases being completed, he took us to an inn where we
regaled him for the trouble he had taken with the above-
mentioned merchant. We were compelled this evening to eat
and sleep ashore, which we did at the inn, The Golden Fleece.

We had heard a great deal said for some days past, and
to-day, of great danger from the Turks, who had taken four
Dutch ships. This caused no small apprehension in our ship,
and especially in Mr. Jan.

19th, *Wednesday*. My companion wrote a letter home from
on board the ship. We did our best this whole day to get our
little merchandise on board, but without success, because it

[1] The Falmouth customs officers had the right, or opportunity by connivance
of the government, to bring in some goods duty-free.

was not yet declared. However, every thing concerning the
ship and the lading was finished to-day; and the passengers
obtained the bills of their goods, and paid them. Having
accomplished nothing the whole day, we returned on board
the ship.

20th, Thursday. My comrade having finished the letters,
we went on shore to Mr. Roggers's, in order to post them in
time, and paid the postage to London. We bought also some
brandy, vinegar and other articles, for we began to see it would
go slim with us on the voyage. We were engaged the whole
day in declaring our goods and carrying them on board, which
was completed early in the evening, and the goods stowed away.
We then paid Mr. Lucas a ducaton[1] for the duties on our goods.
He told us what the duties on the whole of the ship's cargo
amounted to, and gave us various other information, all very
willingly, because, after he heard that I was somewhat acquainted with the wine business, he desired some particulars
in regard to it from me, which I gave him in writing to his
satisfaction. We were now all cleared.[2] . . .

[September] 21st, Thursday. The hatches of the hold were
all opened yesterday evening, and we began to make the cables
fast to the anchors, which we finished this morning. As soon
as the sun rose, every one climbed aloft in order to look for
land and some of them immediately cried out "land," but they
soon discovered they were mistaken. Our course was north,
with the wind E. N. E. I said the land we would see was in
front of us, and we could not see it yet because it was in latitude 40° 20', and we had 39°, a difference of eighty miles, and
as we had sailed only from twenty-four to twenty-eight miles
at the most during the night, we were still fifty-two to fifty-
six miles off, and if we continued to sail as we were doing, it
would be noon or two o'clock before we would see it. I must
say a word here in relation to our cat; how she was always
sick and lame for some days before a storm, and could not
walk, and when the storm was over, was lively and nimble

[1] A Dutch silver coin, worth about $1.25.
[2] The *Charles* set sail from Falmouth the next day, July 21, 1679. The account of the voyage is here omitted. It is a somewhat interesting picture of the
hardships, discomforts, and other incidents of an Atlantic voyage in the seventeenth century, but it is excessively long.

again. She had now been very playful for several days, running here and there over the ship, but this morning she was unusually gay. She came running with a spring, leaping into the rigging and going far aloft, turning her head about and snuffing the land, as much as to say, there is the land you should look out for; and causing great laughter among the folks, who said the cat was on the lookout for land. When she came down she mewed. But a thick fog coming from the land, cut off all view and hopes of going inside, as we turned at once from the shore. I obtained, however, the latitude, to wit: 40° 5′. The distance was reckoned to be sixty-four miles. In the mean time the deep lead was thrown many times, and 22, 21, 19, 17, 16, 14 fathoms of water found, at one time more and at another less, for the bottom is uneven. We did this in order not to run ashore during the fog. It, however, cleared away, and we wore over again, and immediately saw the land distinctly, which caused new rejoicing. We perceived clearly that we had been sailing, since yesterday, along the shore, although it was too far off to be seen. Rentselaer's Hook,[1] which adjoins Sandy Hook, was in front or north of us; and we had sailed N. N. E. and N. by E. It was about one o'clock when we first saw the land. It is not very high, but like a dome, only it is a little higher. Long Island is not very high; Rentselaer's Hook, which is the most westerly point of the bay, is the highest of all. Sandy Hook is low, and stretches out about three miles eastwardly from Rentselaer's Hook, and makes the channel. You must be close on Sandy Hook before you can see Long Island. We intended to run in, but could not well do so this evening, in consequence of the mist continually intercepting the sight of the land. As the weather was calm, and the sea smooth, we came to anchor, in thirteen fathoms of water, and lay there quietly all night.

22d, Friday. When the day began to break, they were all in an uproar; but the weather continued misty, with a northeast wind, for which reason we judged we could not make the channel. All those who were so joyful and merry yesterday, were now more sober, as we were compelled to keep off land, so as not to be caught on a lee shore, from which it is very difficult to get away. The fog cleared up a little about ten

[1] Navesink.

o'clock, and we sailed again towards the shore, when we perceived we were approaching the west side. It rained a part
of the time, and was misty, so that sometimes we could only
see the land dimly, and for a moment, and Sandy Hook hardly
at all. We durst not yet venture to run in, and wore off again.
About noon we saw a ketch to the sea-ward of us, but we did
not speak to her. She was laying her course to the west.
This coast surely is not very easy to enter, especially in the
autumn. Our captain had trouble enough, though our mate
did not agree with him. Sailing onward, we had 13, 14, 15,
16 fathoms of water, but very uneven bottom as we approached
the shore. We laid our course N. N. E. and N. E. by N. and
from the shore, S. S. W. and S. At four o'clock in the afternoon we determined to run in, if it were possible. We could
see the land a little better, and also Rentselaer's Hook. Everybody, therefore, was very industrious, some in looking after
the sails, ropes and tackle, so as to be able to turn and tack
ship quickly; others were constantly on the lookout for land
and especially to discover Sandy Hook, in order to secure the
best channel which is next to that point; for not far from it,
on the other side, are the east banks, which are very dangerous. We did our best, first in a calm, then with a little breeze,
to enter. We caught sight of Sandy Hook at last, but it was
soon hid by the fog. We observed how the land lay by the
compass, and so sailed accordingly, expecting a good flood tide
which would begin to make at six o'clock. The deep lead was
thrown constantly, and we found five and four fathoms in the
shallowest places, near the channel. It was low water, and
the wind was N. E. and E. N. E., which took us soon inside,
short around the point of Sandy Hook, into the bay towards
the highlands of Rentselaer's Hook. Upon passing the Hook
which was now west of us, we found deeper water, 5, 6, 7 and 8
fathoms, and ran, as I have said, immediately for the highlands, and came to anchor in ten fathoms of water, praising
the Lord again, and thankful for the many instances of His
goodness towards us. This is a very fine bay, where many
ships can lie, protected from all winds, except the S. E., which,
however, cannot do much damage, because the east banks lie
before it; and at the worst, the ship can only be driven in the
wind. They determined this evening, to go up early in the

morning, in the jolly-boat, to Staten Island or Long Island, for a pilot.

23d, Saturday. It rained the whole night. Our ship lay as quiet as if she were made fast to the piles at Amsterdam, which was very unusual for us. The wind being west in the morning, they changed their resolution of going up for a pilot, and as the wind was so favorable determined to take her up themselves. The anchor was therefore raised, and we sailed on, for the purpose of passing between Staten Island and Long Island, where there are two high points of land, for that reason called the *Hoofden*.[1] We turned gradually from Sandy Hook to the right, in order to avoid the shoals of the east bank, and so sailed to the Hoofden. We had a good flood tide, and four to five fathoms of water at the shoalest part; but the wind shifted again to the north, and we were compelled to tack, which rendered our progress slow, for it was quite calm. Coming to the Hoofden, and between them, you have 10, 11, and 12 fathoms of water. As soon as you begin to approach the land, you see not only woods, hills, dales, green fields and plantations, but also the houses and dwellings of the inhabitants, which afford a cheerful and sweet prospect after having been so long upon the sea. When we came between the Hoofden, we saw some Indians on the beach with a canoe, and others coming down the hill. As we tacked about we came close to this shore, and called out to them to come on board the ship, for some of the passengers intended to go ashore with them; but the captain would not permit it, as he wished, he said, to carry them, according to his contract, to the Manathans, though we understood well why it was. The Indians came on board, and we looked upon them with wonder. They are dull of comprehension, slow of speech, bashful but otherwise bold of person, and red of skin. They wear something in front, over the thighs, and a piece of duffels, like a blanket, around the body, and this is all the clothing they have. Their hair hangs down from their heads in strings, well smeared with fat, and sometimes with quantities of little beads twisted in it out of pride. They have thick lips and thick noses, but not fallen in like the negroes, heavy eyebrows or eyelids, brown or black eyes, thick tongues, and all of them

[1] "Headlands," at the Narrows.

black hair. But we will speak of these things more particularly hereafter. After they had obtained some biscuit, and had amused themselves a little, climbing and looking here and there, they also received some brandy to taste, of which they drank excessively, and threw it up again. They then went ashore in their canoe, and we having a better breeze, sailed ahead handsomely. As soon as you are through the Hoofden, you begin to see the city, which presents a pretty sight. The fort, which lies upon the point between two rivers, is somewhat higher; and as soon as they see a ship coming up, they raise a flag on a high flag-staff, according to the colors of the sovereign to whom they are subject, as accordingly they now flew the flag of the king of England. We came up to the city about three o'clock, where our ship was quickly overrun with people who came from the shore in all sorts of craft, each one inquiring and searching after his own, and his own profit. No custom-house officers came on board, as in England, and the ship was all the time free of such persons. We came to anchor, then, before the city at three o'clock. Every one wanted to go ashore immediately. We let those most in a hurry go before us, when, leaving our property in charge of Robyn,[1] we also went in company with a passenger, named Gerrit,[2] who took us to the house of his father-in-law, where we lodged.

It is not possible to describe how this bay swarms with fish, both large and small, whales, tunnies and porpoises, whole schools of innumerable other fish, which the eagles and other birds of prey swiftly seize in their talons when the fish come up to the surface, and hauling them out of the water, fly with them to the nearest woods or beach, as we saw.

We had finally arrived where we had so long wished to be, but from whence we were soon to depart, because we had come only to do the will of Him who watches over us, and who after our longest voyage, will cause us to arrive, by His favor, as it pleases Him. Meanwhile unto Him be given all honor, and

[1] Robert Sinclair.

[2] Gerrit Evertsen van Duyn, carpenter and wheelwright, emigrated in 1649 from Nieuwerkerk in Zeeland, married Jacomina, daughter of Jacob Swarts Hellekers, lived mostly in New Utrecht and Flatbush, and died in 1706. He had returned to the Netherlands in 1670, but was now coming out for good.

praise and glory for what He does, to all eternity. Amen; yea, amen.

Leaving the ship on our arrival, it would seem proper that this narrative concerning the voyage should here be brought to an end; but as the sea over which we passed is wide and broad, and various things are to be noted, which could only be found out in process of time, I will here add them each by its kind.

Observations upon the Sea and the Voyage.

1. I have uniformly found it true, that the bottom causes the change in the color of the sea, and makes the color lighter or darker according as it may happen to be; as we experienced from the beginning to the end of our voyage. And this is the reason: the water of itself has no color, but, as it is transparent, the bottom shows itself, such as it is, through the clearness of the water, according to its depth; but something must be allowed for the sky, clouds and other bodies in the atmosphere, which, although they do not change the water, nevertheless shine in it, and throw a shadow or reflection.

2. The banks or shoals of Newfoundland extend further south than they are laid down on the charts, and as far as 36° or less of latitude, as we observed from the color of the water, although it may be deeper there than about Newfoundland.

3. There is a stream running from the river Amazon, in fact from Cape ——, along the coast of Guiana, through the Gulf of Mexico and the channel of the Bahamas, along the coast of Florida, Virginia and New Netherland, to the banks of Newfoundland, where, uniting with another stream, coming from the north out of Davis's Strait and river St. Lawrence, it goes again south, and afterwards S. W., to the Bermudas, but mostly to the east of them, the particular causes and reasons of which we will notice in its proper place.

4. This stream has its course along the gulfs, capes and bays of the coast, the same as we experienced near or west of Cape Cod or Staten Hook, where for two days successively, without headway on the ship, and in a calm, we were carried by it a degree to the north. This should be kept in mind, and one should regulate himself accordingly.

5. The storm of the Bermudas has been mentioned in its place.[1]

6. I have heretofore exposed mistakes on the large plane chart, and it is not material to enter further into that subject.

7. After we approached and passed the Bermudas the wind did not turn round the compass with the sun, which happened to us four or five times, and frequently does so, as is said by experienced persons.

8. Therefore, in navigating this passage for this place, it is best, when there are no reasons to the contrary arising from the Turks[2] or otherwise, to run just above or below the Azores, to latitude 34 and 33, and even to 32 and 31, in order to get into the stream, and yet I also consider it well to sail to the eastward of these islands; or if you avoid the Azores, then to sail from Newfoundland or its latitude, due south, or S. S. E., to the before mentioned latitude; but, in returning, it is best to follow the coast to Newfoundland, in order to fall into the stream and wind. The home voyage is almost always the shortest, inasmuch as the stream runs mostly along the coast.

9. When a change occurs in the color of the water, and at other times, the deep lead should be much used. It should be of 25 or 30 pounds weight. The ship or vessel should lie as still as possible, or the jolly-boat should be used, whether the lead be thrown with a certainty as to where you may be, or for the discovery of other bottom.

10. In storms or hurricanes never be without stern-sails, however small, unless you can sail before the wind, but no longer than that; for it is too dangerous, and too uncomfortable, both for the ship and the persons in her.

Some other observations in regard to the art of navigation and the management of ships, of minor importance we will reserve for another occasion.

[1] The mate told him, September 1, off the Bermudas, that one never failed to have storms there; and that one dark night " it seemed as if the air was full of strange faces with wonderful eyes standing out of them " (*cf.* Shakespeare's *Tempest*); and then he remembered to have read the same, in his youth, in a little book called *De Silver Poort-Klock* (The Silver Gate-Bell).

[2] Corsairs from North Africa, who at that time constantly infested the seas near England and concerning whom the narrative of the first part of the voyage shows frequent alarms.

The Persons with whom we made our Voyage.

Although this is such a miserable subject, that I deliberated long whether it were worth while to take any notice of it, yet since one does not know when a matter can be serviceable, I will nevertheless say something.

The persons who belonged to the ship were:

The captain, Thomas Singelton, an Englishman, and a Quaker, from London, I believe. He had his wife with him, who was quite young, about 24 or 26 years old, and he was surely a person of 40 or 45. He was not the best or most experienced seaman by a long distance. He was proud and very assiduous or officious to please people, especially Margaret and her man; yet he had some amiable qualities, he was affable. He was stingy; for when many mackerel were caught, he would not give one to the poor sailors; they all hung there and spoiled. He was even displeased if the sailors came with their fish lines to fish too near the place where he was, because the fish might come to their lines instead of his. His wife was a young, worldly creature, who had not the least glimmer of Quakerism, of which nevertheless she made profession, but entirely resembled an English lady fashioned somewhat upon the Dutch model. She was so proud that she wore much silver and gold; and when Margaret once spoke to him about it, he said, "I did not give it to her." Whereupon Margaret asked, "Why did you give her money to buy them?" To which he replied, "She wanted it."

The English mate, who afterwards became captain, was a passionate person, inwardly still more than he showed outwardly, a great man-pleaser where his interest was to be promoted. He was very close, but was compelled to be much closer in order to please Margaret.

The Dutch mate, Evert, was a wicked, impious fellow, who also drank freely. He was very proud of his knowledge and experience, which were none of the greatest.

The boatswain, Abram, of Plymouth, was rough and wicked in his orders, but he was a strong and able seaman. Robyn was the best.

I cannot permit myself to go further; it is too unpleasant a subject.

The passengers and crew were a wretched set. There was no rest, night or day, especially among the wives—a rabble I cannot describe. Day and night without cessation it was as if one were in the fish market or apple market, where, indeed, some of them had obtained their living, or as if indeed one were in still worse places. There were nine or ten of them always together. Among the men there were some who drank like beasts, yes, drank themselves dead drunk, as you may judge from the fact that two or three of them drank 3½ ankers[1] of brandy, from the time we left England or Holland, besides the wine which they had with them—it is too horrible. As to Margaret and Jan, it is not to be told what miserable people Margaret and Jan were, and especially their excessive covetousness. In fine, it was a Babel. I have never in my life heard of such a disorderly ship. It was confusion without end. I have never been in a ship where there was so much vermin, which were communicated to us, and especially not a few to me, because being in the cordage at night I particularly received them. There were those whose bunks and clothes were as full as if they had been sown. But I must forbear.

When we first came on board the ship we ate where we were, and with those we found there, but afterwards the messes were regulated, and we were placed on deck with five or six uncouth youngsters; where, nevertheless, we continued. This so exercised the other passengers, seeing us submit so willingly, that they themselves could no longer endure it, and desired us to come with them, and make a mess of eight. We had been compelled to buy our stores in England, as what we had were spoiled, or not sufficient. There was not a bit of butter or vinegar on the food during the whole voyage, except what we had purchased at Falmouth. I do not know how long it was we had nothing to eat except heads of salt fish, and those spoiled for the most part. We had to eat them till they were thrown overboard. Most of the time we had white peas, which our cook was too lazy to clean, or were boiled in stinking water, and when they were brought on the table we had to throw them away. The meat was old and tainted; the pork passable, but enormously thick, as much as six inches; and the bread was mouldy or wormy. We had a ration of

[1] An anker was about ten gallons.

beer three times a day to drink at table. The water smelt very bad, which was the fault of the captain. When we left England they called us to eat in the cabin, but it was only a change of place and nothing more. Each meal was dished up three times in the cabin, first for the eight passengers, then for the captain, mate and wife, who sometimes did not have as good as we had, and lastly for Margaret and Mr. Jan, who had prepared for them hardly any thing else except poultry and the like. But this is enough.

After we left England, I took upon myself, out of love of the thing, and because there were so few persons to work the ship, namely, ten in all, including the captain, to watch and attend the rudder, as well as to make observations in navigation; but when I perceived the sailors, on this account, became lazy and depended upon me, I left the rudder-gang. Nevertheless, when an English ship came near running us down in the watch off Cape Cod, causing thereby much uproar and confusion in our ship, I did my best to unfasten a rope which they could not make loose, at which the mate raved and swore, and for which he would have almost struck or killed me. When my comrade heard of it he wished me not to do any thing more, and that was my opinion. I could not, however, refrain from helping to the last, but I abandoned the watch, and so caused the mate to feel that we were not insensible, for there was nothing else to be done to him. He, nevertheless, invited us daily more than any one else. Finally, when the voyage was completed, there was no one, either captain, or mate, or sailor, or Margaret, who said "We thank you," except our poor Robyn. We had a little package put in the ship at Falmouth, about a foot and a half square, on which the captain charged us four guilders freight, in the money of Holland. We represented to Margaret how we had managed with only one chest between us, although each passenger was entitled to have one of his own, but it was all to no purpose. Four guilders it must be. It was not that we had any difficulty in giving it, but it was only to be convinced of her unblushing avarice. The mate's wife was the least evil-inclined, and listened most to what was said to her, which we hope will bear fruit. We have truly conducted ourselves towards all in general and each one in particular, so that not only has every one reason to be edified and convinced, but, by the grace of God, every one renders us testimony that we have edified and convinced them as well by our lives as our conversation.   Let Him alone who is the author of all grace, receive therefore all the glory, to all eternity.   Amen.[1]

[1] After this the original manuscript begins a new pagination.   See introduction to this book.

JOURNAL OF OUR TRAVELS THROUGH NEW NETHERLAND,

From the Time of our Arrival until our Departure for the Fatherland.

HAVING then fortunately arrived, by the blessing of the Lord, before the city of New York, on Saturday, the 23d day of September, we stepped ashore about four o'clock in the afternoon, in company with Gerrit, our fellow passenger, who would conduct us in this strange place. He had lived here a long time and had married his wife here, although she and his children were living at present at Zwol.[1] We went along with him, but as he met many of his old acquaintances on the way, we were constantly stopped. He first took us to the house of one of his friends, who welcomed him and us, and offered us some of the fruit of the country, very fine peaches and full grown apples, which filled our hearts with thankfulness to God. This fruit was exceedingly fair and good, and pleasant to the taste; much better than that in Holland or elsewhere, though I believe our long fasting and craving of food made it so agreeable. After taking a glass of Madeira, we proceeded on to Gerrit's father-in-law's, a very old man, half lame, and unable either to walk or stand, who fell upon the neck of his son-in-law, welcoming him with tears of joy. The old woman was also very glad. This good man was born in Vlissingen, and was named Jacob Swart.[2] He had been formerly a master carpenter at Amsterdam, but had lived in this country upwards of forty-five years. After we had been here a little while, we left our travelling bag, and went out to take a walk in the fields. It was strange to us to feel such stability under us, although it seemed as if the earth itself moved under our

[1] Zwolle in the Netherlands.

[2] *I. e.*, "black Jacob." His name was Jacob Hellekers, and his house, in which the Labadists lodged while in New York, stood where now stands no. 255 Pearl Street, near Fulton Street.

feet as the ship had done for three months past, and our body also still swayed after the manner of the rolling of the sea; but this sensation gradually passed off in the course of a few days. As we walked along we saw in different gardens trees full of apples of various kinds, and so laden with peaches and other fruit that one might doubt whether there were more leaves or fruit on them. I have never seen in Europe, in the best seasons, such an overflowing abundance. When we had finished our tour and given our guide several letters to deliver, we returned to his father-in-law's, who regaled us in the evening with milk, which refreshed us much. We had so many peaches set before us that we were timid about eating them, though we experienced no ill effects from them. We remained there to sleep, which was the first time in nine or ten weeks that we had lain down upon a bed undressed, and able to yield ourselves to sleep without apprehension of danger.

24th, Sunday. We rested well through the night. I was surprised on waking up to find my comrade had already dressed himself and breakfasted upon peaches. We walked out awhile in the fine, pure morning air, along the margin of the clear running water of the sea, which is driven up this river at every tide. As it was Sunday, in order to avoid scandal and for other reasons, we did not wish to absent ourselves from church. We therefore went, and found there truly a wild worldly world. I say wild, not only because the people are wild, as they call it in Europe, but because almost all the people who go there to live, or who are born there, partake somewhat of the nature of the country, that is, peculiar to the land where they live. We heard a minister preach, who had come from the up-river country, from Fort Orange, where his residence is, an old man, named Domine Schaets,[1] of Amsterdam. He was, it appears, a Voetian, and had come down for the purpose of approving, examining, ordaining and collating a student; to perform which office the neighboring

[1] Rev. Gideon Schaets was settled as pastor at Rensselaerwyck in 1652, later at Beverwyck and Albany, continuing in service there till he died in 1694, aged 86. Peter Tesschenmaker had come up from Dutch Guiana, and had supplied the pulpits at Esopus and at Newcastle on the South River (Delaware River), for about a year in each place. The history of his formal call, examination, ordination in October, 1679, and appointment, is set forth in *Ecclesiastical Records*

ministers come here, as to the capital, and in order that the
collation may be approved by the governor, who, at this time,
was not at home, but was at Pemequick, in the northerly parts
of New England.[1] This student, named Tessemaker, from
Utrecht, I believe, was a Voetian, and had found some ob-
stacles in his way, because the other ministers were all Cocceians, namely: Do. Niewenhuisen, of [New] Amsterdam, the
one of Long Island, and Do. Gaesbeck, of Esopus, whose son
is sheriff of this city. He was to minister at the South River,
near the governor there, or in the principal place, as he himself told us. The governor was expected home every day,
and then Tessemaker supposed he would be dispatched.

The governor is the greatest man in New Netherland, and
acknowledges no superior in all America, except the viceroy,
who resides upon Jamaica.

This Schaets, then, preached. He had a defect in the left
eye, and used such strange gestures and language that I think
I never in all my life have heard any thing more miserable;
indeed, I can compare him with no one better than with one
D. van Ecke, lately the minister at Armuyden, in Zeeland,
more in life, conversation and gestures than in person. As it
is not strange in these countries to have men as ministers who
drink, we could imagine nothing else than that he had been
drinking a little this morning. His text was, "Come unto me
all ye," etc., but he was so rough that even the roughest and
most godless of our sailors were astonished.

The church being in the fort, we had an opportunity to
look through the latter, as we had come too early for preaching. It is not large; it has four points or batteries; it has no
moat outside, but is enclosed with a double row of palisades.
It is built from the foundation with quarry stone. The para-
pet is of earth. It is well provided with cannon, for the most

---

of New York, I. 724–735. The only three other Dutch Reformed ministers in
the province at this time were those named below: Rev. Wilhelmus van Nieuwenhuysen of New York (1672—d. 1681), Rev. Casparus van Zuuren of Flushing,
Brooklyn, and Flatlands (1677–1685), and Rev. Laurentius Gaasbeeck of Esopus
(1678—d. February, 1680).

[1] Pemaquid, on the coast of Maine, where this governor had built a fort in
1677, on territory embraced in the Duke of York's patent. The governor was Sir
Edmund Andros (1674–1681). He visited Pemaquid in the autumn of 1679.
He was of course nowise subordinate to the governor of Jamaica.

part of iron, though there were some small brass pieces, all bearing the mark or arms of the Netherlanders. The garrison is small. There is a well of fine water dug in the fort by the English, contrary to the opinion of the Dutch, who supposed the fort was built upon rock, and had therefore never attempted any such thing. There is, indeed, some indication of stone there, for along the edge of the water below the fort there is a very large rock extending apparently under the fort, which is built upon the point formed by the two rivers, namely, the East River, which is the water running between the Mahatans and Long Island, and the North River, which runs straight up to Fort Orange. In front of the fort, on the Long Island side, there is a small island called Noten Island (Nut Island),[1] around the point of which vessels must go in sailing out or in, whereby they are compelled to pass close by the point of the fort, where they can be flanked by several of the batteries. It has only one gate, and that is on the land side, opening upon a broad plain or street, called the Broadway or Beaverway. Over this gate are the arms of the Duke of York. During the time of the Dutch there were two gates, namely, another on the water side; but the English have closed it, and made a battery there, with a false gate. In front of the church is inscribed the name of Governor Kyft, who caused the same to be built in the year 1642.[2] It has a shingled roof, and upon the gable towards the water there is a small wooden tower, with a bell in it, but no clock. There is a sun-dial on three sides. The front of the fort stretches east and west, and consequently the sides run north and south.

After we had returned to the house and dined, my comrade not wishing to go to church, sat about writing letters, as there was a ship, of which André Bon was master, about to leave in a few days for London; but in order that we should not be both absent from church, and as the usual minister[3] was to

[1] Governor's Island.

[2] The inscription, on a stone extant till 1835, is here quoted almost literally. It ran, "Anno Domini 1642, W. Kieft, director general, has caused the commonalty to build this temple." Willem Kieft was director-general of New Netherland from 1638 to 1647. A plan of town and fort may be seen at p. 420 of *Narratives of New Netherland*, in this series.

[3] Nieuwenhuysen. The text is in I Timothy v. 17, "Let the elders that rule well, be accounted worthy of double honor."

preach in the afternoon, I went alone to hear him. He was a thick, corpulent person with a red and bloated face, and of very slabbering speech. His text was, the elders who serve well, etc., because the elders and deacons were that day renewed, and I saw them admitted. After preaching, the good old people with whom we lodged, who, indeed, if they were not the best on all the Manathans, were at least among the best, especially the wife, begged we would go with their son Gerrit to one of their daughters, who lived in a delightful place, and kept a tavern, where we would be able to taste the beer of New Netherland, inasmuch as it was also a brewery.[1] Some of their friends passing by requested Gerrit and us to accompany them, and so we went for the purpose of seeing what was to be seen; but when we arrived there, we found ourselves much deceived. On account of its being to some extent a pleasant spot, it was resorted to on Sundays by all sorts of revellers, and was a low pot-house. Our company immediately found acquaintances there and joined them, but it being repugnant to our feelings to be there, we walked into the orchard to seek pleasure in contemplating the innocent objects of nature. Among other trees we observed a mulberry tree, the leaves of which were as large as a plate. The wife showed us pears larger than the fist, picked from a three year's graft which had borne forty of them. A great storm of rain coming up in the evening compelled us to go into the house, where we did not remain long with the others, but took our leave of them, against their wishes. We retraced our steps in the dark, exploring a way over which we had gone only once in our life, through a salt meadow and over water, upon the trunk of a tree. We nevertheless reached home, having left the others in their revels. While in their company we conversed with the first male born of Europeans in New Netherland, named Jean Vigné. His parents were from Valenciennes and he was now about sixty-five years of age. He was a brewer and a neighbor of our old people.[2] When we had come

[1] Rebecca, daughter of Jacob Hellekers's wife by her former husband, was married to Arie or Adrian Corneliszen, who had a license to sell wines and other liquors, and lived a little out of town, beyond the Fresh Water.

[2] Jean Vigné had in previous years been four times one of the schepens, or municipal councillors, of New Amsterdam. If he was born in New Netherland

back we said to our old woman what it was fitting should be said to her, regarding her daughter and her employment, in order to free our minds, though she herself was quite innocent in respect to it.

A ketch came in from sea this evening, of which David Jochemsen was the master. She left England three weeks before us, and was the same one we saw the day we came in. The captain said he recollected to have seen us, but observing us tacking several times, he did not dare follow us, for fear of being misled.

25th, Monday. We went on board the ship this morning in order to obtain our travelling bag and clothes for the purpose of having them washed, but when we came on board we could not get ashore again, before the afternoon, when the passengers' goods were to be delivered. All our goods which were between decks, were taken ashore and carried to the public storehouse, where they had to be examined; but some time elapsed before it was done in consequence of the examiners being elsewhere. At length, however, one Abraham Lennoy,[1] a good fellow apparently, befriended us. He examined our chest only, without touching our bedding or any thing else. I showed him a list of the tin which we had in the upper part of our chest, and he examined it and also the tin, and turned up a little more what was in the chest, and with that left off, without looking at it closely. He demanded four English shillings for the tin, remarking at the same time, that he had observed some other small articles, but would not examine them closely, though he had not seen either the box or the pieces of linen. This being finished we sent our goods in a cart to our lodgings, paying for the two heavy chests and straw beds, and other goods from the public storehouse, to the Smit's

in or about 1614, there must have been at least one European woman in the colony at an earlier date than has been supposed, namely, back in the years of the first Dutch trading along that coast. But many things concerning the earliest years of New Netherland must remain in uncertainty until the publication of a certain group of documents of that period, evidently important, which were sold in 1910 by Muller of Amsterdam and are now in private possession in New York, and withheld from public knowledge.

[1] Abraham de la Noy was a schoolmaster. See *post*, p. 63, note 2. Probably the writer means Peter de la Noy, who was clerk under the collector of the port. Later he was one of the chief supporters of Leisler.

Valey[1] (which is about as far as from the Elve to Wilken's house),[2] sixteen stuivers of zeawan, equal to three stuivers and a half in the money of Holland.[3]   This finished the day and we retired to rest.

26th, Tuesday.   We remained at home for the purpose of writing, but in the afternoon finding that many goods had been discharged from the ship, we went to look after our little package, which also came.   I declared it, and it was examined. I had to pay 24 guilders in zeawan or five guilders in the coin of Holland.   I brought it to the house and looked the things all over, rejoicing that we were finally rid of that miserable set and the ship, the freight only remaining to be paid, which was fixed at four guilders in coin.   We went first to Margaret in relation to the freight, who said she had nothing more to do with it, and that we must speak to her husband about it, which it was not convenient to do that evening, and we therefore let it go, waiting for an opportunity to speak to her and her husband with the captain and perhaps also Mr. Jan.

27th, Wednesday.   Nothing occurred to-day except that I went to assist Gerrit in bringing his goods home, and declaring them, which we did.   We heard that one of the wicked and godless sailors had broken his leg; and in this we saw and acknowledged the Lord and His righteousness.   We visited Jean Vigné in order, as he was one of the oldest inhabitants, to obtain from him information on various matters relating to the country.

28th, Thursday.   We remained at home to-day.   I performed some little errands.   Monsr. de La Grange[4] called upon us, dressed up like a great fop, as he was.   My comrade did

---

[1] The Smith's Flats, a tract of low-lying land along the East River, outside the palisade of the town, and extending from present Wall Street to Beekman.

[2] Perhaps a reminiscence from the days (1671–1675) when the Labadists lived on the Elbe, at Altona.

[3] The stiver of Holland money was equivalent to two cents.   Six white beads of wampum to the stiver was the rate established by authority in 1673.

[4] Arnoldus de la Grange and his wife Cornelia (Fonteyn), resident at this time in New York, removed soon after to Newcastle, on the Delaware River, where he had various tracts of land and where he in 1681 erected a windmill. In 1684–1685 he was concerned in the purchase from Augustine Herrman of land in Bohemia Manor for the Labadist settlement, and later is found as a member of their community.

not fail to speak to him seriously on the subject.   He requested us to go with him immediately to his house, as I at length did. His house was not far from our lodgings on the front of the city.   He had a small shop, as almost all the people here have, who gain their living by trade, namely, in tobacco and liquors, thread and pins and other knick-knacks.   His wife welcomed me, and instantly requested that we would come to their house and stay there as long as we were here, for which I thanked them.   They had lost a child by the small pox, and they had been sick with the same disease.   He said he intended to go to the South River[1] within three weeks, and hearing we were inclined to travel, he desired our company, being willing to take us everywhere and to give us every information.   I thanked him, but gave him no assurances, telling him we would see what the Lord would will of us.

29th, Friday.   We finished our letters, and intended to go to-day over to Long Island.   At noon a person came to us in our chamber and requested that we would be pleased to go to their minister, who was in the next house, as he was desirous of seeing and conversing with us, having already heard much good of us.   We excused ourselves on the ground that we were busy writing, endeavoring to finish our letters, in order, if it were possible, to go over to Long Island in the afternoon, with which he went away.

As soon as we had dined we sent off our letters; and this being all accomplished, we started at two o'clock for Long Island.   This island is called Long Island, not so much because it is longer than it is broad, but particularly because it is the longest island in this region, or even along the whole coast of New Netherland, Virginia and New England.   It is one hundred and forty-four miles in length, and from twenty-four to twenty-eight miles wide, though there are several bays and points along it, and, consequently, it is much broader in some places than others.   On the west is Staten Island, from which it is separated about a mile, and the great bay over which you see the Nevesincke.   With Staten Island it makes the passage through which all vessels pass in sailing from or to the Mahatans, although they can go through the Kil van Kol, which is on the other side of Staten Island.   The ends of

[1] Delaware River.

these islands opposite each other are quite high land, and they
are, therefore, called the Hoofden (Headlands), from a comparison with the Hoofden of the channel between England and
France, in Europe. On the north is the island of Mahatans
and a part of the mainland. On the east is the sea, which
shoots up to New England, and in which there are various
islands. On the south is the great ocean. The outer shore
of this island has before it several small islands and broken
land, such as Coninen [Coney] Island, a low sandy island of
about three hours' circuit, its westerly point forming with
Sandy Hook, on the other side, the entrance from the sea.
It is oblong in shape, and is grown over with bushes.
Nobody lives upon it, but it is used in winter for keeping
cattle, horses, oxen, hogs and others, which are able to obtain
there sufficient to eat the whole winter, and to shelter themselves from the cold in the thickets. This island is not so cold
as Long Island or the Mahatans, or others, like some other
islands on the coast, in consequence of their having more sea
breeze, and of the saltness of the sea breaking upon the shoals,
rocks and reefs, with which the coast is beset. There is also
the Bear's Island and others, separated from Long Island by
creeks and marshes overflown at high water.[1] There are also
on this sea coast various miry places, like the Vlaeck, and others
as well as some sand bays and hard and rocky shores. Long
Island stretches into the sea for the most part east by south
and east-southeast. None of its land is very high, for you
must be nearly opposite Sandy Hook before you can see it.
There is a hill or ridge running lengthwise through the island,
nearest the north side and west end of the island. The south
side and east end are more flat. The water by which it is
separated from the Mahatans, is improperly called the East
River, for it is nothing else than an arm of the sea, beginning
in the bay on the west and ending in the sea on the east.
After forming in this passage several islands, this water is as
broad before the city as the Y before Amsterdam, but the ebb
and flood tides are stronger. There is a ferry for the purpose
of crossing over it, which is farmed out by the year, and yields
a good income, as it is a considerable thoroughfare, this island

[1] Beeren Eylandt, afterward called Barren Island, lay east of Coney Island,
between it and Jamaica Bay. Vlaeck means "the flat."

being one of the most populous places in this vicinity. A considerable number of Indians live upon it, who gain their subsistence by hunting and fishing, and they, as well as others, must carry their articles to market over this ferry, or boat them over, as it is free to every one to use his own boat, if he have one, or to borrow or hire one for the purpose. The fare over the ferry is three stuivers in *zeewan*[1] for each person.

Here we three crossed over, my comrade, Gerrit, our guide, and myself, in a row-boat, as it happened, which, in good weather and tide, carries a sail. When we came over we found there Jan Teunissen, our fellow passenger, who had promised us so much good. He was going over to the city, to deliver his letters and transact other business. He told us he would return home in the evening, and we would find him there. We went on, up the hill, along open roads and a little woods, through the first village, called Breukelen, which has a small and ugly little church standing in the middle of the road.[2] Having passed through here, we struck off to the right, in order to go to Gouanes. We went upon several plantations where Gerrit was acquainted with almost all of the people, who made us very welcome, sharing with us bountifully whatever they had, whether it was milk, cider, fruit or tobacco, and especially, and first and most of all, miserable rum or brandy which had been brought from Barbados and other islands, and which is called by the Dutch *kill-devil*. All these people are very fond of it, and most of them extravagantly so, although it is very dear and has a bad taste. It is impossible to tell how many peach trees we passed, all laden with fruit to breaking down, and many of them actually broken down. We came to a place surrounded with such trees from which so many had fallen off that the ground could not be discerned, and you could not put your foot down without trampling them; and, notwithstanding such large quantities had fallen off, the trees still were as full as they could bear. The hogs and other animals mostly feed on them. This place belongs to the oldest European woman in the country. We went immediately into

[1] Less than half a cent.

[2] The second church building in Brooklyn, erected in 1666, and standing till 1766. It stood in the middle of what is now Fulton Street, near Lawrence Street. Gowanus was a distinct hamlet to the southward from Breukelen.

her house, where she lived with her children. We found her sitting by the fire, smoking tobacco incessantly, one pipe after another. We enquired after her age, which the children told us was an hundred years. She was from Luyck [Liège], and still spoke good Wals.[1] She could reason very well sometimes, and at other times she could not. She showed us several large apples, as good fruit of that country, and different from that of Europe. She had been about fifty years now in the country, and had above seventy children and grandchildren. She saw the third generation after her. Her mother had attended women in child-bed in her one hundred and sixth year, and was one hundred and eleven or twelve years old when she died. We tasted here, for the first time, smoked *twaelft* [twelfth], a fish so called because it is caught in season next after the *elft* [eleventh].[2] It was salted a little and then smoked, and, although it was now a year old, it was still perfectly good, and in flavor not inferior to smoked salmon. We drank here, also, the first new cider, which was very fine.

We proceeded on to Gouanes, a place so called, where we arrived in the evening at one of the best friends of Gerrit, named Symon.[3] He was very glad to see us, and so was his wife. He took us into the house, and entertained us exceedingly well. We found a good fire, half-way up the chimney, of clear oak and hickory, which they made not the least scruple of burning profusely. We let it penetrate us thoroughly. There had been already thrown upon it, to be roasted, a pail-full of Gouanes oysters, which are the best in the country. They are fully as good as those of England, and better than those we ate at Falmouth. I had to try some of them raw. They are large and full, some of them not less than a foot long, and they grow sometimes ten, twelve and sixteen together, and are then like a piece of rock. Others are young

[1] French of the Walloon variety. See p. 70, note 1, *post.*

[2] Striped bass and shad, respectively. In reality the word *elft* has nothing to do with *eleven*, for *elft*=Fr. *alose* or Eng. *allice.*

[3] This settler was Simon Aertsen De Hart, who came to New Netherland in 1664 and settled at Gowanus Cove. The house in which he entertained the travellers was till lately still standing, near Thirty-ninth Street, west of Third Avenue, Brooklyn, but was destroyed to make room for the terminal buildings of the Thirty-ninth Street ferry. A picture of it as it appeared in 1867 is plate XII. in Mr. Murphy's edition of this journal.

and small.   In consequence of the great quantities of them, everybody keeps the shells for the purpose of burning them into lime.   They pickle the oysters in small casks, and send them to Barbados and the other islands.   We had for supper a roasted haunch of venison, which he had bought of the Indians for three guilders and a half of *seewant,* that is, fifteen stivers of Dutch money,[1] and which weighed thirty pounds. The meat was exceedingly tender and good, and also quite fat.   It had a slight spicy flavor.   We were also served with wild turkey, which was also fat and of a good flavor; and a wild goose, but that was rather dry.   Everything we had was the natural production of the country.   We saw here, lying in a heap, a whole hill of watermelons, which were as large as pumpkins, and which Symon was going to take to the city to sell.   They were very good, though there is a difference between them and those of the Caribbee Islands; but this may be owing to its being late in the season, and these were the last pulling.   It was very late at night when we went to rest in a kermis bed, as it is called,[2] in the corner of the hearth, along side of a good fire.

30*th, Saturday.*   Early this morning the husband and wife set off for the city with their marketing; and we, having explored the land in the vicinity, left after breakfast.   We went a part of the way through a wood and fine, new made land, and so along the shore to the west end of the island called Najack.[3]   As we proceeded along the shore, we found, among other curiosities, a highly marbled stone, very hard, in which we saw muscovy glass[4] lying in layers between the clefts, and how it was struck or cut out.   We broke off a small piece with some difficulty, and picked out a little glass in the splits. Continuing onward from there, we came to the plantation of the Najack Indians, which was planted with maize, or Turkish wheat.   We soon heard a noise of pounding, like thrashing, and went to the place whence it proceeded, and found there an old Indian woman busily employed beating Turkish beans

---

[1] Thirty cents.   [2] Shake-down, bed on the floor.

[3] Pronounced Nyack; the region around the present site of Fort Hamilton, on the eastern side of the Narrows.   It was at that time largely surrounded by a marsh and hence is referred to in the text as an island.

[4] Mica.

out of the pods by means of a stick, which she did with astonishing force and dexterity. Gerrit inquired of her, in the Indian language, which he spoke perfectly well, how old she was, and she answered eighty years; at which we were still more astonished that so old a woman should still have so much strength and courage to work as she did. We went from thence to her habitation, where we found the whole troop together, consisting of seven or eight families, and twenty or twenty-two persons, I should think. Their house was low and long, about sixty feet long and fourteen or fifteen feet wide. The bottom was earth, the sides and roof were made of reed and the bark of chestnut trees; the posts, or columns, were limbs of trees stuck in the ground, and all fastened together. The top, or ridge of the roof was open about half a foot wide, from one end to the other, in order to let the smoke escape, in place of a chimney. On the sides, or walls, of the house, the roof was so low that you could hardly stand under it. The entrances, or doors, which were at both ends, were so small and low that they had to stoop down and squeeze themselves to get through them. The doors were made of reed or flat bark. In the whole building there was no lime, stone, iron or lead. They build their fire in the middle of the floor, according to the number of families which live in it, so that from one end to the other each of them boils its own pot, and eats when it likes, not only the families by themselves, but each Indian alone, according as he is hungry, at all hours, morning, noon and night. By each fire are the cooking utensils, consisting of a pot, a bowl, or calabash, and a spoon also made of a calabash. These are all that relate to cooking. They lie upon mats with their feet towards the fire, on each side of it. They do not sit much upon any thing raised up, but, for the most part, sit on the ground or squat on their ankles. Their other household articles consists of a calabash of water, out of which they drink, a small basket in which to carry and keep their maize and small beans, and a knife. The implements are, for tillage, a small, sharp stone, and nothing more; for hunting, a gun and pouch for powder and lead; for fishing, a canoe without mast or sail, and without a nail in any part of it, though it is sometimes full forty feet in length, fish hooks and lines, and scoops to paddle with in place of oars. I do not know whether there are not some others of a trifling nature. All who live in one house are generally of one stock or descent, as father and mother with their offspring. Their bread is maize, pounded in a block by a stone, but not fine. This is mixed with water, and made into a cake, which they bake under the hot ashes. They gave us a small piece when we entered, and although the grains were not ripe, and it was half baked and coarse grains, we nevertheless had to eat it, or, at least, not throw it away before them, which they would have regarded as a great sin, or a great affront. We chewed a little of it *with long teeth*, and managed to hide it so they did not see it. We had also to drink out of their calabashes the water which was their drink, and which was very good. We saw here the Indians who came on board the ship when we arrived. They were all very joyful at the visit of our Gerrit, who was an old acquaintance of theirs, and had heretofore long resided about there. We presented them with two jewsharps, which much pleased them, and they immediately commenced to play upon them, which they could do tolerably well. Some of their *patroons* (chiefs), some of whom spoke good Dutch, and are also their medicine-men and surgeons as well as their teachers, were busy making shoes of deer leather, which they understand how to make soft by continually working it in their hands. They had dogs, fowls and hogs, which they learn by degrees from the Europeans how to manage better. They had, also, peach trees, which were well laden. Towards the last, we asked them for some peaches, and they answered, "Go and pick them," which showed their politeness. However, in order not to offend them, we went off and pulled some. Although they are such a poor, miserable people, they are, nevertheless, licentious and proud, and given to knavery and scoffing. Seeing a very old woman among them, we inquired how old she was, when some young fellows, laughing and jeering, answered twenty years, while it was evident to us she was not less than an hundred. We observed here the manner in which they travel with their children, a woman having one which she carried on her back. The little thing clung tight around her neck like a cat, where it was kept secure by means of a piece of daffels, their usual garment. Its head, back and buttocks were entirely flat. How that happened to be so we will relate hereafter, as we now only make mention of what we saw.

These Indians live on the land of Jaques , brother-in-law of Gerrit.[1] He bought the land from them in the first instance, and then let them have a small corner, for which they pay him twenty bushels of maize yearly, that is, ten bags. Jaques had first bought the whole of Najack from these Indians, who were the lords thereof, and lived upon the land, which is a large place, and afterwards bought it *again*, in parcels. He was unwilling to drive the Indians from the land, and has therefore left them a corner of it, keeping the best of it himself.[2] We arrived then upon the land of this Jaques, which is all good, and yields large crops of wheat and other grain. It is of a blackish color, but not clayey, and almost like the garden mould I have seen in Holland. At length we reached the house of this Jaques, where we found Monsr. de La Grange, who had come there in search of us, to inform us further concerning his departure for the South River, and to take us to his house. We spoke to him in regard to this and other matters, as was proper, and shortly afterwards he left. This Jaques is a man advanced in years. He was born in Utrecht, but of French parents, as we could readily discover from all his actions, looks and language. He had studied philosophy in his youth, and spoke Latin and good French. He was a mathematician and sworn land-surveyor. He had also formerly learned several sciences, and had some knowledge of medicine. But the worst of it was, he was a good Cartesian,[3] and not a good Christian, regulating himself, and all externals, by reason and justice only; nevertheless, he regulated all things better by these principles than most people in these parts do, who bear the name of Christians or pious persons. His brother-in-law and ourselves were welcomed by him and

---

[1] Jacques Cortelyou. He came out from Utrecht as tutor to the children of Cornelis van Werckhoven, to whom this New Utrecht tract was first granted by the Dutch West India Company. He became the official surveyor of the province, made in 1660 a map of New Netherland, and founded New Utrecht, on Long Island, and a settlement in New Jersey.

[2] There is probably here some confusion between the original grant to van Werckhoven and subsequent regrants to Cortelyou.

[3] Follower of René Descartes (1596–1650), the celebrated French philosopher and mathematician, founder of Cartesianism and of modern philosophy in general.

his wife. He treated us with every civility, although two of
his sons being sick, and he very much confined in attending upon them, he was much interrupted in attending to us,
since they more than we afflicted his head and that of his wife.
We went looking around the country, and towards evening
came to the village of New Utrecht, so named by him. This
village was burned down some time ago, with every thing
about it, including the house of this man, which was almost
half an hour distant from it[1] Many persons were impover-
ished by the fire. It was now almost all rebuilt, and many
good stone houses were erected, of which Jaques's was one,
where we returned by another road to spend the night. After
supper, we went to sleep in the barn, upon some straw spread
with sheep-skins, in the midst of the continual grunting of
hogs, squealing of pigs, bleating and coughing of sheep, barking of dogs, crowing of cocks, cackling of hens, and, especially,
a goodly quantity of fleas and vermin, of no small portion of
which we were participants; and all with an open barn door,
through which a fresh northwest wind was blowing. Though
we could not sleep, we could not complain, inasmuch as we
had the same quarters and kind of bed that their own son
usually had, who had now on our arrival crept in the straw
behind us.

OCTOBER 1st, *Sunday.* We went, this morning, on a tour of
observation of the country and of the neighbors, some of whom
were better situated than others, but all of them had more or
less children sick with the small pox, which, next to the fever
and ague, is the most prevalent disease in these parts, and
of which many have died. We went into one house where
there were two children lying dead and unburied, and three
others sick, and where one had died the week before. This
disease was more fatal this year than usual. We spoke to
these afflicted people what was suitable and they could
bear.

Finding myself afterwards alone upon a small eminence,
I made a sketch, as well as I could, of the land surrounding the

---

[1] See Governor Andros's recommendation to the constables and overseers of
Brooklyn to contribute to the relief of Cortelyou and the other inhabitants of
New Utrecht, on account of their losses by fire, 1675, in Stiles, *History of Brooklyn,*
I. 198.

great bay, that is, Coney Island, the entrance from the sea, Rentselaer's Hook, and so further to the right, towards Kil van Kol.[1]

After dinner we intended to leave for a place called the bay,[2] where Jan Theunissen, our fellow passenger, lived, who had made us great promises of friendship; besides, my companion was desirous, as they said there would be preaching, to hear the minister of the island,[3] who was very zealous and a great Cocceian, and, perhaps, a Cartesian. But Jaques persuaded us from it, because the house where Jan Theunissen lived with his father was so full of people on Sundays, who came from all directions to attend preaching, that you could scarcely get in or out. As the minister was not in the village where he dwelt, he remained over with many other persons; and he (Jaques) said he would accompany us there the next morning. So we let it pass, and took another walk to New Utrecht, where we drank some good beer a year old, and coming back again to the house, indulged in peaches on the road. I went along the shore to Coney Island, which is separated from Long Island only by a creek, and around the point, and came inside not far from a village called Gravesant,[4] and again home. We discovered on the road several kinds of grapes still on the vines, called *speck* (pork) grapes, which are not always good, and these were not; although they were sweet in the mouth at first, they made it disagreeable and stinking. The small blue grapes are better, and their vines grow in good form. Although they have several times attempted to plant vineyards, and have not immediately succeeded, they, nevertheless, have not abandoned the hope of doing so by and by, for there is always some encouragement, although they have not, as yet, discovered the cause of the failure.

[1] This sketch is still preserved, accompanying the manuscript of this journal in the possession of the Long Island Historical Society. It bears the legend, in Dutch, "Views of the land on the south side and southwest side of the great bay between the Nevesincks and Long Island, six [Dutch] miles from New York. . . . All as it appears from . . . Jaques [*blank*]'s house at Najaq." It is reproduced as plate II. in Mr. Murphy's edition.

[2] Flatlands, where Elbert Elbertsen Stoothoff, father-in-law of Jan Theunissen, and a man of prominence, lived.

[3] Niewenhuisen.

[4] Gravesend, still farther down the south shore of Long Island.

2d, Monday. Having slept the night again at Najack, we four went, after breakfast, to the bay, where we arrived about ten o'clock. We did not find Jan Theunissen at home, as he had driven to the city to bring his goods; but the father and mother bade us welcome, and took us around into their orchards to look at them. My comrade spoke to him as opportunity offered of godly things, but he seemed to be a little disposed to play the part of a religious and wise man, and he defended himself and the evil as much as he could, going to work somewhat coldly with us. We took the time, however, to go around and see every thing thoroughly, and found the land, in general, not so good as that at Najack. There is towards the sea a large piece of low flat land which is overflowed at every tide, like the *schorr* with us, miry and muddy at the bottom, and which produces a species of hard salt grass or reed grass. Such a place they call *valey* and mow it for hay, which cattle would rather eat than fresh hay or grass. It is so hard that they cannot mow it with a common scythe, like ours, but must have the English scythe for the purpose. Their adjoining corn lands are dry and barren for the most part. Some of them are now entirely covered with clover in blossom, which diffused a sweet odor in the air for a great distance, and which we discovered in the atmosphere, before we saw the fields. Behind the village, inland, are their meadows, but they also were now arid. All the land from the bay to the Vlacke Bos[1] is low and level, without the least elevation. There is also a tract which is somewhat large, of a kind of heath, on which sheep could graze, though we saw none upon it. This marsh, like all the others, is well provided with good creeks which are navigable and very serviceable for fisheries. There is here a grist-mill driven by the water which they dam up in the creek; and it is hereabouts they go mostly to shoot snipe and wild geese. In the middle of this meadow there is a grove into which we went, and within which there was a good vale cleared off and planted. On our return from this ramble we found Jan Theunissen had come back with his company. He welcomed us, but somewhat coldly, and so demeaned himself all the time we were there, as to astonish my comrade at the change, but not me entirely, for I had observed this falling off

[1] Flatbush.

while we were yet at sea and were approaching the land and even before that, and had remarked it to my colleague, but he had more confidence in him. The day having been thus passed, we remained here for the night to sleep. In the evening we made the acquaintance of one Jan Poppe, formerly a skipper in the West Indies, whom I had known when I lived there.[1] He did not know me by name or by vocation, but only that I lived there, and had conversed with him there, but not much. He was tired of the sea, and not having accumulated much, he had come to settle down here, making his living out of the business of a turner, by which he could live bountifully.

3d, *Tuesday*. This whole day it did nothing except rain, with an E. and E. N. E. wind, so that we were compelled to sit in their house, as in a prison all the time; and it was so much the worse because the house was constantly filled with a multitude of godless people; for this father or father-in-law of Jan Theunissen,[2] being the principal person in the place, was their captain, and having many children of his own besides, there was a continual concourse at his house. We had to remain, although it grieved us a great deal. But as we had heard that there was an Englishman residing at Gravesend, named Bouman, who went every year about this time with horses and sheep to the South River, and would probably go there again in about three weeks time, we resolved, when the rain was partly over, to go and talk to him, which we did, arriving there towards evening. We found him at home, and inquired of him as to the situation. He said, he intended to leave in fourteen days or at the longest in three weeks, with horses, and would be happy to have our company on the road. He told us several things touching the situation of the South River, where he had a large tract of land which he intended soon to put under cultivation. It being evening, and nearer Jaques's house than the bay, we determined to go there as we had previously intended. Mr. Bouman had the kindness to conduct us a portion of the way so that we could not go astray. We arrived at Jaques's house, where we were welcome. The

[1] This may mean Surinam (Dutch Guiana). Later, in 1683, a Labadist colony went out to Surinam, but failed; Danckaerts went out to join them, but returned.

[2] Elbert Elbertsen.

land around Gravesant is also flat, but not so flat or so barren as in the bay, and yields good crops.

4th, Wednesday. We slept for the night in our old place. In the morning the horses were harnessed to the wagon for the purpose of carrying us to the city, and bringing back some medicines which had arrived for him (Jaques) from Holland in our ship. We breakfasted to our full, and rode first to the bay, where we had left our travelling bag. Seeing there was nothing to be accomplished with our Jan Theunissen, all his great promises having vanished without the least result, though they had cost us dearly enough, we let that rest quiet, and taking our leave, rode on to the Vlacke Bos, a village situated about an hour and a half's distance from there, upon the same plain, which is very large. This village seems to have better farms than the bay, and yields full as much revenue. Riding through it, we came to the woods and the hills, which are very stony and uncomfortable to ride over. We rode over them, and passed through the village of Breukelen to the ferry, and leaving the wagon there, we crossed over the river and arrived at home at noon, where we were able to rest a little, and where our old people were glad to see us. We sent back to Jaques half of our tincture Calaminaris, and half of our balsam Sulpherus and some other things.[1] He had been of service to us in several respects, as he promised to be, and that with perfect willingness.

5th, Thursday. We remained at home this morning, my comrade having been a little indisposed the preceding day and night, and betook ourselves to writing. At noon we visited Mons. de La Grange, who was busily employed in his little shop, packing and marking a parcel of ribbons which he was going to send to Barbados, because, as he said, he could not dispose of them here to advantage, that is, with sufficient profit. We let him first finish his work, and after that he took us to his counting room, where his wife was. We did not fail to converse kindly with him and his wife in relation to those matters in which we believed they were sinning, notwithstanding all the little reasons which pious people of that description are accustomed to advance in extenuation of their sin and

---

[1] Tincture of calamus; sulphur balsam, a mixture of olive oil and sublimed sulphur.

avarice. As there were plenty of books around, my comrade inquired of him what book he liked or esteemed the most. Upon this he brought forward two of the elder Brakel, one of which was, *De Trappen des Geestelycken Levens*.[1] He also took down another written by a Scotchman, of whom my comrade had some knowledge, and translated by Domine Koelman. On my return home, the son of our old people asked me if I would not go to their usual catechizing, which they held once a week at the house of Abraham Lanoy, schoolmaster, and brother of the clerk in the custom house.[2] I accompanied him there, and found a company of about twenty-five persons, male and female, but mostly young people. It looked like a school, as indeed it was, more than an assembly of persons who were seeking after true godliness; where the schoolmaster, who instructed them, handled the subject more like a schoolmaster in the midst of his scholars than a person who knew and loved God, and sought to make him known and loved. They sang some verses from the Psalms, made a prayer, and questioned from the catechism, at the conclusion of which they prayed and sang some verses from the Psalms again. It was all performed without respect or reverence, very literally, and mixed up with much obscurity and error. He played, however, the part of a learned and pious man, *enfin le suffisant et le petit precheur*. After their departure, I had an opportunity of speaking to him and telling him what I thought was good for him. He acknowledged that I convinced him of several things; and thus leaving him I returned home.

6th, Friday. We remained in the house during the forenoon, but after having dined we went out about two o'clock

[1] "The Gradations of the Spiritual Life," by Theodorus à Brakel (1608–1699), an orthodox clergyman of note in the Reformed Church of Holland. Jacobus Koelman was originally a minister of the same church, in Zeeland, but became a schismatic and a Labadist and was forbidden to preach. In 1682 the people on the South River made much effort with the Classis of Amsterdam to have him sent over to be their minister, but in vain, and shortly after he left the Labadists, and in 1683 published a book against them. The book here spoken of was probably one of the works of Rev. John Brown of Wamphray in Scotland, written during his exile in Holland, 1663–1679.

[2] Abraham de la Noy seems to have taught in New York from 1668 to his death in 1702, conducting at this time a private school, but from 1686 serving as master of the Dutch parochial school.

to explore the island of Manathans. This island runs east
and west, or somewhat more northerly. On the north side of
it is the North River, by which it is separated from the main
land on the north; on the east end it is separated from the
main land by a creek, or rather a branch of the North River,
emptying itself into the East River. They can go over this
creek at dead low water, upon rocks and reefs, at the place
called Spyt den Duyvel. This creek coming into the East
River forms with it the two Barents Islands.[1] At the west end
of these two running waters, that is, where they come together
to the east of these islands, they make, with the rocks and
reefs, such a frightful eddy and whirlpool that it is exceedingly
dangerous to pass through them, especially with small boats,
of which there are some lost every now and then, and the persons in them drowned; but experience has taught men the way
of passing through them with less danger. Large vessels have
always less danger because they are not capable of being carried along so quickly. There are two places where such whirl-
ing of the stream occurs, which are on account of the danger
and frightfulness called the Great and Little Helle Gadt. After
these two streams are united, the island of Manathans is separated on the south from Long Island by the East River,
which, beginning at the bay before New York, runs eastwardly,
after forming several islands, again into the sea. This island [2]
is about seven hours' distance in length, but it is not a full hour
broad. The sides are indented with bays, coves and creeks.
It is almost entirely taken up, that is, the land is held by private
owners, but not half of it is cultivated. Much of it is good
wood land. The west end on which the city lies, is entirely
cleared for more than an hour's distance, though that is the
poorest ground; the best being on the east and north side.
There are many brooks of fresh water running through it,
pleasant and proper for man and beast to drink, as well as
agreeable to behold, affording cool and pleasant resting places,
but especially suitable places for the construction of mills, for
although there is no overflow of water, yet it can be shut off
and so used. A little eastward of Nieu Haerlem there are two

---

[1] Named from Barent Blom, a settler. Later called Great and Little Barn
Islands, now Ward's and Randall's Islands.
[2] Of Manhattan.

ridges of very high rocks, with a considerable space between them, displaying themselves very majestically, and inviting all men to acknowledge in them the majesty, grandeur, power and glory of their creator, who has impressed such marks upon them. Between them runs the road to Spyt den Duyvel.[1] The one to the north is most apparent; the south ridge is covered with earth on its north side, but it can be seen from the water or from the main land beyond to the south. The soil between these ridges is very good, though a little hilly and stony, and would be very suitable in my opinion for planting vineyards, in consequence of its being shut off on both sides from the winds which would most injure them, and is very warm. We found blue grapes along the road which were very good and sweet, and as good as any I have tasted in the Fatherland.

We went from the city, following the Broadway, over the *valley*, or the fresh water. Upon both sides of this way were many habitations of negroes, mulattoes and whites. These negroes were formerly the proper slaves of the (West India) company, but, in consequence of the frequent changes and conquests of the country, they have obtained their freedom and settled themselves down where they have thought proper, and thus on this road, where they have ground enough to live on with their families. We left the village, called the Bowery,[2] lying on the right hand, and went through the woods to New Harlem, a tolerably large village situated on the south[3] side of the island, directly opposite the place where the northeast creek and the East River come together, situated about three hours' journey from New Amsterdam, as old Harlem, in Europe, is situated about three hours' distance from old Amsterdam. As our guide, Gerrit, had some business here, and found many acquaintances, we remained over night at the house of one

---

[1] The road was finished in 1673. Traced along the modern streets, it ran up Broadway, Park Row, the Bowery, Fourth Avenue (to Union Square), Broadway (to Madison Square), and then irregularly to the Harlem River at Third Avenue and 130th Street. The heights spoken of east (northeast) of the village of New Harlem were the present Mount Morris and Mott Haven.

[2] So called because its main street ran through the farm or *bouwery* of Peter Stuyvesant.

[3] Or east.

Geresolveert,[1] schout (sheriff or constable), of the place, who had formerly lived in Brazil, and whose heart was still full of it. This house was constantly filled with people, all the time drinking, for the most part, that execrable rum. He had also the best cider we have tasted. Among the crowd we found a person of quality, an Englishman, named Captain Catrix, whose father is in great favor with the king, and he himself had assisted in several exploits in the king's service. He was administrator, or captain general, of the English forces which went, in 1666, to retake St. Christoffel, which the French had entirely conquered, and were repulsed.[2] He had also filled some high office, during the war, in the ship of the Duke of York, with two hundred infantry under his command. The king has given to his father, Sir [George] Catrix, the entire government of the lands west of the North River, in New Netherland, with power to appoint as governor whom he pleases; and at this present time there is a governor over it, by his appointment, another Carteret, his nephew, I believe, who resides at Lysbethstaun [Elizabethtown], in N. Jarnisee[3] [New Jersey].[4] From this Catrix, in England, the Quakers have

[1] Resolved Waldron (1610–1690), elected constable in October, 1678. He was the chief man of the place, had been deputy fiscael of New Netherland in the time of Governor Stuyvesant, and held many provincial and local offices. In 1659 he and Augustine Herrman went to Maryland on an embassy for Stuyvesant; see its journal in *Narratives of Early Maryland*, in this series, pp. 309–333. Thus it may have been he who told Danckaerts and Sluyter of Herrman and of Bohemia Manor. It is almost certain that he never was in Brazil; but Hendrick Vander Vin, clerk and *voorleser* of Harlem, whom our travellers may have met at Waldron's house, had had an important official position there.

[2] Catrix for Carteret. Captain James Carteret, son of Sir George Carteret, the proprietary of New Jersey, had commanded a ship at the reduction of St. Christopher in 1667, had come to New Jersey in 1671, and had allowed himself to be made leader of the malcontents in an uprising in that province in 1672. In 1673 he married the daughter of the mayor of New York, and set out for Carolina, where he was a "landgrave," but returned to New York, and ultimately (1680) to Europe.

[3] The diarist is perhaps confusing the two Channel Islands of Jersey and Guernsey.

[4] Philip Carteret, a distant cousin, not a nephew, of Sir George, is the person here meant. He was appointed governor of New Jersey under the joint proprietorship of Lord Berkeley and Sir George Carteret, in 1664, and of East Jersey in 1674, under the sole grant to Sir George. He resigned in 1682, and died in December of that year, in this country. "This Carteret in England" means of

purchased the privilege of a government of their own, over a
large tract of territory which they have bought and settled
within his dominion; and it is but little different from their
having bought the entire right of government of the whole of
his land. This son is a very profligate person. He married
a merchant's daughter here, and has so lived with his wife
that her father has been compelled to take her home again.
He runs about among the farmers, and stays where he can
find most to drink, and sleeps in barns on the straw. If he
conducted himself properly, he could be not only governor
here, but hold higher positions, for he has studied the moral-
ities, and seems to have been of a good understanding; but
that is all now drowned. His father, who will not acknowledge
him as his son, as before, allows him yearly as much only as is
necessary for him to live.

7th, Saturday. This morning, about half-past six, we set
out from the village, in order to go to the end of the island;
but before we left we did not omit supplying ourselves with
peaches which grew in an orchard along the road. The whole
ground was covered with them and with apples, lying upon the
new grain with which the orchard was planted. The peaches
were the most delicious we had yet eaten. We proceeded on
our way, and when we were not far from the point of Spyt den
Duyvel, we could see on our left hand the rocky cliffs of the
main land on the other side of the North River,[1] these cliffs
standing straight up and down, with the grain, just as if they
were antimony. We came then to the end of the island, which
was alluvial ground, and crossed over the Spyt den Duyvel in
a canoe, and paid nine stivers fare for us three, which was very
dear. We followed the opposite side of the land, and came to
the house of one Valentyn,[2] a great acquaintance of our Gerrit.
He had gone to the city, but his wife, though she did not know

course Sir George. The half of New Jersey called West New Jersey, first granted
to Fenwick and Byllynge, came as a trust into the hands of Penn, Lawrie, and
Lucas (see *Narratives of Early Pennsylvania, West New Jersey, and Delaware*, in
this series, pp. 177–195), who used it for Quaker colonization.

[1] The Palisades.

[2] Valentine Claessen, whose sons took the surname of Valentine. He was
a Saxon from Transylvania; his wife, Marritie Jacobs, was a Dutch woman, of
Beest in Gelderland.

Gerrit or us, was so much rejoiced to see Hollanders, that she hardly knew what to do for us. She set before us what she had. We left after breakfasting there. Her son showed us the way, and we came to a road which was entirely covered with peaches. We asked the boy why they left them lying there, and did not let the hogs eat them. He answered, We do not know what to do with them, there are so many; the hogs are satiated with them and will not eat any more. From this we may judge of the quantity of them. We pursued our way now a small distance through the woods and over the hills, then back again along the shore to a point, where one Webblingh,[1] an Englishman, lived, who was standing ready to cross over. He carried us over with him, and refused to take any pay for our passage, offering us at the same time some of his rum, a liquor which is everywhere. We were now again at New Harlem, and dined with Geresolveert, at whose house we slept the night before, and who made us welcome. It was now two o'clock; and leaving there, we crossed over the island, which takes about three-quarters of an hour to do, and came to the North River, which we followed a little within the woods, to Sappokanikke.[2] Gerrit having a sister and friends there we rested ourselves, and drank some good beer, which refreshed us. We continued along the shore to the city, where we arrived in an hour in the evening, very much fatigued, having walked this day about forty miles. I must add, that in passing through this island we sometimes encountered such a sweet smell in the air that we stood still, because we did not know what it was we were meeting.

8th, Sunday. We staid at home this morning for the purpose of writing and resting ourselves. Gerrit requested me to shave him, as did also an old countryman of Nevesinck who lodged at our house, which was the first time in my life that I had ever shaved any one. It afforded us an opportunity of speaking to this countryman about various matters touching the country. We intended in the afternoon to attend the English service, but, on going to the fort, the sentinel told us there was no English preaching in the afternoon, and we returned home.

[1] Walter Webley, nephew of Colonel Lewis Morris.
[2] Greenwich.

9th, Monday. We remained at home to-day, except that
I went out to ascertain whether there was any way of going
over to Staten Island. Meanwhile we began to dispose of
some of our large merchandise. Gerrit went out to Sapokan,
to do some carpenter's work. We tasted to-day some very
fine grapes.

10th, Tuesday. Finding no opportunity of going to Staten
Island, we asked our old friend Symon, who had come over
from Gouanes, what was the best way for us to get there,
when he offered us his services to take us over in his skiff,
which we accepted; and at dusk accompanied him in his boat
to Gouanes, where we arrived about eight o'clock, and where
he welcomed us and entertained us well.

11th, Wednesday. We embarked early this morning in his
boat and rowed over to Staten Island, where we arrived about
eight o'clock. He left us there, and we went on our way.
This island is about thirty-two miles[1] long and four broad. Its
sides are very irregular, with projecting points and indented
bays, and creeks running deep into the country. It lies for
the most part east and west, and is somewhat triangular. The
most prominent point is to the west. On the east side is the
narrow passage which they call the channel, by which it is
separated from the high point of Long Island. On the south
is the great bay which is inclosed by Nayaq, Conijnen Island,
Rentselaer's Hook, Nevesinck, etc. On the west is the Raritans. On the north or northwest is New Garnisee [Jersey],
from which it is separated by a large creek or arm of the river,
called Kil van Kol. The eastern part is high and steep, and
has few inhabitants. It is the usual place where ships, ready
for sea, stop to take in water, while the captain and passengers
are engaged in making their own arrangements and writing
letters previous to their departure. The whole south side is
a large plain, with much salt meadow or marsh, and several
creeks. The west point is flat, and on or around it is a large
creek with much marsh; but to the north of this creek it is
high and hilly, and beyond that it begins to be more level, but
not so low as on the other side, and is well populated. On the
northwest it is well provided with creeks and marshes, and the
land is generally better than on the south side, although there

[1] In fact, about fourteen.

is a good parcel of land in the middle of the latter.   As regards the middle or most hilly part of the island, it is uninhabited, although the soil is better than the land around it; but, in consequence of its being away from the water, and lying so high, no one will live there, the creeks and rivers being so serviceable to them in enabling them to go to the city, and for fishing and catching oysters, and for being near the salt meadows. The woods are used for pasturing horses and cattle, for being an island, none of them can get off.   Each person has marks upon his own by which he can find them when he wants them. When the population of the country shall increase, these places will be taken up.   Game of all kinds is plenty, and twenty-five and thirty deer are sometimes seen in a herd.   A boy who came into a house where we were, told us he had shot ten the last winter himself, and more than forty in his life, and in the same manner other game.   We tasted here the best grapes.   There are now about a hundred families on the island, of which the English constitute the least portion, and the Dutch and French divide between them about equally the greater portion.   They have neither church nor minister, and live rather far from each other, and inconveniently to meet together.   The English are less disposed to religion, and inquire little after it, but in case there were a minister, would contribute to his support.   The French and Dutch are very desirous and eager for one, for they spoke of it wherever we went, and said, in the event of not obtaining Domine Tessemaker, they would send, or had sent, to France for another.   The French are good Reformed churchmen, and some of them are Walloons.[1]   The Dutch are also from different quarters.

We reached the island, as I have said, about nine o'clock, directly opposite Gouanes, not far from the watering place. We proceeded southwardly along the shore of the high land on the east end, where it was sometimes stony and rocky, and sometimes sandy, supplied with fine constantly-flowing springs with which at times we quenched our thirst.   We had now come nearly to the furthest point on the southeast, behind which I had observed several houses when we came in with the ship. We had also made inquiry as to the villages through which

[1] French-speaking persons from those provinces of the Low Countries then remaining under the rule of Spain, but now constituting the kingdom of Belgium.

we would have to pass, and they had told us the Oude Dorp[1] would be the first one we should come to; but my comrade finding the point very rocky and difficult, and believing the village was inland, and as we discovered no path to follow, we determined to clamber to the top of this steep bluff, through the bushes and thickets, which we accomplished with great difficulty and in a perspiration. We found as little of a road above as below, and nothing but woods, through which one could not see. There appeared to be a little foot-path along the edge which I followed a short distance to the side of the point, but my comrade calling me and saying that he certainly thought we had passed by the road to the Oude Dorp, and observing myself that the little path led down to the point, I returned again, and we followed it the other way, which led us back to the place from where we started. We supposed we ought to go from the shore in order to find the road to the Oude Dorp, and seeing here these slight tracks into the woods, we followed them as far as we could, till at last they ran to nothing else than dry leaves. Having wandered an hour or more in the woods, now in a hollow and then over a hill, at one time through a swamp, at another across a brook, without finding any road or path, we entirely lost the way. We could see nothing except a little of the sky through the thick branches of the trees above our heads, and we thought it best to break out of the woods entirely and regain the shore. I had taken an observation of the shore and point, having been able to look at the sun, which shone extraordinarily hot in the thick woods, without the least breath of air stirring. We made our way at last as well as we could out of the woods, and struck the shore a quarter of an hour's distance from where we began to climb up. We were rejoiced, as there was a house not far from the place where we came out. We went to it to see if we could find any one who would show us the way a little. There was no master in it, but an Englishwoman with negroes and servants. We first asked her as to the road, and then for something to drink, and also for some one to show us the road; but she refused the last, although we were willing to pay for

[1] The Oude Dorp (Old Town or Old Village) stood near the present South Beach on the east side of the island. The steep bluff spoken of was at what is now called Fort Wadsworth.

it. She was a cross woman. She said she had never been in the village, and her folks must work, and we would certainly have to go away as wise as we came. She said, however, we must follow the shore, as we did. We went now over the rocky point, which we were no sooner over than we saw a pretty little sand bay, and a small creek, and not far from there, cattle and houses. We also saw the point to which the little path led from the hill above, where I was when my comrade called me. We should not have had more than three hundred steps to go to have been where we now were. It was very hot, and we perspired a great deal. We went on to the little creek to sit down and rest ourselves there, and to cool our feet, and then proceeded to the houses which constituted the Oude Dorp. It was now about two o'clock. There were seven houses, but only three in which any body lived. The others were abandoned, and their owners had gone to live on better places on the island, because the ground around this village was worn out and barren, and also too limited for their use. We went into the first house which was inhabited by English, and there rested ourselves and ate, and inquired further after the road. The woman was cross, and her husband not much better. We had to pay here for what we ate, which we had not done before. We paid three guilders in zeewan, although we only drank water. We proceeded by a tolerably good road to the Nieuwe Dorp,[1] but as the road ran continually in the woods, we got astray again in them. It was dark, and we were compelled to break our way out through the woods and thickets, and we went a great distance before we succeeded, when it was almost entirely dark. We saw a house at a distance to which we directed ourselves across the bushes. It was the first house of the Nieuwe Dorp. We found there an Englishman who could speak Dutch, and who received us very cordially into his house, where we had as good as he and his wife had. She was a Dutch woman from the Manhatans, who was glad to have us in her house.

12th, *Thursday.* Although we had not slept well, we had to resume our journey with the day. The man where we slept set us on the road. We had now no more villages to go to, but went from one plantation to another, for the most part belong-

[1] Still called New Dorp; a village some two miles east of Richmond.

ing to French, who showed us every kindness because we conversed with them in French, and spoke of the ways of the Lord
according to their condition. About one-third part of the distance from the south side to the west end is still all woods,
and is very little visited. We had to go along the shore, finding sometimes fine creeks well provided with wild turkeys,
geese, snipes and wood hens. Lying rotting upon the shore
were thousands of fish called *marsbancken*,[1] which are about
the size of a common carp. These fish swim close together
in large schools, and are pursued so by other fish that they are
forced upon the shore in order to avoid the mouths of their
enemies, and when the water falls they are left there to die,
food for the eagles and other birds of prey. Proceeding thus
along we came to the west point where an Englishman lived
alone some distance from the road.[2] We ate something here,
and he gave us the consolation that we should have a very bad
road for two or three hours ahead, which indeed we experienced, for there was neither path nor road. He showed us as
well as he could. There was a large creek to cross which ran
very far into the land, and when we should get on the other
side of it, we must, he said, go outward again along (the shore).
After we had gone a piece of the way through the woods, we
came to a valley with a brook running through it, which we
took to be the creek or the end of it. We turned round it as
short as we could, in order to go back again to the shore,
which we reached after wandering a long time over hill and dale,
when we saw the creek, which we supposed we had crossed,
now just before us. We followed the side of it deep into the
woods, and when we arrived at the end of it saw no path along
the other side to get outwards again, but the road ran into the
woods in order to cut off a point of the hills and land. We
pursued this road for some time, but saw no mode of getting
out, and that it led further and further from the creek. We,
therefore, left the road and went across through the bushes, so
as to reach the shore by the nearest route according to our
calculation. After continuing this course about an hour, we

[1] Menhaden.
[2] Perhaps Christopher Billop of Bentley. The creeks next spoken of are
Richmond Creek and Main Creek, which make well into the island from its west
side.

saw at a distance a miserably constructed tabernacle of pieces of wood covered with brush, all open in front, and where we thought there were Indians; but on coming up to it we found in it an Englishman sick, and his wife and child lying upon some bushes by a little fire. We asked him if he were sick. "Do you ask me whether I am sick? I have been sick here over two months," he replied. It made my heart sore indeed, for I had never in all my life seen such poverty, and that, too, in the middle of a wood and a wilderness. After we obtained some information as to the way, we went on, and had not gone far before we came to another house, and thus from one farm to another, French, Dutch, and a few English, so that we had not wandered very far out of the way. We inquired at each house the way to the next one. Shortly before evening we arrived at the plantation of a Frenchman, whom they called Le Chaudronnier (the coppersmith), who was formerly a soldier under the Prince of Orange, and had served in Brazil. He was so delighted, and held on to us so hard, that we remained and spent the night with him.

13th, *Friday*. We pursued our journey this morning from plantation to plantation, the same as yesterday, until we came to that of Pierre le Gardinier, who had been a gardener of the Prince of Orange, and had known him well.[1] He had a large family of children and grandchildren. He was about seventy years of age, and was still as fresh and active as a young person. He was so glad to see strangers who conversed with him and his in the French language about the good, that he leaped for joy. After we had breakfasted here they told us that we had another large creek to pass called the Fresh Kil, and there we could perhaps be set across the Kil van Kol to the point of Mill Creek, where we might wait for a boat to convey us to the Manhatans. The road was long and difficult, and we asked for a guide, but he had no one, in consequence of several of his children being sick. At last he determined to go himself, and accordingly carried us in his canoe over to the point of Mill Creek in New Jersey behind the Kol.[2] We learned

[1] Pierre Cresson, a Picard, who after many years in Holland came out to New Netherland in 1657, and lived at Harlem till 1677, when he obtained this grant on Staten Island. His son Jacques embraced the Labadist views.

[2] *I. e.*, behind the Kill van Kull. Mill Creek is probably the stream now known as Elizabethtown Creek.

immediately that there was a boat up this creek loading with brick, and would leave that night for the city. After we had thanked and parted with Pierre le Gardinier, we determined to walk to Elizabethtown, a good half hour's distance inland, where the boat was. From the point to this village there is a fine wagon road, but nowhere in the country had we been so pestered with mosquitos as we were on this road. The land about here is very poor, and is not well peopled. We found the boat, and spoke to the captain who left about two hours afterwards; but as the wind was against going out of the creek, he lay by and waited for the tide. We returned by evening to the point where we were to stay until morning. There was a tavern on it, kept by French papists, who at once took us to be priests, and so conducted themselves towards us in every respect accordingly, although we told them and protested otherwise. As there was nothing to be said further we remained so in their imaginations to the last, as shown both in their words and actions, the more certainly because we spoke French, and they were French people. We slept there this night, and at three o'clock in the morning we set sail.

14th, Saturday. Being under sail, as I have said, it was so entirely calm that we could only float with the stream until we came to the Schutters Island,[1] where we obtained the tide again. It was now about four o'clock. In order to protect ourselves from the air which was very cold and piercing, we crept under the sail which was very old and full of holes. The tide having run out by daylight, we came under sail again, with a good wind which brought us to the city at about eight o'clock, for which we were glad, and returning thanks to God, betook ourselves to rest.

15th, Sunday. We went at noon to-day to hear the English minister, whose services took place after the Dutch church was out. There were not above twenty-five or thirty people in the church. The first thing that occurred was the reading of all their prayers and ceremonies out of the prayer book, as is done in all Episcopal churches. A young man then went into the pulpit and commenced preaching, who thought he was performing wonders; but he had a little book in his hand out of which he read his sermon which was about a quarter of an

---

[1] Now Shooter's Island, opposite Mariner's Harbor.

hour or half an hour long.[1]   With this the services were concluded, at which we could not be sufficiently astonished. This was all that happened with us to-day.

16th, Monday.   I was occupied to-day in copying my journal.   In the morning there came an Indian to our house, a man about eighty years of age, whom our people called Jasper, who lived at Ahakinsack or at Ackinon.[2]   Concerning this Indian our old people related that when they lived on Long Island, it was once a very dear time; no provisions could be obtained, and they suffered great want, so that they were reduced to the last extremity; that God the Lord then raised up this Indian, who went out fishing daily in order to bring fish to them every day when he caught a good mess, which he always did.   If, when he came to the house, he found it alone, and they were out working in the fields, he did not fail, but opened the door, laid the fish on the floor, and proceeded on his way.   For this reason these people possess great affection for him and have given him the name of Jasper, and also my nitap,[3] that is, my great friend.   He never comes to the Manhatans without visiting them and eating with them, as he now did, as among his old friends.   We asked him why he had done so much kindness to these people.   "I have always been inclined," he answered, "from my youth up to do good, especially to good people known to me.   I took the fish to them because Maneto[4] said to me, you must take fish to these people, whispering ever in my ear 'You must take fish to them.'   I had to do it, or Maneto would have killed me."   Our old woman telling us he sometimes got drunk, we said to him he

[1] This was the Rev. Charles Wolley, the only English minister then in the province.   A graduate of Emmanuel College, Cambridge, he came out with Governor Andros in 1678 as chaplain to the garrison, and remained in New York till 1680.   He published in 1701 (London, two editions) a pleasant though fragmentary little book entitled A Two Years Journal in New York, well worth reading in comparison with Danckaerts's account of the province.   Two reprints of it have been issued (New York, 1860; Cleveland, 1902), the former edited by Dr. E. B. O'Callaghan, the latter by Professor Edward G. Bourne.

[2] Hackensack.

[3] The word, in the form neetup, has survived in local speech in some parts of New England.   "What cheer, neetup?" was the Indian's salutation to Roger Williams on his arrival at Seekonk.

[4] The chief (evil) spirit.

should not do so any more, that the Great Sakemacker[1] who is
above, was offended at such conduct and would kill him.
"No," said he, laughing as if that were a mistake of ours, "it
is Maneto who kills those who do evil, and leaves those who do
good at peace." "That is only," we replied, "because Maneto
is the slave and executioner of the Great Sakemacker above;"
and we then asked him if he believed there was such a great
and good *sakemacker* there? "Undoubtedly," he said, "but
he remains above, and does not trouble himself with the earth
or earthly things, because he does nothing except what is good;
but Maneto, who also is a *sakemacker*, is here below, and governs all, and punishes and torments those men who do evil
and drink themselves drunk." Hereupon we inquired of him
why he did so then. "Yes," he said, "I had rather not, but
my heart is so inclined that it causes me to do it, although I
know it is wrong. The Christians taught it to us, and give
us or sell us the drink, and drink themselves drunk." We
said to him: "Listen! if we came to live near you, you would
never see us drunk, nor would we give or sell you or your people
any rum." "That," he replied, "would be good." We told him
he must not make such a difference between himself and a
Christian, because one was white and the other red, and one
wore clothes and the other went almost naked, or one was
called a Christian and the other an Indian, that this great and
good Sakemacker was the father of us all, and had made us
all, and that all who did not do good would be killed by Maneto
whether they were called Christians or Indians; but that all
who should do good would go to this good *sakemacker* above.
"Yes," said he, "we do not know or speak to this *sakemacker*,
but Maneto we know and speak to, but you people, who can
read and write, know and converse with this *sakemacker*."

We asked him, where he believed he came from? He answered from his father. "And where did your father come
from?" we said, "and your grandfather and great-grandfather,
and so on to the first of the race?" He was silent for a little
while, either as if unable to climb up at once so high with his
thoughts, or to express them without help, and then took a
piece of coal out of the fire where he sat, and began to write upon
the floor. He first drew a circle, a little oval, to which he made

[1] Sachem, lord.

four paws or feet, a head and a tail. "This," said he, "is a tortoise, lying in the water around it," and he moved his hand round the figure, continuing, "This was or is all water, and so at first was the world or the earth, when the tortoise gradually raised its round back up high, and the water ran off of it, and thus the earth became dry." He then took a little straw and placed it on end in the middle of the figure, and proceeded, "The earth was now dry, and there grew a tree in the middle of the earth, and the root of this tree sent forth a sprout beside it and there grew upon it a man, who was the first male. This man was then alone, and would have remained alone; but the tree bent over until its top touched the earth, and there shot therein another root, from which came forth another sprout, and there grew upon it the woman, and from these two are all men produced." We gave him four fish-hooks with which he was much pleased, and immediately calculated how much in money he had obtained. "I have got twenty-four stivers' worth," he said. He then inquired our names, which we gave him, and wished to know why he asked for them? "Well," he replied, "because you are good people and are true *nitaps;* and in case you should come into the woods and fall into the hands of the Indians, and they should wish to kill or harm you, if I know or hear of it I might help you, for they will do you no injury when they know me." For he was the brother of a *sakemaker*. We told him that we did not give them to him on that account, but only from regard because he was a good person, although the good will or thankfulness which he wished to show thereby was good. "Well," he said, "that is good, that is good," with which, after eating something, he departed.

But at noon he returned with a young Indian, both of them so drunk they could not speak, and having a calabash of liquor with them. We chided him, but to no purpose, for he could neither use his reason nor speak so as to be understood. The young Indian with him was a *sackemaker's* son, and was bold. He wanted to have a piece of meat that was on the table, and on which we all had to make our dinner, when we told him it was not for him. "Yes," said he, "I see it is so;" nevertheless, and although we offered him something else to eat, he was evilly disposed and dissatisfied, and would take nothing except the piece of meat alone; but that was not given to him. Whereupon Jasper told him he must be quiet, that the old people and we were all his *nitaps*, and by degrees quieted him, they sitting together by the fire and drinking their rum. They left afterwards for Long Island.

17*th, Tuesday.* Nothing transpired to-day.

18*th, Wednesday.* In the afternoon Jasper, the Indian, came back again, and proceeded confidently to our room in the rear of the house, but sober and in his senses. He told us how he had been with his nephew, the *sackemaker's* son, to Long Island, among the other Indians; and that he had given away, not only his fish-hooks, but also his shoes and stockings. We found fault with him at first for having become so drunk, contrary to his promise, and when he well knew it was wrong. To which he said he had to buy some nails for an Englishman who lived near him, from another Englishman here, who had sold and given him the rum.

I must here remark, in passing, that the people in this city, who are almost all traders in small articles, whenever they see an Indian enter the house, who they know has any money, they immediately set about getting hold of him, giving him rum to drink, whereby he is soon caught and becomes half a fool. If he should then buy any thing, he is doubly cheated, in the wares, and in the price. He is then urged to buy more drink, which they now make half water, and if he cannot drink it, they drink it themselves. They do not rest until they have cajoled him out of all his money, or most of it; and if that cannot be done in one day, they keep him, and let him lodge and sleep there, but in some out of the way place, down on the ground, guarding their merchandise and other property in the meantime, and always managing it so that the poor creature does not go away before he has given them all they want. And these miserable Christians are so much the more eager in this respect, because no money circulates among themselves, and they pay each other in wares, in which they are constantly cheating and defrauding each other. Although it is forbidden to sell the drink to the Indians, yet every one does it, and so much the more earnestly, and with so much greater and burning avarice, that it is done in secret. To this extent and further, reaches the damnable and insatiable covetousness of most of those who here call themselves Christians. Truly, our hearts grieved when we heard of these things, which call so grievously upon the Supreme Judge for vengeance. He will not always let His name be so profaned and exposed to reproach and execration.

We asked Jasper why he had given away his hooks and stockings. He said, it was a custom among them, for the lesser to give to the greater. We replied the *sackemaker* was richer than he, and he should, therefore, have kept them. "No," he said, "I did it as a mark of respect and obedience." We gave him four more fish-hooks, and told him he must take care of them for himself. "I will bring you fish as soon as I catch any," he said as he went away, promising also that he would get drunk no more.

From this time until the 22d of October, nothing special took place, except that we spoke to one Ephraim, a young trader, who was just married here, and who intended to go with his wife to the South River, where he usually dwelt, for which purpose he was only waiting for horses and men from there.[1] He tendered us his services and his horses, if we would accompany him, and offered to carry us in his own boat everywhere on that river, from the falls [of the Delaware], to which we should have to travel by land, and where the boat would be waiting for him to take him down the river; since he himself would have to touch at many places on the river, in going down. As Bouman, who was going there with horses, did not make his appearance, we accepted the offer with thankfulness, waiting only for the time.

24th, Tuesday. Margaret's ship in which we arrived here, being ready to leave, but she not going in it, as it was said, we set about writing letters, which we might give to our Robyn, and finished them to-day, and also the copying of my journal.

25th, Wednesday. Having closed up our letters, we had Robyn at our house, and gave them to him in his own hands, as we had heard from the supercargo himself that he would run into Falmouth again for the purpose of paying the duties;

[1] Ephraim Herrman, eldest son of Augustine Herrman of Bohemia Manor, had on September 3, 1679, six weeks before this date, married Elizabeth Rodenburg, daughter of Lucas Rodenburg, formerly vice-director of Curaçao. South River is the Delaware.

we gave Robyn money to post our letters over London, together with something for his trouble, and with this, wishing
him the blessing of the Lord, we took leave of him; but recol-
lecting afterwards that we had forgotten to put a date to the
letters, which was very necessary, I had to go in search of
Robyn again, whom I found at last, and took back from him
the letters. When we had resealed them, I went after him
again, but he had gone on board the ship. I waited for an
opportunity and went on board myself, and handed them to
him again. He was glad to see me on board; and while there
I went looking around to see how the ship was laden, and found
her so full that the poor sailors had scarcely room to eat or
sleep. The boatswain, who had now become mate, because
the Dutch mate, Evert, had become captain of a ketch, treated
me with much kindness; but as the boat and sailors were
continually ashore, it was dark before I could reach the
land.

26th, Thursday. We inquired whether our journey to the
south would soon take place, and were informed it would not
be this week. We resolved not to remain idle, and to embrace
the opportunity to cross to-morrow over the North River opposite the fort to a place called Gamoenepaen,[1] as soon as we
could find the means of passage.

27th, Friday. We went after breakfast to see if we could
be taken over the river. We found a boat going soon, but we
must wait a little. In the meanwhile we made the acquaintance of a person from Zeeland, or who had lived there a long
time, for he himself was a Hollander. He had been an appren-
tice to Jaques Fierens, printer, at the Globe in the Gi street,[2]
and, although I had been often enough in that house, and he
knew my face, he did not know me particularly. He came to
this country with Cornelis Everts of Zeeland, and had assisted

---

[1] Communipaw, in New Jersey, founded in 1658. It is uncertain whether
the name is of Indian origin (Gamoenipaen), or is a Dutch name made up from
that of Pauw. The former is more likely.

[2] Jacques Fierens was from 1642 to 1669 a noteworthy printer, bookseller,
and publisher at Middelburg in Zeeland, where Danckaerts (see the introductory
note B to this volume) then lived. Fierens's shop, as we know from other sources,
was at the sign of the Globe in Gistraat or Giststraat (*i. e.*, Heilige Geest Straat,
Holy Ghost Street).

in taking it from the English in 1674.[1]   He had remained here since and married.   He sometimes bound old books, and was the only bookbinder in the country.

It was about noon when we crossed over.   Our old woman at the house had told us of another good woman who lived at this place, named Fitie,[2] from Cologne, and recommended us to visit her, which we did as soon as we landed.   We found her a little pious after the manner of the country, and you could discover that there was something of the Lord in her, but very much covered up and defiled.   We dined there and spoke to her of what we deemed necessary for her condition.   She has many grandchildren, all of whom are not unjust.   We continued our journey along a fine broad wagon road to the other village, called Bergen, a good half hour or three-quarters inland from there,[3] where the villagers, who are almost all Dutch, received us well, and were rejoiced to see us.   They inquired and spoke to us about various things.   We also found there the cook of the vessel in which we came over.   He was sick of the ship, and was stopping ashore with his relations here in order to recruit himself.   He entertained us according to his ability, and gave us some *hespaen*[4] to eat, a wild animal somewhat larger than a cat.   It was very fat, and of a good flavor, almost like a pig.   The skins of these animals are good peltry, and are sent in great quantities to Europe.   We had also some good cider.   Our cook took a short walk with us over the country, and showed us the situation of the plantations around there, as he had lived there a long time, and consequently was acquainted with all these farms.   The soil was very good, and indeed of the best that we had seen anywhere.   This good ground was for the most part on the declivities of the hills, and so on below.   Snake Hill, of which I had heard much, and which I had imagined to myself was a large projecting hill, lies close by and is only a small round hill; and is so

[1] In 1673, after the Duke of York and the English had held New York nine years, two Dutch commodores, Cornelis Evertsen and Jacob Binckes, retook it for the States General.   The Dutch, however, held it only a year.

[2] Fytje Hartman, widow of Michael Jansen Hartman.   She had seven children.

[3] Bergen was founded in 1661.   Both it and Communipaw are now in Jersey City.

[4] Raccoon.

named on account of the numerous snakes which infest it. It stands quite alone, and is almost entirely encircled by the North Kil.[1] It is nothing but rocks and stones, with a little earth up above where a plantation could be formed. We returned to the village by evening, and lodged with one Claes Fransen, who had brought us over the river. He had a good old mother,[2] and also a brother living there. His other brothers were married, and lived in the same village. We conversed with these people about spiritual things, and had great enjoyment therein. We were entirely welcome. We slept upon some straw on the floor, and it was lucky for us that he sold blankets, some of which he used to cover us. We have nowhere, to my knowledge, seen or eaten finer apples. One kind was very large, fair, and of good taste, fifty-six of which only could be put in a heaped up bushel, that is, half a bag. Another variety, somewhat smaller, but not less fair in appearance, and of a better flavor, my comrade was acquainted with, and said they were called the Double Paradise. He acknowledged they were very delicate.

28th, Saturday. Early this morning Claes prepared to cross over to the Manhatans, to carry to market some fine fat mutton from a sheep which he had killed the night before. He sold it for two *blanken*[3] a pound, reckoned in Holland money and Amsterdam weight. It was rainy the whole morning, and it had stormed so hard in the night that we could not find a dry place in the house to lie in. We were apprehensive of hearing of some misfortune to the ships, especially two lying under Staten Island, one of which was Margaret's, and was bound for Holland. Claes was alarmed for his boat, in which we had to cross over; but going to the shore about eleven o'clock, he found it there, but half full of rain water. The mast which he had left standing was overboard, and to be looked for, but was afterwards found, and the mast bench and socket were out of their places, and in pieces. He had, therefore, some repairs to make. It cleared up gradually, and he resolved to cross over, which he was the more anxious to do, because he was going to bring back Domine Tessemaker, who had promised to come the next day and preach for them

---

[1] Hackensack River.
[2] Immetie Dirx, widow of Frans Claesen.   [3] Say three cents.

before his departure; for although there is a considerable congregation in this vicinity, and they are abundantly able to support a minister, they have none; for it is not easy to obtain one, and there is no probability of their doing so as long as the country belongs to the English, though they intend to build a church next spring.   For the present they have nobody except a *voorleser*,[1] who performs his service for them on Sundays, in the school house, where they assemble.   They have, however, agreed with the minister of the city to administer there the Lord's Supper three times a year, for which he receives thirty bushels or fifteen bags of wheat.   This service he performs on week-days, because he cannot be absent from the city on Sundays, where he is the only minister.   This Gmoenepaeu is an arm of the main land on the west side of the North River, beginning at Constable's Hook, directly opposite Staten Island, from which it is separated by the Kil van Kol.[2]   On the east is the North River; on the north the mainland Pavoni or Haverstroo, or indeed Hackingsack; and on the west, the North Kil, which separates it from New Jersey and Elizabethtown.   It is almost an hour broad, but has large salt meadows or marshes on the kill.   It has many bays and inlets, and lies very commodiously for the inhabitants, because it is everywhere accessible by water from the city.   The village of Bergen lies about in the middle of the tract, and has been reasonably strong in time of the war with the Indians.[3]   It has very fine farms which yield well.

As we were about to cross, an Indian came up, who also desired to be carried over.   He asked the skipper whether he might go over with him, who replied he had too much freight.   "Well," said he, "I will pay you for that.   How much freight do the people give you?"   The skipper answered six stivers in seewan."   "Well then," said the Indian, "I will give you

[1] Parish clerk, precentor, and (usually) schoolmaster.   The church records of Bergen go back to 1664, and the first church edifice was built in the next year, 1680.

[2] Now Constable's Point.   Pavonia was the domain of Michael Pauw. Haverstraw lay well to the northward, Hackensack to the northwestward, of the Bergen peninsula.

[3] "The Town is compact and hath been fortified against the Indians." Captain Nicolls, in George Scot, *The Model of the Government of East New Jersey*, p. 142.

seven." This made us all laugh, because he valued himself less and bound himself to pay more than the others. We, therefore, took him with us. The river here is full four miles wide, and when it blows, especially from the north or northwest, there is sometimes a rolling sea, making it dangerous to cross over, particularly in small boats. While we were in the village of Bergen, a person came to us who was willing to take us up through the Northwest Kil, where we were inclined to go, because Jaques[1] of Long Island and his associates had bought for a trifle, a piece of land there of twelve thousand *morgen*,[2] and he had related wonders to us about it; and that above his land, and above the falls which are more than an hour's distance from it, there was another tract still better, which was corroborated by almost every one, especially in Bergen, whose inhabitants were very well acquainted there, and some of whom had bought a large piece of land close by.[3] The before mentioned tract was considered by them the best in all New Netherland. We, therefore, did not reject the offer of this person, but only postponed it until a later opportunity, perhaps after our return from the South River. They said this piece of land was very large, and could be increased to twenty-five or thirty thousand *morgen*, which the Indians were disposed to sell, and we could buy for a small price. When we reached home we showed our old people the apples which we had brought with us, and they confessed that as long as they had lived in the country, they had never seen any finer or larger.

29th, Sunday. We had been last Sunday to hear the Quakers, but the greater portion of them were on Long Island, so that nothing was done.[4] My comrade had a mind to go again to-day, but I remained at home. After waiting two hours, he went to hear the Episcopalians and then returned to the Quakers, who had remained all this time sitting silent and gazing. He then took a walk out for a considerable time, and

[1] Jacques Cortelyou and his associates had a large grant of land at Aquack-anonck (Passaic). Northwest Kill is the Passaic River.

[2] A *morgen* was about two acres.

[3] Deed of March 28, 1679, from the Indian sachem Captahem to a group of Bergen men.

[4] There were few Friends yet in New York, but on Long Island there were already quarterly and half-yearly meetings.

went back again and found them still in the same position. Being tired out, he would wait no longer, and came home. We went in the afternoon to see Ephraim for the purpose of inquiring of him how soon our journey to the South River would commence, and whether we would have time first to take a trip to Aquakenon[1] with the man from Bergen, of whom we have spoken above; but we did not find Ephraim at home.

30th, Monday. We went again this morning to speak to him. He said we should have time to go there, and allowing the utmost it might take us, he would still wait a day or two. We went immediately to Sapokanikke, where [Gerrit] was engaged in building, whom we wished to accompany us, because he knew several of those Indians and spoke their language, and because he had said all along that he wished to see the land of his brother-in-law, since Jaques had promised him as much of it as he would cultivate; but we found him indisposed with a sore leg, and unable to go. Nevertheless, we crossed over the river in the evening, at the same time the two ministers were returning, namely, Tessemaker who preached there on Sunday as we have stated, and Niewenhuisen who had administered the Lord's Supper there to-day. We went over with Claes, and it was dark when we arrived at Gmoenepaen. We followed Claes, who took us to his house, where we were made welcome by his old mother. My comrade went with Claes, yet this evening, to see the man who was to take us up the kill, so that in case he had any thing to make ready it might be done this evening. He said it would be noon before the tide would serve to-morrow and that he had nothing else to do in the morning. We learned he was a most godless rogue, which caused us to be cautious in what we had to do with him. We conversed this evening with the old woman in whose house we slept, and this poor woman seemed to have great enjoyment and fruition, as did also her sons and others with whom we occasionally conversed. It appeared, indeed, as if the Lord might have there the seed of the elect, which He will bring forth in His own time, if it please Him. Truly these are the best people whom we have found in these parts.

31st, Tuesday. We went this morning to look about the country a little, which pleased us very much, and thus occupied

---

[1] Passaic.

ourselves until noon, when we proceeded to look after our guide and arrange matters with him. As soon as he came in the house, we inquired of him what he wanted for his trouble for the journey. He demanded a cloth *innocent* or coat, and that not of the poorest. His wife, who was the worst woman, I think, I have ever beheld in my life, did the best also to cheat us. We asked him what he thought such a coat would cost. "Well," said he, "call it a hundred guilders." We told him we did not intend to give so much. He replied, "I cannot take less for so long a time." "And how long do you expect to be gone," we asked. "You must not," he said, "think of being back before Monday." We then asked him how much he demanded a day, and he said eight guilders. We made an agreement with him for seven guilders a day, that is, twenty-eight stivers, Holland money. We then started to get some provisions, which the old woman, where we slept, had cheerfully given us; but we took nothing, except two half loaves of rye bread, and some apples in our travelling bag, but this Dirck provided himself better for making the journey. When we were ready, we went over the salt meadow or marsh to the kill, which was full half an hour's distance; but when we came to the canoe, the ebb tide was still running strong, and we required the flood. The canoe lay in a bend of a small creek, and it was impossible to get it out of this bight and over the mire, except at high water, which would not take place until evening. We were, therefore, brought to a stand, whether to proceed in the evening, to which we were not much inclined, or await until the next morning, which was too much of a delay in view of our journey to the south. We had, besides, felt some misgivings in our hearts on account of the godlessness of the person who was to conduct us. We saw that the Lord plainly shewed what we had to do, and we, therefore, abandoned the trip, and told him we had not so much time to lose, and should embrace another opportunity. He cursed and swore at those who had told him the tide would serve at noon. In truth he had not been careful and had nobody to blame but himself. We were glad we were rid of him. We gave our apples and bread back to the old woman, who, as well as all the villagers, who heard we were not going up, were rejoiced, and declared we should not have been satisfied. Afterwards, several others offered their services to accompany us by land, either on foot or horseback, or otherwise, and go with us themselves, which we did not reject, but only postponed until we should see what the Lord would do in His time.

We went immediately to the strand to see whether we could still cross over to the other side; but Claes had left for the city, and did not return until evening, and there was no other boat. We were, therefore, compelled to remain; but, in the meantime, we visited the before mentioned Fytie, where we met several Indians, who lived upon and owned the very land we had intended to visit. They had heard we had gone up to look at their land, and wondered at seeing us back there. They manifested pleasure at our wishing to visit them, and examine their land; shook hands with us, and said we were great and good *nitaps*. They were in hopes we would come and live on their lands, where we would always be good *nitaps*. Meanwhile Claes having arrived, we went back with him to Bergen, and passed the night again at his house.

NOVEMBER 1st, *Wednesday*. As soon as Claes had taken his freight on board, we crossed over with him to the city. Our old people where we lodged were glad we had not gone with that person, for they also knew him well. About noon Claes came to the house, wishing to buy something of us, which he did. We presented him and the good people of this place with *Christelyke Grondregelen*,[1] in Low Dutch, because we hoped, after what we had seen, it would serve for their instruction and edification, and the glory of God, who will bring forth the fruits thereof in His own time if it please Him.

2d, *Thursday*. This day, and for the rest of the week, nothing transpired worthy of note, except we informed Ephraim that our trip was not to take place, and therefore he need not wait on our account. I have wished several times that I could sketch in order to employ the art sometimes when it might be serviceable, especially upon this voyage. I, therefore, have practised it some, because it was convenient, and I thought I succeeded in it reasonably well, but I have done it, without any regularity or assiduity, and only to amuse myself occasionally.[2]

[1] The Dutch translation of Jean de Labadie's *Points Fondamentaux de la Vie vrayement Chrestienne* (Amsterdam, 1670).

[2] Several very interesting pen-and-ink drawings accompany the manuscript of this journal. See the introduction to the volume.

5th, Sunday. My comrade, who was exercising himself in the English language, went again to hear the English minister preach.

6th, Monday. We went again to ascertain whether our journey to the South River would soon be undertaken; for although this opportunity would suit us very well and we should not miss it, nevertheless the best time was passing by, and the winter was close at hand. There was a horse offered us elsewhere, which had to be taken to the South River; and a yacht also was ready to sail there. The time, therefore, was to be looked to; and we went again to Ephraim, who assured us that he would not delay it longer than the ensuing Thursday. But we heard that Domine Tessemaker was going with him, by which we were entrapped, for it was one of the reasons why we did not leave with de La Grange, who had now been gone fourteen days, that he always told us Domine Tessemaker and some other persons would accompany him. However, as the Lord had thus ordered it, we were glad to submit to His will, who always knows why He does thus and so.

Nothing worth mention happened between this and Thursday. Meanwhile, however, Domine Tessemaker had abandoned the journey with Ephraim, and resolved to proceed by sea in the yacht or boat, in which he sailed the next day. Whether he had some special reasons for going by water we do not know, although we guessed so. Ephraim had ordered a shallop or yacht, which was to land us at the Rarytans, and was to be ready, he said, Thursday evening or Friday morning without fail, but of that he would give us timely notice. We, therefore, remained at home until Friday morning, the

10th, when, as we did not see him, we went to ascertain the cause and why the journey was not begun. He said it was not his fault, but that his wife could not leave her mother so soon, and he had given her time until next Monday, and had, therefore, let the sloop make a trip. This did not please us very much, for our time was fast running away, and we were able to accomplish nothing. We bethought ourselves, therefore, whether we could not make some progress, and as our Jaques [Cortelyou], had promised to show us the laws of the country, we determined to go and see whether we could not finish what we had to do therein before our departure. We both left about noon to go over to Long Island, and passed through Breukelen and the Vlacke Bos, over Nieu Uytrecht[1] on large, fine wagon roads to Najack, where we arrived about three o'clock. It had been very warm during the day, and we were all in a perspiration and fatigued. Jaques's wife bade us welcome, but he himself was in the fields. After we had rested ourselves and eaten something, we went outside upon the banks of this beautiful bay, to breathe a little air, and look at various vessels, going and coming. In the meantime he came with his son to meet us. They had been to the fish *fuyck*,[2] which they had lying there upon the shore and out of which they had taken at noon some fine fish, but at present the water was too high. Another of his sons had been out shooting, but had not shot anything; though the day before he had shot a woodcock and a partridge before the door of the house, which we must taste this evening with still some other things. Also because we were there the *fuyck* must be lifted again, from which they took out two fine bass, of a kind we had not yet seen. They are quite large, and of a good shape. They have seven black stripes on the body, extending from the head to the tail. We ate of them also in the evening, and found them very fine, and had not yet tasted any better in the country. They were fat and hard, with a little of the flavor of the salmon. The other suited us very well.

We had much conversation together, and informed ourselves in relation to various matters. He gave us some me-- dicinal roots, which we have mentioned heretofore. He also let us look at the laws, which were written in a folio volume, but in very bad Dutch, for they had been translated from English into Dutch.[3] As it was a large book, and we saw we could not copy it there, we requested him to let us take it home with us for that purpose. He consented upon condition that if we left for the south, we would then deliver it to his brother-in-

[1] Brooklyn, Flatbush, New Utrecht.

[2] Large stationary net.

[3] The reference is to Governor Nicolls's code, commonly called the Duke's Laws, first promulgated in 1665, for Long Island and the Delaware River region, and reissued by Governor Lovelace in 1674.   Copies were sent to each Long Island township, and thus to New Utrecht.   The code was printed in 1809 in the first volume of the *Collections* of the New York Historical Society, and may also be found in a Pennsylvania issue, *Charter to William Penn*, etc. (Harrisburg, 1879).

law, Gerrit, who intended to come over shortly, and would
hand it to him. We lodged this night at his place, but somewhat better than we had done in the barn, for we slept in his
dwelling, still so that we could well feel where we had slept.

11th, Saturday. As soon as we awoke we determined to
return home and finish up our matters in the little time remaining. We left, therefore, about eight o'clock, after taking
some breakfast. He conducted us to New Utrecht. We lent
him Les Pensées de Pascal [1] which we judged would be useful
to him. We returned by the same roads as we came, and
reached home about eleven o'clock. We had observed that
although the previous day had been pretty warm, this night
had not only been frosty but ice had formed as thick as the
back of a knife. We commenced at noon copying the most
necessary [laws], and afterwards the rest of them.

12th, Sunday. We continued making extracts, and finished
about the middle of the day all that we deemed it necessary to
make, omitting minor matters pertaining to the duties of particular officers. Still, what shall we say, they were laws and
nothing else.

13th, Monday. We took care that Jaques should receive
the papers back again, and then went to see whether our journey with Ephraim would be made. We found the boat lying
at the dock, laden with fire-wood, and that the day would
necessarily be occupied in discharging, so that at the best, it
could not be undertaken before the next day. The time was
finally fixed for the journey for the next day, and every thing
was this day arranged.

JOURNEY TO THE SOUTHWARD BEGINS.[2]

14th, Tuesday. Having taken leave of all our acquaintances, we set off at ten o'clock, this morning, in company with
Ephraim, his wife, his wife's mother, two of her sisters, and a
young brother, who were to accompany her as far as Pescatteway.[3] We stepped into the boat, where we found three

[1] The Pensées of Blaise Pascal had been published, posthumously, in 1670.

[2] These words appear as a marginal note in the original manuscript.

[3] Piscataway, N. J., founded in 1666, some seven or eight miles up the
Raritan River from its mouth at Perth Amboy. Achter Kol, below, was the

horses, two Quakers, and another Englishman.   We were not long in starting.   The wind was from the west, which is a head wind for sailing to Achter Kol.   The sky began to be heavily overcast, and the wind to freshen up more, so that we had to tack.   Ephraim being afraid the wind might shift to the northwest, and blow hard, as it usually does when it is from that quarter, wished to return, and would have done so, if the skipper had not tried to go ahead more than he did.   The tide running out, and the boat advancing but little, and being fearful of the flood tide, which would delay us, if it did not drive us back, and as there was room to work with the rudder, I went and took hold of the tiller myself, and brought the boat, with the flood tide, just within the point of Staten Island, where we found a ketch bound for Achter Kol, and further up to Snake Hill.   Having now the tide with us, we tacked about, and quickly passed by Schutters Island, lying in the mouth of a kill, on the north side of the Kil achter Kol.   This island is so called, because the Dutch, when they first settled on the North River, were in the practice of coming here to shoot wild geese, and other wild fowl, which resorted there in great numbers. This kill, when the water is high, is like a large river, but at low water it is dry in some places.   Up above it divides itself into two branches, one of which runs about north to Snake Hill and Ackingsak; and the other, called the Northwest Kill, because it extends in that direction, runs to Aquakenom, of which we will speak hereafter.[1]   We sailed inside of Schutters Island, although the passage is very small, and thus obtained the in-running current; because the flood tide which came from Achter Kol, and that from the North River, strike each other here, and thus shoot together in this kill.   With much effort we reached the point of Elizabeth's Kill, where we were compelled to come to anchor, at four o'clock.   We all went ashore, and lodged for the night in the house of the French people, of whom we have spoken before, and who were not yet rid of the suspicion they had conceived, notwithstanding the declarations we had made to the contrary.   We all slept

Dutch name for what is now corruptly called Arthur Kill, and, by extension, for Newark Bay and the portion of New Jersey immediately west of Staten Island, Arthur Kill, and the Kill van Kull.

[1] Hackensack and Passaic Rivers.

on the floor, and supped upon what we had brought with us. We were no sooner in the house, than it began to rain and blow hard from the northwest, and to be very cold. We saw herein the good providence of the Lord again, whom we had so many times, during our journeying, so visibly perceived, watching and protecting so faithfully those who cared for nothing, except for Him and to do His will.

15th, *Wednesday.* It still blew stiff out of the northwest, so that our skipper had little disposition to weigh anchor and get under sail, especially with the horses on board, although we would have willingly proceeded. It was, therefore, determined that the horses should go by land with the servant and brother of Ephraim, and the Quakers resolved to do the same. The rest of the company went on board the boat, and after taking in a large reef, we got under sail, with a head wind, but ebb tide. It blew hard and squally, and we had to look out well, with sheets in hand. We made good progress, and came to Smokers Hoeck, which is about half way of Kil achter Kol. We came to anchor here, because the next reach was directly against the wind, and it blew too hard to tack. We all stepped ashore here, and went on foot to an English village called Wout Brigg,[1] where we should find the horses. Smoker's Hoeck is the easterly point of the kill, which runs up to Wout Brigg, and we would have sailed up this creek, but it was ebb tide. We passed over reasonably fair and good land, and observed particularly fine salt meadows on the creek, on which there was built a good grist mill,[2] and over which we had to cross. We arrived about noon or one o'clock, at this English village. Ephraim, not wishing to go with his family to the ordinary tavern, went to another house or tavern, where he had been many times before, and where the people were under some obligations to him. But he could not lodge there now; and we were, therefore, compelled to go to the common tavern, which was full of persons, sitting drinking, and where nothing was to be obtained except that vile rum. Nevertheless, we had to pass the day there, waiting for the boat and the baggage; but these did not come up to-day, in consequence of the hard wind. We had, therefore, to lie down here upon

---

[1] Woodbridge, N. J., founded in 1665.

[2] The mill of Jonathan Dunham, whose house was standing till 1871.

the ground all together, on a little hay, as we had done last night.

16*th, Thursday.* The weather moderated and it cleared up, but we had to wait till about noon, before the goods arrived from the boat, which the skipper had to bring up in a canoe, because the boat could not come. We obtained here another horse, making five horses we had, and another servant of Ephraim. We then dined, and politely took our leave of Madam van B.[1], the mother of Ephraim's wife, and of her two sisters, who had come to conduct her as far as here, and from here were to return home again in the same boat, but the little brother went with us to the south, to live with Ephraim. It was then about three o'clock, when we mounted the horses, namely, Ephraim and his wife upon the best one, my comrade and myself each upon the one we had obtained at Woodbridge, his brother and servant on one, and the other servant upon another. *Our* horses, like the riders, were very poor. We proceeded on, however, and about four o'clock arrived at Pescatteway, the last English village in New Jersey, for thus the government of the Governor my Lord Catrix [Carteret] is called; which begins on the west side of the North River, and extends about half way to the South River, though this division did not seem to me to be well made. We rode about two English miles through Pescatteway, to the house of one Mr. Greenland,[2] who kept a tavern there. We had to pass the night here, because it was the place of crossing the Milstoons [Millstone] River, which they called the falls. Close by there, also, was the dwelling of some Indians, who were of service to this Mr. Greenland, in many things. We were better lodged and entertained here, for we slept upon a good bed, and strengthened ourselves against the future.

17*th, Friday.* As the water was high in the kill or Millstone River, Ephraim would not ride over the fall, on account of the current of water, which made it dangerous. He, there-

[1] Madame van Brugh, *née* Katrina Roelofs, later Madame van Rodenburg, now the wife of Johannes Pieterszen van Brugh.

[2] Dr. Henry Greenland, formerly a resident of Newbury, Mass., and of Kittery, Maine. The route which travellers at this time took through New Jersey crossed the Raritan at the present site of New Brunswick, and then proceeded to what is now Trenton. The crossing of the Raritan is not mentioned in the journal.

fore, determined after breakfast we should be set across in a
canoe, and the horses should swim across, as they did. We
reached the other side about nine o'clock, and proceeded on
horseback. The road from here to the falls of the South
River, runs for the most part W. S. W., and then W. It is
nothing but a foot-path for men and horses, between the trees
and through the small shrubs, although we came to places
where there were large plains, beset with a few trees, and grown
over with long grass, which was not the worst. When you
have ridden a piece of the way, you can see over the lands of
the Nevesink, far off on the left hand, into the ocean, affording
a fine view. The land we rode over was neither the best, nor
the worst. The woods consist of reasonably straight oak and
hickory, with some chestnut, but they are not very close.
They would, therefore, afford tolerably good tillable land; but
we observed the best pieces lay here and there, along the creeks.
We saw many deer running before us, out of the road, sometimes five or six together, starting off at the sound of the horses.
When about half way, you come to a high, but very rocky hill,
which is very difficult for man or beast to walk upon. After
crossing it, you come to a large valley, the descent to which,
from this hill, is very steep, by a very shrubby road; and you
must dismount, in order to lead your horses down carefully,
as well as to descend carefully yourselves. We were in the
middle of this valley, when a company met us on horseback,
from the South River. They were acquaintances of Ephraim,
and some of them were his relations. They wished each other
welcome, and mutually inquired after various matters, after
which we separated, exchanging one of our horses, which
Ephraim's brother rode, and was to be sent back to the Manathans, for one of theirs, which must return to the South River.
We rode on a little further, and came to Millstone River again,
which runs so crookedly, that you cross it at three different
places. After we crossed it now, we took the bridles from the
horses, in order that they might eat something, while we sat
down and dined together, upon what we had in our travelling
bags. We remounted in about an hour, and rode on, continuing our way and course as before. About three o'clock we
came again to Millstone River, which we again waded over,
but it had gradually become smaller. Resuming our route,

we arrived at the falls of the South River about sundown, passing a creek where a new grist-mill was erected by the Quakers, who live hereabouts in great numbers, and daily increase.[1] But it seemed to us as if this mill could not stand long, especially if the flow of water were heavy, because the work was not well arranged. We rode over here, and went directly to the house of the person who had constructed it, who was a Quaker, where we dismounted, and willingly dismissed our horses. The house was very small, and from the incivility of the inmates and the unfitness of the place, we expected poor lodgings. As it was still daylight, and we had heard so much of the falls of the South River, or, at least, we ourselves had imagined it, we went back to the river, in order to look at them; but we discovered we had deceived ourselves in our ideas. We had supposed it was a place, where the water came tumbling down in great quantity and force from a great height above, over a rock into an abyss, as the word *falls* would seem to imply, and as we had heard and read of the falls of the North River, and other rivers. But these falls of the South River are nothing more than a place of about two English miles in length, or not so much, where the river is full of stones, almost across it, which are not very large, but in consequence of the shallowness, the water runs rapidly and breaks against them, causing some noise, but not very much, which place, if it were necessary, could be made navigable on one side. As no Europeans live above the falls, they may so remain. This miller's house is the highest up the river, hitherto inhabited. Here we had to lodge; and although we were too tired to eat, we had to remain sitting upright the whole night, not being able to find room enough to lie upon the ground. We had a fire, however, but the dwellings are so wretchedly constructed, that if you are not so close to the fire as almost to burn yourself, you cannot keep warm, for the wind blows through them everywhere. Most of the English, and many others, have their houses made of nothing but clapboards, as

[1] In 1675 the moiety of Berkeley and Carteret's grant called West New Jersey came into the hands of three English Friends, Penn, Lawrie, and Lucas, as trustees. In the four years since that time more than a thousand Friends had settled in the province. The owner of the mill was Mahlon Stacey, a Yorkshire Quaker, who had just built it, on Assanpink Creek, in what is now Trenton.

they call them there, in this manner: they first make a wooden
frame, the same as they do in Westphalia, and at Altena,[1] but
not so strong; they then split the boards of clapwood, so that
they are like cooper's pipe staves, except they are not bent.
These are made very thin, with a large knife, so that the thickest
end is about as thick as a little finger, and the other is made
sharp, like the edge of a knife. They are about five or six feet
long, and are nailed on the outside of the frame, with the ends
lapped over each other. They are not usually laid so close
together, as to prevent you from sticking a finger between them,
in consequence either of their not being well joined, or the
boards being crooked. When it is cold and windy the best
people plaster them with clay. Such are almost all the English
houses in the country, except those they have which were built
by people of other nations. Now this house was new and
airy; and as the night was very windy from the north, and
extremely cold with clear moonshine, I shall not readily forget
it. Ephraim and his wife obtained a bed; but we passed
through the night without sleeping much.

18th, Saturday. About ten o'clock, after we had breakfasted, we stepped into a boat, in order to proceed on our
journey down the river. The ebb tide was half run out.
Although there is not much flood tide here, as it is stopped by
the falls, yet, the water rises and falls with the ebb or flood,
or through the ebb or flood, because the water, although it
runs down, increases through the flood, in consequence of its
being forced up, and is diminished with the ebb, because the
ebb gives it so much the more course to run down. We went
along, then, moving with the tide; but as Ephraim was suffering with the quartan ague, and it was now its time to come on,
we had to go and lie by the banks of the river, in order to make
a fire, as he could not endure the cold in the boat. This continued for about an hour and a half. The water was then rising, and we had to row against the current to Borlinghton
[Burlington], leaving the island of Matinakonk [2] lying on the
right hand. This island, formerly, belonged to the Dutch

---

[1] The Labadists had dwelt at Herford in Westphalia from 1670 to 1672, and
at Altona in Holstein from 1672 to 1675.

[2] Matinnaconk Island lies in the Delaware River between Bordentown and
Burlington.

governor, who had made it a pleasure ground or garden, built good houses upon it, and sowed and planted it. He also dyked and cultivated a large piece of meadow or marsh, from which he gathered more grain than from any land which had been made from woodland into tillable land. The English governor at the Manathans now held it for himself, and had hired it out to some Quakers, who were living upon it at present. It is the best and largest island in the South River; and is about four English miles in length, and two in breadth. It lies nearest to the east side of the river. At the end of this island lies the Quakers' village, Borlington, which east side of the river the Quakers have entirely in their possession, but how they came into its possession, we will show in another place.[1] Before arriving at this village, we stopped at the house of one Jacob Hendrix, from Holstein, living on this side. He was an acquaintance of Ephraim, who would have gone there to lodge, but he was not at home. We, therefore, rowed on to the village, in search of lodgings, for it had been dark all of an hour or more; but proceeding a little further, we met this Jacob Hendrix, in a canoe with hay. As we were now at the village, we went up to the tavern, but there were no lodgings to be obtained there, whereupon we reembarked in the boat, and rowed back to Jacob Hendrix's, who received us very kindly, and entertained us according to his ability. The house, although not much larger than where we were the last night, was somewhat better and tighter, being made according to the Swedish mode, and as they usually build their houses here, which are block-houses, being nothing else than entire trees, split through the middle, or squared out of the rough, and placed in the form of a square, upon each other, as high as they wish to have the house; the ends of these timbers are let into each other, about a foot from the ends, half of one into half of the other. The whole structure is thus made, without a nail or a spike. The ceiling and roof do not exhibit much finer work, except among the most careful people, who have the ceiling planked and a glass window. The doors are wide enough, but very low, so that you have to stoop in entering. These houses are quite tight and warm; but the chimney is placed in a corner. My comrade and myself had some deer skins, spread upon the

[1] See *post*, pp. 154–156.

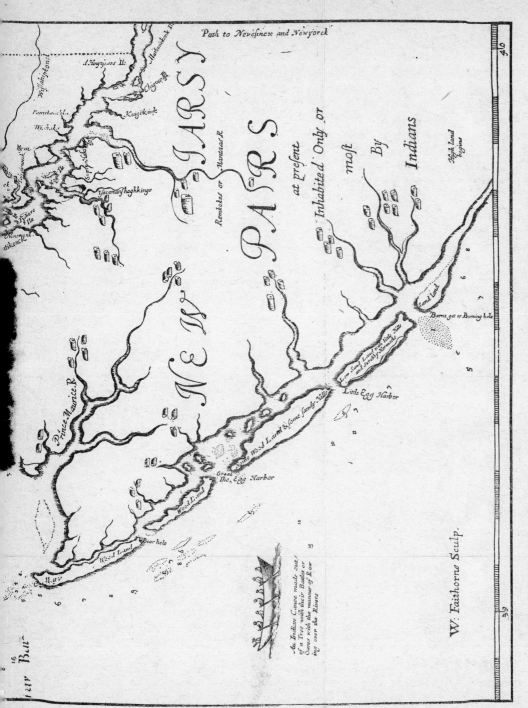

THE NORTHEAST PORTION OF AUGUSTINE HERRMAN'S MAP OF MARYLAND, 1673

From Mr. P. L. Phillips's facsimile

floor to lie on, and we were, therefore, quite well off, and could
get some rest. It rained hard during the night, and snowed
and froze, and continued so until the

19th, *Sunday*, and for a considerable part of the day,
affording little prospect of our leaving. At noon the weather
improved, and Ephraim having something to do at Borlinton,
we accompanied him there in the boat. We went into the
meeting of the Quakers, who went to work very unceremoni-
ously and loosely. What they uttered was mostly in one tone,
and the same thing, and so it continued, until we were tired
out, and went away. We tasted here, for the first time, peach
brandy, or spirits, which was very good, but would have been
better if it had been more carefully made. Ephraim remained
there for the evening, and we returned back to our former
lodgings, where we slept on a good bed, the same that Ephraim
and his wife had the night before. This gave us great comfort,
and recruited us greatly.

20th, *Monday*. We went again to the village this morning,
and entered the ordinary exhorters' house, where we breakfasted with Quakers, but the most worldly of men in all their
deportment and conversation. We found lying upon the window a volume of Virgil, as if it were a common hand-book, and
also Helmont's book on *Medicine*,[1] whom, in an introduction,
which they have made to it, they make pass for one of their
sect, although in his life time he did not know anything about
Quakers; and if they had been in the world, or should have
come into it, while he lived, he would quickly have said, no,
to them; but it seems these people will make all those who
have had any genius, in any respect, more than common, pass
for theirs; which is certainly great pride, wishing to place
themselves far above all others; whereas, the most of them,
whom I have seen as yet, are miserably self-minded, in physical
and religious knowledge. It was then about ten o'clock, and
it was almost noon before we left. The boat in which we had
come as far as there with its owner, who intended to return in

---

[1] Jean Baptiste van Helmont (1577–1644), an eminent Belgian chemist, physi-
ologist, and physician. Of his collected writings, *Ortus Medicinae*, there were
many editions and translations, and one of the English versions may have been
edited with sympathy by a Quaker, for with much scientific acuteness Van Helmont combined much mystical philosophy.

it, was exchanged for another, belonging to Oplant [Upland],[1] of which a Quaker was master, who was going down with several others of the same class; but as it was half ebb tide, and the shallop was lying far up in the mud, no one of these zealous people was willing to bring her through it, into the water. Ephraim, in order to get started, and to shame them, did not hesitate long, and followed by his servant and both of us, very soon had the boat afloat in the water. Pursuing our journey, we arrived about two o'clock at the house of another Quaker, on the west side of the river, where we stopped to eat our dinner and dry ourselves. We left there in an hour, rowing our best against the flood tide, until, at dark, we came to Takany,[2] a village of Swedes and Finns, situated on the west side of the river. Ephraim being acquainted, and having business here, we were all well received, and slept upon a parcel of deer skins. We drank very good beer here, brewed by the Swedes, who, although they have come to America, have not left behind them their old customs.

21st, *Tuesday*. The tide falling, we set out with the day, and rowed during the whole ebb and part of the flood, until two or three o'clock, when we arrived at the island of Tynakonk,[3] the fifth we had passed. Matinakonk and this Tinakonk are the principal islands, and the best and the largest. The others are of little importance, and some of them, whose names we do not know, are all meadow and marsh, others are only small bushes. The pleasantest thing about them is, they afford an agreeable view and a variety to the traveller, and a little *divertissement* to those who go up and down the river; also some conveniences for fishing in the river, and other accommodations for the planters.

This Tinakonk is the island of which M. Arnout de La Grange[4] had said so much; but we were much disappointed in comparing it with what he had represented, and what M.

---

[1] Chester, Pennsylvania.   [2] Tacony, Philadelphia County.

[3] Tinicum Island, a few miles below the present site of Philadelphia (which, it should be remembered, was not founded till 1682). On this island the Swedish governor Johan Printz had in 1643 built his stronghold of Nya Göteborg, or New Gothenburg, and his mansion; and here, after his return to Sweden, his daughter Armegot Printz, wife of his lieutenant and temporary successor Johan Papegoia, lived from 1654 to 1662, and from 1673 to 1675.

[4] Here and in many other places the diarist spells the name Grangie.

La Motte has written about it. The first mistake is in the name, which is not Matinakonk—the name rather of the island of which we have spoken before—but Tinakonk. It lies on the west side of the river, and is separated from the west shore, not as he said, by a wide running branch of the river, as wide as the Eemster, near Amsterdam, but by a small creek, as wide as a large ditch, running through a meadow. It is long and covered with bushes, and inside somewhat marshy. It is about two miles long, or a little more, and a mile and a half wide. Although there are not less miles than he said, he did not say they were English miles, which are only one-fourth the length of Dutch miles, of fifteen to a degree. The south-west point, which only has been and is still cultivated, is barren, scraggy, and sandy, growing plenty of wild onions, a weed not easily eradicated. On this point three or four houses are standing, built by the Swedes, a little Lutheran church made of logs,[1] and the remains of the large block-house, which served them in place of a fortress, with the ruins of some log huts. This is the whole of the manor. The best and pleasantest quality it has, is the prospect, which is very agreeable, and one of the principal things for which Mons. La Motte recommends it, namely, *belle videre*. I have made a sketch of it, according to my ability.[2] But as to there being a mine of iron ore upon it, I have not seen any upon that island, or elsewhere; and if it were so, it is of no great importance, for such mines are so common in this country, that little account is made of them. Although Ephraim had told us every thing in regard to the condition of the land, as well as the claim which Mons. de La Grange makes to it, yet we ourselves have observed the former, and have ascertained the latter, from a person who now resides there, which is as follows: When the Swedish colony was flourishing under its own government, this island belonged to a Mr. Papegay [Papegoia], the Swedish governor, who lived upon it, and cultivated it, the church and the fort still existing there as monuments to prove the fact. Although the Swedes have had fortresses, from time to time, in several other places, at this time, this was called New Gottenburg. This governor died, leaving a widow;[3] and she, Madam Papegay, sold the

---

[1] Built by Governor Printz in 1646.
[2] This sketch is not preserved with the manuscript.
[3] Papegoia returned to Sweden in 1656, but did not die till 1667.

island, which was then very flourishing, to the father of de La
Grange, for six thousand guilders, in the money of Holland,
though the person who now lives upon it says it was seven
thousand guilders, to be paid in several installments, here in
New Netherland.   Some of the first payments were duly made
by de La Grange, but the last two, I think, he was not so ready
to make, as he had to procure the money from Holland, and
that, I know not why, did not come.   Thereupon Mons. de
La Grange determined to go to Holland himself, and bring the
money with him; but he died on the voyage, and the payments
were not made.   It remained so for a long time, and at length
the widow Papegay cited the widow de La Grange before the
court, claiming as her right, payment in full, or restitution of
the land, as de La Grange had been in possession of the land
for some years, and had enjoyed the profits, and the time for
the last payment had also expired some years before.   In the
mean time comes one M. La Motte, who it seems was to assist
Madam de La Grange, either by discharging the debt or by
defending the suit, and in order the better to do so, he buys
the island from the widow de La Grange, seeking her also in
marriage.   But as Madam Papegay persevered, and the affair
of Mons. La Motte and the widow de La Grange came to
nothing, and on the other hand the widow de La Grange
could not deliver the land to La Motte, and La Motte could
not pay, the widow de La Grange was therefore condemned
to restore the island to Madam Papegay, and pay her costs,
and also to pay the income which she had received from the
island for the time she had lived upon it, and for the buildings
which she had allowed to go to waste.   Madam de La Grange,
conceiving this decree to be unjust, appealed to the high
court—the country having in the mean time been taken by
the English—and was again condemned, and therefore, had to
deliver up the land.[1]   Now, in this last war with Sweden,[2]
Madam Papegay, who has two brothers in Sweden, in the service of the crown,[3] was sent for by them to come home, where-

[1] This suit of Madame de La Grange against Madame Papegoia took place
at New York in 1672.

[2] The Scanian War, 1675–1679.

[3] Her only brother, it appears, had died.   But she had three sons in the
Swedish military and naval service in 1675.

upon, she sold the island to Mr. Otto Kuif [1] a Holsteiner, who now lives upon it, for fifteen hundred guilders in *zeewant,* as it was very much decayed and worn out. This is three hundred guilders in the money of Holland. Hereupon, Madam Papegay delivered full possession thereof to this Otto. Now, M. Arnout de La Grange, as heir of his father, when he was here last year laid claim to the island from Mr. Otto, who told him he did not know him in the matter, and if M. de La Grange had any lawful claim, he must not apply to him, but to the court, as his possession was under its judgment; but if M. de La Grange wished to buy it from him, he would let him have it for three hundred pounds sterling, or as they might agree. Whereupon, de La Grange flew into a passion, and threatened to appeal to London. "That you can do," said Otto, "if you have money enough. All this affects me not, since I have bought and paid for it, and have been put in possession of it by order of the court." De La Grange has not proposed to purchase the island again of Mr. Otto, although he could do it very favorably, notwithstanding Mr. Otto asked so much for it. Ephraim told me that Mr. Otto had said to him, confidentially, that in case he could obtain for it what it had cost him, he would let it go, as he had other land lying elsewhere, and that he had asked so much for it, merely to hear what he [de La Grange] would say, and in order to scare him. Should you lay out three hundred guilders in Holland for merchandise, and sell it here, which usually yields an hundred per cent. profit, or is so reckoned in barter, you could have this island almost for nothing, or at least for very little. But there is better land to be bought cheaper. De La Grange has let this slip by, and it seems as if he had not much inclination to stir the subject any more. He has given me to understand that he disregards it, or at least regards it as little now, as he formerly prized and valued it; as indeed he shows, for he has now bought land on Christina Creek, consisting of two or three old plantations, which, perhaps, are not much better than this island, and cost him enough. He has obtained another piece from the governor, lying between Burlington and the falls, on

---

[1] Otto Ernst Koch or Kock, a justice of the peace of the court held at Upland during this period when the region on the right bank of the Delaware River was under the administration of the Duke of York.

the west side, but will not accomplish much with it.   I forgot to mention that de La Grange, four years ago when he was in Holland, gave one Mr. Peter Aldrix,[1] who now resides on the South River, and is one of the members of the court, authority to make this man deliver the island to him, which Aldrix refused, and advised him that he was well assured he could not accomplish anything with it.   Yet to satisfy La Grange he laid the matter before Mr. Otto, who gave him the same answer he had given La Grange.   As I understand and have heard, La Grange bases his claim under the English law, that the son is the heir of the father's possessions; but the possession of the father being disputed, and he himself disinherited by two courts, the claim is null and of no value.[2]

When we arrived at this island, we were welcomed by Mr. Otto, late *medicus*, and entertained at his house according to his condition, although he lives poorly enough.   In the evening there also arrived three Quakers, of whom one was their greatest prophetess, who travels through the whole country in order to *quake*.   She lives in Maryland, and forsakes husband and children, plantation and all, and goes off for this purpose. She had been to Boston, and was there arrested by the authorities on account of her quakery.   This worthy personage came here in the house where we were, although Ephraim avoided her.[3]   They sat by the fire, and drank a dram of rum with each other, and in a short time afterwards began to shake and groan so, that we did not know what had happened, and supposed they were going to preach, but nothing came out of it.   I could not endure them, and went out of doors.   They left for Upland, which is three or four miles from there on the same side of the river, in the same boat in which we came.

[1] Peter Alrichs, a Dutchman of Nykerk near Groningen, had been commandant of the region during the brief Dutch reoccupation of 1673–1674, and was now a justice of the Newcastle court.   He was a nephew of Jacob Alrichs, governor of the region 1657–1659, under the rule of the city of Amsterdam.

[2] In the next year, 1681, Arnoldus de La Grange sued Kock in the Upland court.   The case was postponed "by reason that there's noe court without Justice Otto, whoe is a party," and, under Penn's government, was decided in favor of La Grange in 1683.

[3] Probably this was Alice Gary, formerly Alice Ambrose, who in 1662 had been whipped at Dover and Hampton, N. H., and Salisbury, Mass., and in 1665 had been punished at Boston, along with Wenlock Christison.   She now lived on West River, in Maryland.

22d, *Wednesday*. It was rainy all this day, which gave us sufficient time to explore the island. We had some good cider which he had made out of the fruit from the remains of an old orchard planted by the Swedish governor. The persons of whom we have before spoken having left for Upland, Ephraim did not wish to go there because he thought they would preach; and it being rainy, and no fit boat at hand, we remained here the whole day. We saw an ox as large as they have in Friesland or Denmark, and also quite fat—a species of which we have observed more among the Swedes, and which thrive well. It clearing up towards evening, we took a canoe and came after dark to Upland. This is a small village of Swedes, although it is now overrun by English. We went to the house of the Quaker who had brought us down, and carried the other persons from Tinakonk. His name was Robert Willemsen or Weert.[1] We found here the prophetess or *apostle-ess*, with her company. Among others, there were two widows, who were at variance, and whom the prophetess with all her authority and spiritual power could not reconcile, or had not endeavored to do so. They would have been compelled to have gone before the court, had not Ephraim striven his best to make them adjust the matter, and brought them to a settlement. One of these widows, named Anna Salters, lived at Takany, and was one of those who, when   [2] gave himself out as the Lord Jesus, and allowed himself to be carried around on an ass, shouted Hosanna as he rode over their garments, for which conduct he was arrested, his tongue bored through with a red-hot iron, and his forehead branded with a B, for blasphemer. She was not only one of those, but she anointed his head and feet, and wiped them with her hair. The other widow, named Lysbeth, was also one of the principal persons. She lived a little lower down than Takoney, on the same side of the river. The state of the difference between them was this. They had agreed between themselves to exchange or

---

[1] Robert Wade, who had come out with Fenwick in 1675, and settled at Salem, N. J., but presently removed to Upland (Chester). He and his wife were probably the first Quakers in Pennsylvania. Penn occupied this house when he first landed in 1682, and here the first assembly of Pennsylvania met.

[2] James Naylor. The episode occurred at Bristol, England, in 1656. Anna Salters was at that time Anna or Hannah Strayer, whose conduct in that episode was as here described.

barter their plantations, and each made a writing and each kept her own. Anna Salters afterwards repented her bargain, and went to Elizabeth, and desired that each should take back the writing subscribed by her; but it so happened that Anna Salters went away, having given up hers, and the other not being then to be found. She had given hers to Elizabeth, supposing she would afterwards obtain the other; but when she went again to demand it, Elizabeth said the paper had become wet, and in her attempting to dry it, was burnt up. It was believed that Elizabeth had the two writings in her possession, and consequently both plantations, which, they said, she wanted to sell privately. Whereupon Anna called upon her to restore either the deed or the plantation. Elizabeth charged that Anna was indebted to her for a certain amount of tobacco, which she had taken to England for her, and of which she had never been able to obtain a correct account. It was really confusion and rascality. Elizabeth, who was a bad person, appealed always to some papers which she said she had not with her. Ephraim who was clerk of both the courts, namely, of Upland and Nieu Castel [Newcastle],[1] wrote down separately from the beginning the claims which they set up against each other, and decided that the plantations should be mutually restored, and the debts balanced, and he made them agree to it, although Elizabeth was very unwilling. Robbert Weert, who is the best Quaker we have yet seen, and his wife, who is a good woman, were both troubled, as they said, as also was the prophetess, that such things should take place among their people before strangers, and be settled through them, and when there were other strangers present. Whereupon Ephraim said, "Who do you suppose we are? Possibly we are as good Christians as you are." And certainly he exhibited something more christianly in reconciling and pacifying them than they who brewed this work had done, or those who would be so very devout that they would neither speak to them authoritatively nor admonish them with kindness to any effect. The Lord has caused us to see this example that we might know that these people are still covetous, and that almost all of them are attached to the world and to themselves—that is, they are worldly people, which shows the holi··

[1] So appointed by Governor Andros in 1676.

ness of the spirit by which they are actuated! As regards
Anna Salters, it was said she was mundane, carnal, covetous,
and artful, although she appeared to be the most pious. Her
sayings and discussions were continually mixed up with prot-
estations of the presence and omniscience of God, and upon
the salvation of her soul, so truly gross that if the ordinary
boors had talked so, they would have been punished and ex-
pelled. But what are not those people capable of, who present themselves to be carried away as we have mentioned
above; as well as others in this country, who publish and
declare, one, that she is Mary the mother of the Lord; another,
that she is Mary Magdalen, and others that they are Martha,
John, etc., scandalizers, as we heard them in a tavern, who not
only so called themselves, but claimed to be really such. For
this reason, Mr. Weert would no longer have them in his house,
making them leave, although it was well in the evening; for
the Weerts said they could not endure it. Indeed, God the
Lord will not let that pass by, for it is not far from blasphemy.
He will bring them to justice, if they be of His elect.

It was very late in the evening, in consequence of this dispute, before we supped and went to sleep. We were taken to a
place to sleep directly before an open window, to which there
was no shutter, so that it could not be closed, and as the night
was very cold, and it froze hard, we could scarcely keep ourselves warm.

23d, Thursday. It was late before we left here, and we
therefore had time to look around a little, and see the remains
of the residence of Madame Papegay, who had had her dwelling here when she left Tinakonk. We had nowhere seen so
many vines together as we saw here, which had been planted
for the purpose of shading the walks on the river side, in between the trees. The dinner being ready, I was placed at the
table next to the beforenamed prophetess, who while they all
sat at the table, began to groan and quake gradually until at
length the whole bench shook. Then rising up she began to
pray, shrieking so that she could be heard as far as the river.
This done, she was quickly in the dish, and her mouth began
immediately to prate worldly and common talk in which she
was not the least ready. When the meal was finished, Ephraim
obtained a horse for himself and his wife, and we followed him

on foot, carrying our travelling bags.   Our host took us to the
path, and Ephraim's servant was to act as our guide.   In
travelling along we observed the difference between the soil
on the North River and this, and also that this difference was
not so great as is usually asserted.   After we had proceeded
about three hours, our guide missed the way, and we had gone
a good distance before he became aware of it, and would have
gone on still further if we had not told him that we thought
the course we were going was wrong.   We therefore left one
road, and went straight back in search of the other which we
at length found.   A man overtook us who was going the same
way, and we followed him.   We crossed the Schiltpads Kill,[1]
where there was a fall of water over the rocks, affording a site
for a grist-mill which was erected there.   This Schilpads Kil
is nothing but a branch or arm of Christine Kill into which it
discharges itself, and is so named on account of the quantities
of tortoises which are found there.   Having crossed it we came
to the house of the miller who was a Swede or Holsteiner whom
they usually call Tapoesie.   He was short in person, but a very
friendly fellow.   Ephraim had told us we would find him such
as we did, for he had ridden there before us.   He had, as it
appeared, several well-behaved children, among whom was a
little girl who resembled very much our little Judith in her
whole countenance and figure, and was about the same age,
and had she met us by our house, I should have considered her
Judith.   Her name was Anne Mary.   We were welcome here,
and were entertained according to the man's circumstances.

24th, Friday.   Ephraim having some business here, we did
not leave very speedily.   This miller had shot an animal they
call a muskrat, the skin of which we saw hanging up to dry.
He told us they were numerous in the creeks.   We asked
them why they gave them that name, and he said because
they smelt so, especially their testicles, which he had preserved of this one, and gave my comrade, remarking that they
were intended for some amateur or other, and he could do
little with them.   The muskrat is not larger than the common
rat.   It has gray hair, and the fleece is sometimes sold with
other peltries, but it is not worth much, although it has some

[1] Turtle Creek, now Shelpot Creek.   At its falls the Swedes had built a mill
in 1662.

odor. It was about noon when we were set across the creek
in a canoe. We proceeded thence a small distance over land
to a place where the fortress of Christine[1] had stood which had
been constructed and possessed by the Swedes, but taken by
the Dutch governor, Stuvesant, and afterwards, I believe, demolished by the English. We went into a house here belonging to some Swedes, with whom Ephraim had some business.
We were then taken over Christine Creek in a canoe, and landed
at the spot where Stuyvesant threw up his battery to attack
the fort, and compelled them to surrender.[2] At this spot there
are many medlar trees which bear good fruit from which one
Jaquet,[3] who does not live far from there, makes good brandy
or spirits, which we tasted and found even better than French
brandy. Ephraim obtained a horse at this Jaket's, and rode
on towards Santhoek, now Newcastle, and we followed him
on foot, his servant leading the way. We arrived about four
o'clock at Ephraim's house, where we congratulated each other,
and were glad, thanking the Lord in our hearts for His constantly
accompanying grace. We found here the young brother of
the wife with the servant, who had come with the horses from
the falls overland, and had been at the house several days.
We also saw here Ephraim's sister, Miss Margaret Hermans,[4]
who showed us much kindness. She was a little volatile, but
of a sweet and good disposition. She had been keeping house
during the absence of Ephraim. Truly the Lord has in all
these things been very good to us, for we knew not where to
go, and He has directed us among these people, who have done
out of love what they have shown us. We knew not where
to lodge, and He has provided us lodgings where we were so

[1] The creek mentioned was Brandywine Creek. Fort Christina stood on a
part of the present site of Wilmington, Delaware. For the Dutch conquest of
it in 1655, see *Narratives of New Netherland*, in this series, pp. 379–386, and *Narratives of Early Pennsylvania*, pp. 167–176.

[2] Fort Christina stood on the north side of Christina Creek. Stuyvesant's
main battery was erected behind the fort, on the land or north side of it, but he
also had works on the opposite or south side of Christina Creek. Lindström's
original plan of the siege may be seen reproduced in Dr. Amandus Johnson's
The Swedish Settlements on the Delaware, II. 602.

[3] Jean Paul Jaquet was vice-director on the Delaware during the initial
period of Dutch control, 1655–1657.

[4] Anna Margareta, eldest of the three daughters of Augustine Herrman of
Bohemia Manor. She afterward married Matthias Vanderheyden.

free and had, according to the circumstances of the time, what we desired. We hope and doubt not the Lord will visit that house in grace, and even gives us some assurances in what we have seen.

25th, Saturday. We rested a little to-day. Ephraim and his wife and we ourselves had several visits from different persons who came to welcome us, as Mons. Jan Moll,[1] whom we had conversed with in New York, and who now offered us his house and all things in it, even pressing them upon us. But we were not only contented with our present circumstances, but we considered that we should not be doing right to leave Ephraim's house without reason. We therefore thanked him, but nevertheless in such a manner, that we took notice of his kindness, and answered accordingly. Pieter Aldrix also showed us much attention, as did others, to all of whom we returned our thanks. We went out to view this little place, which is not of much moment, consisting of only forty or fifty houses. There is a fine prospect from it, as it lies upon a point of the river where I took a sketch.[2]

26th, Sunday. We went to the church, but the minister, Tessemaker, who has to perform service in three places, over the river, at the Sandhook, and at Apoquemene,[3] was to-day over the river, and there was, therefore, nothing done, except what was done by a poor limping clerk, as he was a cripple and poor in body. He read from a book a sermon, or short explanation, and sang and made a prayer, if it may be called such, and then the people went home. In the afternoon there was a prelection again about the catechism.

27th, Monday. The weather was sharp and windy. We had intended to proceed on our journey but we could not very well do so. My comrade had also been indisposed in the night. We therefore waited for the opportunity which the Lord would present. Meanwhile we had another visit. Ephraim advised us to wait a day or two until his brother, Kasparus Herman,[4]

---

[1] Presiding justice of the court at Newcastle. See *post*, p. 144.

[2] This Newcastle sketch seems not to have survived.

[3] Appoquinimink Creek, in the lower part of Newcastle County, Delaware.

[4] Kasparus Herrman, second son of Augustine Herrman of Bohemia Manor. Andros in 1676 had confirmed him in the possession of lands on the northeast side of Augustine Creek in Delaware, a part of St. Augustine Manor (see note 2 on page 112), and here we may assume that he was living, near Reedy Isle.

whom he expected there, should arrive, and who would conduct us farther into Maryland.

28th, *Tuesday.* Little transpired while we were waiting to-day, except that we spoke to several persons of the way of the Lord, and particularly to the sister of Ephraim, Miss Margaret, who received with some favor what was said to her, and also to Ephraim and his wife, who we hope will bring forth the seed the Lord has sown in them, in His own time.

29th, *Wednesday.* We were still waiting, although Ephraim nad sent for his brother; but we obtained tidings that he had gone to Maryland, and was coming back home immediately, as he had gone to visit his father who lives at the entrance into Maryland and was sick.

30th, *Thursday.* The weather had been cold and windy, but had now cleared up; so that some of the servants of Kasparus came, who confirmed the account that their master had gone to Maryland, but they were expecting him home. Whereupon Mons. Moll, who had to go to one of his plantations lying on the road leading to Kasparus's house, requested us to accompany him, so that the servants of Kasparus on their return home would find us at his place and take us on to the house of Kasparus. We accordingly started, Mr. Moll riding on horseback and we following him on foot, carrying our travelling sacks, but sometimes exchanging with him, and thus also riding a part of the way. This plantation of his is situated about fifteen miles from the Sandhook. It was about ten o'clock in the morning when we took leave of our friends and left. We passed through a tolerably good country, but the soil was a little sandy, and it was three o'clock in the afternoon when we reached the plantation. There were no persons there except some servants and negroes, the commander being a Parisian. The dwellings were very badly appointed, especially for such a man as Mons. Moll. There was no place to retire to, nor a chair to sit on, or a bed to sleep on. For their usual food the servants have nothing but maize bread to eat, and water to drink, which sometimes is not very good and scarcely enough for life, yet they are compelled to work hard. They are brought from England in great numbers into Maryland, Virginia and the Menades and sold each one according to his condition, for a certain term of years, four, five, six, seven or more. And thus they are by hundreds of thousands compelled to spend their lives here and in Virginia and elsewhere in planting that vile tobacco, which all vanishes into smoke, and is for the most part miserably abused.[1] It is the chief article of trade in the country. If they only wished it they could have everything for the support of life in abundance, for they have land and opportunity sufficient for that end; but this insatiable avarice must be fed and sustained by the bloody sweat of these poor slaves. After we had supped, Mr. Moll, who would be civil, wished us to lie upon a bed that was there, and he would lie upon a bench, which we declined; and as this continued some length of time I lay down on a heap of maize, and he and my comrade afterwards did the same. This was very uncomfortable and chilly, but it had to go so.

December 1st, *Friday*. Mr. Moll wishing to do us every kindness, as he indeed did do many, wrote addresses which might be serviceable to us in Maryland, for he was not only very well known there, but had influence among the people by reason of the trade they had with each other, and of his being a member of the court, and having some authority. He also gave us some letters of recommendation and credit in case we might have any necessity for the latter, in all which he indeed showed he had an affection for us. After we had breakfasted, the servants of Kasparus not having arrived, he himself conducted us to one of the nearest plantations where his cooper was, who had also something to do for Kasparus, and would conduct us farther on, as took place; and we arrived about three o'clock at the house of Kasparus. But he had not yet come home nor had the servants arrived, for whom we had been waiting.

2d, *Saturday*. We waited here all this day, and had time and opportunity to explore this place, which they call St. Augustine.[2] We found that it was well situated, and would

[1] Great numbers of indented white servants came into Maryland, Delaware, and Pennsylvania. See E. I. MacCormac, *White Servitude in Maryland*, in *Johns Hopkins University Studies*, XXII.

[2] This was one of Augustine Herrman's estates. His possessions included Bohemia Manor and Little Bohemia (acquired in 1662), St. Augustine's Manor (1671), and Misfortune, or the Three Bohemian Sisters (1682). All lay in the region between Elk River and the Delaware. Bohemia Manor was the tract in present Maryland between Bohemia River (and Great Bohemia Creek) and Back

not badly suit us.   There are large and good meadows and marshes near it, and the soil is quite good.   It has much good timber and a very fine prospect, for looking from the strand you can see directly south into the mouth of the bay, as this place lies on the west side of the river in a bend.   There is much land attached to it, which he purchased from the Indians for almost nothing, or nothing to signify.   Towards evening two Englishmen and a Quaker stopped here to pass the night who were also going to Maryland.

3d, Sunday.   The Englishmen left this morning at daylight, and after breakfast we determined also to leave, delivering a letter, which Ephraim had given us for his brother, to his wife.   We started at nine o'clock, and followed a large broad wagon road, which Kasparus had made through the woods, from his house to his father's, who lived in the uppermost part of Maryland, that is, as high up as it is yet inhabited by Christians.   This road is about twenty-two miles long, and runs almost due west, but a little more northerly than southerly.[1]   When we were about half way we met Kasparus on horseback with a cart, his wife having described him to us. We told him we had been to his house waiting for him, and had left a letter there for him from his brother.   He regretted, he said, he had not known it and was not at home, but he hoped,

Creek, Little Bohemia that between Great and Little Bohemia Creek, the Three Bohemia Sisters a tract north of Back Creek, and St. Augustine, the tract in present Delaware east of Bohemia Manor and extending from St. George's Creek or the present line of the Chesapeake and Delaware Canal southward to Appoquinnimink or perhaps Blackbird Creek.   The tract which the Labadists afterward purchased lay in the southeast part of Bohemia Manor, east of the manor-house, and on the north side of Great Bohemia Creek.   Their house was still standing a few years ago.   Our travellers had gone down the Delaware River some fifteen miles from Newcastle, and were now near the present Port Penn, Delaware.

[1] In 1671 the New York authorities ordered those at Newcastle to clear one-half of a road from there to Augustine Herrman's plantation, the Marylanders having agreed to clear the other half.   In a rare tract, *Copies of some Records and Depositions Relating to the Great Bohemia Manor* (1721), Herrman van Barkelo, an elderly resident, describing the "old Highway Road or Delaware Path about Thirty eight Years ago," and giving some reminiscences of Ephraim Herrman about the same time (1683), when the deponent lived with the Labadists on Bohemia Manor, adds that as he then "travelled the . . . Delaware Road, . . . he observed the Trees marked or notched along the said Delaware Road Sides, that the Notches seemed to him to be made about Eight or Ten Years before that Time."

and so did we, that we should be able to converse together on our return, and with this we pursued our respective roads. It was very warm to-day, and we were all in a perspiration. We reached Augustynus Hermans[1] the father of these two brothers, about three o'clock. This Augustynus Hermans is a Bohemian, and formerly lived on the Manathans, and had possessed farms or plantations there, but for some reason, I know not what, disagreeing with the Dutch governor, Stuyvesant, he repaired to this place, which is laid down upon a complete map, which he has made of Maryland and Virginia, where he is very well acquainted, which map he has dedicated to the king. In consequence of his having done the people of these two countries a great service, he has been presented with a tract of land of about a thousand or twelve hundred acres, which he, knowing where the best land was, has chosen up here, and given it the name of Bohemia.[2] It is a noble piece of land, indeed the best we have seen in all our journey south, having large, thick, and high trees, much black walnut and chestnut, as tall and straight as a reed.

It was, then, on this day and at this plantation, that we made our entry into Maryland, which was so named, I believe, in Queen Mary's time,[3] when it was discovered or began to be settled. It is a large territory, but has as yet no fixed boundaries, except only on the south where it is separated from Virginia by a straight line running westerly from   [4] to the

[1] See the Introduction, p. xvii. Augustine Herrman, born in Prague in 1608, seems to have resided at New Amsterdam most of the time from 1633 to 1659. In the latter year he was sent on an embassy into Maryland. His journal of that embassy is printed in *Narratives of Early Maryland*, in this series, pp. 309–333. From 1662 to his death in 1686 he lived on his estates in Maryland, already described, and was the great man of northeastern Maryland. His house stood till 1815, when it was destroyed by fire.

[2] Twenty thousand acres, rather, or perhaps twenty-four thousand. The map, one of the finest ever executed in English America in the seventeenth century, is entitled *Virginia and Maryland, As it is Planted and Inhabited this present Year* 1670 *Surveyed and Exactly Drawne by the Only Labour and Endeavour of Augustin Herrman Bohemiensis*. It was engraved by Faithorne. Only one copy is now known, that in the British Museum. A facsimile was lately published by Mr. P. Lee Phillips (Washington, 1911).

[3] Queen Henrietta Maria, consort of Charles I.

[4] On the east side of Chesapeake Bay the line of division between Maryland and Virginia ran east from Watkins Point on the bay shore to the Atlantic. On the west side the boundary was the Potomac.

river. All north of this line is Maryland, and all south of it
Virginia. On the east it is bounded by New Netherland, but
that line is undefined; and on the north and west indefinitely
by the Indians. It comprises four great provinces, as   .
The principal rivers are on the east side of the bay of   .¹

Maryland is considered the most fertile portion of North
America, and it were to be wished that it was also the most
healthy, though it is more healthy than its neighbor, Virginia,
which has to give passage by water through the great bay of
         ,¹ to Maryland. It is also very rich in fish as well as
in all kinds of water fowl. There are few Indians in comparison with the extent of country. When the English first discovered and settled Virginia and Maryland, they did great
[wrong] to these poor people, and almost exterminated them.²

To return to Augustine Hermans, he was sick when we
arrived at his house.³   We found there the three Englishmen
before mentioned, who had left the house of Kasparus in the
morning. They were about proceeding further on their journey. We delivered to Augustine a letter from his son Ephraim,
and related to him how we had travelled with him from the
Manathans, and how he was, which rejoiced him. Becoming
thus acquainted he showed us every kindness he could in his
condition, as he was very miserable, both in soul and body.
His plantation was going much into decay, as well as his body,
for want of attention. There was not a Christian man, as
they term it, to serve him; nobody but negroes. All this was
increased by a miserable, doubly miserable wife;⁴ but so miserable that I will not relate it here. All his children have been
compelled on her account to leave their father's house. He
spoke to us of his land, and said he would never sell or hire it
to Englishmen, but would sell it to us cheap, if we were inclined to buy. But we satisfied ourselves and him by looking
at it then, hoping that we might see each other on our return.
We were directed to a place to sleep, but the screeching of the

---

¹ Chesapeake.

² The travellers had no first-hand knowledge of the subject, and their com-
ment is without authentic value.

³ "My father is and has been all this winter extreme weakly." Ephraim
Herrman to Secretary Matthias Nicolls, Newcastle, January 17, 1680.

⁴ A second wife, of whom little is otherwise known.

wild geese and other wild fowl in the creek before the door, prevented us from having a good sleep, though it answered.

4th, Monday.   After breakfast we were set over this creek, or Bohemia River, in a canoe, after Augustine had, as the head man of the place, signed the passport which Mr. Moll, Ephraim and Aldrix had given us.   Our first address was to one Mr. van Waert,[1] who had arrived from England the day before, and who gave us little news, except that a certain skipper Jacob, who lived at the Manathans, had left England some days before him, bound there.   We were glad of this, thinking we would receive some letters from Fatherland, as we had, when we were at Newcastle, written to our hostess at New York, that in case the skipper Jacob had letters for us, she should send them to the South River.   Towards evening we came to a Swede's, named Mouns,[2] where we had to be put across a creek, after we had mistaken the road.   We spent the night with him, and were entirely welcome.   He and his wife and some of his children spoke good Dutch, and conversed with us about various matters concerning the country.

5th, Tuesday.   We left after breakfast, and he took us upon the road to go to Captain Frisby's.[3]   Leaving Mr. Blacstoon's [Blackstone's] plantation on the right hand of Frisby's, we came to the court house standing on the Sassafrix [Sassafras] River, which is also an ordinary.   We requested to be taken over the river, as there is a ferry here, which they did, and it cost us each an English shilling.   We then travelled along the river until we came to a small creek, which runs very shallow over the strand into the river.   Here we had to take off our shoes and stockings in order to cross over, although it was piercing cold.   We continued some distance further, along the river, to the Great Bay, when we came to another creek and called out to be taken across, which was done.   The road was shown us further on to Mr. Howel's, where we had a letter of

[1] Probably Captain Henry Ward, several times member of assembly from Cecil County, who had a plantation in Sassafras Neck.

[2] Probably Måns Andersson.   He and Hendrick Hendrickson, mentioned below, are known as petitioners for naturalization in 1674.

[3] Captain James Frisby, member of the Maryland assembly for Cecil County in 1678.   George Fox held a notable meeting at his house in 1672.   The first court-house of Cecil County was erected on the north side of Sassafras River, a short distance east of what is still called Ordinary Point.

recommendation and credit to deliver Captain Seybry,[1] who was not at home, but had gone to the ships which had arrived. So we gave the letter to Mr. Howel, to hand to Mr. Seybry. We slept here this night, and were welcome.

6th, *Wednesday*. This morning we crossed a creek, and were shown the way to another plantation, where we would be set over still another. To this plantation we soon came, but the people excused themselves from taking us over, saying that their canoe was not at home, and sent us to another plantation on the right. We crossed there and saw on almost every tree one or two grape-vines, and that for a long distance along the road until we reached the plantation of one Hendrick Hendricksen, where no one was at home except a woman, who nevertheless lent us a canoe with which we might not only cross over, but go a considerable distance down the creek, trusting her canoe to us. We arrived in this at the plantation of Mr. Hopkins, who was not at home. Being fatigued, and not having yet breakfasted, we asked for something to drink that clear water from, and afterwards for something to eat; but we could obtain nothing except a piece of maize bread with which we satisfied ourselves. The worst was, she would not show us the way, which, however, we found ourselves. We arrived at noon at Salsberry's, who also was not at home. They had all sailed down below to the ships. But we found a good old woman who immediately put before us something to eat, and gave us some exceedingly good cider to drink. We were, therefore, somewhat strengthened. This plantation is one of the most pleasantly situated I have seen, having upon the side of the great bay a fine prospect, and a pretty view in the distance, as the sketch shows.[2] We left here about three o'clock, and were taken across the creek and put upon the road, and at evening came to the house of one Richard Adams, an Englishman, who had a Dutch wife born at Deventer. The husband was not at home, and she had almost forgotten her

[1] Captain Nathan Sybrey was a member of assembly for Cecil County in 1678. The Great Bay, above, means the Chesapeake. "Howel's Point" is noted on Herrman's map, at the mouth of Sassafras River.

[2] The sketch is not preserved. The place would seem to be west of Newtown, Maryland, where Herrman's map indicates "Salsbury Creek." Richard Adams was a petitioner to the Maryland assembly from Cecil County in 1681.

Dutch. However, we were welcome, and we remained there for the night, and rested reasonably well.

7th, Thursday. We left there after breakfast, and were put across a creek which runs by the door, and shown the road to go to an English plantation. The owner was not at home, but we first passed a small plantation where an Amsterdamer was engaged in carpenter work, who very willingly pointed out the road. We found at the Englishman's a young man from Middelburgh,[1] who had been sold as a servant, but had served out his time. He was in the last English war, had been taken by a privateer and carried to Virginia, and there sold for four years, which having expired, he thought of returning to Fatherland next year. We were unacquainted with each other, but he was glad to see one of his countrymen. He took us to the road, and we proceeded on to a plantation where the people were in the woods working, to whom we went to inquire the way. The master of the plantation came to meet us, accompanied by his wife and a person who spoke high Dutch.[2] The owner's name was Miller. We told him we wished to learn the road to Mr. Hosier's. He was about to show us the way, but as this was far around, his wife said he had better let us be taken over a creek which ran in front of his plantation, and we would have a less distance to go, whereupon he gave us directions that it should be so done. We thanked him, and went to his plantation for the purpose of going over, but we were not there soon enough, for there was a man gone over who was now almost on the other side, who called out to us that he was not coming back, because there was another canoe on this side where there was a woman. This I immediately launched in the water, as we had permission, and went over, and the woman took it back. We had here as company the man who had crossed over before us, for a piece of the way, and he directed us to another plantation, also with a creek in front of it where we had to cross. There was no one here except some women attending upon another sick woman. The man who had travelled with us a part of the way, afterwards came up and again directed us, but we came to a different plantation from what we intended. If we had gone to the right hand, we should have proceeded straight, for we should

---

[1] Where Danckaerts had lived.   [2] German.

then have found Mr. Commegys, a Dutchman, whom we were
in search of according to the address Mr. Moll had given us,
and for whom we had inquired.[1] We should have found him
with many of his people bringing slaughtered meat over the
creek. The owner of the plantation we had come to, had no
canoe at home; but he assisted us by going with us himself,
where a son of Mr. Commegys, as he said, worked a plantation,
who, if he heard us call, would certainly come and take us over.
But when we came to the creek we saw all those people who
had carried the meat over in the boat, but this man did not
know them, and doubted whether they were Commegys's
men. We arrived at last at Cornelis's, the son of Commegys,
and called out to him, and he brought a canoe which relieved
us, as it was close on to evening. We thanked the person who
had brought us, and stepped into the canoe. Cornelis, who
was an active young man, was pleased to meet Hollanders,
although he himself was born in this country. We found Mr.
Commegys on the next plantation, who bade us welcome, and
after we had drunk some cider, accompanied us with one of
his company to Mr. Hosier's, who was a good generous-hearted
man, better than any Englishman we had met with in this
country. He had formerly had much business with Mr. Moll,
but their affairs in England running behindhand a little, they
both came and settled down here; and, therefore, Mr. Moll
and he had a great regard for each other. He showed us very
particular attention, although we were strangers. Something
was immediately set before Mr. Commegys and ourselves to
eat, in which the wife manifested as much kindness as the
husband. This was not unacceptable, for we had eaten nothing all day. They requested Mr. Commegys and us very
urgently to stay all night, but he desired to go home, although
it was two or three hours distant from there, and it already
began to grow dark. However, we left with him on foot, but
he obtained a horse on the road which enabled him to travel
better than we could with our wearied feet. We reached his

---

[1] An act of assembly of 1671 naturalized Cornelius Commegys the elder,
Millementy [so in the act as printed, read Willemtje] his wife, and his four children, Cornelius, Elizabeth, William, and Hannah, the first born in Virginia, the
younger three in Maryland. He settled at Quaker Neck on the Chester River,
in Kent County, below Chestertown.

house about eight o'clock, where he and his wife bade us welcome. We were well entertained, and went easily to sleep,
having travelled during the day a great distance.

8th, Friday. We advised this morning with Mr. Commegys as to proceeding further down to Virginia, and crossing the bay, in pursuance of the address which we had received
from Mr. Moll, and our recollection, to wit, that arriving at
Mr. Commegys's we should then consult him, and he would
give us further information. In talking the matter over with
him, he said, he saw no probability of our being able to accomplish this, and advised us against it, for several reasons. First,
the country below there was full of creeks and their branches,
more so than that we had passed over, and it was difficult to
get across them, as boats were not always to be obtained, and
the people were not very obliging. As to going by water,
either down or across the bay, there was not much navigating
at this time of year, the winter being so close at hand, and
the worst of it would be to get back again. To go by sea to
the South River, or New York, there was not much opportunity, and it was attended with great danger and inconvenience. As to exploring the land, he assured us we had seen
the best; the rest of it was poor and covered with bushes,
especially in Virginia. It would cost us much at this time,
and we would have to do with a godless and very crafty people,
who would be the more so towards us, because we were strangers
who could not speak their language, and did not understand
the customs of the country, and so forth, all which we took
into consideration. After breakfast a man arrived with a
letter from Mr. Miller, requesting Commegys to go with him
in his boat across the bay to the ships. Commegys not wishing to go, answered the letter, and said to us in general terms
something about a man who wished to cross the bay in a boat,
but he did not express himself fully, and we also did not understand him well. We supposed the man was at his plantation
with a boat, and after waiting awhile without perceiving anything of him, we asked him where the man was with the boat.
He said he was not there, but that it was Captain Miller's
boat which was going, and he lived about ten or twelve miles
off. We immediately resolved to go there, which we did,
about noon, after having breakfasted and dined together. Mr.

Commegys was from Vianen,[1] and had had a Dutch woman
for a wife, who had taught her children to speak the Dutch
language; they therefore had a kind disposition towards Hollanders. After her death he married an English woman, and
he had himself learned many of the English maxims, although
it was against his feelings; for we were sensible that he dared
not work for us with an open heart. He told us he would
rather live at the Cape of Good Hope than here. "How is
that," said I, "when there is such good land here?" "True,"
he replied, "but if you knew the people here as well as I do,
you would be able to understand why."

We departed from his house over the same road by which
we had come, thinking that if nothing more should result from
this opportunity, we would at least have advanced so far on
our way back. We arrived at about three o'clock at Mr.
Hosier's,[2] who received us kindly, and would have cheerfully
kept us all night, but understanding our intention, he not only
let us go and showed us the road, but went with us himself in
order to facilitate our getting over the creek; but on arriving
at the next plantation on the creek, there was no canoe to put
us over, and he therefore took us to another, the same one
where we had found the Commegys, and where we now found
his son, of whom I have before spoken, who soon had his boat
ready, when thanking Mr. Hosier, and taking our leave of
him, we crossed over. Young Commegys showed us the road,
which we followed to a creek, where we found a canoe, but no
person with it. We took ourselves over in it, and came to the
house where we left the sick woman before spoken of. There
were now some men at home whom we requested to show us
the road, and the same person who brought us here over the
same road, accompanied us a part of the way, and gave us
directions how to proceed. We struck the creek directly opposite Mr. Miller's plantation, as it began to get dark, and on
calling out were taken over. We inquired of Mr. Miller
whether he intended to cross the bay in his boat and when,

---

[1] Vianen is in South Holland, near the borders of Utrecht. The act of naturalization and the record of their marriage at New Amsterdam in 1658 speak of
him as born in Lexmont (Leksmond, a village near Vianen) and his wife in Bar-
neveld, a village near Amersfoort.

[2] Henry Hosier was a member of the assembly from Kent County in 1679.

and whether he would take us with him. He said yes, but he did not know whether he would leave the next day or not. He would start as soon as the weather would permit, as he had some casks of tobacco to carry over, with which we might help him; but he did not know how we would manage on the other side, as he had to go further up the river from there, and he saw no chance for us to go down the bay or to cross back again. We finally concluded we would go with him, and remain on board the ships until he came back to take us with him, he promising not to leave there without coming for us. We also found here the person who spoke high Dutch, and of whom we have before said a word. We were able to converse with him, but my companion could do so the best.[1] He resided on this plantation, and was a kind of proctor or advocate in the courts. We passed the evening with him. We were well entertained here, and had a good bed to sleep on, which was very agreeable.

9th, *Saturday*. We expected the trip would be made this morning, but no mention was made of it, and we asked him at last whether it would not be proceeded with. He said the weather was not fit, and that as soon as it was suitable we would start. But about noon the wind blowing very fresh from the west, which was straight ahead, we gave up all hope of going to-day. Seeing that the same difficulty might exist on Monday and the following days, as he said he would not go over on Sunday, we determined to proceed, after we had dined, with our journey back to Newcastle, which we did, excusing ourselves on the ground that we could not wait so long, and that time pressed us. So we took our leave and went to Richard Adams's as we had promised his wife when we went on, to stop there on our return; but missing the way, or not knowing it, we came to a plantation and house about three o'clock, where there was neither man nor beast, and no one from whom we could inquire the road. We chose the one we thought best, and walked on till evening. We came to a plantation on the point of the creek where Richard Adams lived on the opposite side, being now on the Great Bay about four miles below where we had to be. We were strangers here, and had no address to these people, who, nevertheless, showed us every kindness and treated us well. They told us we had

[1] Sluyter, though Dutch, came from the German town of Wesel.

lost the way at the empty house, by taking the road to the left instead of the right.

10*th*, *Sunday*. The son, who went out to shoot at daylight, put us on the road which would lead us to the creek directly opposite Richard Adams's house, taking us back to the empty plantation which we now left on the right hand. We arrived at the place about eight o'clock, and were taken over the creek by Richard Adams himself. He and his wife were glad to see us, and bade us welcome. As it was Sunday, and we had promised to write a letter to Holland for his wife, we remained there this day, writing the letter after dinner, and having time also to look around a little. These people were so delighted at the service we were to do them in Holland, of posting a letter to Steenwyk,[1] and sending an answer back to them, that they did not know what to do for us. He gave us some French brandy to drink, which he had purchased of the captains of the ships who had brought it from England; but as it was an article prohibited on pain of forfeiture, it was not to be bought here, and scarcely anything else, for he had made a useless journey below, not being able to obtain shoes and stockings for his little children who were bare-legged.

I have nowhere seen so many ducks together as were in the creek in front of this house. The water was so black with them that it seemed when you looked from the land below upon the water, as if it were a mass of filth or turf, and when they flew up there was a rushing and vibration of the air like a great storm coming through the trees, and even like the rumbling of distant thunder, while the sky over the whole creek was filled with them like a cloud, or as the starlings fly at harvest time in Fatherland. There was a boy about twelve years old who took aim at them from the shore, not being able to get within good shooting distance of them, but nevertheless shot loosely before they flew away, and hit only three or four, complained of his shot, as they are accustomed to shoot from six to twelve and even eighteen and more at one shot. After supper we ate some Maryland or Virginia oysters which he had brought up with him. We found them good, but the Gouanes oysters at New York are better.

[1] Steenwijk is in Overyssel.

11*th, Monday*.   We left there after breakfast, the man conducting us to the path which led to the plantation of Mr.
Stabley, whose address we had from Mr. Moll, but he was
sick.   We were here a little while, but nothing was offered us
to eat, and we only asked to drink.   We wished to be put
across the Sassafras River here, but could not accomplish it,
although we were upon the bank of the river.   We were
directed to the ferry at the court house, which was about two
miles west, but difficult to find through the woods.   A person
gave us a letter to take to the Manathans, who put us in the
path leading to the ferry, where we arrived about two o'clock,
and called out to them to come and take us over.   Although
the weather was perfectly still and they could easily hear us,
we were not taken over, though we continued calling out to
them until sundown.   As no one came for us, we intended to
go back to the plantation of Mr. Stabley, or one of those lying
before us, and to proceed there along the strand, but a creek
prevented us, and we had to search for the road by which we
came.   We missed this road, although we were upon it, and
could not find that or any other plantation, and meanwhile it
became dark.   Although the moon shone we could not go
straight, for it shone above, and did not give us light enough
to see through the trees any houses or plantations at a distance,
several of which we passed as the result proved.   We were
utterly perplexed and astray.   We followed the roads as we
found them, now easterly and then westerly, now a little more
on one side, and then a little more on the other, until we were
completely tired out, and wished ourselves back again upon the
strand.   We had to keep on, however, or remain in the woods,
and as the latter did not suit us, we chose the former, fatigued
as we were, and uncertain as was the issue.   I plucked up courage and went singing along, which resounded through the
woods, although I was short of breath through weariness.   My
comrade having taken his compass out of his sack in order to
see how we were going, had put it back again, and we were
walking on, when he discovered he had by that means lost his
sword; though we had gone some distance, we returned again
to look for it, and I found it at last.   We continued on westerly
again, but as we came to no end, we determined to go across,
through the thickets and bushes, due north, in order that if we

could not discover any plantation, we might at least reach the strand. It was now about nine o'clock in the evening. After having proceeded about an hour in that direction, we heard directly in front of us a dog barking, which gladdened us. It was a remarkable circumstance, as dogs are used to keep men away from dwellings, but served to bring us to them, and was remarkable also for the providence of the Lord, who caused this dog to bark, who, the nearer we approached, heard more noise made by us among the leaves and bushes, and barked the more, calling to us as it were, to come straight up to him, which we endeavored to do. We soon came, however, to a very deep hollow, where we could see over the tops of the trees in it, and on the other side what seemed to be a shed of a plantation in which the dog was barking. This encouraged us, but we had yet to go through the hollow, where we could see no bottom, and the sides were steep. We scrambled down I know not how, not seeing whether there was water or a morass there; but on reaching the bottom, we found it was a morass grown up with bushes. My comrade, who followed me, called out to know whether we could not pass round it, but we had to go through it. We came at length to a small brook, not broad, which we crossed and clambered up the side again, when we came to the shed where the dog continued barking, and thus led us to the house. His master was in bed, and did not know what noise it was he heard. On our knocking, he was surprised to hear such strange people at the door, not knowing whether we were few or many, or whether he dared invite us in or not, but he did. We had then little trouble. When we entered the house he was astonished to see us, inquiring what people we were, where we came from, where we were going, but especially how we reached there. No one, he said, could get there easily in the day time, unless he were shown or knew the way well, because they were very much hidden, and he would come to all the other plantations sooner than this one. We told him our adventures, at which he was as much astonished as we were rejoiced. We had reason to behold the Lord in all this, and to glorify Him as we did silently in our hearts. The wife arose and offered us a little to eat of what she had, and afterwards gave me some deer skins, but they were as dry and hard as a plank. I lay down upon them, and crept under them, but was little covered and still less warmed by them. My companion went to lie with a servant in his bunk, but he did not remain there long before a heavy rain came—before which the Lord had caused us to enter the house against all appearances—and compelled him to evacuate his quarters very quickly. The water entered in such great quantities that they would otherwise have been wet through, though already it did not make much difference with my comrade. We passed the night, however, as well as we could, sitting, standing, or lying down, but cold enough.

12*th*, *Tuesday*. This plantation was about four miles below the court house or ferry, westerly towards the bay, and we did not know if we went to the ferry that we would not be compelled again to remain there calling out, uncertain when we would be carried over. We therefore promised this servant if he would put us across we would give him the money, which we would otherwise have to pay at the ferry. The master made some objections on account of the servant's work and the distance from the river, and also because they had no canoe. The servant satisfied him on these points, and he consented. We breakfasted on what we could get, not knowing how or where we would obtain anything again. We three, accordingly, went about two miles to the strand, where we found a canoe, but it was almost entirely full of water, and what was the worst of it, we had nothing with which to bale it out. However, by one means and another we emptied it and launched the canoe. We stepped in and paddled over the river to the plantation of a Mr. Frisby. I must not forget to mention the great number of wild geese we saw here on the river. They rose not in flocks of ten or twelve, or twenty or thirty, but continuously, wherever we pushed our way; and as they made room for us, there was such an incessant clattering made with their wings upon the water where they rose, and such a noise of those flying higher up, that it was as if we were all the time surrounded by a whirlwind or a storm. This proceeded not only from geese, but from ducks and other water fowl; and it is not peculiar to this place alone, but it occurred on all the creeks and rivers we crossed, though they were most numerous in the morning and evening when they are most easily shot.

Having crossed this river, which is of great width, we came

to the plantation of Mr. Frisby, which stands upon an eminence and affords a very pleasant prospect, presenting a view
of the Great Bay as well as the Sassafras River. When we
first came on, we stopped here, but the master was not at home;
and as we had a letter of recommendation and credit to him,
he found it at his house when he returned. When we arrived
there now, we intended merely to ask his negroes for a drink,
but he being apprised of our arrival, made us go into the house,
and entertained us well. After we had partaken of a good
meal, he had horses made ready for us immediately to ride to
Bohemia River, which hardly deserves the name of a river in
respect to other creeks. We mounted on horseback, then,
about ten o'clock, he and one of his friends leading a piece of
the way. Upon separating, he left us a boy to show us the
path and bring back the horses. This boy undertaking more
than he knew, assured us he was well acquainted with the
road; but after a while, observing the course we rode, and the
distance we had gone, and that we had ridden as long as we
ought to have done, if we had been going right, we doubted no
longer we had missed the way, as truly appeared in the end;
for about three o'clock in the afternoon we came upon a broad
cart road, when we discovered we had kept too far to the
right and had gone entirely around Bohemia River. We supposed we were now acquainted with the road, and were upon
the one which ran from Casparus Hermans's to his father's,
not knowing there were other cart roads. We rode along this
fine road for about an hour or an hour and a half, in order to
reach Augustine Hermans, when we heard some persons calling out to us from the woods, "Hold, where are you riding to?"
Certain, as we supposed we were, in our course, we answered,
"to Augustine Hermans." "You should not go that road
then," they rejoined, "for you are out of the way." We therefore rode into the bushes in order to go to them, and learned
that we were not upon the road we thought we were, but on
the road from Apoquemene, that is, a cart road made from
Apoquemene, a small village situated upon a creek, to Bohemia
Creek or river. Upon this road the goods which go from the
South River to Maryland by land, are carried, and also those
which pass inland from Maryland to the South River, because
these two creeks, namely, the Apoquemene and the Bohemia,

one running up from Maryland, and the other from the Delaware River, as the English call the South River, come to an
end close to each other, and perhaps shoot by each other, although they are not navigable so far; but are navigable for
eight miles, that is two Dutch miles of fifteen to a degree.
When the Dutch governed the country the distance was less,
namely, six miles. The digging a canal through was then
talked of, the land being so low; which would have afforded
great convenience for trade on the South River, seeing that
they would have come from Maryland to buy all they had need
of, and would have been able to transport their tobacco more
easily to that river, than to the great bay of Virginia, as they
now have to do, for a large part of Maryland. Besides, the
cheap market of the Hollanders in the South [River] would
have drawn more trade; and if the people of Maryland had
goods to ship on their own account, they could do it sooner
and more readily, as well as more conveniently in the South
[River] than in the Great Bay, and therefore, would have chosen
this route, the more so because as many of their goods, perhaps,
would for various reasons be shipped to Holland, as to England.
But as this is a subject of greater importance than it seems
upon the first view, it is well to consider whether it should not
be brought to the attention of higher authorities than particular governors. What is now done by land in carts, might
then be done by water, for a distance of more than six hundred
miles.[1]

We had, then, come on this road with our horses to the
carrying-place into Maryland and more than three miles from
where we supposed we were. To go there we would have had
to pass through woods and over small morassy creeks. The
sun was nearly down, and we therefore advised with the persons before mentioned. One of them was a Quaker who was
building a small house for a tavern, or rather an ale-house, for
the purpose of entertaining travellers, and the other was the
carpenter who was assisting him on the house, and could speak
good Dutch, having resided a long time at the Manathans.
We were most concerned for the young man and the horses.
The Quaker, who had put up a temporary shed, made of the

---

[1] This suggestion was finally realized by the cutting of the Chesapeake and
Delaware Canal, completed in 1829.

bark of trees, after the manner of the Indians, with both ends open, and little larger than a dog's kennel, and where at the best we three might possibly have been able to lie, especially when a fire was made, which would have to be done, offered us his lodgings if we wished, and as good accommodations as he had, which were not much. He had nothing to eat but maize bread which was poor enough, and some small wild beans boiled in water; and little to lie on, or to cover one, except the bare ground and leaves. We would not have rejected this fare if the Lord had made it necessary, and we were afterwards in circumstances where we did not have as good as this; but now we could do better. The other person, an Irishman, who lived about three miles from there, did not urge us much, because, perhaps, he did not wish us to see how easily he would make two English shillings for which we had agreed with him to take the horses and boy to the creek, and put them on the path to reach home. We were to walk to his house, conducted by the Quaker, while he rode round the creek with the horses. We had to cross it in a canoe, which, when we were in it, was not the breadth of two fingers above water, and threatened every moment to upset. We succeeded, however, in crossing over, and had then to make our way through bushes by an untrodden path, going from one newly marked tree to another. These marks are merely a piece cut out of the bark with an axe, about the height of a man's eyes from the ground; and by means of them the commonest roads are designated through all New Netherland and Maryland; but in consequence of the great number of roads so marked, and their running into and across each other, they are of little assistance, and indeed often mislead. Pursuing our way we arrived at the house of Maurits, as the carpenter was called, where he had already arrived with the horses, and had earned two shillings sooner than we had walked three miles, and more than he had made by his whole day's work. We went into the house and found his Irish wife, engaged in cooking, whereby we made reprisals in another way. After we had thus taken a good supper, we were directed to a place to sleep which suited us entirely and where we rested well.

13th, Wednesday. As soon as it was day we ate our break-fast and left, after giving this man his two shillings, who also immediately rode off with the young man and the horses, to put him on the path to Sassafras River, while the Quaker who had remained there during the night, was to take us to the broad cart-road where he had found us. But neither he nor we could follow the new marked trees so well in the morning light, and we soon missed the way, and no wonder, for we now had the marks behind the trees. We went again through the thickets and bushes of the woods, to and fro, for full three hours without any prospect of getting out, and that within a distance of not over three-quarters of an hour. We struck a foot-path at last which led us to Bohemia Creek, directly opposite the house which was being built. We descended in order to wade over it, the bottom appearing to be hard on this side, and promising a good passage; but when we were in the middle of it, we sank up to our knees in the mud. When we were over we went into the Quaker's hut, who warmed up some beans, and set them before us with maize bread. Not to leave him like an empty calabash, we gave him an English shilling for leading us astray, and other things. We had now a fine broad cart-road to follow, eight miles long, which would lead us to Apoquemene, as it did, and where we arrived about noon. They are almost all Dutch who live here, and we were again among the right kind of people, with whom we could at least obtain what was right. We stepped into a house and were welcome. Some food was immediately set before us to eat, and among other things butter, cheese, and rye bread which was fresh and so delicious that my companion said it was to him like sweet cake. We left there after we had taken dinner, a boy leading us upon the way as far as a long wooden bridge or dam over a meadow and creek, and proceeded on to Kasparus Hermans's, the brother of Ephraim, about six miles from there, where we arrived at three o'clock, but again found him absent from home. As the court was sitting at Newcastle he had to be there as one of its members. We were, however, welcomed by his wife. Her name was Susanneken, and his, Kasparus or Jasper; which led my thoughts further, communing with God in His love, who makes the past as well as the future to be present, and who consumes the present in Him with the future and the past, as it proceeds from Him with all our sensations.[1]

[1] The meaning of this passage is made clear only by the discovery of the facts mentioned in Note B prefixed to this volume. The names Jasper and Susan-

We passed the night there, and had to sleep with a Quaker who was going next day to Maryland.

14*th*, *Thursday*. While we were waiting for Casparus, we embraced the opportunity to examine his place again, which pleased us in all respects, and was objectionable only because it lay on the road, and was therefore resorted to by every one, and especially by these miserable Quakers. He returned home in the afternoon, and was glad to find us. We spoke to him in relation to a certain tract of land which we wished to look at, and Ephraim and his father had told us of; and when we heard what it was, it was a part of Bohemia, which we had already tolerably well looked at on our way to Maryland, being that which lies on the creeks and river, and which, on our return and twice losing the way, lay higher up in the woods; but we reserved the privilege in case we should winter on the South River, of riding over it thoroughly on horseback, with him and his brother Ephraim.[1] For the present, time compelled us to see if we could not yet reach the Manathans for the winter; and we were the more induced to the attempt because a servant of Ephraim had arrived this evening by water in a boat, and would be ready to return with it to Newcastle early in the morning. We therefore excused ourselves and let the subject rest. We heard here that his father Augustine Hermans was very sick and at the point of death, and that Miss Margaret had gone there to attend upon him in that condition.

15*th*, *Friday*. It was flood tide early this morning, and our servant slept a little too long, for it was not far from high water when he appeared. We hurried, however, into the boat and pushed on as hard as we could, but the flood stopped running, when we were about half way. We continued on rowing, and as the day advanced we caught a favorable wind from the west and spread the sail. The wind gradually increasing brought us to Newcastle about eight o'clock among our kind friends again, where we were welcome anew. We were hardly ashore before the wind, changing from the west to the northwest, brought with it such a storm and rain that, if we had

neken (a diminutive of Susanna) appeal to Danckaerts and excite these reflections because they were the names of himself and his wife, who had died in 1676.

[1] It was upon the piece of land here alluded to that the colony of the Labadists was afterward planted. See p. 112, note 2, *supra*.

still been on the water, we should have been in great peril, and if we had been at Kasparus's we should not have been able to proceed in such weather.   We here again so clearly perceived the providence of the Lord over us, that our hearts were constrained to ascend to Him, and praise him for what He is and does, especially towards His children.   As we have confined ourselves quite strictly to the account of our journey, we deem it serviceable to make some observations upon some general matters concerning Maryland, in addition to what we have before remarked.

As regards its first discoverer and possessor, that was one Lord Balthemore, an English nobleman, in the time of Queen Maria.   Having come from Newfoundland along the coast of North America, he arrived in the great bay of Virginia, up which he sailed to its uppermost parts, and found this fine country which he named Maryland after his queen.   Returning to England he obtained a charter of the northerly parts of America, inexclusively, although the Hollanders had discovered and began to settle New Netherland.   With this he came back to America and took possession of his Maryland, where at present his son, as governor, resides.[1]

Thereafter, at the time of Queen Elizabeth, the settlers preferred the lowest parts of this great bay and the largest rivers which empty into it, either on account of proximity to the sea, and the convenience of the streams, or because the uppermost country smacked somewhat of the one from whom it derived its name and of its government.   They have named this lower country Virginia, out of regard to Queen Elizabeth.   It has been the most populous, though not the best land, and a government was established in Virginia distinct from that of Maryland.   A governor arrived while we were there, to fill the place made vacant by the death of his predecessor.[2]

[1] The first Lord Baltimore, George Calvert, who secured the patent of 1632, never voyaged to Maryland as here described. Also, the grant was definite in bounds, from the Potomac to 40° N. lat. Cecilius Calvert, the second lord, died in 1675. Charles Calvert, the third, was at this time both proprietary and governor, having come out to his province this winter, arriving in February, 1680. The writer erroneously attributes the granting of Maryland to Queen Mary Tudor, predecessor of Queen Elizabeth, instead of to Queen Henrietta Maria.

[2] Lord Culpeper came out to Virginia as governor this year, arriving in May, 1680. His predecessor as *governor*, Sir William Berkeley, had been recalled and

As to the present government of Maryland, it remains firm upon the old footing, and is confined within the limits before mentioned. All of Maryland that we have seen, is high land, with few or no meadows, but possessing such a rich and fertile soil, as persons living there assured me that they had raised tobacco off the same piece of land for thirty consecutive years. The inhabitants, who are generally English, are mostly engaged in this production. It is their chief staple, and the money with which they must purchase every thing they require, which is brought to them from other English possessions in Europe, Africa and America. There is, nevertheless, some-times a great want of these necessaries, owing to the tobacco market being low, or the shipments being prevented by some change of affairs in some quarter, particularly in Europe, or indeed to both causes, as was the case at this time, whereby there sometimes arises a great scarcity of such articles as are most necessary, as we saw when there. So large a quantity of tobacco is raised in Maryland and Virginia, that it is one of the greatest sources of revenue to the crown by reason of the taxes which it yields. Servants and negroes are chiefly employed in the culture of tobacco, who are brought from other places to be sold to the highest bidders, the servants for a term of years only, but the negroes forever, and may be sold by their masters to other planters as many times as their masters choose, that is, the servants until their term is fulfilled, and the negroes for life. These men, one with another, each make, after they are able to work, from 2,500 pounds to 3,000 pounds and even 3,500 pounds of tobacco a year, and some of the masters and their wives who pass their lives here in wretched-ness, do the same. The servants and negroes after they have worn themselves down the whole day, and come home to rest, have yet to grind and pound the grain, which is generally maize, for their masters and all their families as well as themselves, and all the negroes, to eat. Tobacco is the only production in which the planters employ themselves, as if there were noth-ing else in the world to plant but that, and while the land is capable of yielding all the productions that can be raised anywhere, so far as the climate of the place allows. As to

had died, but Colonel Jeffreys and Sir Henry Chicheley had meantime been lieu-tenant-governors successively.

articles of food, the only bread they have is that made of Turkish wheat or maize, and that is miserable. They plant this grain for that purpose everywhere. It yields well, not a hundred, but five or six hundred for one; but it takes up much space, as it is planted far apart like vines in France. This grain, when it is to be used for men or for similar purposes, has to be first soaked, before it is ground or pounded, because the grains being large and very hard, cannot be broken under the small stones of their light hand-mills; and then it is left so coarse it must be sifted. They take the finest for bread, and the other for different kinds of groats, which, when it is cooked, is called *sapaen* or *homina*. The meal intended for bread is kneaded moist without leaven or yeast, salt or grease, and generally comes out of the oven so that it will hardly hold together, and so blue and moist that it is as heavy as dough; yet the best of it when cut and roasted, tastes almost like warm white bread, at least it then seemed to us so. This corn is also the only provender for all their animals, be it horses, oxen, cows, hogs, or fowls, which generally run in the woods to get their food, but are fed a little of this, mornings and evenings during the winter when there is little to be had in the woods; though they are not fed too much, for the wretchedness, if not cruelty, of such living, affects both man and beast. This is said not without reason, for a master having a sick servant, and there are many so, and observing from his declining condition, he would finally die, and that there was no probability of his enjoying any more service from him, made him, sick and languishing as he was, dig his own grave, in which he was to be laid a few days afterwards, in order not to busy any of the others with it, they having their hands full in attending to the tobacco.[1]

A few vegetables are planted, but they are of the coarsest kinds and are cultivated in the coarsest manner, without knowledge or care, and they are, therefore, not properly raised, and do not amount to much as regards the production, and still less as to their use. Some have begun to plant orchards,

---

[1] Despite these criticisms as to slavery, it appears, if we can accept the hostile testimony of Dittelbach, *Verval en Val der Labadisten* (Amsterdam, 1692), that Sluyter, when in control of the Labadist plantation at Bohemia Manor, employed slave labor without hesitation and with some harshness.

which all bear very well, but are not properly cultivated. The
fruit is for the greater part pressed, and makes good cider, of
which the largest portion becomes soured and spoiled through
their ignorance or negligence, either from not putting it into
good casks, or from not taking proper care of the liquor afterwards. Sheep they have none, although they have what is
requisite for them if they chose. It is matter of conjecture
whether you will find any milk or butter even in summer; we
have not found any there at this season of the year. They
bestow all their time and care in producing tobacco; each
cask or hogshead, as they call it, of which pays two English
shillings on exportation, and on its arrival in England, two
pence a pound, besides the fees for weighing and other ex-
penses here, and freight and other charges beyond sea.
When, therefore, tobacco only brings four or five pence, there
is little or nothing left for the owner.

The lives of the planters in Maryland and Virginia are
very godless and profane. They listen neither to God nor
his commandments, and have neither church nor cloister.
Sometimes there is some one who is called a minister, who
does not as elsewhere, serve in one place, for in all Virginia
and Maryland there is not a city or a village[1]—but travels for
profit, and for that purpose visits the plantations through the
country, and there addresses the people; but I know of no
public assemblages being held in these places; you hear often
that these ministers are worse than anybody else, yea, are an
abomination.

When the ships arrive with goods, and especially with
liquors, such as wine and brandy, they attract everybody,
that is, masters, to them, who then indulge so abominably
together, that they keep nothing for the rest of the year, yea,
do not go away as long as there is any left, or bring anything
home with them which might be useful to them in their subsequent necessities. It must therefore go hard with the household, and it is a wonder if there be a single drop left for the
future. They squander so much in this way, that they keep
no tobacco to buy a shoe or a stocking for their children, which
sometimes causes great misery. While they take so little care
for provisions, and are otherwise so reckless, the Lord some-

[1] No cities, of course, but some villages.

times punishes them with insects, flies, and worms, or with
intemperate seasons, causing great famine, as happened a few
years ago in the time of the last Dutch war with the English,[1]
when the Lord sent so many weevils that all their grain was
eaten up as well as almost all the other productions of the
field, by reason of which such a great famine was caused that
many persons died of starvation, and a mother killed her own
child and ate it, and then went to her neighbors, calling upon
them to come and see what she had done, and showing them
the remains of her child, whereupon she was arrested and condemned to be hung.   When she sat or stood on the scaffold,
she cried out to the people, in the presence of the governor,
that she was now going to God, where she would render an
account, and would declare before him that what she had done
she did in the mere delirium of hunger, for which the governor
alone should bear the guilt; inasmuch as this famine was
caused by the weevils, a visitation from God, because he, the
governor, undertook in the preceding summer an expedition
against the Dutch residing on the South River, who maintained themselves in such a good posture of defense, that he
could accomplish but little; when he went to the Hoere-kill on
the west side of that river, not far from the sea, where also he
was not able to do much; but as the people subsisted there
only by cultivating wheat, and had at this time a fine and
abundant harvest in the fields—and from such harvests the
people of Maryland generally, and under such circumstances
as these particularly, were fed—he set fire to it, and all their
other fruits, whether of the trees or the field; whereby he committed two great sins at the same time, namely, against God
and his goodness, and against his neighbors, the Dutch, who
lost it, and the English who needed it; and had caused more
misery to the English in his own country, than to the Dutch
in the enemy's country.   This wretched woman protesting
these words substantially against the governor, before Heaven
and in the hearing of every one, was then swung up.

In addition to what the tobacco itself pays on exportation,

---

[1] The war of 1672–1674. But the attack on the Hoere-kill (Whorekill, now
Lewes, Delaware) was not an act of war against the Dutch, but an attack by
Marylanders on inhabitants who were under the jurisdiction of the Duke of
York, in a territory disputed between him and Lord Baltimore.

which produces a very large sum, every hundred acres of land, whether cultivated or not, has to pay one hundred pounds of tobacco a year, and every person between sixteen and sixty years of age must pay three shillings a year. All animals are free of taxation, and so are all productions except tobacco.

It remains to be mentioned that those persons who profess the Roman Catholic religion have great, indeed, all freedom in Maryland, because the governor makes profession of that faith, and consequently there are priests and other ecclesiastics who travel and disperse themselves everywhere, and neglect nothing which serves for their profit and purpose. The priests of Canada take care of this region, and hold correspondence with those here, as is supposed, as well as with those who reside among the Indians. It is said there is not an Indian fort between Canada and Maryland, where there is not a Jesuit who teaches and advises the Indians, who begin to listen to them too much; so much so, that some people in Virginia and Maryland as well as in New Netherland, have been apprehensive lest there might be an outbreak, hearing what has happened in Europe,[1] as well as among their neighbors at Boston; but they hope the result of the troubles there will determine many things elsewhere. The Lord grant a happy issue there and here, as well as in other parts of the world, for the help of His own elect, and the glory of His name.

We will now leave Maryland, and come back to Sandhoeck [Newcastle], on the South River, where, in the house of our friend Ephraim Hermans, the Lord had brought us, and our friends received and lodged us with affectionate hearts.

16th, Saturday. Mr. Moll, who is the president [of the court] and one of the principal men here in the South, having finished his business in the court which was now ended, had intended to ride this morning to a plantation which he had recently purchased on Christina Kill, and would have been pleased to have had us accompany him, and look at the lands about there, which he said were very good; but as the hard

---

[1] The reference is to the Popish Plot in England; in respect to Boston, it is probably to King Philip's War, 1675–1676, and the hostilities along the Maine coast in 1677, though there is no reason to attribute these to French or Jesuit instigation. Yet possibly the great fire of August 8–9, 1679, is meant; see p. 269, note 1, *infra*.

and rainy weather of yesterday had not yet cleared up, he put off the journey until Monday, in hopes he would then have our company, when he would provide a horse for each of us, and Ephraim would also go with us. Meanwhile we went to see whether there would be any means of returning to the Manathans notwithstanding the ice, either by land or sea. If we should return by water, we should be able to see the lower parts of this river, the Hoere-kill and others; but no opportunity presented itself, because it was so late in the year, there being no navigating in consequence of every one being afraid of the ice.

17th, *Sunday*. We had an opportunity to-day to hear Domine Tessemaker, which we did, but never heard worse preaching, and I, therefore, had little desire to go again in the afternoon, though I was misled by the ringing of the bell. He is a man who wishes to effect some *établissement* or reform here, but he will not accomplish much in that respect, as he not only has no grace therefor, but there seems to be something in his life which will hereafter manifest itself more. For the present we can say with truth that he is a perfect worldling.[1] It seems that in these spiritually, as well as physically, waste places, there is nevertheless a craving of the people to accept anything that bears even the name of food, in order to content rather than satisfy themselves therewith. Nevertheless the Lord will take pity upon these his lands, as we hope, for it appears indeed that the seed of the elect is here, especially among those of European descent.

18th, *Monday*. We four, namely, Mr. Moll, Ephraim, my comrade and myself, after we had breakfasted, started about nine o'clock, on horseback, from Newcastle for Christina Kill. We observed the land through which we rode was sometimes only common soil, until we reached a plantation which Mr. Moll and Ephraim owned together, lying on a branch of that creek, and which was a good piece of land. Ephraim having finished the business for which he had come here, of having planks sawed for boarding a new clap-board house he had

---

[1] Domine Petrus Tesschenmaker remained in charge of the church in Newcastle till 1682. After brief sojourns in New York and on Staten Island, he was called to the church in Schenectady. There he served from 1685 to 1690, when he was killed in the Indian massacre of that year.

built, left us and rode back to Newcastle, and we continued on
after we had looked at a grist-mill which the Swedes had constructed upon one of the branches of the creek, a considerable
distance along another of them. We discovered here and there
pieces of good land, but they were not large, and were along
the creek. The greater portion of the country was only common land. Evening coming on, we rode back to the plantation
of a Mr. Man, lying upon a neck of land called Cheese-and-
bread Island, which is a good piece of ground, and up to which
the creek is navigable for large boats or barks.[1] This man is
a great friend of Mr. Moll. We were, therefore, very welcome,
and slept there this night.

19th, Tuesday. After breakfast we rode out in company
with Mr. Man, to look at several pieces of land which they
very highly recommended to us, but it was because, as they
said, they wished to have good neighbors, though sometimes
neighbors did not amount to much. It was now in the afternoon, and we rode towards home, over a plain where the deer
ran out of the road in herds. Coming to the large creek,
which is properly called Christina Kill, we found Mr. Moll
had not correctly calculated the tide, for he supposed it would
be low water or thereabouts, whereas the water was so high
that it was not advisable to ride through it with horses, and
we would have to wait until the water had fallen sufficiently
for that purpose. While we were waiting, and it began to
get towards evening, an Indian came on the opposite side of
the creek, who knew Mr. Moll, and lived near there at that
time, and had perhaps heard us speak. He said that we
should have to wait there too long; but if we would ride a
little lower down, he had a canoe in which he would carry us
over, and we might swim the horses across. We rode there at
once, and found him and his canoe. We unsaddled the horses,
and he swam them over one by one, being in the canoe and
holding them by the bridle. When we were over, we quickly
saddled them and rode them as fast as they could run, so
that they might not be cold and benumbed. It was entirely

---

[1] Bread and Cheese Island lay up Christina Creek, some ten miles west of
present Wilmington, Delaware, and at the junction of Red Clay Creek and White
Clay Creek. The planter was Abraham Mann, who in 1683 was sheriff and member of assembly for Newcastle County.

dark, and we remarked to each other the providence of the
Lord in this Indian coming there; for otherwise we should not
have known how to find the way through the woods in consequence of the great darkness.   It was bad enough as it was,
on a path that both the horses and Mr. Moll were acquainted
with, for we could scarcely see each other sometimes.   We
reached Newcastle happily about eight o'clock in the evening,
much rejoiced, and thanking Mr. Moll.

20th, *Wednesday*.   While we were in Maryland, and were
crossing over the Sassafras River, we saw a small English
ship lying there, which they told us would leave about the
English Christmas.[1]   We now learned from Mr. Moll, that he
was going to write by her, and was willing if we wrote, to allow
our letters to go to London under cover of his; and also that
he should soon go to Maryland to attend the court now about
to be held there.   We determined, therefore, not to permit the
opportunity to pass by of writing home.

21st, *Thursday*.   We finished our letters to-day.   We perceived it would be in vain to wait for a chance to go to the
Manathans by sea, and there would be no opportunity to go
up the river.   We, therefore, finally concluded to hire a canoe
and a person to take us up the river; and accordingly agreed
with one Jan Boeyer,[2] for fifty guilders in *zeewan*, and a dollar
for the canoe a day, to leave the next day if it were possible.
Whereupon, Ephraim and his wife, who had done their best
herein, as well as other friends, set about writing letters for us
to take to the Manathans.   Meantime, Ephraim received news
that his father was near his end, and had to be handled by one
or two men to turn him in bed, and that he desired once more
to speak to him.

22d, *Friday*.   It had frozen some this morning, and Jan
Boeyer manifested little disposition to go up the river, declar-
ing that with such a frost as this, the river above was all frozen
up; and though there was no probability of it, we had to wait.
Ephraim and Mr. Moll left together for Maryland to see
Ephraim's father, who wanted to speak to him, as we heard,

[1] Our travellers used the new style, current in Holland (though not in Friesland), the English and their colonists the old.   Christmas of old style was January
4 of new.

[2] Jan Boeyer was constable of Newcastle the next year.

in relation to the land or manor which he possessed there; for while he had given portions to all his other children, namely, one son and three daughters, he had made Ephraim, his oldest son, heir of his rank and manor, according to the English law, as *fils de commys*,[1] that is, Ephraim could enjoy the property during his life, and hire or sell it for that period, but upon his death, it must go to his oldest son, and so descend from heir to heir. Mr. Moll was the witness of this, and had the papers in his care. It seemed that the father wished to make some change because we had been there, and he had offered us a part of the land.[2] We, therefore, think we shall hear what he shall have done in the matter.

Although it had frozen hard, yet when the sun rose high about nine o'clock, it was ordinarily pleasant and handy weather, but there was no decision on the part of our skipper to leave. In the meantime we had the house with Ephraim's wife alone, and, therefore, more freedom and opportunity to speak to her of God, and godly things, which she well received. We expect something good from her as well as from Ephraim.

23d, Saturday. The weather was milder, and there was some fog which cleared away as the sun rose. We went to see Jan Boeyer again, but he had no intention to make the journey. We heard it was not so much on account of the ice, as of the small-pox, which prevailed very much up the river, and which he had never had. There was no use of striving

[1] For *fideicommissum*.

[2] Augustine Herrman did not die till 1686. In 1684 he executed his final deed of conveyance to Peter Sluyter *alias* Vorsman, Jasper Danckaerts *alias* Schilders, Petrus Bayard of New York (nephew of Governor Stuyvesant and ancestor of all the Bayards of Delaware), John Moll, and Arnoldus de La Grange, conveying the "Labadie Tract" of some 3750 acres on the north side of Bohemia River. Moll and de La Grange immediately released their interest in the land to Danckaerts and Sluyter, Bayard did so in 1688, and Danckaerts in 1693, from Holland, conveyed to Sluyter all his rights. Augustine Herrman at his death conveyed the rest of Bohemia Manor to his son Ephraim as an entailed estate. But evidently he had by that time repented of his dealings with the Labadists, for a codicil to his will appoints trustees to carry it out because "my eldest Sonn Ephraim Herman . . . hath Engaged himself deeply unto the labady faction and religion, seeking to perswade and Entice his Brother Casparus and sisters to Incline thereunto alsoe, whereby itt is upon Good ground suspected that they will prove no True Executors of This my Last Will of Entailement . . . but will Endeavour to disanull and make it voide, that the said Estates may redound to the Labady Communality." MS., Md. Hist. Soc.

with him, and we determined, therefore, to hire somebody else, if we could find any person.   Mr. Peter Aldrix made inquiry for us, but to no purpose, and we had to wait and depend upon God's providence.   We heard, however, of some people who had arrived in a canoe from Christina Kill, and that even in that creek there was no ice yet, or up the river.

24th, Sunday.   Domine Tessemaker being at Apoquemene, there was no preaching to-day at Newcastle but some reading. We went, however, to the church, in order not to give offense. Much of the reading we could not bear, but we hope others were more edified than we expected to be.

It was very fine weather and it annoyed us that we had to wait so.   This evening there arrived a canoe with Swedes, who had come from half way below the falls, and of whom we inquired whether there were any ice up the river.   They said there was not, and they were going back the next day.   We endeavored to make an agreement with them to carry us, but they asked entirely too much, namely, an anker[1] of rum, which would amount to about 120 guilders in *zeewan:* whereupon we rebuked them for their exorbitancy.   The Swedes and Finns, particularly, have this fault, and generally towards strangers; but as it seemed to me they had drunk a little too much, we let the matter rest in the hope they would talk more reasonably tomorrow.

25th, Monday.   The weather being good, we spoke again to our Swedes, but they continued obstinate; and also to Jan Boeyer, but nothing could be done with him either.   While we were standing on the shore talking with them about leaving, I saw coming down the river a boat which looked very much like that of the Quaker of Upland,[2] as indeed it was. He landed at Newcastle and was going to Ephraim's house, where he had some business to transact, intending to leave the next day.   We asked him if he was willing to take us with him, and he said he would do so with pleasure.   We were rejoiced, observing the providence of the Lord who took such fatherly care of us.   There stood Jan Boeyer and the Swedes cheated by their own covetousness.   Robert Wade and his wife lodged at Ephraim's, which assured us our journey would be commenced the next day.

---

[1] About ten gallons.   [2] Robert Wade. See p. 105.

26th, Tuesday. All the letters having been collected together, which we were to take with us and deliver, and the Quaker having finished his business, we breakfasted together, and courteously took leave of all our acquaintances; but especially with some love, of Madame Ephraim, named Elizabeth van Rodenburgh. She had shown us much kindness, and given us good hope that the Lord will not forget her therein.

We will observe before leaving Sand-hoek, that it has always been the principal place on the South River, as well in the time of the English as of the Dutch. It is now called Newcastle by the English. It is situated on the west side of the river upon a point which extends out with a sandy beach, affording a good landing place, better than is to be found elsewhere on that account. It lies a little above the bay where the river bends and runs south from there, so that you can see down the river southerly, the greater portion of it, which presents a beautiful view in perspective, and enables you to see from a distance the ships which come out of the great bay and sail up the river. Formerly all ships were accustomed to anchor here, for the purpose of paying duties or obtaining permits, and to unload when the goods were carried away by water in boats or barks, or by land in carts. It was much larger and more populous at that time, and had a small fort called Nassau; but since the country has belonged to the English, ships may no longer come here, or they must first declare and unload their cargoes at New York, which has caused this little place to fall off very much, and even retarded the settlement of plantations. What remains of it consists of about fifty houses, almost all of wood. The fort is demolished, but there is a good block-house, having some small cannon, erected in the middle of the town, and sufficient to resist the Indians or an incursion of Christians; but it could not hold out long. This town is the capital of justice, where the high court of the South River is held, having three other courts subordinate to it, from which appeals lie to it, as they do from it to New York, and from New York to England. These three minor courts are established, one at Salem, a small village of Quakers newly commenced on the east side of the river not far from Newcastle[1]; another is at Upland, on the west

[1] Salem, New Jersey, had been founded by John Fenwick in 1675.

side above Newcastle, a Swedish village, and the third is at Burlington, a new Quaker village on the east side of the river above Newcastle. Newcastle is about eighty miles from the falls, and the same distance from the mouth of the river or the sea. The water in the river at Newcastle at ordinary flood tide is fresh, but when it is high spring tide, or the wind blows hard from the south or southeast, it is brackish, and if the wind continues long or it is hard weather it becomes a little saltish. With a new or full moon it makes high water at Newcastle at five o'clock. The principal persons whom we have seen are Mr. Moll and his wife, Ephraim Hermans and his wife, Pieter Aldrix and his wife, and Domine Tessemaker.

As regards Mr. Moll, he lived in his youth at Amsterdam, in order to learn business. He afterwards went to Bristol, in England, where he carried on a reasonably large business which he had begun to do at Amsterdam. In the war between England and Holland, he lost so much that he failed, or made an agreement with his creditors. He, therefore, immigrated to this country, and after trading in Virginia and Maryland some time, came to Newcastle to live, where he has two or three plantations, upon which he raises tobacco, more for the purpose of paying his creditors, as he himself informed me, than because he seeks this manner of gain and life, intending, as soon as he can release himself, to go and live upon the land, and support himself by what God may be pleased to give him. Touching the hope of grace discoverable in him it is very slight, although he has listened with attention to all we have said to him, requesting us to continue, and that he might be favored with a letter from us on the subject, or some books such as we might deem necessary, and willing, with a full heart, to do us every service in his power in these quarters or elsewhere, as he had done many, and endeavored to do still more. The Lord will do for him as it pleases him.

The wife of Mr. Moll is an English woman, a pious Independent. When he married her, she lived in a large house where many persons dwelt together, separate from all other assemblies and the attachments of the world, seeking nothing except to serve God in peace and uprightness, and having their own preacher and other ministers. But with all this she remains a great *mundane*, as to which we have spoken to her. They have only one son.

Ephraim Hermans is the oldest child of Augustine Hermans, there being two brothers and three sisters, one of whom lives now at Amsterdam. They are all of a Dutch mother, after whose death their father married an English woman, who is the most artful and despicable creature that can be found. He is a very godless person, and his wife, by her wickedness, has compelled all these children to leave their father's house and live elsewhere. Ephraim, the oldest, having gone into business, settled at Newcastle, his oldest sister keeping house for him. He had for a long time sought in marriage at New York, a daughter of the late governor of the island of Carsou [Curaçao], in the Caribbean Sea, belonging to the Dutch West India Company, whose name was Johan van Rodenburgh.[1] She lived with her mother on the Manhatan, who, after the death of her husband, Rodenburgh, married one Joannes van Burgh, by whom she had several children. Her daughter, Elizabeth van Rodenburgh, being of a quiet turn of mind, and quite sickly, had great inclination to remain single. Ephraim, however, finally succeeded in his suit, and married her at New York. He brought her with him to Newcastle on the South River, and we accompanied them on the journey. Ephraim had been a bad, artful fellow in his youth, and lived in all godless ways, but the Lord seized his heart, whereby he began to repent, and saw that he must live otherwise, the Lord compelling him. He found, however, no ground or strength, but having a good conception of spiritual matters or religion, as far as could be the case in such a man, he saw nothing but untruth, falsehood, and deception in all that was done in relation to God and godly things, and great hypocrisy in the best persons with whom he was acquainted. Convinced of this, and seeing no better result, he remained in suspense, although he professed the doctrines of the Reformed, and was a member of their church. Seeing our life, and hearing us speak, he has begun to see the difference, and discover the truth received in the heart. He has examined himself in several things, and corrected them, and was disposed to do more, as we had persuaded him. May the Lord bestow upon him His

[1] *Lucas* Rodenburgh was vice-director of Curaçao from 1644 to 1655.

true grace, who puts it in our hearts to beseech this for him with confidence. We commit all to Him.

His wife, Elizabeth van Rodenburgh, has the quietest disposition we have observed in America. She is politely educated. She has had through her entire youth a sleeping sickness of which she seems now to be free. She has withdrawn herself much from the idle company of youth, seeking God in quiet and solitude. She professes the Reformed religion, is a member of that church, and searches for the truth which she has found nowhere except in the word and preaching, which she therefore much attended upon and loved, but which never satisfied her, as she felt a want and yearning after something more. She was so pleased at our being near her, and lodged at her house, she could not abstain from frequently declaring so, receiving all that we said to her with gratitude, desiring always to be near us; and following the example of her husband, she corrected many things, with the hope and promise of persevering if the Lord would be pleased so to give her grace. We were indeed comforted with these two persons, who have done much for us out of sincere love. The Lord pities them, and will keep His promise to this house.

Margaret Hermans possesses a good disposition, although a little wild, according to the nature of the country. She complained that she was like a wild and desolate vine, trained up in a wild and desolate country; that she had always felt an inclination to know more of God quietly, and to serve Him, hoping the Lord would be merciful to her. She treated us with great affection, and received thankfully and acceptably what we said to her. We did not see her on our return, as she had gone to attend upon her father; and we therefore have not conversed much with her. The Lord will do with her as it pleases Him.

As to Mr. Pieter Aldrix he is a man of Groningen. He came to this country in the year '63 or '64, for the Lord Burgomasters of Amsterdam, as chief of their cargoes and storehouse in respect of the trade with the Indians, and thus was at the head of their office on the South River. Whether he had been in this country before or not, I do not know.[1] He did not occupy his place long, for the English shortly afterwards took

[1] Peter Alrichs came over in 1657.

the country and deprived him of all he had; yet he has remained here, gaining his livelihood by various means as well as he can, and seems to have gradually succeeded. He had a ketch made for the purpose of trading to the [West India] Islands, and elsewhere. He has a large family of children, and others. He sought to render us as much service as he could, but for the things of grace he is not inclined. He is a mundane, but is not vicious. The Lord can use him as it pleases Him.

These are the persons at Newcastle with whom we have some acquaintance, and such the hope they have given us. We have promised them to continue it, and write to them, and send them such books as we might deem necessary for them.

Returning now to our boat, it left about ten o'clock for a place a little higher up the river where they had to take in some wheat, and where we were to go on foot, with the Quaker's wife. We reached it about noon, and found the boat laden, and lying high up on the land, so that we had to wait until the tide was half flood. We saw there a piece of meadow or marsh, which a Dutch woman had dyked in, and which they assured us had yielded an hundred for one, of wheat, notwithstanding the hogs had done it great damage. The boat getting afloat, we left about three o'clock, and moved up with the tide. The weather was pleasant and still, with a slight breeze sometimes from the west, of which we availed ourselves; but it did not continue long, and we had to rely upon our oars. We arrived at Upland about seven o'clock in the evening, and it was there only half flood, so much later does the tide make there than at Newcastle. The Quaker received us kindly, gave us supper, and counselled with us as to how we should proceed further. We were shown a better place to sleep than we had when we were here before.

27th, Wednesday. It rained some during the night and it was very misty early in the morning. Before the tide served to leave, we agreed with this man who had brought us up, to send us in his boat to Burlington, with two boys to manage it, paying him twenty guilders for the boat, and three guilders a day to each of the boys for three days, amounting in the whole to thirty-eight guilders; but one of the boys wishing too much, he determined to take us up himself. A good wind coming out of the south, we breakfasted and dined in one meal, and left about ten o'clock, with a favorable wind and tide, though at times the wind was quite sharp. We sailed by Tinakonk again, but did not land there. It began at noon to rain very hard, and continued so the whole day, and also blew quite hard. We ran aground on the lee shore upon a very shallow and muddy place, from which we got off with difficulty. On account of this and other accidents, if we had had the boys it would have been bad for us. We arrived at Wykakoe,[1] a Swedish village on the west side of the river, in the evening at dusk, where we went, all wet, into the house of one Otto, who had three children lying sick with the small-pox. We dried ourselves here partly. He gave us supper and took us to sleep all together in a warm stove room, which they use to dry their malt in and other articles. It was very warm there, and our clothes in the morning were entirely dry.

28th, Thursday. It was flood at daylight when we left, but had not gone far before I discovered I had left one of my gloves behind, whereupon we ran the boat ashore, and I went back and found it. My comrade was more unfortunate, for after we had proceeded full two hours, and when we were going to breakfast on what our female friend had given us, he found he had left his knife and fork; but we had gone too far to lose the time to go back for them. The weather was foggy, but when the sun had risen a little, it cleared away and became pleasant and calm. We therefore advanced rapidly, rowing with the tide, and reached Takany of which we have before spoken, about ten o'clock, and where we landed a person who had come up with us. We continued on, and as the tide just commenced rising there we had a constant flood tide with us to Burlington, where we arrived about two o'clock. We were put ashore on an island of Peter Aldrix[2] who had given us a letter of recommendation to a person living there, and working for him. We paid Robert Wade who and his wife are the best Quakers we have found. They have always treated us kindly.

---

[1] Wicacoa was in the southeastern part of the present area of Philadelphia, where Gloria Dei Church, still standing, was erected by the Swedes in 1697.

[2] A manuscript map of the upper Delaware, which accompanies the journal, shows a plantation of Peter Alrichs on the right bank, opposite Matinnaconk Island and Burlington, and near the present Bristol, Pennsylvania.

He went immediately over to Burlington where he did not
stop long, and took the ebb tide and rowed with it down the
river. It was not high tide for an hour and a half after we
arrived at the island, and there is, therefore, a difference of
eleven hours or more in the same tide from Newcastle.

The man who lived on this island was named Beerent
       , and came from Groningen. He was at a loss to
know how to get us on further. Horses, absolutely, he could
not furnish us; and there was no Indian about to act as a
guide, as they had all gone out hunting in the woods, and none
of them had been at his house for three weeks. To accompany us himself to Achter Kol or the Raritans, and return,
could not be accomplished in less than four days, and he would
have to leave his house meantime in charge of an Indian woman
from Virginia, who had left her husband, an Englishman, and
with two children, one of which had the small-pox, was living
with him; and she could be of no use to any one, whether
Indians or other persons who might come there. We were
compelled again to wait upon the providence of the Lord.

About three o'clock in the afternoon a young Indian arrived with whom we agreed to act as our guide, for a duffels
coat which would cost twenty-four guilders in *zeewant*, that is,
about five guilders in the money of Holland; but he had a fowl-
ing-piece with him which he desired first to take and have
repaired at Burlington, and would then come back. He accordingly crossed over, but we waited for him in vain, as he
did not return. The greatest difficulty with him was, that we
could not speak the Indian language, and he could not speak
a word of anything else. He not coming, we asked Beerent
if he would not undertake the task, which, after some debate,
he consented to do. He arranged his affairs accordingly, and
prepared himself by making a pair of shoes or foot-soles of
deer skin, which are very comfortable, and protect the feet.
That was done in half an hour. We were to give him thirty
guilders in *zeewant*, with which he was satisfied.

29th, Friday. We breakfasted, and left about ten o'clock
in a canoe, which set us on the west side of the river, along
which a foot-path runs a part of the way, in an east-northeast
direction, and then through the woods north-northeast. We
followed this path until we came to a plantation, newly begun

by a Quaker, where we rested and refreshed ourselves.   We
agreed with this man, who came in the house while we were
there, that he should put us over the river for three guilders
in *zeewant*.   We crossed over about one o'clock, and pursued
a foot-path along the river, which led us to a cart-road, and
following that we came to the new grist-mill at the falls, which,
in consequence of the great flow of water, stood in danger of
being washed away.[1]   Crossing here, we began our journey in
the Lord's name, for there are no houses from this point to
Peskatteway, an English village on the Raritans.   We had
now gone twelve or thirteen miles from Peter Aldrix's island,
and it was about two o'clock in the afternoon.

We must here make some general observations in relation
to the South River.   The Dutch, who first discovered and took
possession of it, so named it, undoubtedly because it empties
into the sea in the most southerly part of New Netherland,
to wit, in latitude 39° north, being one degree and twenty
minutes, or more, further south than the mouth of the North
River.   It runs up from the sea northwesterly, making a fine,
large bay, much better than that of the North River, or Godyn's
Bay.[2]   It is not only of greater length, which is about forty
miles, with a breadth of six or seven miles; but it has a fine
bottom of sand, and gravel reefs all along the banks.   The
water is purer up above.   From the inside or middle of the
bay, its course to the narrow part, or river, is mostly south
[north] or bent gradually from northwest to north, with here
and there a small bay, and it continues running so, from twenty
to twenty-four miles, or more, to Newcastle, where it bends
to the east to northeast, with several bays on both sides, to
Upland and Tinakonk, a distance of twenty-four miles.   At
Tinakonk, it runs about east or east-northeast, but having
passed that island it bears off again, north to northeast; also,
with several bays to Wykakoe about twenty miles, and continuing so to Takany, sixteen miles.   From Takany to Burlington, it runs again more easterly and east-northeast twenty
miles, thence due east six miles, where there is a round bay
turning north to north-northwest to the falls four miles, so

---

[1] See p. 96, note 1.
[2] New York Bay; so named from Samuel Godyn, one of the earliest patentees
of New Netherland.

that from the falls to the sea coast it is about eighty English
miles, or twenty Dutch miles, from Newcastle each way. It
has numerous fine navigable creeks on both sides of it, which
are like small rivers running far inland, but how far is not yet
known; nor is it known how far the South River extends above
the falls, as they have not explored above them. This river
is generally very clear. I do not know that there is anything
above to be avoided, except occasionally a muddy point on
the margins. Heavy ships, drawing ten, twelve, and fourteen
feet water, go up the river as far as Burlington, and higher;
but in the great bend where it runs to the falls, it can be
navigated close to the falls by boats, drawing five and six feet
and more. The land on the east side is generally lower than
on the west, and is not so good. It continues very flat, deep
into the country, as you go far down. On the west side the
land is tolerably high, immediately off from the river, and is
generally good all the way down. Both sides being low, this
river is better to navigate than the North River, for that has
very high banks, which being frightfully steep and rocky, it is
subject to great whirlwinds and squalls, which, coming sud-
denly over the hills, fall upon the river, which is no small inconvenience. The water which comes over the falls is pure
and clear, and is quite blue, but running lower down, it gradually becomes muddy, but is entirely clear again at Takany,
and reasonably so at Wikakoe; further on it becomes thick,
but it is always good. As to the salubrity of the climate of
which we did not say anything when we spoke of Maryland, it
is certain that Virginia being the lowest on the sea, is the
most unhealthy where they [die] by thousands sometimes of
the epidemical disease of the country. In Maryland, which
lies higher up from the sea than Virginia, it is more healthy,
although it is subject to the epidemic. Therefore, all those
who come into the country, must undergo this sickness without escape. Even the children who are born there are not
excepted, as those who live there and have experienced it told
us when we were there. And although their manner of life is
the cause of much irregularity in their health, there is nevertheless something in the atmosphere which produces disease:
but this will become gradually better, as the country is meas-
urably populated, and thereby becomes more cleared, as ex-

perience shows is true of all the lands in America which have been unhealthy. The uppermost parts of Maryland are more healthy than those lowest down. The South River is more salubrious than Maryland, as it lies higher. It partakes however somewhat of the nature of Maryland, especially below, but with great difference, which every year increases. The higher the more healthy; although at the Hoerekil, which is near the sea, it is as healthy as anywhere, because it is well populated. In the upper part of the river it is as healthy as it can be anywhere, and for myself, I believe that New Netherland has not a place in it which is not healthier than any part of old Netherlands in the United Provinces, and is becoming every day more salubrious, especially if they live here as they do in Holland. The North River is entirely healthy, for it lies much higher up than the South River, that is further to the north, and although it is nearer the sea than where they live in Maryland and on the South River, it is nevertheless more wholesome, which shows that it is not the air of the sea which causes the insalubrity, but other reasons which I will not consider at present.

As the Hollanders were the first discoverers of this river, they were also the first residents, settling themselves down in small numbers at the Hoerekil and thereabouts, and at Santhoeck, though the most people and the capital of the country were at the Manhatans, under the rule and authority of the West India Company.[1] The Indians killed many of them because they did not live well with them, especially with their women, from which circumstance this kill derives its name. Others fled to the Manhatans, but afterwards returned, and have since continued in possession of the river, although in small numbers and with little strength. Meanwhile some Swedish soldiers, who had been in the service of the West India Company, went to Sweden, and there made known the fact that the country was so large the Hollanders could not possess it all, especially the river called the South River, lying

[1] The settlement at the Whorekill was Swanendael, founded by David de Vries and other Dutch patroons in 1631. See his Notes in *Narratives of Early Pennsylvania, West New Jersey, and Delaware*, in this series. The origin of New Sweden was quite different from what is stated in the text. It sprang from commercial companies formed in Sweden, allied with Dutch merchants.

next to Virginia, their old friends, and that it was only necessary to go there with a small number of people to take possession of it, as no one in that country was powerful enough to prevent it.   They accordingly ordered a levy to be made of men, half of them under the name of soldiers, and half of boors, and sent them under a certain commander to settle on the west side of the river, well knowing where the best and healthiest climate was, namely, up the river, and being thus near their friends, the English.   Whether these good friends, here or in Europe, have not assisted them in this matter, is not known.   They thus established themselves there, the Hollanders either being not strong enough or too negligent to prevent them, whilst the West India Company began gradually to fail, and did not hinder them.   The Swedes therefore remained, having constructed small fortresses here and there, where they had settled and had Swedish governors.

The Hollanders did not abandon this river, but they, as well as the Swedes, sought to advance their settlements; but although the whole country belonged to them, they were nevertheless unable to possess it, the company either having too much to do elsewhere, or not ability sufficient, or sending over too few people.   They always however had their forts, without hindrance or molestation from the Swedes, or being brought under their dominion.   This continued during the time the burgomasters of the city of Amsterdam had this territory under their protection, up to the year 1664, when Governor Stuyvesant went there with a large force, planted himself before the fortress of Christina on Christina Kill, cannonaded it and compelled them to surrender it with all their government to him, in the name of the city of Amsterdam.[1]   In that year the whole country was reduced under the dominion of the crown of England, which put an end to the rule of the Hollanders, who had then recently conquered the Swedes.

The east side of the river, which is now entirely in the pos-

[1] The conquest of New Sweden by the Dutch under Stuyvesant took place in 1655; narratives of it are in the volume just named and in *Narratives of New Netherland*, in this series.   The surrender was of course not demanded in the name of the city of Amsterdam but in that of the Dutch republic, the United Provinces. The Dutch West India Company in 1656 sold a part of the territory to the city of Amsterdam.

session of the Quakers, has never been claimed by any one, although here and there lived a Swede, as also among the Swedes, here and there dwelt a Hollander. But when the whole country, in the year 1664, came to the crown of England under the Duke of York,[1] the duke or the king gave the land lying between the two rivers, namely, the North River and the South River, the easterly part to my Lord Catrix [Carteret], and the westerly part to my Lord Barklay [Berkeley], but without a boundary line between them. This remained so till the year

a Mr. Pennel,[2] a brewer of London, failed there. Berkeley, who was a great friend of his, as were also many other courtiers, and frequented his brewery daily, came to his brewery and told him that as he, the brewer, was a broken man, he could advise him how to recover his fortune; that if he would furnish him a sum of money, he would, by authentic writings, make over to him a tract of land which the king had given him. This suited the brewer very well, who succeeded in obtaining the money from his friends, and this land was accordingly transferred to him. But as the affairs of the brewer would not permit him to act himself, he had a friend named Phenix [Fenwick], also a Quaker, who was to transact the business in his own name, for him the brewer, in consideration of which Fenwick was to enjoy a tenth of the whole westerly part. Fenwick managed it in his name so well that he would soon have stripped the other of all, but means were afterwards employed to compel him to be satisfied with his tenth. Fenwick had letters printed and circulated everywhere, in which he described this portion of the country in glowing colors; that it was a veritable Paradise, especially for those people who were of the same religious sentiments as him-

---

[1] Came to the crown of England and was conferred by King Charles II. on his brother, James, duke of York, afterward James II. The duke's grant of New Jersey to Berkeley and Carteret in 1664 conveyed it to them undivided. The partition was effected by the new grants of 1674 and the Quintipartite Deed of 1676, creating East New Jersey and West New Jersey.

[2] A strange corruption of the name of Edward Byllynge; less altered is the name of the other proprietor of West Jersey, mentioned below, John Fenwick, who founded Salem in 1675. West Jersey in that year fell into the hands of Penn, Lawrie, and Lucas as trustees. Their letter in *Narratives of Pennsylvania,* pp. 177–185, explains the system of land sales, of which our censorious traveller takes so dark a view.

self.   Many persons of this belief thereupon bought pieces of
land, parcelled out only on the map, according to the imper-
fect knowledge which they then possessed, first into tenths,
of which Fenwick had one, and then each tenth into hundredths,
embracing water, morasses, swamps and marshes, so that these
poor people bought they knew not what.   Fenwick hereupon
came over to this country, with a portion of these people, in
order to take possession of what they had bought; but he,
being in debt in England, was arrested on the eve of departure,
and compelled to leave the original letters of authorization in
the hands of his creditors, and could himself obtain nothing
but copies thereof.   With these he arrived in the South River,
and demanded the country from the chief rulers there, who
required the production of his authority, which he refused a
long time, but not being able to obtain justice, he brought
forward his copies to show them, whereupon these principal
men referred him to their sovereign governor at New York,
who has not yet been able either to reject or admit the claim.
They landed however after some tumult, but without blood-
shed, and have remained there, constantly bringing more
people, and the governor tolerating them.   Every one of the
purchasers who arrives here is at a loss to know where he has
bought, and so settles down where he thinks best, leaving it
to be determined hereafter; and finding more land has been
sold than can be delivered, looks out for himself.   Inasmuch
as they are thrown under the government of New York, they
have two small courts to decide trifling cases, in order thereby
to save travel.   Meanwhile the country was recovered by the
Hollanders in 1673, and then again, by treaty of peace, sur-
rendered to the crown of England, whereby the Dutch lost all
their right to the westerly part a second time, unless the provision in the treaty that all things should remain as before the
war, should restore them their pretended right.   But if this
clause only relates to the two peacemaking parties, it remains
justly with the crown of England.   Finally, there is the utmost confusion without any good foundation for it.

There are Quakers who either are more wise, or through
poverty act so, who do not buy any land on the east side of
the river, but buy on the west side, where it is cheaper in consequence of the Indians being there.   The Quakers have en-

deavored to break up the Dutch and others not of their religion, who have lived of old on the east side of the river, but resist them, and are sustained by the authorities. How far this may be carried, and what may be the result, time will show. The Indians hate the Quakers very much on account of their deceit and covetousness, and say they are not Englishmen, always distinguishing them from all other Englishmen, as is also done by almost all other persons. The Indians say "they are not Christians, they are like ourselves." The deeds of all lands bought on the South River from the government of New York contain a provision that they must be settled upon within three years, or they will revert to the king. Every acre of land, whether cultivated or not, pays a bushel, that is, one schepel and a fifth of wheat. The meadows pay nothing. The swamps, cattle and men, are free. The outgoing good [*blank*].

We will now go back, and resume our journey. When we passed by the mill, a Quaker was there who gave us a letter, and told us it was difficult travelling, on account of the height of the water in the creeks; that about eight miles further on, some Indians had come to live, a little off the path on the left hand. We thought we should reach there by evening. We left the falls about two o'clock, following the ordinary path, which is the same for men and horses, and is grown up on both sides with bushes, which wore our breeches, stockings and shoes, as much as all the woods in Maryland together. The road runs from here east-northeast. When we came upon the land above, we found an extraordinary quantity of water, not only upon the flats and in the valleys, brooks, and morasses, but also upon the high, solid ground. We supposed this was caused by shutting up the creek by the mill dam, whereby the water did not have shoot sufficient to run down, but it was not that alone. We pursued our way, however, courageously, but discovered no Indians up to evening. We called aloud to ascertain whether they were about there, as they would answer if they were; and as our guide could speak the Indian language well, we thought it would all come right. But it was to no purpose; we perceived no Indians. We had gone about twelve miles from the falls, and it began to grow dark, when we came to a hill descending to a creek or small river called Millstone River, whence we saw fire at a distance, and supposed

that Indians or other people might be about there.   We therefore called out again several times, but received no answer.
On arriving at the creek we found it so full of water, and running so swiftly, there was no prospect of crossing it that evening, the more so as it was almost entirely dark.   We looked
about for some wood, though there was not much at this place,
and collected as much as we thought we should want to burn
for the whole night.   We made a good fire, and after warming
and drying ourselves, ate our supper from what we had brought
in our travelling bag.   At last we lay down around the fire
and fell asleep, having travelled twenty-five miles during the
day; but our rest did not continue long, as it began to rain
hard before midnight, and we soon awoke and arose to attend
to our fire, in order that it might not be extinguished.   The
rain continued so long and increased so that we could not sit
down, because the place was so full of water.   We had to take
care and protect the fire from going out, which gave us enough
to do.   It was quite calm, or blew very little, the wind coming
from all quarters; nevertheless, we could not dry ourselves,
although we kept turning continually round towards the fire.
We were wet through, and could do nothing better than to
stand straight up, whereby from the length of time and the
weight of our clothes we became very weary instead of having
the repose we so much needed.   Walk or sit, we could not,
because it was too dark, and the land too full of water for the
former, and for the other it was too wet.   We were compelled
to wait with patience in this position until daylight, which
seemed to tarry, because we longed for it so much.   It was one
of the shortest days in the year, with dark and rainy weather.
Each one looked out for the day as if we could thereby cause
it to appear sooner.   Finally, as our wood was consumed, the
day began.

30th, Saturday.   As soon as we could see, we went to the
creek, to ascertain whether we could cross over, but it was as
full and the water ran as swiftly as the evening before, because
it had rained continually, and was still raining; although we
had hoped that, if the weather had remained dry, the water
would have subsided.   As it was, there was no other course
than to wade over, and although we were stiff and cold, we
had to take off our stockings, and put our bare feet in the shoes

to protect them from treading on anything sharp, and our stockings were the dryest articles we had. We bound up our breeches as high as we could. "Now," said I, "let each one of us take a good stick in his hand in order to prop himself up against the current, and prevent his being washed away." Our guide went ahead even before I had found a stick; but when he reached the middle of the creek, he cried out, "Help, help, if you do not help me, I shall be carried away." I ran, took off my breeches, placed them on top of my head, and struggling, stick in hand, with the stones washing from under my feet and stick, went to him and took from him my travelling sack with which he was bent down. I kept on and was nearly across when my foot slipped on a smooth stone, and I fell forward into the water. However, by the aid of the stick, and the short distance to go, I succeeded in crossing, the sack being thoroughly wet. Our guide, who had on leather breeches, which became full of the running water, whereby he could not get along, now rolled them up, and by that means the water ran out below and lightened him, and thus he got over. My companion was yet on the other side, with his travelling bag and two swords. He did the same as I had done, and placed his breeches on top of his head, tied the rest on well, and followed us; but he was scarcely in the middle of the creek when he cried out to us to come and meet him, and relieve him of the sack if we wished him to come over, for he could not go any further. Whereupon I went in the creek again to him, and took from him the sack. Thus we all three waded over. We dressed ourselves quickly, for it was very cold, putting on our stiff legs the wet stockings, which chafed them, and over them the water-soaked shoes and the breeches which were wet through with the rain and very heavy; and then taking a mouth full of rum, we set out again on the way, stiff as we were. We were now anxious in relation to crossing this Millstone at half way, where it would be much broader and fuller of water. We proceeded then badly conditioned, wet, cold, and weary enough. We had thirty-six miles to travel to-day and more if we missed the road. We kept up our spirits, however. We found the land above so full of water, that we were most of the time over shoes in it, and sometimes half leg deep. After we had gone four or five miles, we saw the houses of the Indians

on the right, and went to them partly for the purpose of drying ourselves, for though the rain seemed at times to abate it
still continued, and partly to inquire the best way to go, in
order to cross the large creek. We entered their dwelling
where we dried ourselves and breakfasted a mouthful out of
our travelling sacks. We presented the Indians some fish-
hooks which pleased them. As to crossing the large creek,
they said it was not advisable to wade over, as the water was
as high as our shoulders or higher, as one of them showed us,
and the current was so swift as to render it impassable. He
said that not far from their house lived a *sackemaker* who had
in the creek a canoe with which he had set a man across the
day before, who had a horse which he swam over; but the
sackemaker was not pleased at his doing so without his permission. We promised him a guilder to take us to the *sackemaker*. While we were in this house a little naked child fell
from its mother's lap, and received a cut in its head, whereupon all who sat around that fire, and belonged to that household, began to cry, husband and wife, young and old, and
scream more than the child, and as if they themselves had
broken their arms or legs. In another corner of this house there
sat around a fire, forming another household, a party whose
faces were entirely blackened, who observed a gloomy silence
and looked very singular. They were in mourning for a deceased
friend. The Indian, having made himself ready, took both
our sacks together and tied them on his back for the purpose
of carrying them, which did not suit us badly, as we were very
tired. He did that without our asking him, and conducted us
in a direction more southeasterly to their king or *sackemaker*,
who lived two or three miles from there. On arriving there,
they immediately offered us some boiled beans in a calabash,
cooked without salt or grease, though they brought us our
own kind of spoons to take them out with. It was the queen
who did this, who was dressed more than the others. She gave
us also a piece of their bread, that is, pounded maize kneaded
into a cake and baked under the ashes. We ate some of it,
more for the purpose of satisfying her people, than our appe-
tite. Meanwhile we agreed with the *sackemaker* to set us
across the river for three guilders in *zeewan*. We presented
fish-hooks to several of them, but especially to the queen who

had entertained us. The *sackemaker* being ready, took one of our sacks to carry, and went on ahead of us; and there went this king, carrying our pack, almost without any clothing on his body. He conducted us to the creek which was two or three miles distant to the north and northeast over a very difficult and rocky hill. On arriving at the creek we saw there certainly would have been no way of going over, for the water was very high, and ran like a sluice. We were then put across, I myself helping the *sackemaker* and our *sack-carrier* in doing it, as it was difficult to go over even in a canoe. He took us a piece of the way, until we came to the right path, and gave us proper directions how to proceed further. He was to come for our guide the next day and carry him back.

We went on through water for the most part east-northeast, until about three o'clock in the afternoon, when the rain began to hold up, and we turned into a road on the right, which runs easterly to the Raritans Kill.[1] We did this because it was nearer, as they said, and also in order to go to a young Dutch-man's and secure good lodgings, of which we were truly in want. The other road led to Piskatteway to Mr. Greenland's, where we stopped a night in going on; yet this road was so long, and it was so difficult to travel continually through the water, that we could hardly proceed any further, as my comrade was entirely exhausted. We were, therefore, half afraid we should be compelled to pass the night in the woods. We picked up courage, however, as well as we could, and arrived at dusk at the house of Cornelis van Langevelt,[2] stepson of Thomas the baker in New York. He lived in that house alone with an Indian, who assisted him in trading with the Indians, but he had some neighbors who were beginning a new village on the land of this Thomas, the baker, directly opposite Pes-catteway, upon the point where the Millstone River unites itself with the Raritans Kill, and flows down to Achter Kol. The begun village had no name yet, but they intended to call it

[1] They took the "lower road" or more easterly path to the Raritan.

[2] Cornelis van Langevelt was married within the ensuing year to Dr. Greenland's daughter; he was probably son of Cornelis van Langevelt of New Amsterdam. Under the name Cornelius Longfield he appears as deputy from Piscataway to the general assembly of East Jersey in 1696–1697. "Thomas the baker in New York" is Thomas Lawrence.

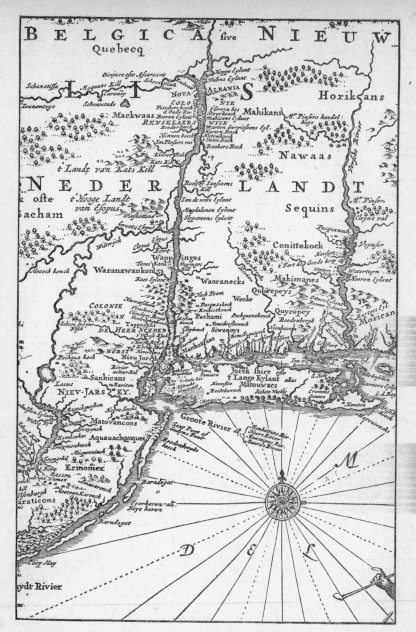

PART OF THE MAP OF NEW YORK AND NEW ENGLAND
IN MONTANUS'S "NIEUWE WEERELD," 1671
From a copy in the New York Public Library

Nassau.[1] This Dutchman was a good acquaintance of Beerent, our guide, and we were, therefore, welcome. He had heard of our being at the South River, and expected we would come over here, perhaps, he said, to be neighbors. He recommended to us a piece of land here, but we had neither time nor inclination to go and look at it.

We had special reasons to thank the Lord, and let our hearts ascend to Him on account of several things which we here take notice of to His glory, and in which His providence and goodness have assisted us. First, if we had taken the before described Indian with us, there is no probability we should have come right, he being a mere boy, without experience, and not well acquainted with the road, especially under such difficult circumstances; and, worst of all, we were not able to speak a word with him. Our guide said several times, and we thought so too, that when he had seen these difficulties, he would have deserted us in the woods and run away, as he could easily have done, and we should have been left alone. In the next place, we did not find the Indian dwelling on the other side of the first crossing, as we had wished, and supposed we should do. And if we had, what advice would there have been for our crossing the second place? We should then have been between the two crossings without any help. And thirdly, notwithstanding all our hardships, our hearts possessed such strength and courage until we happily arrived. To Him be glory therefor forever.

Millstone River is not, as is usually supposed, the Raritans Kill,[2] for that runs near this house on the right hand, due west, and a little more southerly beyond, and this one before the house, runs on the left hand, west-northwest, and a little more northerly beyond. It has its source above the falls of the South River, not far from that river, and runs for the most part north, and coming from thence, makes several great bends, and therefore, in going from Piscatteway to the South River, you must cross it three times. As far as known, it is about twelve or fourteen Dutch miles to this place on the Raritan. The Millstone is not very wide, which causes the current to run so much swifter when there is much upper water. It has

---

[1] At or near the present site of New Brunswick.

[2] It is an affluent of the Raritan, coming into it from the south.

several falls, and is shallow in dry weather.   It is therefore not navigable, though the Indians sometimes come down in their little canoes, made of the bark of trees.

31*st, Sunday*.   As we proposed to rest ourselves, we kept ourselves quiet to-day.   We paid our guide, giving him two ducatoons,[1] that is, thirty-two guilders in *zeewant*, because he had a little more trouble than either he or we had expected, and presented him with one hundred fish-hooks in addition. He was well satisfied and thanked us.   He left after breakfast to return home.   Meanwhile we expected a boat which they said was coming to load with wood, but it did not come.

1680, January 1*st, Monday*.   The boat not arriving, and Christmas, according to the old style, being near, at which time there is not much boating, every one endeavoring to be at home, we were apprehensive it would not come.   We therefore made an agreement with one of the neighbors, that he should take us in a canoe to the French tavern, which we have mentioned before, at Elizabethtown point, Kill achter Kol, for twelve guilders in *zeewant*.   We accordingly left about ten o'clock in the morning, through a beautiful creek, which is more like a river, with fine large meadows or marshes on both sides of it.   We came to a bank, from the broken point of which a beautiful white clay is taken, as fine as I have ever seen anywhere, or as Cologne earth[2] can be.   At the same place there are also red earth, and earth entirely black, which would be suitable for various purposes.   At the point of the Raritans Kill, we arrived at a place called Amboy, a very proper site for a city or place of business.   From there you can look over the great bay between the Nevesinck and the west point of Staten Island into the sea.   As regards view, therefore, it lies as well as New York, and is quite safe to be reached by ships.   The land around it is tolerably good, and therefore the place is reserved from sale.   There is an abundance of oysters on the shore, considered to be of the best.   The ebb tide being spent, we entered the Kill achter Kol with a good wind and, rowing ahead, arrived at about three o'clock at the point of Woodbridge Creek.   We landed here on Staten Island to drink at the house of the Frenchman *Le Chaudronnier*, where we formerly passed a night in making our tour of Staten

---

[1] Say, two dollars and a half.   [2] Cologne earth is a brown ochre.

Island. He set before us something to eat, and related to us what strange opinions every one, as well as he himself, entertained of us, which were certainly false enough, and whereof we disabused him. From there we made good speed past Smokers Hook, and by evening arrived at the point of Elizabethtown Creek, in the tavern before mentioned, where we lodged for the night; but there was nothing to be had there except to warm us. We were no sooner in the house than it began to rain and blow hard. We were therefore lucky in being housed, for to be in such weather and darkness upon the water in a canoe, is not without danger. We again perceived the Lord's goodness and care, for which we rendered Him thanks. We discovered no chance of going to the city immediately, but heard that two boats had gone down this afternoon, and were expected back the next day, which made us glad. We had something left in our travelling sack, upon which we made our supper, and then laid ourselves down to sleep in our old fashion upon a little hay, before the fire.

2d, Tuesday. On looking out at daybreak, we found quite calm, good weather, but no boats; but when it grew lighter, we saw a boat lying at anchor below the point. She appeared to be laden, and we therefore could not be certain that she would come up further. It was in consequence of her being laden that she had waited there for daylight, although she had a good tide to sail up to the city. We ascertained she was one of those which had gone down the evening before; and thereupon looked about to see how to get on board of her, as it would not be long before she would leave. The landlord took us and another person in a canoe to put on board, but before we had paddled half way, we saw them weigh anchor, and get under sail. We called out, and pulled with all our might, and, as it was calm, overtook her in time, and went on board. They were Dutchmen from the city, and were even our neighbors. They cheerfully received us; we paid our landlord, who immediately rowed back.

The wind began to blow gradually more and more from the west-northwest, so that when we arrived in the North River, we had as much as we could carry. It brought us up to the city about nine o'clock, where we had not yet set a foot on shore, before such a storm burst out of the northwest, of rain, hail, and snow together, that every thing seemed to bend and crack. It was at the same time so cold, it appeared as if this weather, whereby the winter was begun, had held back until we had arrived in the city to spend the winter. We cannot pass this circumstance by without some reflections upon the special goodness and providence of the Lord, which we experience so constantly; that he caused us to reach the land and house on the point of Elizabethtown Creek before the storm came up there; that the boat came to anchor there and took us on board, when she had a good tide and wind, but the darkness prevented her from keeping on, and we believe no more boats went there afterwards, not only during Christmas, but during the whole winter; and thirdly, that as soon as we had landed in the city, such a great storm and the winter began at the same time; to which may be added a fourth, that we hired the canoe on the Raritans, for being in the city, I spoke to the skipper of the boat, and he said he did not expect to go there again during the winter. Certainly if we did not regard all this with an humble and thankful heart, we should be guilty indeed.

But before we depart from New Jersey, we must remark that my Lord Carteret, having obtained this government, sent here his nephew[1] Carteret, to manage the same in his own way. This Carteret arriving here from England, accordingly, for the purpose of governing it, went first to New England,[2] where he so recommended his plan of government, and promised the people so much if they would go with him, that he caused a large number of persons to follow him here from Piscataway and Woodbridge, two places so called in New England, and settle down in New Jersey, where they have built two villages, called Piscataway and Woodbridge, after the names of the places where they had lived in New England. And indeed they did not do badly in view of the soil, because it is much richer here than where they were, although they did not choose the best land here by far. Besides these people, he found here

[1] Governor Philip Carteret was a cousin of the proprietary.

[2] Sent word, rather. Governor Carteret arrived in New Jersey late in 1665. Piscataway was so named from Piscataqua in New Hampshire (Portsmouth), and Woodbridge from the Rev. John Woodbridge of Newbury, Massachusetts, from which two places the first settlers came.

already a large number of other persons at Gmoenepa, Bergen, etc.

We were welcomed on our arrival by our old people, and we rejoiced and praised God, for we had seen the storm coming while we were on the water. We rested and warmed ourselves, then refreshed ourselves a little, and in the afternoon, delivered a portion of the letters which had been entrusted to us from the South River, and Maryland. Those which we had from Ephraim and his wife, we gave to her mother and father[1] who welcomed us. We told them of the good health of their children, and the comfort and hope which they gave us, which pleased them.

3d, *Wednesday.* We put our chamber in order this morning, and in the afternoon delivered the rest of the letters. We went also to M. de Lagrange's, where we saw a newly drawn map of the South River, from the falls to Burlington, made by the land surveyor there. He told us the governor had given him a grant of a piece of land on the South River between those places.

But what grieved us was, on arriving here to find no letters by Captain Jacob, when we had so much expected them, and did not know the cause of there being none. But we consoled ourselves in Him who is the consolation of all those who know Him and trust in Him; as we praised and thanked Him for His fatherly protection, His constant care and guidance, through His providence, which has been so continual and so manifest in our whole journey. He causes us to put our trust in Him, to lose ourselves in Him, and worthily to walk in such grace that He may be glorified in us and through us here, during our lives, in grace, and hereafter in glory. Amen. So may it be.

It would serve very well to add now a general description of the country through which we have travelled, and of each part in particular; but as we intend to give ourselves expressly to this work, we will omit it here, and proceed, meanwhile, with our journal.

End of the Journey to the Southward.

[1] Step-father; Johannes van Brugh. See p. 94, note 1, *supra.*

[IN NEW YORK.]

Continuation, of what happened in New York during the Winter.

4th, Thursday. It was now Christmas, according to the old style. It had frozen very hard during the night. We went to church, in order to hear Do. Niewenhuise preach, but more to give no offense to the people, than either on his or our own account.

5th, Thursday [Friday]. We began writing.

6th, Friday [Saturday]. It continued to freeze hard, though during the day the weather was more moderate. The ice was strong and mixed with snow.

13th, Saturday. It felt like a change of weather. In all this time nothing occurred worthy of note except the ships left the harbor in front of the city, on Thursday, for Deutel Bay, a cove of Long Island in the East River, about three miles east of the city, opposite Hellgate, where they lie during the winter, to be out of the way of the floating ice, which is sometimes very great.[1] On Friday, the governor's yacht arrived from Virginia, having been twenty-two days on the way. They had brought a *sackemaker* from there with whom the governor had negotiated for peace between the Indians and English in that quarter. In all this frost and cold we have discovered little difference from the cold in Holland, except that when the sun is high, that is, about nine o'clock in the morning, it is a little milder here. It thawed every day until the

16th, Tuesday, when all the ice and snow disappeared. De la Grange having a new small map of a portion of the South River, I copied it.

24th, Wednesday. Fred. Flipsen[2] met me, and told me the

---

[1] Deutel Bay was a small bight in the East River, about at the foot of Forty-seventh Street. The name was later corrupted into Turtle Bay. It was not a cove of Long Island.

[2] See p. 5, note 1, *supra*.

governor had been at his house, and spoken to him about us, and that he desired to see us and talk with us. We, therefore, determined to call upon him, and at the expiration of three days of rain and stormy weather, on the

25th [26th], *Friday*, we went to Fredryck Flipsen, that he might take us to the governor, as he had promised, and as he did do. The governor received us kindly, and told us he had wondered at our being so long in the country without coming to see him. We replied, that we should undoubtedly not have failed in doing so, if he had been in the city, for when we arrived here he was at Penequik,[1] and afterwards when he had been only a few days at home, with much business to occupy him, he left for Fort Albany just as we were going to the South River. We parted politely from each other.

30th [29th], *Monday*. A person who, they said, was the thief-catcher, came to our house in the evening, and, by order of the governor, summoned us to appear at eight o'clock the next morning at the house of   Rombouts,[2] the mayor of the city, and give our names and further information as to our doings and condition, as all strangers now and henceforth, whether men or women, must do. We were somewhat astonished, since they had told us, as was certainly true, that such had never been the custom. What induced them to adopt this course, we do not know.

31st [30th], *Tuesday*. We went in company with the old woman where we lodged, to Mayor Rombouts, at the appointed time. When we arrived, there was a magistrate's officer or two in attendance, and some came in while we were there. Addressing us, he said: "Friends, we have summoned you here, not because we have anything to say to you, or have any debt to claim, or because any one has sought of us to demand of you any such thing, or to summon you." The reason, he said, was because we had been so long in the country without having reported our names, who we were, our profession, trade or business, condition and purpose. We answered, we would by no means have been in default, if there were any law or order which required us to do so, or if we had been informed

---

[1] Pemaquid, on the Maine coast, where Governor Andros had caused a fort to be erected, which he visited in the autumn of 1679.

[2] Francis Rombouts was mayor of New York in 1679–1680.

that it was customary, or had ever been done; and it therefore
surprised us that they complained and charged us with neglect
of duty, or found fault with us, or wished to convict us of a
matter where there was no law, obligation, custom, or even
precedent; that this treatment struck us as very strange, since
there were several foreigners who had come over in the ship
with us, from whom they had not required what they required
of us. "You know well," he said, "it is the custom in Europe."
We replied, "it was not so in any of the United Provinces or
any other places except upon the frontiers." "Well," he continued, "we are no frontier, but a capital, and it must and shall
be so in the future." He then inquired after our names, trade
or profession, and place of residence in Fatherland, all of which
we told him, namely, that my comrade was a theologian, and
had studied at Leyden;[1] that I was a wine-racker, and that we
both lived near Leeuwarden, in Friesland. He asked further
what we came there to do, or what was our purpose or intention. We told him it was to look at the country. "How, look
at the country?" he asked: "some come here to look at the
cities, others at the fortifications; some to learn the mode of
government and policy, others the manner of regulating the
militia; others again to learn the climate, and times, and
seasons, and you run and travel through the country without
giving us any notice why." We replied, we had come here
and travelled through the country in order to make ourselves
acquainted generally with the nature and fertility of the soil,
as was convenient, or we might perhaps go around mornings
and evenings. He inquired further of us how we wished to be
regarded in the future, whether as citizens or foreigners. We
answered, as foreigners. "Well then," he proceeded, "you
are forbidden to carry on trade, particularly with the inhabitants, that is, to sell anything to private persons, but you may

[1] The *Album Studiosorum Academiae Lugduno-Batavae* (Hague, 1875) contains the entry of "Petrus Sluyter Vesaliensis" (*i. e.*, of Wesel) as entering the
University of Leyden in 1666 as a student of theology, at the age of twenty-one.
Also, Sluyter in 1670 told Paul Hackenberg at Herford that he had studied three
years in the Palatinate (without finding one truly pious pastor or teacher).
Domine Selyns, in a letter to Rev. Willem à Brakel, says that Sluyter gave himself out as a physician, but unsuccessful in practice, Danckaerts as a wine-
racker, as here. Danckaerts is understood from Zeeland sources to have been
originally a cooper for the Dutch West India Company at Middelburg.

dispose of it to merchants who sell to private individuals."
He said the privilege, or burgher right cost   beavers,[1]
each beaver reckoned at five guilders in Holland money, or
twenty-five guilders in *zeewan,* and was prohibited to all persons who reside out of the city; and as we resided out of the
city, we must be treated like others. We replied to this, we
would cheerfully obey the law. We were also told to travel
nowhere, particularly to Albany, without special permission
from the governor, which we said we would ask from his
Excellency, and thereupon we left.

On arriving at our house, we found there Simon of Gouanes,[2]
who had brought a boat-load of wood, and with whom my
companion went to Long Island, but I remained at home; the
Lord exercising me somewhat, I was rather quiet. We had
been to the strand several days, watching for Claes, the ferry-
man, or some other opportunity to cross over to Gamoenepaen,
but we found none; and as there was some difficulty between
this governor and the governor of New Jersey, we were contented to wait and follow the providence of the Lord therein,
although our purpose in going over was not on that account.

FEBRUARY 1st [*January* 31], *Wednesday.* Gerrit, the son-
in-law of our host, having been a long time upon Long Island,
came over with a cask of tobacco, which he intended to ship
in the ship *Beaver;* he repacked it, and I helped him cooper it.[3]
He said he had another one to bring over from the island, and
then he would take Simon's boat and go with us to Ackquak-
enon. After he had finished packing this one, the boat going
to Gouanes after wood, I left along with him on the

3d [*2nd*], *Friday,* at nine o'clock in the morning. I heard
that my companion had gone from the Bay to Najack, where
I proposed to follow him, because we might not be able to
obtain these people who, in order to go to Ackqueqenon, re-
solve upon it half a year beforehand, for when one can go, the
other cannot, and we were not able to wait. Simon told us
now he could not accompany us. The other person was uncertain, and Gerrit was not any more sure. I arrived at

---

[1] Six beavers, according to a municipal ordinance of 1676.

[2] Simon Aertsen de Hart.

[3] The *Beaver* was the ship by which Gerrit van Duyn's wife had just come out.
For the writer as a cooper see p. 168, note.

Najack in the evening, and my comrade also arrived there from the bay, in company with Jaques.[1] He concluded to return to the city with me in the morning.

4th [*3d*], *Saturday.* Our resolution was defeated. We started on the road, but were compelled to return, as it had rained hard the whole night, and continued to do so all day.

5th [*4th*], *Sunday.* It snowed all night and until about nine o'clock in the morning, when it cleared up, and we set out on our journey. We reached the ferry at one o'clock, where we waited three hours to be taken over by the lame brother-in-law of Jan the baker, or Jan Theunissen.[2]

6th [*5th*], *Monday evening.* M. de la Grange came to call upon us, being somewhat under concern of mind, and giving us some hope. His wife, being touched also, has been to see us several times; and certainly the Lord will comfort us about His people. I will take some other occasion to speak more particularly in relation to this matter, if the Lord continue it. Meanwhile, I had translated the *Verheffinge des Geestes tot God*[3] into Dutch, for Elizabeth Rodenburgh, wife of Ephraim Hermans, in order to send her a token of gratitude for the acts of kindness enjoyed at her house, as she had evinced a great inclination for it, and relished it much, when sometimes we read portions of it to her while we were there. I also began a translation of the last exercise of the *Heylige Decades.*[4] Nothing further occurred worthy of mention, except that the snow, frost, rain and inclement weather prevented us from going to Ackquequenon.[5]

11th, Sunday. We received letters from the South River, from Mr. Ephraim Hermans, and Heer Johan Moll, which consoled us as to their state, and gave us some hope at least of great progress, as appears by the same. We answered them, and dispatched our letters by the same person who brought theirs, and who was to return on the

---

[1] Jacques Cortelyou.

[2] Probably a mistake for Jacob Theunissen, who was a baker at this time.

[3] "The Liftings up of the Soul to God"; one of Labadie's publications (Dutch, Amsterdam, 1667), of which, however, Danckaerts evidently had with him only the original French, *Élévations d'Esprit à Dieu* (Montauban, 1651).

[4] *Les Saintes Décades des Quatrains de Piété Chrestienne* (Amsterdam, 1671), poems by Jean de Labadie.

[5] Passaic.

14*th, Wednesday*, and with whom we sent the translation of the *Verheffinge des Geestes* with a small package of knitted baby-clothes. The ship *Beaver* came out of Deutel Bay, and was up for Europe and Holland immediately. Therefore, on the

15*th, Thursday*, we began writing to our friends in the Fatherland. The winter gradually passing away, the weather was during the last of February, and first of March, as pleasant as if it were the month of May. I finished the translation of the *Decades*.

MARCH 2*d, Saturday*. M. de la Grange has chartered a yacht to go to the South River, with a lot of merchandise, and to take to his land there the boor, whom he had brought for that purpose from the Fatherland. This person came from near Sluis,[1] and had done nothing here as yet, because De la Grange had not gone to Tinaconcq, as he had first intended. He designed to take him now to the land he had bought on Christina Kill, and have it put in order. He had obtained exemption from tax on his merchandise, and was the first one who had enjoyed this advantage, that is, from the second tax, he having paid the first tax when the goods were unladen here. All merchandise pays a second tax when it is sent to the South River, or Albany. I gave him *Les Paroles de Salut*[2] for Heer Johan Moll, who had urgently requested us to send him some religious book or other, writing to him what was necessary on the subject.

We had waited till this time to go to Ackquekanon, either on account of the weather, or because it was not convenient for the persons on Long Island. We finally determined to go with Gerrit, who could speak very good Indian, and who had sent word to us from Long Island, that we must be at Simon's house in Gouanes for that purpose on Sunday morning in order to go in his boat. We accordingly prepared ourselves.

3*d, Sunday*. We both went over to Long Island, at eight o'clock; and as we were entering the ferry boat, Madame de la Grange came aboard with her nephew, Kasparus Rein-

---

[1] Sluis in Staats-Vlanderen, now in Zeeland.

[2] What appears to be the Dutch version of this, *Handboekje van Godsaligheid*, by Labadie, was published at Amsterdam in 1680.

derman, who, when they had landed, took a wagon, and rode on to the bay. We went through Breukelen to Gouanes, where we arrived about ten o'clock, and found Gerrit was not yet there. Several families of Indians had erected their huts upon the beach, whereby Simon's house was very accessible. This was done with the consent of his wife, with whom he had left the profit from the Indians. While we were engaged in obtaining some oysters, Gerrit with Jaques and his son and daughter rode up in a wagon. Jaques had come for the purpose of attending to a sick horse of Simon, which had a certain disease, they call here the staggers, to which their horses are subject, and with which the creatures whether going or standing constantly stagger, and often fall; this increasing they fall down at last, and so continue till they die. It is cured sometimes by cutting the tip end of the tail, and letting the blood drip out; then opening a vein, giving the animal a warm drink and making a puncture in the forehead, from which a large quantity of matter runs out. The boat being leaky, and a right calculation not having been made as to the tide, we remained here to-day, intending to leave early in the morning, and, therefore, made every preparation. We had expected another person to go with us, but there were only us three.

4th, Monday. We left Gouanes Bay at high water, about eight o'clock, with a southerly wind, but calm, and rowed with the current to Gheele Hoeck,[1] where we made sail, and crossed the bay to Achter Kol, where we knew there were some Indians lying behind Constables Hook. We sailed there in order to request one of them, named Hans, to go with us as a guide. Hans had long frequented among the Dutch, and spoke the Dutch language tolerably well. He was a great *nitap,* that is, friend of Gerrit. He refused at first to accompany us, saying he had just come from there; and when we urged it upon him, he said, "would you Christians do as much for us Indians? If you had just been there and had come back tired and weary, and some Indians should come and ask you in the midst of your children, in your own houses, while busied with your occupation, would you be ready immediately to go back with them?" We answered yes, upon proper terms. He said, "I do not think so, I know well what you would do."

[1] Yellow Point.

We told him, we would fully satisfy him.   He wished to make
a bargain beforehand, which we did not, as we wanted to see
whether he would earn anything.   He allowed himself to be
persuaded; "but," he said, "I will lose so much time in making
zeewant," which is their money and consists only of little beads.
"I am very cold; you are all well clothed and do not feel the
cold; I am an old man (as he was), and have nothing but a
little worn-out blanket for my naked body."   We must give
him a blanket and then he would be willing to go with us.
We said we had none with us.   "Well," he replied, "I do not
ask you to give it to me now, but when I come to the city."
We told him he should be satisfied, and have no cause of complaint.   After he had fitted himself out a little he went with
us.   We had some of the flood tide left; but before we reached
Schutters Island the wind changed, and it was quite calm.
We therefore struck our sails and went to rowing in order to
strike the current.   By scraping along we reached the Slangenbergh, on the west point of the Northwest Kill,[1] where there
is a very large piece of salt meadow, and where the tide ran so
strong against us we could not proceed any further.   We
therefore lay to and went ashore, in order to walk about a
little.   This was the largest, cleanest, and most level piece of
salt meadow that we had observed anywhere.   After having
been an hour or a little more on shore, a light breeze sprang
up out of the east, when we took the boat again and putting
off, came to Milfor,[2] an English village, lying upon high land
on the south side of the creek, having left Santfort on the right
hand, which is an English village also, lying on the west side
of Hackingsackse Kill.   We then came to high land; and the
wind falling, we rowed up against the ebb tide to a house on
the northeast side belonging to one Captain Berry, where it
being evening and commencing to rain, we stopped, made the
boat fast, and took every thing out of her.   We entered the
house which was large enough, but poorly furnished.   We

[1] Passaic River.

[2] Milford, *i. e.*, Newark, founded in 1666 by settlers from Milford, Connecticut, and other Connecticut towns.   Opposite, between the Hackensack and Passaic rivers, lay Captain William Sandford's plantation (granted 1668), afterward
called New Barbadoes.   North of his grant lay that of Captain John Berry (1669),
still higher that of Jacques Cortelyou and his partners.

found nobody there except a negro who could speak nothing but a little broken French. We warmed ourselves, and ate from what we had brought with us, Hans, the Indian, sharing with us. In the meanwhile we engaged in conversation with him, and he told us certain things which we had never heard any Indian or European mention, the opinion of the Indians in relation to the Godhead, the creation, and the preservation and government of all things.

We acknowledge, he said, a supreme first power, some cause of all things, which is known by all the Indians of North America, hereabouts, whether Mahatans, Sinnekes, Maquaas, Minquaas, southern or northern Indians, not only by the name of *Sackamacher* or *Sachamor* (which the Dutch for the sake of convenience will pervert into *Sackemacher*), that is to say, lord, captain, or chief, which all persons bear who have any power or authority among them, especially any government or rule over other persons and affairs, and that name, it appeared to him, was used by others to express God, more than by themselves; but the true name by which they call this Supreme Being, the first and great beginning of all things, was Kickeron,[1] who is the origin of all, who has not only once produced or made all things, but produces every day. All that we see daily that is good, is from him; and every thing he makes and does is good. He governs all things, and nothing is done without his aid and direction. "And," he continued, "I, who am a captain and *Sakemaker* among the Indians, and also a medicine-man (as was all true), and have performed many good cures among them, experience every day that all medicines do not cure, if it do not please him to cause them to work; that he will cure one and not another thereby; that sickness is bad, but he sends it upon whom he pleases, because those upon whom he visits it are bad; but we did not have so much sickness and death before the Christians came into the country, who have taught the people debauchery and excess; they are therefore much more miserable than they were before. The devil, who is wicked, instigates and urges them on, to all kinds of evil, drunkenness and excess, to fighting and war, and to strife and violence amongst themselves, by which many men are wounded and killed. He thus does all kind of evil to

[1] Probably connected with *Kitchi*, great.

them." I told him I had conversed with Jasper or Tantaqué, another old Indian,[1] on the subject, from whence all things had come, and he had told me they came from a tortoise; that this tortoise had brought forth the world, or that all things had come from it; that from the middle of the tortoise there had sprung up a tree, upon whose branches men had grown. That was true, he replied, but Kickeron made the tortoise, and the tortoise had a power and a nature to produce all things, such as earth, trees, and the like, which God wished through it to produce, or have produced.

It was now time to see if we could not take some rest in a place not very well protected against the cold, and where there was nothing to lie upon except the naked floor; but the negro wishing to favor my comrade and myself, showed us a bunk, in which there was nothing save a few leaves of maize, and those thin enough. We lay down there, but suffered greatly from the cold. We slept very little, and lay shivering all night, and the slave sometimes shaking us and waking us up. We were so stiff we could not move; but the night passed on as well as it could, and we rose early. It had rained, and we started at daylight to the boat, and rowed into the stream. Gerrit grumbled very much. He was a coarse, ignorant man, and had not well calculated the tide. We went ashore about eight or half-past eight to breakfast, and had great difficulty in making a fire, for all the brush was wet through with the rain. We were fortunate enough, however, at last, to succeed. We took a walk for a short distance into the woods, which were not the poorest. In the meanwhile the ebb had ended; the water was calm, and taking a little of the flood, we rowed on until we arrived at Ackquekenon, about one o'clock in the afternoon. Ackquekenon is a tract of land of about twelve thousand *morgen*, which Jaques of Najack, with seven or eight associates, had purchased from the Indians, the deed of which we have seen, and the entire price of which amounted to one hundred or one hundred and fifty guilders in Holland money, at the most. It is a fine piece of land, the best tract of woodland that we have seen except one at the south. It is not very abundant in wood, but it has enough for building purposes and fuel. On one side of it is the Northwest Kill, which is navigable

[1] See pp. 76–78, *supra*.

by large boats and yachts thus far, but not beyond. On the other side, there is a small creek by which it is almost entirely surrounded, affording water sufficient, both summer and winter, to drive several mills.

When we reached here, we took our provisions and whatever was loose out of the boat into a hut of the Indians, of whom there is only one family on this whole tract. We ate our dinner by their fire, and determined to go in the afternoon to the falls, although it had already begun to rain. We started off accordingly under the guidance of Hans, the Indian. The rain gradually increased, with snow, and did not hold up the whole day. After we had travelled good three hours over high hills, we came to a high rocky one, where we could hear the noise of the water, and clambering up to the top, saw the falls below us, a sight to be seen in order to observe the power and wonder of God.[1] Behind this hill the land is much higher than on the other side, and continues so as far as is known. A kill or river runs through this high land between the hills, formed by several branches coming down from still higher land. This river, running along the valley to seek the sea, comes to this hill where it runs over a large blue rock, which is broken in two, obliquely with the river. One part is dry, which is the hill before mentioned; the other is where the river, running over a crevice or fissure between both, appears to be eight or ten feet wide, having on either side smooth precipices like walls, but some parts broken between them. The river finding this chasm pours all its water into it headlong from a height, according to guess, of about eighty feet; and all this pouring water must break upon the undermost piece of stone lying in the crevice, which causes a great roaring and foaming, so that persons standing there, side by side, have to call out loud before they can understand each other. By reason of the breaking of the water, and the wind which the falling water carries with it, there is constantly spray ascending like smoke, which scatters itself like rain. In this spray, when the sun shines, the figure of a rainbow is constantly to be seen trembling and shaking, and even appearing to move the rock. The water in this fissure runs out on the south; and there at the end of the rock or point it finds a basin, which is the begin-

[1] The falls of the Passaic, at Paterson, New Jersey.

ning of the lower kill.   This point is, I judge, about one hundred feet above the water, and is steep like an upright wall.
When the fish come up the river, this basin is so full of all
kinds of them, that you can catch them with your hands, because they are stopped there, and collect together, refreshing
themselves, and sporting in and under the falling fresh water,
which brings with it, from above, bushes, green leaves, earth,
and mire, in which they find food.   The water runs hence east
and northeast to Ackquekenon.   The Indians come up this
river in canoes to fish, because it is one of the richest fisheries
they have; but the river is not navigable by larger boats,
though in case the country were settled the navigation could
be improved.   The falls lie among high hills, especially on the
south, so that the sun does not penetrate there well except in
summer.   We found heavy ice there at this time, although it
had all thawed away below.   When I saw this ice at a distance,
I supposed it was the foam.   I took a sketch[1] as well as I
could, very hastily, for we had no time, and it rained and
snowed very much.   What I did is not very happily done.   I
regret I could not crayon it, for it is worth being portrayed.
Night coming on, we had to leave.   We were very wet and cold,
especially in the feet.   It was dark, and slippery walking on
such precipices, and crossing little streams.   Tired and weary,
wet and dirty, we reached the place which we had started from,
about eight o'clock in the evening, and went into the hut of
the Indians, having to-day rowed constantly from early dawn
until one or two o'clock, and then walked, through heavy
weather, twenty-four to twenty-eight miles.

We endeavored to warm and dry ourselves in this cabin as
best we could.   We could not stand up on account of the smoke,
and there were no means of sitting down unless flat on the
ground, which was very bad for us, on account of our being so
wet, but we did the best we could.   We took our supper, and
distributed some of our bread among the Indians, with which
they were as much pleased as children with sweet cake.   We
gave each man four fish-hooks, and the women and children
each two.   We also gave them two small trumpets, and then
they were great *nitaps* or friends.   We had to lie down there,
and at first, as long as it was warm, it went very well; but the

[1] Not preserved.

fire being almost burned out, and the hut rather airy, and the wind being no longer kept out by the heat in the opening, through which the smoke escaped, we became stiff in the knees, so that I could not, through weariness and cold, move mine without great pain and difficulty. The longed-for day came, and we went out in the snow to look through the woods, and along the little stream, to see whether it would be worth the trouble to erect a saw-mill there for the purpose of sawing timber for sale, as Jaques had supposed. But although we found the stream suitable for mills, we did not discover proper wood sufficient for the purpose. The soil seemed to promise good, and the place is as well situated as it can be, to make a village or city. The land on both sides of the Northwest Kill is all taken up, and the prospect is that the whole region will soon be inhabited. It is already taken up on the south side as high up as the falls. Eating our breakfast about eight o'clock, we went on board of the boat, it being now the

6th, *Wednesday*. We set off with a westerly wind, though light and gusty. If the wind in this river do not come straight from behind, you cannot derive much benefit from it, in consequence of the land on both sides of it being so high, and the bay so winding. The river is the pleasantest we have yet seen. It is gratifying to look upon the continually changing views which present themselves in going either up or down, with its evergreens of pine and cedar, and other species, the names of which I do not know, and its clean bottom and clear fresh water. We rowed and sailed as well as we could, until the flood tide stopped us, when we went ashore to eat our dinner, and make a good fire to warm ourselves. When the ebb began to make, we proceeded on our way. Our poor Indian, who did nothing in the boat, sat all the time benumbed with cold in his poor little blanket. But as the day advanced it was better. The tide serving us, and the wind being stronger as we came below the high land, we reached Achter Kol before evening, and set the Indian ashore at his hut, who told us he would come and see us on Monday. It was calm, with the wind more and more favorable, and we crossed over the bay, and arrived at Gouanes Bay about eight o'clock.

I had asked Hans, our Indian, what Christians they, the Indians, had first seen in these parts. He answered the first were Spaniards or Portuguese, from whom they obtained the maize or Spanish or Turkish wheat, but they did not remain here long. Afterwards the Dutch came into the South River and here, on Noten Island,[1] a small island lying directly opposite the fort at New York, and to Fort Orange or Albany, and after them the English came for the first, who nevertheless always disputed the first possession. But since the country has been taken several times by the one and the other, the dispute is ended in regard to the right of ownership, as it is now a matter of conquest.

When we arrived at Gouanes, we heard a great noise, shouting and singing in the huts of the Indians, who as we mentioned before, were living there. They were all lustily drunk, raving, striking, shouting, jumping, fighting each other, and foaming at the mouth like raging wild beasts. Some who did not participate with them, had fled with their wives and children to Simon's house, where the drunken brutes followed, bawling in the house and before the door, which we finally closed. And this was caused by Christians. It makes me blush to call by that holy name those who live ten times worse than these most barbarous Indians and heathen, not only in the eyes of those who can discriminate, but according to the testimony of these poor Indians themselves. What do I say, the testimony of the Indians! Yes, I have not conversed with an European or a native born, the most godless and the best, who has not fully and roundly acknowledged it, but they have not acknowledged it salutarily, and much less desisted, disregarding all convictions external and internal, notwithstanding all the injury which springs therefrom, not only among the Indians, but others, as we will show in its proper place. How will they escape the terrible judgment of God; how evade the wrath and anger of the Lord and King, Jesus, whom they have so dishonored and defamed, and caused to be defamed among the heathen? Just judgment is their damnation. But I must restrain myself, giving God all judgment and wrath, and keeping only what he causes us to feel therefor. Such are the fruits of the cursed cupidity of those who call themselves Christians for the very little that these poor naked people have. Simon

[1] Governor's Island. The Spaniards spoken of may have been Verrazano's men.

and his wife also do their best in the same way, although we spoke to them severely on the subject.   They brought forward this excuse, that if they did not do it, others would, and then they would have the trouble and others the profit, but if they must have the trouble, they ought to have the profit; and so they all said, and for the most part falsely, for they all solicit the Indians as much as they can, and after begging their money from them, compel them to leave their blankets, leggings, and coverings of their bodies in pawn, yes, their guns and hatchets, the very instruments by which they obtain their subsistence. This subject is so painful and so abominable, that I will forbear saying anything more for the present.

These Indians had *canticoyed* there to-day, that is, conjured the devil, and liberated a woman among them, who was possessed by him, as they said; and indeed, as they told us, it had that appearance, but I have never seen it.[1]

We fared better this night than the last, and whether from fatigue or other reasons, slept soundly.

7th, Thursday. We had intended to go to Najacq, to Jaques's, and afterwards to Elbert's in the bay, in order to report to them how we had found their land, but Gerrit having promised his father-in-law some firewood, he had to take Simon's boat for the purpose, and Simon's wife also had some errands in the city. We, therefore, determined to go with them, as we did, leaving Gouanes at ten o'clock, and seeing the Indians putting up their huts which they had entirely thrown down during their intoxication, although it was not much trouble, as it was not much to make them.   With a tolerably fair wind we reached the city at noon, where we gave ourselves up to rest.

We wished now to make a voyage to the Nevesinkx, Rentselaer's Hoeck, and Sant Hoek, but we could find no opportunity, for the reason that this route is very little navigated in the winter and spring, because it is somewhat dangerous. Meanwhile, the weather continued very variable; sometimes we had frost and severe cold, then rain and snow, wind and squalls, until the time of the sun's crossing the line, when it began to become warm, but continued still variable, though it improved daily.

[1] The *canticoy* of the Indians was wild dancing.

20th, Wednesday. While my comrade sat writing, he observed a change in his vision, being able to see better than before, when he had to look extremely close in writing. It happened thus: writing as he was accustomed to do, his sight in an instant became entirely obscured, so that he had to stop, not being able to write any more. Not knowing what it was, he shut his eyes and rubbed them, as they usually do when anything obstructs the sight, and then undertook to write as he had done before, but yet he could not see well; when raising his head higher from the paper, he saw much clearer than when he had to look close to it. Had he kept his eyes up so high before, he would scarcely have been able to see at all. You could also perceive that his writing was different afterwards.

A yacht arrived down the river from the Hysopes,[1] from which they learned that the navigation was open, though boats going up would have to tug through the ice. It brought news of the death of the minister, Domine Gaesbeck, a Cocceian, which had caused great sorrow.[2] They had determined to call another minister from Holland, or Tessemaker from the south. They had built a new church in the Hysopus, of which the glass had been made and painted in the city, by the father of our mate, Evert Duiker, whose other son, Gerrit, did most of the work.[3] This Gerrit Duiker had to take the glass to the Hysopes, and having heard we had a mind to go there, he requested our company, which we would not refuse him when the time came. He promised to teach me how to draw.

23d, Saturday. The first boat arrived from Fort Orange[4] to-day, bringing scarcely any news except that a great number of Indians had died in the early part of the winter of small pox, and a large party of them had gone south to make war against the Indians of Carolina, beyond Virginia, for which

---

[1] Esopus, founded in 1652. See pp. 220–221, *post*.

[2] Rev. Laurentius van Gaasbeeck, licentiate in theology and doctor of medicine (M. D., Leyden, 1674), had come to the Esopus in September, 1678, and had preached at its three villages of Kingston, Marbleton, and Hurley. He died in February, 1680. A letter from the church, asking for another minister, is in *Ecclesiastical Records of New York*, II. 748. Tesschenmaker had served the church temporarily before Gaasbeeck's arrival.

[3] Evert Duyckinck the elder and his son Gerrit were painters and glaziers; the father is also designated in the Dutch church records as "Schilder," maker of pictures.   [4] Albany.

reason the hunting of beaver had not been good, and there would be a great scarcity of peltries this year, which was the chief trade of New Netherland, especially in this quarter.

There was something published and posted by this government to-day against that of New Jersey or Achter Kol, but I do not know precisely what it was.[1] We found to-day an opportunity to go to Nevesinck. An Englishman who had a little boat, and small enough, was going on Monday without fail, and he had, he said, about sixteen passengers.

24th, Sunday, and 25th, Monday. It stormed hard from the northwest, and he could not go, but he came to tell us he would give us notice when he would sail.

26th, Tuesday. He came and told us he would leave next day at sunrise, and in passing by the house, he would come in and call us.

27th, Wednesday. We waited for him from an early hour, but it was nearly ten o'clock before we saw him. We went to his boat which was poor enough, very small, light, and lank, though it had been repaired some; it had an old sail and piece of a foresail, and yet this captain was as stern and arrogant with his boat, as if it were a ship-of-war. We waited there for the passengers, but they had melted away to three, my comrade, myself and one other person. We started about eleven o'clock with a good wind and tide, though it was almost low water. When we reached the Narrows, the wind veered round to the southeast, which was against us. We discovered the boat to be so leaky that she had a foot or two of water in her, which he sought to excuse, but every word he said on the subject was untrue. The pump was stopped up, and we had to help him clear it out, which was accomplished after much trouble and bungling. We cleared it out, but we had that to do three times, because in repairing the boat they had left all the chips and pieces of wood lying in the hold between the planks, and when we pumped, this stuff would continually obstruct the pump, though we succeeded in getting out most of the water. Meanwhile the wind changed to the south and southwest, with which there was every prospect of getting

[1] Governor Andros's proclamation of March 13/23, 1680, against Governor Carteret's assuming to exercise powers of government in New Jersey. It may be found in *New Jersey Archives*, I. 293.

outside. We tacked about and reached Coney Island, a low, sandy island, lying on the east side of the entrance from the sea. We came to anchor under its outermost point, when we should have gone inside of Sandy Hook, in a creek, as we were able yet to do; but he said, we must go outside of Sandy Hook, round by sea, and then make for a creek there. I began now to have other thoughts. To put to sea in such a light, low, decayed, and small boat, with rotten sails, and an inexperienced skipper, and that at night, did not suit me very well. The sea began already to roll round the point of Coney Island, and I apprehended bad weather from pain in my breast and other indications. He said the place where we were lying was entirely shoal, and he therefore dared not go near the shore, as there was only eight or ten feet water. But he was much mistaken, for when he let the anchor fall, it ran out six fathoms of rope before it struck the bottom. I had seated myself all the time at the helm, and observed he was a miserable person. It was then about half flood, and having put things somewhat in order, he asked us if we would go ashore with him. I said yes, and I did so for the purpose of ascertaining how the westerly point of this island was situated on the sea entrance. My comrade and the other passenger, having no wish to go, remained on board. Upon reaching the shore, we saw immediately a large ship coming up the bay from Sandy Hook, which we supposed to be Margaret's ship, which she had left to be repaired at Falmouth, as we have before mentioned.[1] I wondered why our skipper did not return on board, but he not only remained ashore and left his boat with two inexperienced persons, but he had not hauled up on the beach his small canoe in which we came ashore, or made it fast. I went with him along the strand, on the sea side, and saw that, close by Coney Island, a strong flood tide was running, which was pressed between the east bank and the island, and that led us to think there was an opening there through which you could sail out and in, which is the fact, as I was afterwards informed by one who was very well acquainted with the place; but it is only deep enough for boats, yachts, and other small craft. This island, on the sea side, is a meadow or marsh intersected by several kills or creeks. It is not large, being about half an

[1] See p. 28, *supra*.

hour or three quarters long, and stretching nearly east and west. It is sandy and uninhabited. They generally let their horses run upon it to feed, as they cannot get off of it. We found good oysters in the creek inside, and ate some of them, but seeing his carelessness, I could not remain longer from the boat, as the canoe might be carried off, on the rise of the water, by the tide or the wind, and my comrade and the other passenger, who was sea-sick, not know what to do, the more so in view of the inexperience and carelessness of the captain. I therefore hurried to the boat, running across the island. On the inside of the island I found a sandy elevation like a dune or high dyke which became gradually lower towards Long Island, and that is all which shows itself here. This elevation is on the land side, and is mostly covered with hollies, which, according to my recollection, I have never seen growing in this region except on dry and very fine sand. When we reached the canoe it was not only afloat, but it had been thrown across the beach by the sea, and was full of water. If it had moved off, we certainly should have been at a loss. The water being high, the sea came rolling in heavily around the point into the bay, and caused the boat lying in the current, which ran strong here, to pitch greatly. We were even fearful about getting on board again, for the canoe could scarcely hold us both. I told him to go on board first, and bring the boat nearer the shore, and then he could take me aboard, but he would not do so, we must go on board together. We therefore both went into it, and reached the boat, though it was very dangerous. As soon as we came aboard, our skipper spoke about leaving there, as we could not lie there well. I asked him where he would go to. He said to the city, which I did not much oppose, and was secretly glad of, seeing it was from the Lord. We therefore had to abandon our design of going to the Nevesinckx at this time. The large ship which we had seen sailed before us; and we found that we had not been mistaken in our supposition, as it was the same vessel we had left in Falmouth. It commenced blowing hard in the evening, and we had as much as we could stand, but we reached the city while it was yet in the evening, very much rejoiced.

28th, *Thursday, and* 29th, *Friday.* There was a severe storm, accompanied with much rain, from the southeast, it being about new moon.   Certainly, if we did not see in this the continual care of the Lord, in His providence, we were worse than beasts, for it was too manifest not to be touched by it.   He gives us grace only to lose ourselves more and more in Him, and to offer ourselves up to His service.

30th, Sunday [Saturday.]   The storm continued the whole day.

31st, Monday [Sunday.]   We determined to make a journey to Albany at the first opportunity, but this could not be done without the special permission of the governor.   Though a regulation exists that no one shall go up there unless he has been three years in the country, that means for the purpose of carrying on trade; for a young man who came over with us from Holland proceeded at once to Albany, and continues to reside there.   We went accordingly to request permission of the governor.   After we had waited two or three hours, his Excellency came in and received us kindly.   We made our request, which he neither refused nor granted, but said he would take it into consideration.   Meanwhile we inquired after vessels, of which there were plenty going up at this time of year.

APRIL 2d [3d], Wednesday.   We went again to the lord governor for permission, who received us after he had dined.   He inquired for what purpose we wished to go above; to which we answered, we had come here to see the country, its nature and fertility; and that we had heard there were fine lands above, such as Schoonechten, Rentselaerswyck, and the Hysopus.[1] "Those are all small places," he said, "and are all taken possession of; but I am ashamed I did not think of this." He then requested us to come some morning and dine with him, when he would talk with us.   We thanked him, and took our leave, reflecting whether it would be advisable to trouble his Excellency any more about the matter, as it was not of such great importance to us, and he, perhaps, considered it of more moment than we did.   We then felt inclined to leave the country the very first opportunity, as we had nothing more to do here, and it was the very best time of year to make a voyage. As we had some of our goods left after we were forbidden to sell any more, we went to see if we could get rid of what we had kept for Ephraim.   As there was no prospect of seeing

[1] Schenectady, Rensselaerswyck, Esopus.

him, we proposed to do the best we could with one of our neighbors, named Cornelius van Kleif, to whom my comrade had spoken, and who was inclined to trade. He entered into negotiations, but was a little timorous. We offered to let him examine the bills of the persons from whom we had bought the goods, and also of the freight and custom-house duties, and he should give us an advance of thirty per cent. on their amount; or, he might see what they were worth, and could be sold for, and we would divide the profits equally with him. After he had looked at them, he did not dare to take them himself alone, but said he would bring another person, in order that with the two of them they might make it safe. He did not say he had no means of payment, though he did remark he had no peltries, which we would willingly have taken in payment. The other person had the means to pay. We told him we would wait until de La Grange returned from the South River; that I had spoken to his wife on the subject, and that he was expected back every day; at all events, that we would wait until we had spoken to some other person. Van Kleif's wife, however, took some fine thread, ribbons, pins, and what she wanted for herself.

7th, *Sunday*. M. de La Grange arrived home from the South River, and came with his wife in the afternoon to visit us, both being under concern of mind. We addressed to them what we thought necessary. He stated he had agreed with his nephew to go in partnership with him, and could not withdraw therefrom, unless God did something special. They both hoped that God would have pity upon them.

We spoke of the remnant of our little stock, and of the time advancing when we must be rid of it, so as to be prepared to leave the country. He said as soon as the boat, which he had chartered, returned from the South River, in which he had some peltries, we would see what we could do with each other.

8th, *Monday*. Van Kleif came to examine the goods again. He had the disposition, but not the means to buy, and wished to bring still another person to make the purchase, whom he named, and who was one of the most miserly persons in the city, which was not agreeable to us. We, therefore, told him we had already spoken to M. de La Grange.

10th, *Wednesday*. The boat of de La Grange arrived from the South River, bringing a letter for us from Ephraim, in which he informed us of his intention to come and visit us the last of April or the first of May, which we much desired.

A certain governor from Harford [Hartford], a place situated to the north, arrived in the city from the West Indies.[1] Our governor entertained him nobly, and parted with him with great civility.

Two vessels sailed for Boston, where we much desired to go, but we were not prepared. The governor investigated whether either of them had taken anything on board below the city.

We left a small piece of brown serge, which stood us in rather dear, but was very fine and strong, and which on account of its high price, we had not been able to dispose of, to be cut up for a coat, waistcoat, and breeches for both of us, with fur in front, so that almost the whole piece was used, De la Grange taking the remnant, with which he was much pleased, for a coat, because he did not know where to obtain such goods in this country. Meanwhile, the barter of our few goods was going on with him at the rate of fifty per cent. profit on the invoices, upon which condition he took almost all of them.

13th, *Saturday*. We called upon the governor, and requested permission to leave. He spoke to us kindly, and asked us to come the next day after preaching, thus preventing our request.

14th, *Sunday*. About five o'clock in the afternoon, we went to the lord governor, who was still engaged, at our arrival, in the Common Prayer; but as soon as it was finished, he came and spoke to us, even before we had spoken to him, and said of a person who was with him, "This is Captain Deyer,[2] to whom I have given directions to write a permit or passport for you to go to Albany." He again asked us where we came from, and where we lived, which we told him. He also inquired something about the prince of Friesland, and the prin-

---

[1] William Leete was governor of Connecticut at this time, but there seems to be no evidence of his leaving his colony to go to the West Indies.

[2] William Dyer had been commissioned by the Duke of York in 1674 as collector of the port of New York, and was still acting as such. The next year, 1680–1681, he was mayor of the city.

cess, and also about the differences of the people of Friesland and His Royal Highness and Their High Mightinesses, which we told him.[1] We then thanked him for his favor, and said the object of our visit was not only to ask permission to go up the river, but also to leave the country. He thereupon stated that there would be no boat going to Boston for two or three weeks, but he intended to send one himself soon to Pennequicq,[2] which was at our service, and we could easily get to Boston from there by a fishing boat or some other vessel. We thanked him for the honor and kindness he had shown us, and further inquired of him whether it would be necessary to have a passport at our departure. He replied no. We inquired also whether it would be necessary to post up our names, as there is an established regulation that it should be done six weeks before leaving. To this he replied, if we were merchants, and owed anybody, it would be proper to do so, and then asked if such was the case with either of us. We answered no; then, he continued, it is not necessary. For all which we thanked his Excellency, and took our leave.

Reflecting upon this matter, we thought whether it would not be more respectful to make the voyage to Albany, than to leave, since we had several times requested permission to do so, and he had now granted it. Should we not go, it would perhaps not be well received by him, the more so as there would not be any vessel going to Boston for some weeks. Nevertheless, it was not bad that we had shown his Excellency it was not so important to us that we could not let it pass.

15th, Monday. We went in search of a boat to go to Albany, and found one ready to leave immediately. The name

[1] Since the revolution of 1672 in Holland, William III., Prince of Orange, afterward king of Great Britain, had been stadholder (governor) of that province, and of four others of the seven provinces of which the Dutch federal republic, the United Provinces, consisted. But the other two provinces, Friesland and Groningen, kept as their chief executive Count Henry Kasimir II. of Nassau-Dietz, a third cousin of the Prince of Orange. The stadholder of Friesland was not on good terms with his great relative, and under his lead Friesland stood somewhat aloof from the policies of the latter and of Their High Mightinesses the States-General of the United Provinces. The title His Royal Highness would be given to the Prince of Orange by Andros because of his recent marriage (1677) to the Princess Mary, daughter of the Duke of York and niece of Charles II.

[2] Pemaquid.

of the skipper was Meus[1] Hooghboom, to whom we agreed to pay, for the passage up and down, one beaver, that is, twenty-five guilders in *zeewant*, for each of us, and find ourselves. We gave him our names, to have them inserted in the passport.

Meanwhile we disposed of all our goods to M. de La Grange, upon the terms before mentioned, and received in pay peltries of every description. But, as we were not experienced in merchandise, and much less in peltries, we deemed it proper to have what we received, examined and valued against the goods sold, by Van Kleif, before named. He valued some of the peltries much less than they had been charged to us. But as there are few merchants who do not *hatchel* each other a little, so standing near this merchant you could see he was not free from this feeling, and you would believe, if he had owned our goods and been free to receive payment for them, in such kind of pay, he would have valued them much higher. However, there were three beavers among them which were not current; these De la Grange cheerfully took back, as they were not his, but had been borrowed by him of his nephew, in consequence of his not having enough of his own.

He was about to return to the South River, in order to bring on more goods, which he had there. His wife was going with him, to see if she would live there; for she seemed to take the subject to heart of separating herself from the sinful attachments of the world, giving up trade, and going to live upon the land and out of the land. His nephew was also going with them, for a pleasure trip, and to see the country, and especially to learn the way of trading. They were to leave this evening, having already dispatched the boat on Monday last.

16th, Tuesday. Before we proceed any further, I must here insert a very remarkable circumstance, for the comfort and joy of God's children, who rejoice with the holy and blessed angels over the repentance of one poor great sinner, more than over ninety and nine just men, who need no repentance. The old man and his wife with whom we lodged had several children, the husband and wife each three by former marriages, and one between themselves. The husband's children by his former wife were two daughters and one son. One of the

---

[1] *Meus* for Bartholomaeus, Bartholomew.

daughters was married to Gerrit, the wheelwright, who had married her in New Netherland, but upon the first change in the government[1] she left for Holland, and he followed her there after a little time, and kept house at Swol [Zwolle]; but not being able, after several years, to succeed very well in the Netherlands, he came back in the same ship with us, leaving his wife and children behind at Zwolle. Finding matters go on here to his wishes, he sent for his family by Captain Jacob, of the ship *Beaver*. This is Gerrit the wheelwright, or carpenter, whom we have mentioned several times in our journal.[2] Another daughter lived still at Amsterdam, for whom he has given us several messages and a letter to take when we leave. His son is a carpenter in the East Indies. The children of the old woman were a daughter named Geesie, married here in New York to one Peter Denis, weighmaster; another daughter, named Rebecca, was also married here with one Arie, who gained his livelihood by cultivating land and raising cattle, but kept a tavern, or drinking house, having a situation therefor, and living upon a delightful spot at the Vers Water (Fresh Water), a little out of town; and a son, named Theunis, who was married and had six children, and who supported himself by farming at Sapokanike. The old couple had one child between them, named Willem, now about twenty-three years old, a carpenter by trade, a little rough and coarse, but otherwise not an unjust kind of a person, according to the world. He lived at home with his parents, where we lodged.[3] He was somewhat wronged in his inheritance, as the old people acknowledged, and we reproved them for it. They promised amendment.

Now the before named Theunis had led a very godless life,

---

[1] When the English conquered New Netherland, in 1664. Zwolle is in the province of Overyssel. The old man was Jacob Hellekers, his daughter's husband Gerrit van Duyn. See p. 36, note 2. In fact, however, Gerrit had not gone back to Holland till 1670, nor his wife till 1671.

[2] See pp. 36, 43, 49, 68, 169, 171, 228.

[3] Jacob Hellekers's wife was Theuntje Theunis. She was thrice married: to Ide ———, to Jacob Hellekers, to Jan Strijker. Peter Denys of Emmerich was farmer of the weigh-house; for Arie or Adriaen Corneliszen, see p. 47, note 1; Theunis Idenszen, a man of forty-one at this time, was assessor of the out ward in 1687, was married to Jannetje Thyssen, and had six children; Willem Hellekers was constable of the east ward in 1691.

and had been wild and reckless, extraordinarily covetous, addicted to cursing and swearing, and despising all religious things; but he was not a drunkard, nor was he unchaste, though he previously had taken something that did not belong to him. In a word, he was ignorant of the truth and a godless man, yet his evil and wickedness were more in the spirit than in the flesh. Nevertheless, it appears that God had purposes of grace in regard to him, and the time was approaching when God would touch him and draw him to Him. He had long since felt his conscience gnawing him for his godless life, and that with a strength which very much increased his chagrin. He became meagre in body, his eyes were sunken in his head, he was sombre of speech, he sought solitude in order to fly from the evil, but found it was augmented manifold; and gradually began to long for deliverance and a better life. The devil had been assailing him for six years past, and he was therefore in a miserable state, of both soul and body. Thus he was when, by God's providence, we arrived in the country, and went to lodge at his mother's house, as we have related. We had been at the house only two or three days, when he also came there. I was writing in the front room, and my comrade was with me. He heard us talking together about God, and the Christian life in general, which so affected him that he said to himself, "O God! what men are these? Where did they come from? Are there such people still in the world?" This he told us afterwards. However, it took such hold of his heart, that he more earnestly resolved to reform his life, while the devil, being more displeased, assailed him the more violently. His wife was a very ill-natured woman, scolding, growling, cursing and swearing at him, as well as at their children, and constantly finding fault with him, through her avarice, because he did not do more work, although he wrought continually, and as much as three other men. Their children, collectively, were very bad and saucy, and cursed and swore at each other, except the oldest, a daughter, who appeared to be the best of them. This man being in such a state was pressed on all sides. He sometimes, but not often, came to our house, and as we knew nothing of his condition, we only addressed to him occasionally a general remark. However, his time and that of the Lord were approaching. He heard a sermon upon the requisites of communicants of the Lord's supper, which he had never as yet enjoyed; and was thrown very much aback, abhorring himself and many others, who went to it, yet pursued as wicked lives as he did. For himself, he saw no probability of his ever being able to partake of it, conscious as he was of his being wicked and unworthy. He saw no means of release, and found no help or consolation wherever he went or came. To go to his minister would, he thought, render him little good, as he knew by several examples. He kept his condition concealed from us, and did not dare speak to us, so that he was in distress for himself, his family, and his entire state, and often wishing to die. This caused him to live in continual variance and quarrelling with his neighbors. He lost several cows and other cattle, by which he suffered great damage. A little daughter, about fourteen years old, who lived with her grandmother, was so badly ruptured, that there was no probability of her being cured, or ever being fit to be married. He had bought a piece of land, in common with Arie, his brother-in-law, to make tillable land out of the rough woods. It was to him like dead fruit. He worked on it three times as much as the other did, in felling and chopping trees, and making the best of it into timber, which was carried to the city with little or no profit to him, but to the people to whom Arie was indebted. Differences arose between them as to the land and labor, and it was therefore proposed to divide it, and separate; but, as has been before mentioned, they had begun to clear off a part of it, and they could not agree which should have the cleared land, where he had bestowed so much labor. Great bitterness sprang out of it, when the mother and friends interposed, and settled the difficulty as well as they could. Theunis obtained the cleared land on condition he should make some indemnity to the other; and a part of the land, where he had worked like a mole, and bought and paid for, should be given up by him. He had a very large and beautiful canoe, which was worth much to him, and had been very serviceable to him; this was entirely dashed to pieces by a northwest storm, as Sapocanikke, where he resided and the canoe lay, makes with this wind a flat lee shore. Although his neighbors could have prevented the breaking of the canoe, if they had done as they ought to have done, they had not at

least attempted to prevent it. He had a fine large negro, a
slave, whom he had long possessed, and taught to work and
speak good Dutch; who had done him great service, and he
had much love for him. The negro was riding on horseback,
when the horse ran away with him, and he fell and was injured
internally in the breast. He became sick, supposing it was a
cold, and died in a few days. This event caused great sorrow
to him, his wife, and his whole family, as also to all his friends;
for it was a severe blow and damage to him. He was once
working in the field, and his wife was called to help one of the
cows which was sick and in a bad condition. This happened
eight or ten times at night as well as in the day, whereby he
and his wife had no rest night or day. He was on one occasion
attending her, when word came to them that one of their little
daughters had fallen dead in the barn, and indeed they knew
no better, for she lay in a swoon as if dead; at which they were
all much frightened and out of their senses. Thus he had one
blow after another. The child, who was about nine or ten
years old, came to, when they thought her arm was broken,
or at least her shoulder out of joint, for she had fallen from a
great height. She was brought in that condition to her grandmother's, at our lodgings, to be cured, which was effected after
some time. He has also had several mishaps in the woods in
chopping and felling trees; and had about this time an accident which broke him down. Having felled a tree, it remained
hanging with its branches in the limbs of another one, and in
endeavoring to pull it out his whole hand was crushed so that
all his fingers festered. This happened shortly after the others.
All these misfortunes depressed this poor man very much, and
daily increased his anguish. He could not sleep, and found
rest nowhere. He did nothing but sigh and complain of inward
trouble. When we heard all these things, we said several times
to each other, the Lord has certainly some intention in regard
to this man and this household: the Lord visits this man; although we did not doubt there was something of the evil one.

About this time he came to our house, and we embraced
the opportunity to speak to him, which we did with great
earnestness and affection, by which he was strengthened, and
went home contented. But it did not continue long. He became very much disturbed and troubled. He went in the fields

to plough, and the horses began to neigh and bellow, and would not stand still an instant, springing and jumping, entangling themselves together, foaming and fuming so that he did not know what course to pursue. As to himself, he became so frightened and perplexed, so confused that he did not know what he did or where he was; he was bewildered, and his whole understanding lost; he was like one blind; he wanted to go to the house, and ran hither and thither, through water and everywhere, his hat off his head, and across the fields, and thus reached home. His wife and children were frightened because he looked so horrible and disfigured. He demanded a rope and wanted to harm himself, for he said he could live no longer. The wife and children cried; neighbors were sent for; one of the children brought the grandmother and Rebecca, his sister, from the city. This was on Tuesday, the 16th of April, in the afternoon. My comrade was in the front room when the news came, though there were no particulars. He came to me in the back room sorrowful, and said to me, "*Vous ne savez que le malin a eu possession sur nostre pauvre homme.*" [1] "What man?" I asked. "Our Theunis," he replied, "word came that he had hanged himself, and afterwards that they did not know whether he was alive." We were alarmed; the old woman, his mother, had gone to him; and after waiting a little time, we also determined to go, and as we were a little quicker on foot we reached Sapocanike almost as soon as she did. As we approached the house we heard the lamentations of the women and children; and on entering we found there no one except the mother, the sister Rebecca, and a female neighbor who was a *faus pieuse.* [2] As soon as we came in, he stood up and came to meet us, holding out his hand, and calling out: "Friends, is there still grace with God, is there still grace for me with God?" We grasped his hand and said: "Yes, there is grace for you with God, and for all repentant sinners." He exclaimed, "What wickedness have I committed! how have I sinned! how have I stolen God's honor, His name profaned with vile oaths, his sabbaths violated, his word despised! how godless have I lived, and run from Him! But He has overtaken me. How has the devil troubled and tempted me, how has

[1] "You do not know that the devil has taken possession of our poor man."
[2] "Woman of pretended piety."

he for six years assailed me, seeing that I no longer wished to serve him! And now when God comes to touch me and draw me, he seeks to devour me; but he shall not have me. God who protects me is stronger than he," and much more of similar import. We then spoke to him according to his state and condition, which did him much good. This *pieuse* prated also after her manner, but we tempered her down a little. She had urged him very strongly to go and sit down and read I know not what kind of a book; for, she said, she had also been in such a state, and that reading had done her much good. She was much astonished at our saying he should not read, which could be done afterwards, and would benefit him when he should be well and quiet, and felt a desire and longing for it; that he should now, if he could, go to work at what had to be done or he had an inclination to do, whether in the barn among the grain or in the stalls among the cattle, or any other necessary work. We exhorted him to put his trust in God, to pray to Him and cleave to Him; the devil would then have no more power over him, as this perhaps was his last attack. He said, "I fear him no more, God will protect me; I feel more tranquil, I will not yield." We told him what he must do in future. He answered, "I hope and trust it will go well." He thanked us very much and added, "Friends, you are the cause that I still live and of my preservation." We told him it was God to whom he must give the honor and thank for His grace and mercy; and that we would perhaps call the next day, if we did not leave, at which he was glad. We wanted to give a strong admonition to his wife and children, for they had great need of it, and in order that a greater impression might be made upon them by this circumstance. Returning home, we were affected by the grace of God towards a poor sinner, who truly told us things from the bottom of his heart which were from God and His Spirit, according to His word and our experience. In leaving we told his wife how she must keep her eye on him, and conduct herself towards him.

17th, *Wednesday.* We went to inquire whether the boat was going up the river to-day, but it could not be got ready. In the afternoon we went to visit Theunis again, whom we found at home quiet and calm. He received us kindly, and we asked him how he was. "Very well," he said, "I am as much relieved as if I had a great burden taken from my shoulders." He had rested well during the night. We praised God, and exhorted him to perseverance, and to trust in Him. "Trust in Him," he said. "I know as well that I am a child of God as that I stand here, and I have no fear of the devil any more. I know he can trouble me, but he shall no longer have power over me." We told him he must take care of his affairs, and work when he felt inclined. "Work," he said, "I have no more work. It is as if it were Sunday. I know that the cattle must be taken care of and other things must be done, but that concerns me not. I have no work, and will not work again as I have done before. God will take care of me." We admonished him that he himself and his whole family ought to go learn and be reformed. "That I will do," he replied, "if it please God, and if she will only listen and learn; but if she will not I cannot help it." We read to him some portions of scripture, as Matt. v. 6, John xvi. 17, Matt. vii. 8, of the carefulness of the world, by which he found himself comforted, and promised he would avoid the world as much as he could, and wished he could fulfill his inclination and go and live alone in the woods, away from wicked men, for it was impossible to live near them and not sin as they do. "Could I only go up the river," said he, "with you and everywhere you go! Oh, that I were a young man; I would not leave you." You could see that he spoke with earnestness and from the uprightness of his soul.

19th, *Friday.* We had been several times for our passport, which we supposed would be a special one granted by his Excellency to us, but in that we were mistaken. Our names were merely added to the common passport to go up and down the river, as the names of all the passengers were written on it. We left New York about three o'clock in the afternoon with a southerly wind, in company with about twenty passengers of all kinds, young and old, who made great noise and bustle in a boat not so large as a common ferry-boat in Holland; and as these people live in the interior of the country somewhat nearer the Indians, they are more wild and untamed, reckless, unrestrained, haughty, and more addicted to misusing the blessed name of God and to cursing and swearing. However there was no help for it; you have to go with those with whom

you are shipped.   We were scarcely in the North River when
we saw a ship coming through the Narrows, but as it was so
far off we could not discern what vessel it was. Each passenger had his own opinion on the subject.   After we had
sailed along for half an hour we heard five or six guns fired
from the fort and otherwise, which was a proof that she was
from sea.   As we were sailing along a boat came up to us but
lost her mast in boarding us.   She was to the leeward and we
were sailing before the wind with a good headway.   She came
too near our yard-arm, which carried away her mast, and it
was lucky she was not upset.   They put on board some tons
of oysters, which are not to be found at Fort Albany or away
from salt water.   In passing Sapocanike we saw Theunis
standing upon an eminence where he was busy ploughing, and
observing us as long as he could.   We made rapid progress,
but with the night the wind slackened, and we were compelled
to come to anchor in order to stem the tide.

   20th, Saturday.   When the day broke we saw how far we
had advanced.   We were at the entrance of the Highlands,
which are high and rocky, and lie on both sides of the river.
While waiting there for the tide and wind another boat came
alongside of us.   They had a very fine fish, a striped bass, as
large as a codfish.   The skipper was a son-in-law of D. Schaets,
the minister at Albany, a drunken, worthless person who could
not keep house with his wife, who was not much better than
he, nor was his father-in-law.   He had been away from his
wife five or six years, and was now going after her.[1]   The wind
coming out of the south about nine o'clock we weighed anchor,
and got under sail.   It gradually increased until we had drifted
through the Highlands, which is regarded as no small advantage whenever they wish to sail up or down the river; because,
if they do not have a fresh breeze aft, they cannot have much
favorable wind, as in blowing crosswise over the Highlands it
blows above the vessel, and sometimes comes down in whirlwinds which are dangerous.   In the evening we sailed before
the Hysopus, where some of the passengers desired to be put
ashore, but it blew too hard and we had too much headway.

   [1] Domine Schaets's son-in-law was Thomas Davidtse Kekebel or Kieckebuls.
His wife had been sent away from Albany by the magistrates.   In 1681 she and
her husband came into a final concord; *Doc. Hist. N. Y.*, quarto ed., III. 534.

It did not seem to be very important. In consequence of the river above the Hysopus being difficult to navigate, and beset with shoals and passages, and of the weather being rainy with no moon, we could not proceed without continual danger of running aground, and so came to anchor.

21st, Easter Sunday. The wind was against us and calm, but we advanced as far as the Noorman's Kill,[1] where we were compelled to come to anchor, on account of the strong current running down the river. We went ashore here to walk about a little. There are two high falls on this kill, where the beautiful green water comes falling over incessantly, in a manner wonderful to behold, when you consider the power, wisdom, and directions of God. The water was the greenest I had observed, not only on the South River, but in all New Netherland. Leaving the cause of it for further inquiry, I mention it merely in passing. At the falls on this river stands a fine saw-mill which has wood enough to saw. The man who lives there, although not the mildest, treated us nevertheless reasonably well. He set before us shad which had been caught the day before, and was very good, better, we thought, than the same fish in Fatherland. I observed along the shore, trees which they call in Holland the tree of life, such as we have in our garden,[2] but they grow here beautiful and large, like firs. I picked up a small stone in which there was some crystal, and you could see how the crystal was formed in the stone.

A breeze springing up from the south caused us to hurry on board the yacht, which we saw was making sail. We reached her after a good time of hard rowing, and were quite tired before we did so. The breeze did not continue a long time, and we came to anchor again. After several stoppages we proceeded to-day as far as Kinderhook.

22d, Monday. We had again this morning a southerly breeze, which carried us slowly along until noon, when we came to anchor before the *Fuyck*, and Fort Albany or Orange.[3]

---

[1] Cats Kill. The falls alluded to are the Kaaterskill Falls.

[2] The garden of the Thetinga State, the manor-house at Wieuwert. The tree is the arbor-vitæ.

[3] The *fuyck* is a hoop-net used for catching fish. Its shape is that of a truncated cone. The ground-plan of Albany (see p. 216, *post*, and the plan of 1695 in Rev. John Miller's *Description of New York*) had that shape.

Every one stepped ashore at once, but we did not know where to go. We first thought of taking lodgings with our skipper, but we had been warned that his house was unregulated and poorly kept. M. van Cleif, wishing to do us a kindness, had given us a letter of recommendation to Mr. Robert Sanders,[1] and M. de la Grange had also presented us to the same friend. We went ashore just as preaching was over, to deliver our letter. This person, as soon as he saw us at his house, was pleased and received us with every attention, and so did all his family, giving us a chamber for our accommodation. We did not remain his debtors in heartily serving him in what was necessary, whether by instruction, admonition or reproof, which he always received kindly, as it seemed, promising himself as well as all his family to reform, which was quite necessary.

23d, *Tuesday.* Mr. Sanders having provided us with horses, we rode out about nine o'clock to visit the Cahoos, which is the falls of the great Maquaas Kill,[2] which are the greatest falls, not only in New Netherland, but in North America, and perhaps, as far as is known, in the whole New World.[3] We rode for two hours over beautiful, level, tillable land along the river, when we obtained a guide who was better acquainted with the road through the woods. He rode before us on horseback. In approaching the Cahoos from this direction, the roads are hilly, and in the course of half an hour you have steep hills, deep valleys, and narrow paths, which run round the precipices, where you must ride with care, in order to avoid the danger of falling over them, as sometimes happens. As you come near the falls, you can hear the roaring which makes everything tremble, but on reaching them and looking at them you see something wonderful, a great manifestation of God's power and sovereignty, of His wisdom and glory. We arrived there about noon. They are on one of the two branches into which the North River is divided up above, of

[1] Robert Sanders of Albany was a prominent Indian trader, skilled in Indian languages.

[2] Mohawk River.

[3] The falls of Niagara had been mentioned by Cartier and by Champlain, but the first full description of them, that of Hennepin in his *Description de la Louisiane,* was not published till 1683.

almost equal size. This one turns to the west out of the high land, and coming here finds a blue rock which has a steep side, as long as the river is broad, which according to my calculation is two hundred paces or more, and rather more than less, and about one hundred feet high.[1] The river has more water at one time than another; and was now about six or eight feet deep. All this volume of water coming on this side fell head-long upon a stony bottom, this distance of an hundred feet. Any one may judge whether that was not a spectacle, and whether it would not make a noise. There is a continual spray thrown up by the dashing of the water, and when the sun shines the figure of a rainbow may be seen through it. Sometimes there are two or three of them to be seen, one above the other, according to the brightness of the sun and its paral-lax. There was now more water than usual in consequence of its having rained hard for several days, and the snow water having begun to run down from the high land.

On our return we stopped at the house of our guide, whom we had taken on the way up, where there were some families of Indians living. Seeing us, they said to each other, "Look, these are certainly real Dutchmen, actual Hollanders." Rob-ert Sanders asked them how they knew it. We see it, they said, in their faces and in their dress. "Yes," said one, "they have the clothes of real Hollanders; they look like brothers." They brought us some ground-nuts, but although the Dutch call them so, they were in fact potatoes, for of ground-nuts, or *mice with tails*,[2] there are also plenty. They cooked them, and gave us some to eat, which we did. There was a canoe made of the bark of trees, and the Indians have many of them for the purpose of making their journeys. It was fifteen or sixteen feet or more in length. It was so light that two men could easily carry it, as the Indians do in going from one stream or lake to another. They come in such canoes from Canada, and from places so distant we know not where. Four or five of them stepped into this one and rowed lustily through the water with great speed, and when they came back with the current they seemed to fly. They did this to amuse us at the request of Mr. Sanders. Leaving there for home,

---

[1] The falls at Cohoes are at present about 900 feet broad and 75 feet high.
[2] Peanuts.

we came again to the house of one Fredrick Pieters,[1] where we had stopped in riding out.   He is one of the principal men of Albany, and this was his farm; he possesses good information and judgment.   My comrade had some conversation with him.   He expected us, and now entertained us well.   My comrade was in pain from eating the ground-nuts.   On arriving home in the evening, the house was full of people, attracted there out of curiosity, as is usually the case in small towns, where every one in particular knows what happens in the whole place.

24th, Wednesday.   My comrade's pain continued through the night, although he had taken his usual medicine, and he thought he would become better by riding on horseback. The horses were got ready, and we left about eight o'clock for Schoonechtendeel,[2] a place lying about twenty-four miles west or north-west of Albany towards the country of the Mohawks. We rode over a fine, sandy cart road through woods of nothing but beautiful evergreens or fir trees, but a light and barren soil.   My companion grew worse instead of better.   It was noon when we reached there, and arrived at the house of a good friend of Robert Sanders.   As soon as we entered my comrade had to go and lie down.   He had a high fever, and was covered up warm.   I went with Sanders to one Adam,[3] and to examine the flats which are exceedingly rich land.   I spoke to several persons of the Christian life, each one according to his state and as it was fit.

25th, Thursday.   We had thought of riding a little further on, and so back to Albany; but my comrade was too sick, and had the chills and fever again.   The weather, too, was windy and rainy.   We concluded therefore to postpone it till the following day; and in the meantime I accompanied Sanders to the before mentioned Adam's.   While we were there, a certain Indian woman, or half-breed, that is, from a European and an

---

[1] No Frederick Pieters seems to be known.   It was perhaps Philip Pieterse Schuyler, progenitor of a distinguished family, who lived on a large farm at the flats below West Troy.

[2] Schenectady, of which Danckaerts tried to make Dutch words, quasi "beautiful section."

[3] Probably Adam Vrooman, who at the time of the general massacre by the Indians, 1690, defended his house with great courage and success.

Indian woman, came with a little boy, her child, who was dumb, or whose tongue had grown fast. It was about four years old; she had heard we were there, and came to ask whether we knew of any advice for her child, or whether we could not do a little something to cure it. We informed her we were not doctors or surgeons, but we gave her our opinion, just as we thought.[1] Sanders told me aside that she was a Christian, that is, had left the Indians, and had been taught by the Christians and baptized; that she had made profession of the reformed religion, and was not of the unjust. Not contenting myself with this account, and observing something in her that pleased me, I asked her to relate to me herself how it had gone with her from the first of her coming to Christendom, both outwardly and inwardly. Looking at me she said, "How glad am I that I am so fortunate; that God should permit me to behold such Christians, whom I have so long desired to see, and to whom I may speak from the bottom of my heart without fear; and that there are such Christians in the world. How often have I asked myself, are there no other Christians than those amongst whom we live, who are so godless and lead worse lives than the Indians, and yet have such a pure and holy religion? Now I see God thinks of us, and has sent you from the other end of the world to speak to us." She had heard me give reasons to the others, and address them generally, before I made this request of her. I answered, that all who professed the Christian religion did not live as that religion required, that such were false professors, and not Christians, bearing the name only, but denying the truth. She had said all this with a tender and affectionate heart, and with many tears, but tears which you felt proceeded from the heart, and from love towards God. I was surprised to find so far in the woods, and among Indians—but why say among Indians? among Christians ten times worse than Indians—a person who should address me with such affection and love of God; but I answered and comforted her. She then related to me from the beginning her case, that is, how she had embraced Christianity. She was born of a Christian father and an Indian

---

[1] But it appears from the report of a physician and several surgeons, printed in *Ecclesiastical Records of New York*, II. 869–871, that in 1683 "Dr. Vorstman" (Peter Sluyter) attempted to practise medicine, and with disastrous results.

mother, of the Mohawk tribes. Her mother remained in the country, and lived among the Mohawks, and she lived with her, the same as Indians live together. Her mother would never listen to anything about the Christians, or it was against her heart, from an inward, unfounded hate. She lived then with her mother and brothers and sisters; but sometimes she went with her mother among the Christians to trade and make purchases, or the Christians came among them, and thus it was that some Christians took a fancy to the girl, discovering in her more resemblance to the Christians than the Indians, but understand, more like the Dutch, and that she was not so wild as the other children. They therefore wished to take the girl and bring her up, which the mother would not hear to, and as this request was made repeatedly, she said she would rather kill her. The little daughter herself had no disposition at first to go; and the mother did nothing more with the daughter than express continually her detestation and abhorrence of the Christians. This happened several times, when the daughter began to mistrust that the Christians were not such as the mother told her; the more so, because she never went among them without being well treated, and obtaining something or other. She therefore began to hearken to them; but particularly she felt a great inclination and love in her heart towards those Christians who spoke to her about God, and of Christ Jesus and the Christian religion. Her mother observed it, and began to hate her and not treat her as well as she had done before. Her brothers and sisters despised and cursed her, threw stones at her, and did her all the wrong they could; but the more they abused and maltreated her, the more she felt something growing in her that attracted and impelled her towards the Christians and their doctrine, until her mother and the others could endure her no longer; while she, feeling her love of the Christians, and especially of their religion, which she called their doctrine, to increase more and more, could no longer live with the Indians. They ceased not seeking to wrong her, and compelled her to leave them, as she did, and went to those who had so long solicited her. They gave her the name of Eltie or Illetie.[1] She lived a long time with a woman, with whom we conversed afterwards, who

[1] Aletta.

taught her to read and write and do various handiwork, in which she advanced so greatly that everybody was astonished. She had especially a great desire to learn to read, and applied herself to that end day and night, and asked others, who were near her, to the vexation and annoyance of the other maids, who lived with her, who could sometimes with difficulty keep her back. But that did not restrain her; she felt such an eagerness and desire to learn that she could not be withheld, particularly when she began to understand the Dutch language, and what was expressed in the New Testament, where her whole heart was. In a short time, therefore, she understood more about it than the other girls with whom she conversed, and who had first instructed her, and, particularly, was sensible in her heart of its truth. She had lived with different people, and had very much improved; she spoke of it with heart-felt delight. Finally, she made her profession, and was baptized.[1] Since that time, she said, the love she felt in her heart had not diminished, but had increased, and she sighed to live near Christians, who were good and faithful, and lived up to their religion. Therefore it was that she was so glad to see us, and that God, who had so loved her before, still so loved her as to permit her to see and speak to us, "*me*," she said, "who have been such a heathen." I told her that God had showed her still more love, as she well knew. She believed it, she said, melting into tears, but she could not express her heart. "Might I only live with such people, how would my heart do good." "Blessed are they who hunger and thirst after righteousness, for they shall be satisfied," I repeated to her, and further expressed what was necessary. "How many times," said she, "have I grieved over these Christians, not daring to speak out my heart to any one, for when I would sometimes rebuke them a little for their evil lives, drunkenness, and foul and godless language, they would immediately say: 'Well, how is this, there is a sow converted. Run, boys, to the brewer's, and bring some swill for a converted sow,' words which went through my heart, made me sorrowful and closed my mouth. But I see that God still thinks of me and loves me, now that he causes me to see and converse with

[1] The record of baptisms of the Dutch church at Schenectady does not begin till 1694.

such people as you." We told her she must so much the more
receive with love and affection what we said to her, out of regard to God and her soul. "Oh!" said she, "what you have
told me is as dear to me as my heart," and she spoke with such
feeling and tenderness, such depth of love, that I cannot describe it, and it affected me. Yes, she expressed to me more
reality of the truth of Christianity, through the emotions of
her heart, although in language according to the genius of the
person, which nevertheless was nothing but loving—more, I
said, than any one, whether minister or other person, in all
New Netherland. She had a brother who was also a half-
breed, who had made profession of Christianity, and had been
baptized, and who was not by far as good as she, but on the
contrary very wicked; though, I believe, he has been better,
and has been corrupted by the conversation of impious Hollanders; for this place is a godless one, being without a minister,
and having only a homily read on Sundays.[1] He was married,
and so was she. She has some children; her husband is not
as good as she is, though he is not one of the worst; she sets
a good example before him, and knows how to direct him.

She has a nephew, a full-blooded Mohawk, named Wouter.
The Lord has also touched him, through her instrumentality.
Wouter speaks no Dutch, or very little. He has abandoned
all the Indians, and his Indian friends and relations, and lives
with his uncle, the brother of Illetie. He has betaken himself
entirely to the Christians and dresses like them. He has suffered much from the other Indians and his friends. He has
such a love and comprehension of God, such reverence and
humility towards Him and what is godly, that it is a joy to
hear him speak. His thoughts are occupied night and day
with God and Jesus Christ, wondering about God and His
mercy, that he should cause him to know Him, to comprehend Him, and to serve Him. He is endeavoring to learn the
Dutch language, so as to be instructed in Christianity, and to
be among good Christians who live like Christians. That was
all his desire, thinking all the time about it, speaking always
with Illetie about it, who assisted and instructed him as much

[1] There was a church, and Domine Gideon Schaets came over from Albany
four times a year to administer the sacrament, but there was no settled minister
till the call of Domine Petrus Tesschenmaker in 1684.

as she could, and always with love, with which God much blessed her. His uncle, with whom he lived, was covetous, and kept him only because he was profitable to him in hunting beaver. He therefore would hardly speak a word of Dutch to him, in order that he might not be able to leave him too soon, and go among the Christians and under Christianity. He sent him to the woods and among the Indians, for the sake of the devilish profit of the world—these are the words of Robert Sanders, and Illetie said not much less; yet this poor creature has, nevertheless, such a great inclination and longing after Christianity.

Besides this inward desire, propensity and feeling, God, the Lord, has given him outward proofs of His love and protection, and among other instances I will relate these two which I well remember. It happened once that his uncle went out a shooting with him in the woods, when the uncle began to sneer at him, saying that he, a mere stupid Indian, could not shoot, but a Christian was a different character and was expert and handy: that he, Wouter, would not shoot anything that day, but he himself would have a good hunt. To which Wouter replied, "It is well, I cannot help it; I will have whatever God sends me." Upon this they separated from each other in the woods, and each went where he thought best. "Now when I was tired out," said Wouter, for we heard it from himself, as well as from his aunt, "and had travelled and hunted the whole day without finding any game, with the evening approaching, grieved that I had shot nothing and troubled at the reproach of my uncle, my heart looked up to God; I fell upon my knees and prayed to Him, that although I was no Christian (he meant baptized), I loved God, and only longed to learn the language in order to be instructed in Christianity, and would receive it with my whole heart; that God would be pleased to send to me a wild animal to shoot, so that the slur, which my uncle had thrown upon me, might be wiped off." While thus down on his knees, with his hat hanging upon a bough which was bent down,[1] his prayer not finished, there comes and stands before him a very young deer, not twenty

---

[1] Methinks he was moved by seeing this bended branch, to bend himself before God, and therefore hung his hat upon it; though I dare not so affirm certainly.—*Note of the journalist.*

paces off; it comes softly up to him; his gun rests alongside
of him loaded; he takes aim, shoots, and hits the deer in the
breast, and the creature drops before him on its two fore feet
and there remains. Without going to the deer, he thanks
God upon his knees that he had heard his prayer and had
turned back the reproach. "Oh," said he, "now do I know
there is a God, who is in the woods also, and hears, loves, and
thinks of me there." He comes to the deer, which is a young
buck two or three years old, as fat and beautiful as he had ever
seen in his life, and takes it upon his shoulders and goes with
joy to his uncle, whom he found, and asked where was his good
hunt and the game he had shot. His uncle was angry and
spoke angrily, saying he had been going the whole day, tired
and weary, without seeing or shooting anything, and had come
there to look after chestnuts. "That is well, that is good,"
said Wouter, "reproach the Indians no more for not being good
shooters. Look at what God has given me upon my prayer;"
for he was very glad at what had occurred. The uncle
stood and looked, and knew not what to say, being ashamed at
what he heard and saw, and of himself. Wouter said further,
"I know there has been no wild animal round about here, for
I have explored the whole place, far and near, without being
able to discover any; and now in so short a time this one presented itself before me, and it is, therefore, certain that God
placed it there or caused it to come there. I have no doubt of
it." Although the uncle was ashamed, he was not much
affected by the circumstance, and still less humiliated or improved. But Elletie had taken it strongly to heart, and when
they both told it to us, we were affected by it ourselves, and
saw God in it more than he had done.

Another occasion was during the last harvest, in the year
1679, while he was out in the woods hunting beavers. He had
then had a successful time and had killed some beavers, the
flesh of which he used for food, and had nothing else to eat.
The flesh of the beaver, although we never relished it, is esteemed by others a great delicacy. Nevertheless, as we have
been told by those who are well acquainted with it, it is a kind
of food with which they soon become satiated. He also became tired of it; and not having anything else became sad.
He felt his heart boil—this is his own expression—and fell

down upon his knees and prayed that God who had heard him before, might be pleased now again to hear him and give him other food, not so much to satisfy him, as to show that he was God and loved him—a God whom the Indians did not know, but for whom he felt he had a greater hunger than his hunger for outward food, or for what the Indians usually were satisfied with, which is beaver and beaver meat, that is, to hunt successfully and trade the skins, which is all they go out hunting for; but that he felt something else, a hunger which could not be satisfied with this food and such like; that he felt more hunger after other food than what the Indians satisfied themselves with; and sought to be a Christian, and no longer to be an Indian.

While in the midst of his prayer, there stood a fine deer before him, which he aimed at and felled at one shot. He quickly loaded his gun again, and had scarcely done so, when he saw close to him a young buffalo. He levelled his gun and brought it down; but on running up to it, he came to himself, his heart was disturbed, and he became anxious and ashamed in considering his covetousness, that he had not thanked God for the first small animal; so that he could go no further from joy and fear. He fell upon his knees before God, in great humility, shame, and reverence, confessing his fault and his want of gratitude, praying God to forgive him, and thanking Him now for both; saying that through his unthankfulness for the first one, he was not worthy to have the second and larger one.

This may be believed as the true meaning and almost the very words of the Indian, for they were repeated to us from him in his presence, Illetie, who first told us, interpreting after him in the presence of five or six persons who were well versed in the Mohawk language, and bore testimony that he said what she interpreted, and that it was not enlarged.

Thus continuing to long after something which he did not have, and being yet in the woods returning home, he came to a bush which was growing in the shape of a man's hand, and which he stopped to look at and speculate upon. He wondered at it, and his heart was disturbed and began to *boil*. He fell down upon his knees by the bush, striking his hands into it, and prayed: "Oh God! you cause to come before me a sign or image of what I want and for which I hunger and long. It is true I have two hands with which I hunt and shoot and do other things, but I feel I still require a hand to help me, more serviceable than those I have and use, and stronger and wiser than mine. I am in want of a third hand. It is true I have forsaken the Indians and have come among Christians, but this cannot help me unless a third power make me a true Christian, and enable me to learn the language, that I may inquire, read, and enter into the grounds of Christianity." This he did with great tenderness and love; and being so much affected, he cut off the bush and took it with him in remembrance of his feelings and the outpouring of his heart to God, more than for the rarity of the figure in which it had grown. This stick or bush we have seen ourselves and had in our hands. He presented it to Robert Sanders, who carried it to Albany.

His aunt, Illetie, had taught him as well as she could, how he must pray, which she recommended to him to do every time he returned home, morning or evening, or on any other occasion which might happen to him, which he always did with concern and anxiety of heart. He always rejoiced at the proofs of God's [care] over him, and was sorry that he could not improve them, hoping and believing that God would yet give him what he still wanted and hungered after. I asked Illetie, who first told me all this, why they did not take him to some place where he could learn the language, and some handiwork, with reading and writing and the like, and especially where he might be brought to the knowledge and practice of Christianity. She said there were two impediments, first his uncle, whom we have mentioned, who only kept him as a kind of servant, such as the English have, for the sake of vile gain; and, although he was free, and bound to nobody, would never speak a word of Dutch to him, so that he might not lose him. The other difficulty was, that as he was of age, 24 or 26 years old, or thereabouts, no one would receive him for his board and clothing, fearful he would not learn the one or other handiwork, and would therefore be a loss to them. Whereupon I said if he would go with us we would give him board and clothing for all his life, and he should never be our servant or slave, and would be free and clear of all obligation; and if God should give him further the grace he would be our brother and as free as we were. "Oh," said she, "how happy he would be if he should be so fortunate, and God so honored him, as I must shame myself for the honor and happiness He causes me in enabling me to speak with you about these things." I spoke to her further what I thought would serve for her edification and consolation; and told her as my comrade was sick and not able to go out, and the weather was too rainy, she must come to us in the evening, and bring Wouter with her, that we might see him, and converse with him.

I thereupon went home and told my comrade my adventure, who was rejoiced at it, and would expect her in the evening. Meanwhile he had become stronger. The parish prelector,[1] who is the son of minister Schaets, came to visit my comrade, and said he had heard of us, and had been desirous to converse with us. He was a little conceited, but my comrade having heard that he was the prelector, gave him a good lesson, at which he was not badly content, and with which he went away.

When evening came, so came Illetie with her husband, and Wouter, and Adam and his wife, with two or three others besides. We conversed together through Illetie, who interpreted to him from us, and to us from him, and he himself repeated all that Illetie had told me, as before related. We spoke to him from the bottom of our hearts, and he to us from the bottom of his heart and out of love to us. We exhorted, encouraged, and comforted him as much as he required, and his condition would permit. He thanked us with tenderness, that God had vouchsafed to cause him to see and speak with true Christians, with people whom he had so longed for, and with whom he wished to spend his life. "What would you be willing to give to do so?" my comrade asked. "Oh," said he, "all that I have in the world, and more if I had it, or it were in my power." We told him he must leave it to God's liberty, who would do what he pleased, would hear him, and release him when his time should come. After several episodes, we inquired of him what was his greatest wish and desire, his greatest hunger and strongest longing. "I know not justly what it is," he replied, "but I am like a person who has three knives or some other articles which are valuable, useful, and necessary,

---

[1] Parish clerk and lay reader. This was Reynier Schaets, chirurgeon and justice of the peace, killed in the massacre of 1690.

but has lost the one he has most need of, or is the most serviceable and necessary, and without which the others are of little
service. Thus I have forsaken my relatives, and all my friends,
my nation and country, which is good, and that is one of the
articles. Moreover, I have come among Christians, and Dutch,
and begun to know something of God, and that also is good,
and is the second one. But I am wanting something more than
these, and without which they are of no service to me, namely,
a knowledge of the Dutch language, ability to enter into the
grounds of Christianity, and become a good Christian." We
encouraged him, and assured him of the way of the Lord, that
God would hear his prayer, and fulfill his desire, according to
the words of the Lord Jesus: "Blessed are they who hunger
and thirst after righteousness, for they shall be satisfied."
"Oh," said he to Illetie, "how I love people who speak so
kindly and mildly, and know how to utter such sweet and
beautiful comparisons. Oh, what love I have for them!"

After we had addressed him and her, earnestly and in love,
and also the bystanders, to their shame and conviction, for
their godless lives, whereby they repelled the heathen and
wronged such as began to be drawn [to God] like these, and as
having a terrible judgment to expect which they could not
escape, Illetie said, yes, there were many Mohawk Indians,
who, if they were taught, as they seek to be, and had good
examples set before them by the Christians, by their lives,
and were not so deceived and cheated by the Christians who
ought to assist them, would listen; but now they were repulsed,
and the Jesuits who were among them, and whom Wouter had
heard preach several times in his own language, corrupted
them all. Having said all that was proper to them at this
time, we invoked upon them the blessing of God.

26th, Friday. Wouter was early at our house, in order to
assist in getting the horses ready. My comrade finding himself better, but still weak, we determined to leave, two of us
on horseback and he in a wagon belonging at Albany, which
we had the good fortune of meeting at Schoonechten, and in
which he could ride over a very comfortable road. It had
frozen quite hard during the night, but when the sun rose a
little, it became warm enough, especially in the woods, where
the wind, which was northwest, could not blow through. I

went to take my leave of several persons with whom I had conversed, and also of Illetie, consoling and strengthening her once more and committing her to God and His grace, and she leaving us with tenderness and many tears. At a place where we were taking our leave, the uncle of Wouter had come, who commenced saying in very good Dutch: "Well, gentlemen, I understand Wouter is going to Holland with you." We answered, we did not know it, nor had we thought of it, but nevertheless our hearts were good and tender enough to help him, both body and soul, in whatever the Lord had wrought in him, or should work in him, as far as we could, which we considered to be our duty, and not only our duty, but the duty of all Christians. If he wished to go to Holland, we would not prevent him, because any person who is free may go there if he chooses; and if he wished to go with us in the same ship in which we should go over, he was free and might act his mind; yes, if he wished to be in our company we should not be able to hinder him, and while he was free no one could prevent him, or ought to, but on the other hand should aid him; especially as all who bore the name of Christians ought to assist in bringing to Christ any one who hungered and thirsted after him as Wouter did. "Well," he asked, without any feeling, "what trade would you teach him?" "Whatever God wished," we answered. "And if he should be taken by the Turks," he continued, "who would be his security, and who would redeem him?" "Well," we asked, "if we were taken by the Turks who would be our security and redeem us? God gives no security and makes no agreement. Whoever wishes to be a Christian must believe and trust in Him, and follow Him in faith, and so must you, and I, and every one, who wishes to be a Christian." Some hard words passed also between Robert Sanders and him, about something relating to himself, namely, that Sanders had said the uncle only sought to keep Wouter on account of the profit to him. As the time called us to depart, we took our leave and left him standing there abashed. Having mounted our horses and entered the wagon, we rode from there about ten o'clock, over a smooth sandy road, and arrived at half-past three at Albany, or Fort Orange, where Sanders's wife was glad to see us, and where we were well received by his whole family.

This Schoonechtendeel is situated, as we have said, twenty-four miles west of Fort Albany, toward the country of the Mohawks, upon a good flat, high enough to be free from the overflowing of the water of the river, which sometimes overflows their cultivated lands which lie much lower. Their cultivated lands are not what they call in that country *valleyen*, but large flats between the hills, on the margin or along the side of the rivers, brooks or creeks, very flat and level, without a single tree or bush upon them, of a black sandy soil which is four and sometimes five or six feet deep, but sometimes less, which can hardly be exhausted. They cultivate it year after year, without manure, for many years. It yields large crops of wheat, but not so good as that raised in the woodland around the city of [New] York and elsewhere, nor so productively; the latter on the other hand produce a smaller quantity, but a whiter flour. The wheat which comes from this place, the Hysopus, and some other places is a little bluer. Much of the plant called dragon's blood grows about here, and also yearly a kind of small lemon or citron, of which a single one grows upon a bush. This bush grows about five feet high, and the fruit cannot be distinguished from any other citron in form, color, taste or quality. It grows wild about the city of New York, but not well. I have not heard of its growing in any other places.

The village proper of Schoon echten [Schenectady], is a square, set off by palisades. There may be about thirty houses, and it is situated on the side of the Maquas Kill [Mohawk River], a stream however they cannot use for carrying goods up or down in yachts or boats.[1] There are no fish in it except trout, sunfish, and other kinds peculiar to rivers, because the Cohoes stops the ascent of others, which is a great inconvenience for the *menage* and for bringing down the produce.

As soon as we arrived in Albany we went to our skipper Meus Hoogboom, to inquire when he was going to the city. He said to-morrow, but he said he would come and notify us of the time. We saw it would run on a much longer time, as it usually does in these parts.

[1] The form of Schenectady a few years later is shown in the map in Miller's *New York* (1695).

27th, Saturday. We went to call upon a certain Madam
Rentselaer, widow of the Heer Rentselaer, son of the Heer
Rentselaer of the colony named the colony of Rentselaerswyck,
comprising twelve miles square from Fort Orange, that is,
twenty-four miles square in all.   She is still in possession of the
place, and still administers it as patroonesse, until one Richard
van Rentselaer, residing at Amsterdam, shall arrive in the
country, whom she expected in the summer, when he would
assume the management of it himself.   This lady was polite,
quite well informed, and of good life and disposition.[1]   She had
experienced several proofs of the Lord.   The breaking up of
the ice had once carried away her entire mansion, and every
thing connected with it, of which place she had made too
much account.   Also, in some visitations of her husband,
death, and others before.   In her last child-bed, she became
lame or weak in both of her sides, so that she had to walk with
two canes or crutches.   In all these trials, she had borne herself well, and God left not Himself without witness in her.
She treated us kindly, and we ate here exceedingly good pike,
perch, and other fish, which now began to come and be caught
in great numbers.   We had several conversations with her
about the truth, and practical religion, mutually satisfactory.
We went to look at several of her mills at work, which she had
there on an ever-running stream, grist-mills, saw-mills, and
others.   One of the grist-mills can grind 120 schepels[2] of meal
in twenty-four hours, that is, five an hour.   Returning to the
house, we politely took our leave.   Her residence is about a
quarter of an hour from Albany up the river.   This day we

[1] The patroonship of Rensselaerswyck was founded in 1630 by Kiliaen van
Rensselaer of Amsterdam.   It was a great manorial estate, extending along the
west bank of the Hudson from Beeren Island to the Mohawk and running so
far back from the river as to embrace about the same area as the present Albany
County, though Albany itself was not a part of it.   The first patroon had died
in 1646, the second, his oldest son Johannes, had also died, and the present heir
was the latter's son Kiliaen.   The lady here described was Maria, the widow of
Jeremias van Rensselaer, the original patroon's third son, who had ruled the colony
from 1658 to 1674.   She was a daughter of Oloff Stevensz van Cortlandt, and
lived till 1689.   Her husband's youngest brother Richard had lived at the colony
from 1652 to 1672, but was now in Holland, treasurer of Vianen, and never came
to America again.
[2] Ninety bushels.

went to visit still other farms and milling establishments on the other side of the river, where there was a water-fall but not large, sufficient to keep about three mills going. This is indeed, I think, the highest that I have seen.

28th, Sunday. We went to church in the morning, and heard Domine Schaets preach, who, although he is a poor, old, ignorant person, and besides is not of good life, yet had to give utterance to his passion, having taken his text largely upon us, at which many of his auditors, who knew us better, were not well pleased, and blamed, condemned, and derided him for it, which we corrected.[1]

In the afternoon, we took a walk to an island upon the end of which there is a fort built, they say, by the Spaniards. That a fort has been there is evident enough from the earth thrown up and strewn around, but it is not to be supposed that the Spaniards came so far inland to build forts, when there are no monuments of them to be seen elsewhere and down on the sea coasts, where, however, they have been according to the traditions of the Indians. This spot is a short hour's distance below Albany, on the west side of the river.[2]

29th, Monday. We should have left to-day, but it was not yet to happen, for our skipper, so he said, could not obtain his passport. We called upon several persons, and among others, upon the woman who had brought up Illetie, the Indian woman, and had first taken her from the Indians, and to whom we have alluded before. This woman, although not of openly godless life, is more wise than devout, although her knowledge is not very extensive, and does not surpass that of the women of New Netherland. She is a truly worldly woman, proud and conceited, and sharp in trading with *wild*[3] people, as well as *tame* ones, or what shall I call them, not to give them the name of Christians, or if I do, it is only to distinguish them from the others. This trading is not carried on without fraud, and she is not free from it, as I have observed. She has a husband,

[1] Rev. Gideon Schaets (1608–1694) was minister of Rensselaerswyck from 1652 to 1657, and of Fort Orange (Beverwyck, Albany) from 1657 to 1694.

[2] With these data may be compared the matter of the Pompey Stone, found in Pompey, N. Y., and bearing apparently a Spanish inscription of 1520.

[3] *Wild*, savage, is the word commonly used by the Dutch of that time to denote the Indians.

which is her second one, and he I believe is a Papist. He remains at home quietly, while she travels over the country to
carry on the trading. In fine she is one of the Dutch female
traders, who understand their business so well. If these be
the persons who are to make Christians of the heathen, what
will the latter be? But God employs such means as pleases
Him to accomplish His purposes. He had given Illetie more
grace than to her, we are very certain.

We were also invited to the fort by the Heer commandant,
who wished to see us, but left it to our convenience. We
went there with Robert Sanders, who interpreted for us. This
gentleman received us politely. He said he was pleased to
receive us, and to learn how we liked the lands up above, and
made a few such common observations. He seemed to be not
unreasonable, and a reliable person. If he was not a Scotchman, he seemed nevertheless to be a good Englishman, and,
as we thought, a Presbyterian. We soon took a friendly leave,
and returned home.

We spoke seriously to Robert Sanders about his pride,
arrogance, temper, and passion, although according to the
world's reputation he is not of bad character. His wife is
more simple and a better person; we spoke to her also, as well
as to their children, especially to the oldest, named Elizabeth,
who was tender-hearted and affectionate. He and all of them
promised to improve and reform themselves somewhat, and
we saw with consolation that they in some things commenced
to do so.

30*th*, *Tuesday*. We were ready to leave early, but it ran
well on towards noon, when with a head wind, but a strong
current down, we tacked over to Kinderhoeck, lying on the
east shore sixteen miles below Albany.

Before we quit Albany, we must say a word about the
place. It was formerly named the Fuyck by the Hollanders,
who first settled there, on account of two rows of houses standing there, opposite to each other, which being wide enough apart
in the beginning, finally ran quite together like a *fuyck*,[1] and,
therefore, they gave it this name, which, although the place is
built up, it still bears with many, especially the Dutch and
Indians living about there. It is nearly square, and lies against

[1] See p. 198, note 3.

the hill, with several good streets, on which there may be about
eighty or ninety houses. Fort Orange, constructed by the
Dutch, lies below on the bank of the river, and is set off with
palisades, filled in with earth on the inside. It is now abandoned by the English, who have built a similar one behind the
town, high up on the declivity of the hill, from whence it can
command the place. From the other side of this fort the inhabitants have brought a spring or fountain of water, under
the fort, and under ground into the town, where they now have
in several places always fountains of clear, fresh, cool water.
The town is surrounded by palisades, and has several gates
corresponding with the streets. It has a Dutch Reformed and
a Lutheran church. The Lutheran minister lives up here in
the winter, and down in New York in the summer.[1] There is
no English church or place of meeting, to my knowledge. As
this is the principal trading-post with the Indians, and as also
they alone have the privilege of trading, which is only granted
to certain merchants there, as a special benefit, who know what
each one must pay therefor, there are houses or lodges erected
on both sides of the town, where the Indians, who come from
the far interior to trade, live during the time they are there.
This time of trading with the Indians is at its height in the
months of June and July, and also in August, when it falls off;
because it is then the best time for them to make their journeys
there and back, as well as because the Hollanders then have
more time outside their farm duties.

We came to anchor at Kinderhook, in order to take in some
grain, which the female trader before mentioned [2] had there
to be carried down the river.

MAY 1st, *Wednesday.* We began early to load, but as it
had to come from some distance in the country, and we had to
wait, we stepped ashore to amuse ourselves. We came to a
creek where, near the river, lives the man whom they usually
call the Child of Luxury,[3] because he formerly had been such
an one, but who now was not far from being the Child of Pov-

---

[1] Rev. Bernhardus Arensius had since 1674 ministered to these two Lutheran
congregations, and continued till his death in 1691.

[2] Illetje's mistress.

[3] This was one Frans Pieterse Clauw, who had come out to Beverwyck
(Albany) in 1656.

erty, for he was situated poorly enough. He had a saw-mill on the creek, on a water-fall, which is a singular one, for it is true that all falls have something special, and so had this one, which was not less rare and pleasant than others. The water fell quite steep, in one body, but it came down in steps, with a broad rest sometimes between them. These steps were sixty feet or more high, and were formed out of a single rock, which is unusual. I reached this spot alone through the woods, and while I was sitting on the mill, my comrade came up with the Child of Luxury, who, after he had shown us the mill and falls, took us down a little to the right of the mill, under a rock, on the margin of the creek, where we could behold how wonderful God is even in the most hidden parts of the earth; for we saw crystal lying in layers between the rocks, and when we rolled away a piece of the rock, there was, at least on two sides of it, a crust or bark, about as thick as the breadth of a straw, of a sparkling or glassy substance, which looked like alabaster, and this crust was full of points or gems, which were truly gems of crystal, or like substance. They sparkled brightly, and were as clear as water, and so close together that you could obtain hundreds of them from one piece of the crust. We broke some pieces off, and brought them away with us as curiosities. It is justly to be supposed that other precious stones rest in the crevices of the rocks and mines as these do. I have seen this sort of crystal as large and pointed as the joint of a finger. I saw one, indeed, at the house of Robert Sanders as large as your fist, though it was not clear, but white, like glassy alabaster. It had what they call a table point. Robert Sanders has much of this mountain crystal at his farm, about four miles from Albany, towards the Cahoos, on the east side of the river, but we have not been there.

On returning to the boat, we saw that the woman-trader had sent a quantity of bluish wheat on board, which the skipper would not receive, or rather mix with the other wheat; but when she came she had it done, in which her dishonesty appeared, for when the skipper arrived at New York he could not deliver the wheat which was under hers. We set sail in the evening, and came to Claver Rack,[1] sixteen miles further down, where we also took in some grain in the evening.

---

[1] "Clover Reach," now Claverack.

2d, *Thursday*. We were here laden full of grain, which had to be brought in four miles from the country. The boors who brought it in wagons asked us to ride out with them to their places, which we did. We rode along a high ridge of blue rock on the right hand, the top of which was grown over. This stone is suitable for burning lime, as the people of the Hysopus, from the same kind, burn the best. Large, clear fountains flow out of these cliffs or hills, the first real fountains and only ones which we have met with in this country. We arrived at the places which consist of fine farms; the tillable land is like that of Schoonechtendeel, low, flat, and on the side of a creek, very delightful and pleasant to look upon, especially at the present time, when they were all green with the wheat coming up. The woodland also is very good for tillable land, and it was one of the locations which pleased me most, with its agreeable fountains. Coming back to the shore, I made a sketch,[1] as well as I could, of the Catskill mountains, which now showed themselves nakedly, which they did not do to us when we went up the river. They lie on the west side of the river, deep in the country, and I stood on the east side of it. In the evening we obtained a still more distinct view of them.

3d, *Friday*. We took on board early the rest of our lading. Our tradress left us here in order to go back to Albany, and we received two other passengers in her stead, a young man of this place, named Dirck, to whom we made mention of our crystal. He said they had at his place a rock, in which there was a yellow, glittering substance like gold, as they firmly believed it was; he did not know we were there, otherwise he would have presented us with a specimen. We spoke to him, as he was a good hearted youth, several times of God and Christ, and of the Christian life, and each time he was much concerned. Truly we discover gradually more and more there is here a hunger and thirst after God, and no one to help them. They go everywhere wandering without a shepherd, and know not where they shall turn. We also spoke to the skipper's daughter, a worldly child, who was not affected by what we said. The Lord will, in His own time, gather together those who are of His elect.

We sailed from there about nine o'clock, but after going

[1] Sketch not preserved.

eight or twelve miles got aground in consequence of our heavy
lading, where we were compelled to remain until four o'clock
in the afternoon, waiting for high water. But what was unfortunate, we missed a fine, fair wind, which sprang up about
eleven o'clock. Meanwhile the passengers went ashore. I
walked a small distance into the country, and came to a fall
of water, the basin of which was full of fish, two of which I
caught with my hands. They were young shad. I went immediately after the other passengers for assistance to catch
more, but when they came, they made such an agitation of the
water, that the fish all shot to the bottom, and remained there
under the rocks. We therefore could obtain no more; but if
we had had a small casting net, we could have caught them in
great numbers, or if I had remained there quiet alone. But as
it was, we had to abandon it. These fish come at high water
from the North River into these little streams, where they find
clear, fresh water, and weeds and herbs. They remain there
eating and sporting, and in the meantime at low water they
are left in these holes or basins, and they are thus caught in
great numbers in many of the streams by the Indians.

The water having risen, and the wind being favorable, we
went on board, and as soon as we were afloat, got under sail.
We proceeded rapidly ahead, and at sundown came to anchor
before the Hysopus, where we landed some passengers who
lived there.

4th, Saturday. We went ashore early, and further inland
to the village. We found Gerrit the glass-maker there,[1] with
his sister. He it was who desired to come up here in company
with us, and he was now happy to see us. He was engaged
putting the glass in their new church, but left his work to go
with us through the country, where he was better acquainted
than we were. We found here exceedingly large flats, which
are more than three hours' ride in length, very level, with a
black soil which yields grain abundantly. They lie like those
at Schoonecte and Claver Rack, between the hills and along
the creek, which sometimes overflows all the land, and drowns
and washes out much of the wheat. The place is square,[2] set
off with palisades, through which there are several gates; it
consists of about fifty houses within the stockade. They were

---

[1] Gerrit Duyckinck.   [2] A ground-plan of Esopus or Kingston, showing the
stockade with its gates, and the houses and fortifications as they are here described, may be found in Miller's *Description of New York.*

engaged in a severe war with the Indians during the administration of the Heer Stuyvesant, which is therefore still called
the Hysopus war, partly because it was occasioned on account
of the people of Hysopus, and because they have had to bear
there the largest burden of it.[1]   In returning to the village we
observed a very large, clear fountain bubbling up from under
a rock.   When we arrived there, we went to the house of the
person who was the head of the village, where some people had
assembled, who, having no minister, and hearing that my comrade was a theologian, requested him to preach for them the
next day.   But our skipper having finished what he had to
do, we left there.   Here and in Albany they brew the heaviest
beer we have tasted in all New Netherland, and from wheat
alone, because it is so abundant.   The glass-maker informed
us that Willem, the son of our old people,[2] was going to follow
the sea, and had left for Barbados; that Evert Duyckert, our
late mate on our voyage out, who had gone as captain of a
ketch to Barbados and Jamaica, had arrived; that it was his
ship we had seen coming in, when we were leaving the city,
and that perhaps he would go with her to Holland.   This place
is about three-quarters of an hour inland.   At the mouth of
the creek, on the shore of the river, there are some houses and
a redoubt, together with a general storehouse, where the farmers bring in their grain, in order that it may be conveniently
shipped when the boats come up here, and wherein their goods
are discharged from the boats, as otherwise there would be too
much delay in going back and forth.   The woodland around
the Hysopus is not of much value, and is nothing but sand and
rock.   We had hardly reached the river, when a man came
running up to us as hard as he could, requesting to speak to
us.   We inquired of him what he desired, when he complained
of being sorely afflicted with an internal disease, and said he
had heard we well understood medicine, and knew what to
prescribe for him.   We told him we were no doctors, and had
only brought a few medicines with us for our own use, and
most of them we had given away.[3]   My comrade told him what
he thought of his disease, and that we could not help him:
whereupon this poor wretched man went sorrowfully back

---

[1] The Esopus war occurred in 1658–1660.   [2] Willem Hellekers.
[3] See p. 202, note.

again, for he had spent much to be cured. We told him, however, we would send him a brackish powder which had done
good in several cases, and which, if it pleased God to bless it,
would perhaps help him. We went on board the boat, and
immediately got under sail, with a favorable but light wind,
and by evening arrived at the entrance of the Highlands.

5th, *Sunday*. The wind was ahead, but it was calm.
When the tide began to fall, we tacked, or rather drifted along,
but with little progress. We passed through the Highlands
however, and came to anchor by the time the ebb was spent.
The weather was very rainy.

6th, *Monday*. The wind was still contrary, and blew hard,
therefore we tacked, but in consequence of our being very
heavily laden we advanced but little. We anchored again
when we went ashore at a place on the east side of the river,
where there was a meadow on fire. We saw there a beautiful
hard stone, as white and as clean as I have ever seen either here
or in Europe, very fine for building; and also many cedar trees
of beautiful color and strong perfume. Some Indians came
alongside of us in their canoes, whom we called on board, and
bought from them a very large striped bass, as large as a codfish in the Fatherland, for a loaf of stale bread worth about
three stivers, Holland money, and some other fish for a little
old salt meat.

7th, *Tuesday*. At daylight the tide served, but the wind
was still ahead, though steady. We continued tacking with
considerable progress, and at ten o'clock arrived before the
city of New York, where we struck upon a rock. The water
was falling, and we therefore immediately carried out an anchor,
and wore the yacht off. A slight breeze soon afterward sprang
up, and took us to the city. The Lord be praised and glorified
for His grace. We delivered our letters, and executed the
orders which were committed to us. We inquired for Ephraim
and de la Grange, but they had not yet arrived.

8th, *Wednesday*. We had now nothing more to do, except
to get ready with all speed to leave for Boston. As we had
ordered some clothes, as we have said, to be made, we urged
the tailor to finish them. We inquired for a boat going to
Boston, and found there were two, but the time was up the
next day for leaving, and we could not be ready so soon. We

went first to visit Theunis, concerning whom there had been
great talk during our absence.   Even the minister Niewenhuyse
dared to say that we had misled him; and he intended to visit
Theunis, for he had been to our house.   But Theunis antici-
pated him, and said he need not give himself so much trouble,
as he could go to him, which he did.   When the domine asked
him about these things, he told the domine he must not have
any such opinion; that we had not misled him, but had led
him straight; that he was not able to compensate us for the
good we had done him, since he was more edified, instructed,
strengthened, and comforted by us, than he had been by any
one in his whole life.   The domine therefore had to be satisfied,
and said, " 'Tis well then, 'tis well then, I did not know that."
Our old woman told us Theunis had been so sad and oppressed
again, they did not know what to advise him.   We therefore
went to see him, and found him at home, in as good a frame of
mind as could be wished for one in such a condition.   We
asked him how he got along.   He said very well; that God was
good to him, and then related to us about his going to the
minister, and his standing upon the eminence when we were
sailing by, looking after us.   We spoke to him affectionately,
exhorting him to faithfulness; that he must instruct his wife
and children, and set them a good example.   He informed us
that his wife was as changed as day from night in many respects, and he hoped she would improve still more; that he
would instruct his children as well as he could, if it pleased the
Lord they should be instructed, which comforted us, and we
returned home.[1]

The North River is the most navigated and frequented
river in these parts, because the country about it is the most
inhabited.   Its larger population as compared with other
places is owing, for the most part, first to the fact that the capital was originally established here, and has ever since remained
here, under whatever government has prevailed, although the
South River was first discovered; secondly, because it is the
most convenient place for the purposes of navigation, I mean
the capital, and is the middle and centre of the whole of New
Netherland; and thirdly, because this place, and indeed the

[1] Theunis Idensen is found becoming a member of the Dutch Reformed
Church at New York in the next month, June 17, 1680.

river, possess the most healthy and temperate climate. We will hereafter speak of New York, and confine ourselves now to the North River; which was so called for two reasons, and justly so: the first of which is because, as regards the South River, it lies in a more northerly latitude, the South River lying in 39°, and the North River in 40° 25′, and being also thus distinguishable from the East River, which although it is more easterly, as its name denotes, nevertheless lies in the same parallel. The other reason is because it runs up generally in a northerly direction, or between north by east and north-northeast. It begins at the sea in a bay; for the sea coast, between the North and South Rivers, stretches northeast by north and northeast, and southwest and southwest by south; and from the North River along Long Island for the most past east and west. Besides this name, which is the most common and the best, it bears several others; such as Maurits River, because it was discovered and taken possession of in the time of Prince Maurice; Montagne River because one De la Montagne was one of the first and principal settlers, and lastly, Manhattans River, from the Manhattans Island, or the Manhattan Indians, who lived hereabouts and on the island of Manhattans, now the city of New York.[1] To be more exact, its beginning, it seems to us, ought to be regarded as at the city of New York, where the East River as well as Kill achter Kol separate from the North River. The waters below the city are not commonly called the river, but the bay; for although the river discharges itself into the sea at Sandy Hook, or Rentselaer's Hook, this discharge is not peculiarly its own, but also that of the East River, Achter Kol, Slangenbergh Bay, Hackingsack Creek, Northwest Creek, Elizabeth Creek, Woodbridge Creek, Milstone River, Raritan River, and Nevesinck Creek, all of which deserve the name of rivers, and have

---

[1] The Figurative Map of 1616 gives the name Riviere van den Vorst Mauritius (River of Prince Maurice). Wassenaer (1624) speaks of the river as "called first Rio de Montagnes, now the River Mauritius." De Laet, in his *Nieuwe Wereldt* (1625), gives "Manhattes River" and "Rio de Montaigne," but says that "the Great River" is the usual designation. In his Latin version of 1633, and French of 1640, he adds a mention of the name Nassau River. As Dr. Johannes la Montagne did not come to New Netherland till 1637, the derivation here given can not hold. River of the Mountains is an obvious enough name, to any one who had sailed up through the Highlands of the Hudson.

nothing in common with the North River, but with Long Island on one side and Staten Island on the other. The water below the Narrows to Sandy Hook is usually called the Great Bay; and that of the Narrows and above them as far as the city, and up to and beyond Sapocanikke,[1] the Little Bay. Although the Great Bay is so called, it is not by any means as large as that of the South River. Above Sapocanikke the river is about two miles wide, and is very uniformly of the same width as far up as the Hysopus and higher, except in the Highlands, where there are here and there a narrow strait and greater depth. Above the Hysopus, which is 90 to 96 miles from the city, it still maintains a fair width, but with numerous islands, shoals, and shallows, up to Fort Albany, where it is narrower. It is easily navigable to the Hysopus with large vessels, and thence to Fort Albany with smaller ones, although ketches and such craft can go up there and load. It carries the ordinary flood tide into the Highlands, but with much of a down flow of water, only up to them; though with an extraordinary flow down and a dead neap-tide, the water becomes brackish near the city. With a slight flow of water down and a spring tide, accompanied by a southeast storm, the flood tide is carried quite through the Highlands, and they said they had had a change in the water even as far up as the Hysopus. The land on both sides of the river is high and rocky, but higher in some places than others, as at the Highlands, eminently so called because they are higher than the others. In passing by the Hysopus you see the Katskil Mountains, a little inland, which are the highest in this region, and extend from there, in the form of a crescent, into the country of the Maquaas. Although these mountains are from 112 to 120 miles distant from the sea, there are skippers who in clear weather have seen them while sailing along the coast. All the reaches, creeks, headlands, and islands, bear the names which were accidentally given them in the first instance: as Antonis Neus (Anthony's Nose) a headland and high hill in the Highlands, because it has a sharp edge running up and down in the form of a man's nose; Donderbergh (Thunder Hill), because it thundered there frightfully at the time the first explorers of the river passed it; Swadel Rack (Swath Reach), a short strait between high hills, where

[1] Greenwich, a district of old New York.

in sailing through they encounter whirlwinds and squalls, and meet sometimes with accidents, which they usually call *swadelen* (swaths or mowing sweeps); Danskamer (Dancing Chamber),[1] a spot where a party of men and women arrived in a yacht in early times, and being stopped by the tide went ashore. Gay, and perhaps intoxicated, they began to jump and dance, when the Indians who had observed them fell upon them in the height of their merriment and drove them away. In remembrance of this circumstance the place has since been called the Dancing Chamber. It is on the west side of the river, just through the Highlands. Boterberg (Butter Hill), and Hoyberg (Hay Hill), the one because it is like the rolls of butter which the farmers in Holland take to market, and the other because it is like a haystack in Holland; 't Claver Rack (Clover Reach), from three bare places which appear on the land;[2] and Kinder Hoeck (Children's Point), Noten Hoeck (Nut Point), Potlepels Eylant (Potladle Island), Kock Achie, etc.

Above Fort Albany there are occasionally good flats on both sides of the river, at the foot of the hills, and also some fine islands up to the Cahoos; which is where the colony of Rentselaerwyck is planted. The river begins above Fort Albany to divide itself, first by islands, and then by the main land, into two arms or branches, one of which turns somewhat towards the west and afterwards entirely west through Schoonechten, towards the country of the Maquaas, and this branch, on which the Cahoos lies, is called the Maquaas Kill. The other preserves the course of the main river for the most part, or a little more easterly, and retains also the name of the North River. It runs far up into the country, and has its source in a lake 120 to 160 miles in length,[3] out of which a stream probably empties into the St. Lawrence, a river of Canada; for not only do the Indians, but the French also,

[1] At a cove in the north part of the town of Newburgh.

[2] As if like a clover-leaf. Noten Hoeck was opposite Coxsackie, Potlepels (now Polopel's) Island opposite Cornwall. Kock Achie or Coxsackie is probably Koeksrackie, the cook's little reach, to distinguish it from the Koeks Rack, cook's reach, the name which the early voyagers gave to a reach far below, near present Peekskill.

[3] Referring, but of course mistakenly, to Lake Champlain, or Lakes Champlain and George.

pass over here in canoes from Canada. We ourselves have
conversed with persons who have thus come over, some by
water, and others by land and on foot. Of the Cahoos we have
already spoken, in relating our journey there. Those falls are
a great and wonderful work of God; but although they have
so much water that the wind causes the spray and moisture
to rise continually in the air, so that spectators who stand two
hundred feet or so higher are made wet, especially when there
are any gusts of wind driving from one side, as happened to
us, yet we regard the falls on the Northwest Kill [the Passaic]
as more curious, though smaller, and having less water. Even
on the North River, there are several small creeks and falls
more rare to see than the Cahoos. Beyond the Cahoos the
land is not so high above the water; and no fish pass from below
into the river above, in consequence of the interruption caused
by the falls, nor can any boats be carried over the falls, up or
down, which is a great inconvenience for those who live above
the Cahoos, at Schenectady and other places, although when
the country shall become more inhabited, and they shall have
more occasion, they will take means to remedy this difficulty.
Through the whole of that extensive country they have no
fish, except some small kinds peculiar to the streams, such as
trout, sunfish, roach, pike, etc.; and this is the case in all the
creeks where there are falls.

The North River abounds with fish of all kinds, throughout
from the sea to the falls, and in the branch which runs up to
the lake. To relate a single instance: some persons near
Albany caught in a single haul of a common seine between five
and six hundred fine shad, bass, perch, and other fish, and
there were, I believe, over five hundred of one kind. It is not
necessary for those who live in the city [of New York], and
other places near the sea, to go to the sea to fish, but they can
fish in the river and waters inside; or even to the Great Bay,
except such as live upon it, and they can by means of *fuycks*
or seines not only obtain fish enough for their daily consumption, but also to salt, dry, and smoke, for commerce, and to
export by shiploads if they wish, all kinds of them, as the
people of Boston do; but the people here have better land
than they have there, where they therefore resort more for a
living to the water.

There is much beautiful quarry stone of all kinds on this river, well adapted for building purposes and for burning lime; and as fine cedar wood as we have seen anywhere. Neverthe- less, for suitableness of navigation, and for rich land on both sides, all the way up, the South River excels the North; but what gives the North River the preference, and crowns it over the South River, is its salubrious climate; though above Chris- tina Creek the South River is healthy, and it is every day be- coming more so, along the whole of that river. On the North River, however, one has not to wait and die before this im- provement may take place.

As soon as we arrived in the city, we resolved upon going to Long Island, for the purpose of taking leave according to promise of the kind acquaintances we had living there; and therefore on the

9th, Thursday, we started about ten o'clock. In crossing the ferry we met Elbert, the father-in-law of Jan Theunissen,[1] who came over with us and professed so much friendship towards us. Elbert was going to the city and intended to return again soon; but we thought it would not be before evening, which would be too long to wait for him. We there- fore proceeded on to his house at the bay, where we arrived at noon. We found there Gerrit the wheelwright;[2] and Jan Theunissen soon came in from the fields; but as the father- [in-law] was not at home we had to tarry, although we had in- tended to go to Najack. While we were sitting there Domine Van Zueren[3] came up, to whom the boors called out as uncivilly and rudely as if he had been a boy. He had a chatting time with all of them. As Jan Theunissen had said to us in the house, that if the domine only had a chance once to speak to us, Oh, how he would talk to us! that we avoided him, and therefore could not be very good people; now, as we were there, we sat near him and the boors and those with whom he was conversing. He spoke to us, but not a word of that fell

---

[1] See pp. 30, 52, 59, 61, supra.   [2] Gerrit van Duyn.

[3] Rev. Casparus van Zuuren, of Gouda in Holland, was one of the four Dutch Reformed ministers now remaining in New York (and Delaware)—Schaets, Nieuwenhuisen, van Zuuren, Tesschenmaker—and was minister of Midwout (Flatbush), Brooklyn, and Amersfoort (Flatlands), but lived at Midwout. He came out from Holland in 1677 and returned to a pastorate there in 1685.

from him. Indeed, he sat prating and gossiping with the boors, who talked foully and otherwise, not only without giving them a single word of reproof, but even without speaking a word about God or spiritual matters. It was all about houses, and cattle, and swine, and grain; and then he went away.

10th, *Friday.* The morning was rainy, and we could not go out early; but the weather became better after breakfast, about nine o'clock, when we took our leave and left for Najack, where we arrived at eleven o'clock at Jaques's. He had been sick with a large ulcer on his neck, but that was now better. We were welcome. Among other matters, he told us that he had heard the report about our Theunis, but he did not know what to believe or think of it. We told him the whole truth about it, as he was capable of believing it, for he was at the best a Socinian. Theunis had formerly lived in that neighborhood [1] and Jaques at that time missed a cow which was pasturing in the woods with the other cattle, as they always do. They made a thorough search after her, but could not find her. Although Jaques had some suspicion of Theunis, he did not manifest it even to those who spoke to him about Theunis in connection with the subject. It happened that Theunis came to Jaques's house, when Jaques embraced the opportunity, and took him on the shore near his house. After talking of various matters, Jaques spoke to him about his cow, how she was carried off, and they never could hear anything about her. He then began to push Theunis a little closer, who laughed at it heartily at first; but by hard pressing and proofs which Jaques gradually brought forward, and especially by appeals to his conscience, whether he had not the fear of God before his eyes, Theunis acknowledged he had done it, and falling on his knees prayed for forgiveness. He had stolen the cow and killed her. Jaques, who is one of the justices, said, "I forgive you from the bottom of my heart, but I do this only to cause you to reflect and desist from your wickedness, and to show you that you do not know or fear God, and that you may fear Him more." Whereupon Theunis was much affected, and went away entirely subdued, while Jaques was rejoiced that he had

---

[1] In 1664 Jacob Hellekers and Theunis Idensen both lived in New Utrecht. *N. Y. Col. Doc.*, II. 481. Jaques is Jacques Cortelyou. Socinian means a Unitarian, a follower of Faustus Socinus.

had the opportunity of relieving his mind about Theunis. Jaques, who had known him from his youth up, said he had been a very godless person, cursing and swearing and, in a word, living in direct hostility to God. We told Jaques that better things were now to be expected from him, at which Jaques was pleased.

We dined with Jaques; and his little son came and presented us a humming-bird he had shot. Jaques impressed us very much with his sincerity and cordiality in everything we had to do with him, or wherein he could be of any service to us. We left with him the little book which we had lent to him, and which he said he had found much pleasure in reading, *Les Pensees de M. Pascal.* We took our leave of him, and went directly through the fields to Gouanes, where we arrived at two o'clock. Simon[1] and his wife were out upon some newly cleared land planting water-melons; for water-melons must always have new ground, or the worms will destroy them. They went into the house with us. They also spoke about Theunis, and we disabused them of several things. They showed us some pieces of ambergris, which their brother had brought from the Caribbean Islands, and which we thought was good. We said to them what we deemed proper for them, and took our leave, reaching the city in good time.

De la Grange and his wife arrived this evening from the South River by land, leaving their nephew behind, who had made arrangements to come over with Ephraim in eight days. Meanwhile we made inquiries about going to Boston, and they informed us that a vessel had sailed during our absence, but we were not ready, and there would be another one going in eight or ten days.

11th, *Saturday*. We finished with our tailor, and paid him 77 guilders in *zeewan*, that is, 25 guilders and 8 stivers in Holland money.[2]

13th, *Monday*. We settled with our old hosts and paid them. We continued our inquiries for an opportunity to leave, but without success.

15th, *Wednesday*. As we were crossing the street, the lord governor, passing by, saw us and called to us. We went to him, and he asked us what we thought of the lands around

---

[1] Simon Aertsen de Hart.   [2] About ten dollars.

Albany. We answered, they were very good, but limited, being flats here and there, and that the woodland, in particular, was not worth much. "But," he said, "you have not been to Wappings Kill." [1] We replied, that we had not. "That is," he rejoined, "a beautiful place, about three-quarters of an hour inland, on a fine creek which you can navigate with yachts, and it lies just through the Highlands, directly opposite the Dans Kamer." And with that he left us.

16th, Thursday. As there was still a portion of our small stock of goods remaining, we traded it with De la Grange, who expected his boat from the South River with peltries and other articles, with which he would pay us.

17th, Friday. The boat which they had said would sail to-morrow, was posted to sail next Wednesday; but we think it will be postponed still longer.

18th, Saturday. We prepared our letters for Patria.

19th, Sunday. A ship arrived from Barbados. One had also arrived last week from London, which had been six weeks and three days on the voyage; but we did not receive any letters, nor did De la Grange, and we could learn nothing certain.

Meanwhile we conversed with several persons who came to visit us, among others with a woman who had undergone, several years ago, some remarkable experiences; of a light shining upon her while she was reading in the New Testament about the sufferings of the Lord Jesus, which frightened her very much. It did not continue long but soon passed off; yet it left, nevertheless, such a joy and testimony in her heart as she could not describe. She kept it to herself, without making it known to any one except only one woman. Some years afterwards, while lying abed in the morning, she heard a voice which said to her, she must make this glory known, which she did do to Domine Nieuwenhuise, who told her he did not know what to say. She had also mentioned it to others, and to one man who played the part of a wise man, but who was not a good man. He said to her, "You must not go any more to church, for you are wise enough, and will become still wiser. You must not go to the Lord's Supper, for the Lord has said, 'do that until I come,'" and many other such things,

---

[1] Wappinger's Creek, in Dutchess County.

in order to frighten the poor woman. He once came to her house and asked her very harshly and roughly, why she continued to do so, and in whose hands she would rather fall, into the hands of God, or the hands of men? She said, poor woman, in the words of David, "Rather in God's hands." "And I not," said he; "I would rather fall in the hands of men," and then went away. This has so sorely disturbed this poor woman that for a long time she has not known what to do; for not to go to church, and to leave the Lord's Supper, she could not in her heart consent. We told her that as regards what had happened to her, many things had occurred to us, and further, what was serviceable therein, without however condemning them in her; but that the person who had so spoken to her was a false teacher, and she must be cautious of him; that for herself in all these and the like matters she must seek for true grace, for a new heart and power unto true repentance of life, and for true humility of soul and renunciation of herself and the world. And thereupon she left. Her name was Marie. She was a Frenchwoman; and her husband, a Frenchman, who had also been to us twice. He was the son of Pierre Jardinier of whom we have before spoken.[1] He had a book with the title of *Le Grand Heraut*, etc., which he highly esteemed; but he was a real reformed, of France, as they said. The other person, who played the wise man, was also a Frenchman. His name was Nicolas de la Pleyne, a relation of hers and professed to be of the reformed.[2] He had not for a long time been to the Lord's Supper, but had now gone to it again. He was a tobacco twister by trade.

We wrote up the river to Robert Sanders of Albany, and to the poor sick man at the Hysopus, sending him a *vomitorium* by Meus Hoogboom. We also went to see the Boston skipper, but he had not obtained any freight.

[1] For Pierre the Gardener, Pierre Cresson, see p. 74. The son referred to was Jacques Cresson, who became a Labadist, and died in 1684. His wife was Marie Renard. His book was Labadie's *Le Héraut du Grand Roi Jésus* (Amsterdam, 1667). After his death his widow went to Curaçao, returned, but removed to Philadelphia, and died there in 1710. The two were among the first members of the Dutch church at Harlem.

[2] Nicolas de la Pleine, of "Bersweer in France," was married in 1658 to Susanna Cresson, native of Ryswyk in Holland, sister of Jacques Cresson. He was constable in 1685.

22nd, Wednesday. Mr. Reinderman arrived overland from the South River, leaving Ephraim still there. He started the same day that De la Grange left there, but was not able to overtake him. He had been all this time on the road, and had had a difficult journey, in consequence of there being so much water upon the land.

23d, Thursday. We went again to inquire after our boat, and found that the time was changed for the voyage, which made it a great inconvenience to us to be here so long, without being able to accomplish anything. But some other Boston vessels had arrived, which, they said, would return the first opportunity.

24th, Friday. Ephraim arrived from the South River at noon to-day, with his wife, and her sister's mother,[1] and other company, overland.

25th, Saturday. We went this forenoon to welcome him. He was still very much attached to us, and so was his wife, and both were persuaded and touched with the love which we had shown them, and the wife particularly, for the favor I had granted her, in sending her the translation of the *Verheffinge des Geestes,* in reading which she had experienced great enjoyment, and had been sometimes tenderly affected. She thanked us for the little parcel of braided goods we had sent her, which had been very agreeable to her. He promised moreover, if it should please God to call us again into this country to live and to establish His beloved church, we need not be at a loss to find a place; that the land which belonged to him, namely, Bohemia in Maryland, where his father lived, and of which we have before spoken, should with his consent be applied to no other purpose; that it should never go into English hands, hoping that God would give him this grace.[2] He had brought with him a piece of spermaceti, a portion of which he presented to us. He told us of the disposition of the heart of the Heer Jan Moll towards us, who showed us so much friendship, as we have before related, and will show us all possible kindness in the future; that he had taken well to heart what we had commended to him, and had even reformed

[1] Apparently this means the mother of Susanna Huyberts, wife of Casparus Heerman. See p. 130, note 1.

[2] See p. 141, note 2, *supra.*

several matters in his household, and otherwise; and how it grieved him that Domine Tessemaker had not grace or ability enough to accomplish anything serious in the congregation there, of which he was the elder, as well as president of the king's court. His wife was so far gone in consumption, that they saw no hope of her recovery.

26th, Sunday. Domine Niewenhuyse being sick, there was no preaching yet to-day.

27th, Monday. We went to call upon Ephraim again, in order to speak to him particularly, but did not succeed in consequence of his being visited so much, the more so because his wife's sister was soon to be married.[1]

28th, Tuesday. The supercargo of the last arrived Boston vessel, named Padechal,[2] was at M. van Clief's, who spoke to him about our wishes, and he promised to give us every attention and accommodation, and that he would leave in the coming week. This inspired us with new hope of getting away finally after so much delay.

29th, Wednesday. The before mentioned Boston trader came to speak with us himself, at the house of M. van Cleif. We talked with him, and he promised us every thing fair. The fare from New York to Boston is twenty shillings in English money for each person, which with the loss of exchange is a pound sterling in the money of Old England, which certainly is dear enough.

30th, Thursday. It was now Ascension Day, according to the old style,[3] a day greatly observed by the English. It reminded us of the day we left home on our travels, which was Ascension Day, old style. We wrote to-day to Robert Sanders at Albany, in order that, as we were so long in New York contrary to our intentions, he might regulate himself in the matter of our poor Wouter, the Indian, who, according to our mutual understanding, was to go to Boston by land, with an address from Mr. Robert Sanders, to one John Pisgeon, mer-

[1] According to the records of the Dutch Reformed Church in New York, Elizabeth's half-sister, Helena van Brugh, was married the day before this, May 26.

[2] Richard Pattishall of Boston. He was killed by the Indians at Pemaquid in 1692.

[3] But it was also Ascension Day of the new style.

chant, of that city,[1] so that we might find him, or he us, in
order to go to Europe with us, which he so earnestly desired,
and we endeavored with our whole heart to effect; and as this
could not well be done by the way of York, on account of the
governor and other hindrances, we had chosen that way, as it
seemed to us the best.

M. de la Grange came with his wife to invite me to accompany them in their boat to the Wale Bocht,[2] a place situated
on Long Island, almost an hour's distance below the city,
directly opposite Correlaers Hoeck, from whence I had several
times observed the place, which appeared to me very pleasant,
although I had never been there. He had an old aunt and other
friends living there. We set off accordingly in the boat, but
the strong flood tide carried us beyond the bay, to a place
called the Burnt Mill, where we could let the tide run out.
Meanwhile we fished a little, but we caught nothing except
a small codfish. From there we landed on the Mahatans, a
little north of the Burnt Mill, on a beautiful farm, having two
fine ponds of water before the door, where a mill was standing.
These ponds were full of sunfish, and other fish, some of which
we caught. The flood having run out at noon, we left there
and arrived about two o'clock at the Wale Bocht. This is a
bay tolerably wide where the water rises and falls much, and
at low water is very shallow and much of it dry. Inside of the
easterly point there was a ship aground, which had struck
on the reef of rocks which put out from Corlaer's Hook towards this bay, and had floated over here and sunk. She was
a French privateer, which had taken some rich Dutch prizes
in the bay of Campeachy and was going through here to New
England, in order to dispose of the goods which would not
bring money enough in New York. There were many goods

---

[1] I do not know who this could be if it were not John Pynchon of Springfield,
assistant and councillor of Massachusetts 1665–1703. He owned much property
in Boston and was often there; his large possessions in western Massachusetts
and his position as the chief trader at Springfield would make it natural to use
him in the way described; and in 1677 he had, at Albany, taken part, as repre-
sentative of his colony, in Governor Andros's negotiations with the Mohawks.

[2] The Walebocht, or bay of the Walloons, was a bight in the Long Island
shore, where the Brooklyn Navy Yard now stands. It was so named from a
group of Walloons who settled there at an early date. The modern form of the
name is Wallabout.

still in the sunken ship, and they have tried several times to raise her, but to no purpose. We went ashore here, and observed several kinds of fish, which I had not seen before in this country, such as flounders, plaice, sole, etc. This aunt of de La Grange is an old Walloon woman from Valenciennes, seventy-four years old. She is worldly-minded, with *mere bonte*,[1] living with her whole heart, as well as body, among her progeny, which now number 145, and will soon reach 150. Nevertheless she lived alone by herself, a little apart from the others, having her little garden, and other conveniences, with which she helped herself.[2] The ebb tide left our boat aground, and we were compelled to wait for the flood to set her afloat. De la Grange having to train next week with all the rest of the people, at New York, bespoke here a man to go as his substitute. The flood tide having made, we arrived home by evening.

31st, Friday. We sold to the wife of Evert, the late mate of our ship, a small looking-glass, a steel thimble, a pound and a half of white darning yarn, and half a pound of brown thread, for which she gave us a piece of eight.[3]

JUNE *1st, Saturday.* Nothing transpired to-day, except that several persons came to converse with us, to each of whom we spoke according to his state.[4]

[1] Meaning, apparently, "with mere human goodness."

[2] This old woman was Catalina Trico (1605–1689), widow of Joris Jansen Rapalie. She was the mother of eleven children, of whom the eldest, Sara, born in 1625 at Fort Orange, is understood to have been "the first born Christian daughter in New Netherland," Jean Vigne (see p. 47, note 2) being the first-born child. Two depositions by her of 1685 and 1688, printed in *Doc. Hist. N. Y.*, III. 31–32, quarto ed., give interesting details of the beginnings of the colony, for she came out "in 1623" (1624, rather) in the *Eendracht* (Unity), the first ship sent out to New Netherland by the Dutch West India Company. After three years at Fort Orange and twenty-two at New Amsterdam, she and her husband settled at the Walebocht. In the second deposition she speaks of herself as born in Paris, not Valenciennes. How she was aunt of de la Grange I do not know. He was the son of Joost de la Grange and Margaret his wife, afterward the wife of Andrew Carr. His wife was Cornelia de la Fontaine. Joining the Labadists in their purchase, he was naturalized by the Maryland assembly in 1684, and in 1692 was understood to be living in their community at Bohemia Manor. *Maryland Archives*, XIII, 126, XX. 163.

[3] A dollar, piece of eight reals.

[4] It was believed by the local ministers that Danckaerts and Sluyter while in New York engaged actively in proselytizing. Thus, Rev. Henricus Selyns, Domine Niewenhuisen's successor, says in a letter to Rev. Willem à Brakel,

2d, Sunday. There was no preaching in consequence of Domine Niewenhuise's continued sickness. Ephraim and his wife, among others, called upon us, and we had several conversations with them, and satisfied them in regard to our departure.

3d, Monday. We went to inquire whether our voyage would take place, as they said, on Wednesday. They now fixed the last of the week, which did not please us a great deal, because there was so much fine weather passing away without our being able to do anything; and also because we discovered that we could depend as little upon the word of the people of New England as of others, although they wished to pass for more upright persons, which we have not been able to perceive.

4th, Tuesday. We were again visited by several persons, and also by Ephraim, and one Pieter Beyaert,[1] a deacon of the Dutch church, a very good sort of person whom God, the Lord, began to touch and enlighten, both in regard to the destruction of the world in general and of himself in particular. He had a good intention to perform, through the grace of God, whatever God convicted him the truth of; for, he said, he had for some time past felt that God had some purpose concerning him, and to incite him to serve God with more earnestness; but it was impossible to do so in the city, and in this city of traders, where he lived; and as he observed the hand and providence of God in this matter because there had fallen to him a good piece of land and farm, without any effort of his, and as he felt that a private life was better for him, and brought him nearer to God, he intended to abandon the city and commerce and go and live upon his farm, which is on the South River, a small distance below where Caspar Hermans lives.

"They regularly attended church and said they had nothing against my doctrines; that they were of the Reformed Church, and stood by the Heidelberg Catechism and Dordrecht Confession. . . . Afterwards, in order to lay the groundwork for a schism, they began holding meetings with closed doors, and to rail out against the church and consistory, as Sodom and Egypt, and saying they must separate from the church; they could not come to the service, or hold communion with us. They thus absented themselves from the church." Murphy, *New Netherland Anthology,* pp. 95, 96.

[1] Pieter Bayard was a nephew of Governor Stuyvesant and a brother of Nicholas Bayard, of the council. He joined in the Labadist purchase, but soon withdrew.

We said to him on this subject what we believed he was in need of, which he received kindly.

The large ship of Frederick Flipsen, of which Singleton was captain, besides being lank of herself, was also very badly stowed and laden. In attempting to run out to sea, she was compelled to put back to Staten Island, in order to be restowed, which delays his voyage for several weeks.

5th, *Wednesday*. We now learned that our voyage was postponed until Monday, and perhaps longer, so little calculation can be made upon voyages in these parts.

6th, *Thursday*. We visited Theunis, whom we found well, the Lord confirming and strengthening him in the grace he had manifested towards Him, which comforted us, and we wished him the blessing of the Lord.

7th, *Friday*. We went to take our leave of the lord governor, who was very much engaged with the officers of the burghers, who were to train the next day, and also with the affair of Lord Carteret,[1] governor of New Jersey. After we had been waiting a long time, he observed us and called us. He asked us what we came to say, not with his accustomed kindness, but a little peevishly, as if he were tired of us and we annoyed him. We answered, we came to take our leave of him, as we intended to leave for Boston, and to thank him for the favor and kindness he had shown us. He enquired with whom we were going; and we named the person. He then asked, when; and we said on Monday. "Well," said he, "you will undoubtedly find there in the east a better opportunity than you have found here." We felt that he said this in irony; and replied, we did not think so, as we had seen several good situations within his government, and had been informed they were not so good at the east. He cut off the conversation by wishing us a happy voyage, for which we thanked him and left. We also went to take leave of Frederick Flipsen,[2] whom we requested, in case any letters addressed to us came into his hands, he would be so kind as to direct them to us in the Fatherland, which order we afterwards changed, and gave to M. de la Grange, because we were apprehensive, as he and the governor were one, it might be that our letters, coming from the Fatherland, had been withheld from

---

[1] Governor Carteret was not a lord.   [2] See p. 5, note 1.

us by them, as some persons had absolutely declared, and others had half insinuated.

8th, Saturday. There was a training and muster to-day, which had not taken place before in two years, because the small-pox had prevailed so much the last year. Some were on horseback, and six small companies were on foot. They were exercised in military tactics, but I have never seen anything worse of the kind. They comprised all the force of New York and the adjacent places. De la Grange, who supposed he could put in a substitute, had to appear on horseback himself, although some who were to come so did substitute others in their places.

This day was the anniversary of our departure from home, and we would have now taken our departure from here, if it had not been postponed.

9th, Sunday. Pinxter (Whitsunday). Domine Niewenhuyse having recovered from his sickness, we went to hear him preach, in order not to give any cause of offense at the last. His text was the usual one.

10th, Monday. The second day of Pinxter. We had several visitors whom we received with love and affection, each one according to his circumstances.

11th, Tuesday. We called upon Ephraim, from whom we received in charge some spermaceti, with orders to send him from Amsterdam a good new Bible. He presented us on behalf of his wife, who was not at home, two beautiful otter skins, which we dared not refuse, and accepted with thanks.

The governor, attended by his whole retinue of ladies and gentlemen, escorted Carteret, the governor of New Jersey, in great pomp home to Achter Kol. As we are now about to leave New York, and the affair of the Heer Carteret appears to be finished, which happening during our stay here we should have noticed from time to time, only we thought it was not well to write then what we saw, for various reasons, we do not regard it improper now to state what we heard of it.

These two governors lived at first in friendship and concord. Carteret came often to New York, and generally to church, when he usually went to the governor's, in the fort. A difference afterwards arose between them, but the cause of it I have not heard, or whether it was personal or public. It is certain, however, that the governor of New York wished to bring Carteret and his government, to some extent, into subordination to him. Carteret claimed to be as perfectly governor of his province as the other was of his, and to possess the same prerogatives as the governor of New York, and even more than he, in respect to trade and other privileges. The governor of New York disputed with him all right of navigation, declaring the North River was under his own jurisdiction, and therefore all persons who passed in or out of it must acknowledge him, pay him duties, and even unlade there, and actually commenced seizing some vessels. Carteret thereupon complained to England, and the governor of New York sent Captain Dyer over there as a commissioner, which he disavowed with an oath, as it is said. This Dyer returned with skipper Jacob, or about that time, but with what instructions I do not know. There also arrived with him a collector for Boston, on behalf of the king, as they said, which was contrary to their privileges of liberties, and he was therefore never acknowledged as such by the merchants there.[1] From this time forth the governor of New York began to act more stringently towards Carteret, and also towards his own subjects. Carteret obtaining information of what had been done in England by Captain Dyer, called together all the principal men among his people, who represented under their signatures the circumstances of the case, and sent the paper to England. The governor of New York went to Staten Island, as to the jurisdiction over which they disagreed, and sent for Carteret to come there in order, as he said, to negotiate with him in peace and friendship. Carteret, probably perceiving his purpose, refused to go, and requested of him if he had anything necessary to communicate to come to him, as he was now not far from his residence, and as he, Carteret, had been so frequently at the fort in New York, he should come once to his house, where he might be assured he would be welcome. Hereupon the governor returned again to New York with his object unaccomplished, and shortly afterwards, by proclamation, declared the nullity of the government of Carteret; that at the most he was only the head of a colony, namely, New Jersey; and that

___

[1] Edward Randolph, the famous royal agent, arrived in New York December 7, 1679.

he was guilty of misusing the king's name, power, and authority. He sent boats several times to Achter Kol to demand
the submission of the place to his authority, which the people
of Achter Kol jeered at and disregarded, being ready to up-
hold the king and their own governor, whom they bound themselves by an oath to maintain. This occurred repeatedly, and
Carteret said that so far from wishing himself to oppose it,
he would, on the contrary, immediately submit, if the governor
of New York would produce the least authority from the king
for what he claimed or did. He however never brought forward anything of the kind, but continued his proceedings;
and at night, and unseasonable hours, and by surprise, took
from New Jersey all the staves of the constables out of their
houses, which was as much as to deprive them of the power
to act. Seeing he could accomplish nothing by force, he declared the inhabitants released from their oaths to the Heer
Carteret; they answered they could not acknowledge any
release from their oaths, unless by the same authority which
had required it of them or the exhibition of a higher one, that
of the king. At length he corrupted one of Carteret's domes-
tics, for Carteret had no soldiers or fortifications, but resided
in a country house only. He then equipped some yachts and
a ketch with soldiers, arms, and ammunition, and despatched
them to Achter Kol in order to abduct Carteret in any manner
it could be done. They entered his house, I know not how,
at midnight, seized him naked, dragged him through the
window, struck and kicked him terribly, and even injured
him internally. They threw him, all naked as he was, into a
canoe, without any cap or hat on his head, and carried him in
that condition to New York, where they furnished him clothes
and shoes and stockings, and then conducted him to the fort
and put him immediately in prison. When they seized him
at Achter Kol the armed boats had gone home, and the seizure
was accomplished through treachery. Two of the head men
of Carteret immediately took possession of his papers, such as
were of importance to him, and travelled, one to Maryland,
and the other, crossing the upper part of the North River, to
Boston overland, and both to England, in order to remonstrate.
The governor sent immediately to Achter Kol, took possession
of the place, posted up orders, and caused inquiries to be made

for the man who had set Carteret over the river, but without success.

While Carteret was in prison he was sick, very sick, they said, in regard to which there were various surmises. Meanwhile a court of assizes was convened, to which on every occasion the governor was conducted by three trumpeters in advance of him. Carteret was brought before the same court, after him. The governor had caused a seat to be erected in the court room high up above all the others, and higher than usual, on which he sat. Governor Carteret, as a criminal, was in the middle. The court being seated, the governor presented Carteret as guilty of misusing the king's name, power, and authority, and usurping the government of New Jersey; that he was only the head of a colony, etc. Whereupon Carteret, having the right to speak, said it was far from his intention to seek to defend his case before that court; he did not acknowledge it as a court having power to decide his case, because in the first place the question could not be determined in a court of assizes, as it did not concern a private right, but the right of the king; in the next place, if such a question could be disposed of in such a court, this nevertheless could not act, because he was not subject to its jurisdiction; and thirdly, because it was a court of one party, and he said this without wishing to offend any of the individual members of the court; yet notwithstanding all this he was content that he and his case should be brought before them in order that they might be witnesses of what was done and to be done. As to what the governor of New York alleged, he said it was wonderful to him that he should be thus treated, and that they should dispute a matter which neither the governor of New York, nor his court, nor any one in the world had ever disputed, or with reason could dispute. The governor said he had never acknowledged him as governor of New Jersey. "It is surprising," said Carteret, "that at one time there can be disavowed before all the world, what has been assented to before all the world at another;" and thereupon he took out of his pocket several letters of the governor of New York, all addressed to the governor of New Jersey. The governor did not know what to say to this except that he had so directed them because Carteret was generally styled governor, and not because he was so in fact;

'"for," said he, "although I have done that, can I therefore
make you governor?" "No," replied Carteret, "but the king
has made me governor, and you as well as all the world have
acknowledged me as such." The acts of the king in relation
to the governorship were then produced, and it was found that
the one to Carteret was some time older than that to the governor of New York, and therefore, said Carteret, it is to be
preferred. The governor of New York replied, "mine is more
recent, and yours is therefore annulled by it." "That is
to be shown," rejoined Carteret. Although the governor of
New York had employed a lawyer, he could not succeed.
When at last the jury retired, in order to consult among themselves, Carteret exhibited letters from the king himself, in
which he called him governor of New Jersey. The jury returned and declared Carteret not guilty of what was charged
against him. The governor made them retire a second time,
saying to them it would be well for them to consider what they
did, as more depended upon the matter than they imagined.
They came back a second time with the same verdict. Whereupon the governor became very angry, and caused them to
go out again with threats that they should look to what they
did, as there was too much depended upon it, for themselves,
their entire condition and welfare. Whereupon Carteret told
them they had nothing to fear in committing themselves into
the king's own hands who had given him authority. Again
the jury returned and gave in the same verdict: that as Carteret was not under them and did not acknowledge them as his
judges, they could not do otherwise in the case; but they advised Carteret to return to his house and business at Achter
Kol as a private individual until the case be decided by higher
authority, which Carteret was willing to do, not because it
was a sentence of theirs against him, or even their advice, but
because he was compelled to do so and could not at that time
do otherwise. And thus the affair stood at our departure,
the governor taking him back to Achter Kol with all the mag-
nificence he could. Some think this was all a made-up piece
of work, and that the governor of New York only sought to
possess the government and had no design against the person
of Carteret; and having obtained what he wanted, had no
other or better means than to release him with some show.

The principal persons who have assisted the governor herein are Captain Dyer before mentioned, Captain Nicols,[1] and some others. This matter transpired before all the world. The principal speeches which were made in court were related to us and as regards the other transactions we saw them. It is fortunate we were there when the affair terminated, as we were thus enabled to understand the nature of this government as well as of the governor.[2]

As to what the governor has done in regard to his own subjects: wherever they lived, they had the right to do whatever they considered best for a livelihood; but as this country yields in abundance everything most essential for life, if the inhabitants so apply it, its shipping does not amount to much, for the reason that they have everything at home, and have little occasion to borrow or buy from their neighbors; and as the exports or imports were not much, and produced few customs or duties, in which his profit consists, there was little bought from the merchants of articles obtained from abroad. There was therefore no profit from that source to them or him —for he also is a merchant, and keeps a store publicly like the others, where you can buy half a penny's worth of pins. They usually make at least a hundred per cent. profit. And here it is to be remarked, that as Fredrick Flipsen has the most shipping and does the largest trade, it is said he is in partnership with the governor, which is credible and inferable from the privileges which Frederick enjoys above the other merchants in regard to his goods and ships. Now one of the principal navigations of this place is that with Barbados, which formerly did not amount to much, for the people could ob-

[1] Captain Mathias Nicolls, secretary of the province.

[2] While it may be doubted whether in strictness the language of the grants to Berkeley and Carteret gave them rights of government, precedents extending from 1665 allowed them the constant exercise of such rights. Andros, however, especially now that Sir George Carteret had died, in January, 1680, asserted that all rights of government remained unimpaired in the Duke of York. Governor Carteret's narrative of the high-handed proceedings by which he tried to exercise these rights may be seen in Leaming and Spicer's *Grants and Concessions*, pp. 683, 684. Substantially it agrees with that of Danckaerts. The arrest took place on April 30, 1680, the trial on May 27. But by additional deeds of release, in August and September, 1680, the Duke conceded governmental rights to the representatives of the proprietaries. Andros was recalled, but remained in favor.

tain the productions of Barbados cheap enough from Boston, which had a great trade with that island, and where its productions are cheap in consequence of their exemptions from duties, for they paid scarcely any duty, customs, or other charges. As no French brandies can come into the English dominions, they can not be imported into New York, though they are free at Boston; and as New Netherland is a country overflowing with grain, much liquor was distilled there from grain, and therefore they had no necessity of going elsewhere to buy strong liquors. This brought no profit to the merchants, but on the contrary a loss, for in the first place a large quantity of grain was consumed in distillation, by which means the grain continued too dear, according to the views of the merchants, who received it from the poor boors in payment of their debts, there being no money in circulation; in the second place, it prevented the importation of rum, a spirituous liquor made from sugar in Barbados, and consequently any duties; and thirdly, the merchants did not realize the double percentage of profit, namely, upon the meal they might send to Barbados, and upon the rum which they would sell here. The governor therefore prohibited the distilling of spirituous liquors, whereby not only were many persons ruined who supported themselves by that business, but the rum which had to be procured from the merchants rose in price, and they sold it as high as they pleased; on the other hand the price of grain fell very much, because it could not be consumed, and the merchants gave no more for it than they chose. And thus the poor farmers soon had to work for nothing, all their sweat and labor going with usury into the pockets of the tradesmen. The trade to Barbados now began to increase, and the merchants and the governor to make more gains. The common people, who could not trade to Barbados, but could buy what they wanted at Boston as cheaply as they could order it from Barbados, sent their flour to Boston, and obtained their goods much cheaper than their own merchants sold them. But as this was contributing too much to Boston, although the trade had always been free there, and was injuring the profits of the merchants of New York, the governor forbade any further trading to Boston; though the people of Boston should have the privilege to come and buy at New York on their own account. This took away almost all the trade with Boston, which had been very large, and straitened the farmers and common people still more, while the merchants became, if not worse, at least great usurers and cheats. The grain by this means fell still lower in price, and while we were there the people could not obtain more than four or five guilders in *zeewan* for a schepel of fine wheat, that is, sixteen stivers or one guilder of Holland money.[1] On the other hand, the merchants charged so dreadfully dear what the common man had to buy of them, that he could hardly ever pay them off, and remained like a child in their debt, and consequently their slave. It is considered at New York a great treasure and liberty, not to be indebted to the merchants, for any one who is will never be able to pay them. The richest of the farmers and common people, however, in company or singly, sent their goods to Barbados, on their own account, and ordered from there what they thought proper; and although they had to pay duties, and freight to the merchants for the goods which were carried in their ships, they nevertheless saved to themselves the profits on the goods. The governor at last has forbidden any flour to be bolted except in the city, or to be exported, unless [the exporters] come and reside in the city, and buy their burger or trader-right, which is five beaver skins, and has forbidden all persons whomsoever from carrying on trade, except those whom he licenses, and who know what they must pay him yearly, according to the amount of their sales. All goods sold outside of the city, in the country, must be bought in New York, and not imported on private account from abroad. Madame Rentselaer had even erected a new bolting mill before the last harvest by his advice, which was not yet in operation, when he prohibited bolting. Such was the situation of affairs when we left there. It is true that all goods imported into the South River from abroad had to pay not only import but also export duties, but those bought in New York, or from the merchants there on their own account, pay little or no export duty. And it would appear as if the whole of the proceedings with Carteret and him were founded in this, if they have no higher cause.

They say now, as he has accomplished these objects in

---

[1] About fifty-five cents for a bushel.

regard to his own people and Carteret, he will turn his attention to the Quakers on the South River, who assert that they are not subject to his government, and also to the people on the Fresh River [Connecticut], who claim to be members of the republic of Boston, and even to those of Boston; but whether all this is designed by him is doubtful.[1]

The shoemakers, in consequence of the abundance of hides and bark in the country, have prepared their own leather; but as it was not necessary that every shoemaker should have his own tannery, some of them have put up several tanneries jointly, and others who were not so rich or had not so much to do, had their leather tanned by them, or tanned it themselves in those tanneries, satisfying the owners for the privilege. The proprietors of the tanneries began to exact too much from those who had their leather tanned, whereupon the poorer ones complained to the governor about it. He seized the opportunity to forbid all tanning whatsoever, and to order that the hides should be sent to Europe, and the leather ordered from there for the purpose of making shoes, or else ready-made shoes imported. By this means the farmers and others would be compelled to come and sell their hides to the merchants, who would give for them what they chose, he would derive taxes and duties from them, and the merchants their freight and percentage of profit; leather which is dear in Europe would pay perhaps taxes once or twice there, and freight and taxes or duties again here; the merchants would have their profit, and then the shoemaker would get the leather for the purpose of making shoes. A pair of shoes now costs 16 or 20 guilders, that is, four guilders in Holland money;[2] what would they cost then? And as labor in Europe is cheaper than here, it is certain that shoes made there would be cheaper than the leather would cost here, and thus all the shoemakers here would be ruined, and all their means go to the governor and the merchants. This subject was under discussion, and

---

[1] By "the Quakers on the South River" the writer means the province of West Jersey, the dealings with Carteret having related to East Jersey alone. The people of Connecticut, it is hardly necessary to remark, did not claim to be members of the *republic* of Boston, though united with it in the New England confederation.

[2] One dollar and seventy cents.

had not yet gone into effect when we left.   As they discovered
that leather is contraband, I think the order is stopped for
that reason.   The intention however is evident.

He has taken away land from several country people, and
given it to others who applied to him for it, because it was not
inclosed, and he wishes, as he says, the land to be cultivated,
and not remain waste.   But it is impossible that all the land
bought in the first instance for the purpose of being cultivated
by the purchasers or their heirs, as they generally buy a large
tract with that object, can be put in fence immediately and
kept so, much less be cultivated.   He has also curtailed all
the farms in the free colony of Rentselaerswyck, as well as their
privileges.   Some persons being discouraged, and wishing to
leave for the purpose of going to live under Carteret, he threatened to confiscate all their goods and effects.   He said to others
who came to him and complained they could not live under
these prohibitions: "If they do not suit you, leave the country,
and the sooner you do it the better."

A certain poor carman had the misfortune to run over a
child which died.   He fled, although the world pitied him, and
excused him because he could not have avoided it.   The court,
according to some law of England, on account of his having
seven sons, acquitted him, provided his wife with her seven
sons would go and prostrate themselves before the governor,
and ask pardon for their husband and father.   The carman
was restored by the court to his business, which he began again
to exercise, when the governor, meeting him on his cart in the
street, asked him who had given him permission to ride again.
The carman replied: "My Lord, it is by permission and order
of the court."   "Come down at once," the governor said, "and
remember you do not attempt it again during your life."
Thus he violated the order of the court, and the poor man had
to seek some other employment to earn his bread.

A citizen of New York had a dog which was very useful to
him.   This dog by accident went into the fort, where madam
the governor's wife was standing, and looked steadily at her,
in expectation, perhaps, of obtaining something from her, like
a beggar.   The lady was much discomposed and disturbed,
and related the circumstance to her husband.   The governor
immediately caused inquiries to be made as to the ownership

of the dog, summoned his master before him, spoke to him
severely, and ordered him to kill the dog forthwith. The man
was very sorry for the dog, and endeavored to save him till
the anger of the governor was over. He placed him on board
of a vessel sailing from and to the city, so as to prevent his
coming on land. The governor being informed of this by
some spy or informer, I know not whom, but of such there is
no lack, summoned the man again before him, and asked him
if he had killed his dog. The man answered he had not, but
had done thus and so, whereupon the governor reprimanded
him severely, imposed a heavy fine upon him, and required, I
believe, two of his sons to be security until he had killed the
dog in the presence of witnesses whom he would send for that
purpose.

This will be enough, I think, to enable such as have understanding, to comprehend him. As for us, we did not have
much difficulty in interpreting him from the first. Grace and
power have been given us to act so that neither he nor any
one else should have any hold upon us. For as we were openly
before the world, he had not much to do with us, the more so
as you could trust no one, because he has people everywhere
to spy and listen to everything, and carry what they hear to
him; so every one endeavors to stand well with him. In a
word he is very politic; being governor and, changeably, a
trader, he appears friendly because he is both; severe because
he is avaricious; and well in neither capacity because they are
commingled. The Lord be praised who has delivered us
safely, and the more, because we were in every one's eye and
yet nobody knew what to make of us; we were an enigma to
all. Some declared we were French emissaries going through
the land to spy it out; others, that we were Jesuits travelling
over the country for the same purpose; some that we were
Recollets, designating the places where we had held mass and
confession; others that we were sent out by the Prince of
Orange or the States of Holland, and as the country was so
easily conquered, to see what kind of a place it was, and
whether it was worth the trouble to endeavor to recover it,
and how many soldiers it would require to hold it; others again
that we had been sent out as the principals to establish a new
colony, and were therefore desirous of seeing and examining

everything. And thus each one drifted along according to his wishes. The Papists believed we were priests and we could not get rid of them; they would have us confess them, baptize their children, and perform mass; and they continued in this opinion. The Quakers said we were Quakers, because we were not expensively dressed, and did not curse and swear, that we were not willing to avow ourselves as such; but they were jealous because we had not associated with them. Some said we were Mennonists; others that we were Brownists, and others again that we were David Jorists.[1] Every one had his own opinion, and no one the truth. Some accused us of holding conventicles or meetings, and even at the magistrate's or burgomaster's, and named the place where and the persons who attended them, some of whom were required to purge themselves of the charge, and others were spoken to in a different way. It was all finally found to be false, and that they were mistaken, though few of them were cured of their opinion. The ministers caused us to be suspected; the world and the godless hated and shunned us; the hypocrites envied and slandered us; but the simple and upright listened to us and loved us; and God counselled and directed us. May He be praised and glorified by all His children to all eternity, for all that He is, and all that He does, for all that He is doing for them, and all that He may do for them, to all eternity.

12th, *Wednesday*. Theunis came to our house and took leave of us with great tenderness and with many tears, he committing us, and we him, to God and His grace, recommending himself to our prayers and the prayers of God's children— his beloved brothers and sisters, he said, to whom, although he had never seen them, he requested us to make his salutations.[2] In the evening Ephraim also came to take leave, intending to go south in order to leave his wife there during her confinement. We said to each of them what we deemed necessary.

13th, *Thursday*. It was first announced that we were to leave on Wednesday, then the following Saturday, afterwards on Tuesday, and again on Thursday without fail. Finally we

[1] A sect of mystical and antinomian Anabaptists, followers of David Joris of Delft (d. 1556); otherwise called Familists, or the Family of Love.

[2] Meaning the community of Wieuwerd.

spoke to the skipper or supercargo, Paddechal, who told us he
could not leave before the governor returned, who had some
letters of importance to send by him.   This evening Annetje
Sluys, of whom we have spoken,[1] came to see us.   She had some
ambergris which she wanted us to take, but we did not know
what to do in regard to the terms.   Among others, we made
three different propositions; namely, we would fix the price at
eight pieces of eight the ounce here, and would endeavor to
sell it in Holland as high as we could, and would take one-half
of what it brought over that valuation for our trouble, provided
we could take our portion of the profit out in ambergris at the
current price; or, we would take it all ourselves at eight pieces
of eight the ounce to be paid for in Holland; or, she should
give us one ounce for our trouble and we would sell the rest
of it for her and send back the proceeds to her in goods.   The
second proposition seemed to be the most profitable, if we had
a correct knowledge of the ambergris, but we had none at all;
and if it were not good it would be a great loss.   The first
proposition might, or might not, yield us a profit, but it seemed
to us too tradesmanlike.   It therefore remained with the last
one.   There were twelve ounces of it good, or what we considered good, and four ounces bad.   One ounce was weighed
off for us, and the rest was taken upon that condition.   My
comrade gave her a receipt, acknowledging it was received
from her on such conditions, and she gave a memorandum of
the goods which she wanted for the proceeds.[2]

[1] Not identified.
[2] At this point there is a break in the journal.   See the Introduction to the
volume.

JOURNAL OF OUR VOYAGE FROM NEW NETHERLAND

Until Our Arrival at Wywert, in Friesland

1680, JUNE 19th, *Wednesday*.   We embarked at noon in the yacht of Mr. Padechal, supercargo and captain, residing in Boston.   The anchor was weighed at last; but as we had to wait a long time for the governor's yacht, the tide was nearly all spent.   The wind was from the northwest.   The crew consisted of three men and a boy, besides the captain; but there was another sailor on board who was a passenger.   Many persons came to escort the captain, and also a woman, who was going with us; and as soon as they had gone we hastened to leave.   The wind being ahead, we tacked and towed, until we anchored at Hellgate, almost at flood tide, at four o'clock, in the afternoon.   The woman who was going over with us was born at Rhode Island, in New England, and was the wife of the captain of the *Margaret*, one of Frederick Flipsen's ships. I have never in my whole life witnessed a worse, more foul, profane, or abandoned creature.   She is the third individual we have met with from New England, and we remarked to each other, if the rest of the people there are to be judged by them, we might perhaps do them great injustice; for the first one from Boston whom we saw was a sailor, or he passed for one, on board the ship in which we sailed from the Fatherland. They called him the doctor, and if he were not or had not been a charlatan, he resembled one; the second was our skipper, Padechal, who had told us so many lies; and now this infamous woman.   They all belong to this people who, it is said, pretend to special devoutness; but we found them, the sailor, and the rest, like all other Englishmen, who, if they are not more detestable than the Hollanders, are at least no better.

20th, *Thursday*.   It was about ten o'clock in the forenoon before the flood began to make.   The wind was southwest, but light.   We weighed anchor and towed through Hellgate, when

252

the wind and tide served us until we passed Whitestone,[1] as far as which the tide, from the direction of New York, usually reaches. We sailed bravely by and obtained the ebb tide in our favor which carried us this evening beyond Milford.

21st, Friday. We had shot ahead very well during the night, with the wind west and south-southwest, on a course due east, so that by morning we reached the end of Long Island. The governor's yacht, which had to stop at Fisher's Island, a little to the leeward of us, which is subject to New England, but which the governor is now endeavoring to bring under his authority, and for that purpose had sent his yacht there with letters, left us this morning with a salute. We observed a vessel ahead of us under sail, running before the wind, and we came up to her about nine o'clock. She was a small flute from Milford, laden with horses and bound for Barbados. We hailed her, and as her captain was an acquaintance of our captain and an Independent, our captain went on board of her, where he staid two hours. When he returned we kept our course, and she sailed to the south in order to get to sea. As soon as we reached the end of Long Island, they began to throw their fish lines, and continued to catch mackerel all day long. I think the European mackerel are better and fatter. We came to an island called Maertens Wingaert,[2] about four o'clock in the afternoon, having the Elizabeth Islands on the larboard and sailing between the two, with our course easterly and a lighter wind. Our captain had prayers every evening, performed in this way. The people were called together, and then, without anything being spoken previously, he read a chapter, then a psalm or part of one was sung, after that they all turned their backs to each other, half kneeling, when a common formulary of prayer was said which was long enough, but irreverently enough delivered. It was not done mornings. From what I have experienced the Hollanders perform it better, are more strict mornings and evenings, and more devout.

There was no moon, and the weather was cloudy. We continued sailing onward until two o'clock after midnight, when the captain going aloft cried out, "Strike the sails! strike

---

[1] In the easterly part of Flushing, Long Island.

[2] Martha's Vineyard. They sailed through Vineyard Sound.

the sails! let them run! let them run! we are on the rocks, let the anchor fall!" This startled me so that I cannot tell how I reached the deck, and ran forward. I saw we were indeed close upon a reef of rocks directly before us, and that we were under considerable headway. We did our best to lower the sails, and throw the anchor over. The headway was checked somewhat, but the anchor would not hold. We found that the spritsail had caught in the anchor-stock in consequence of the hurry in lowering the sail and throwing anchor, but it was some time before we could discover what was the matter and get the anchor loose; it then held fast in three fathoms of water at a musket shot's distance from the reef and about as far from the shore. We lay there until daylight on a lee shore, but fortunately it did not blow hard.

22d, *Saturday.* As soon as the day broke, and we saw where we were, we got under sail again with the wind, the same as before. In sailing between the land, namely Maertens Wyngaert, and the reef, the course is to the point of the island, running east-southeast in three and two and a half fathoms till you have this point on the side, and then you have passed the reef. We continued on until we reached the westerly point of the island of Nantoeket, along which we sailed to the easterly point, and thence due north until noon; but the flood tide running in strong, and the vessel not being well steered, we were carried to the west among the shoals. The weather was rather rough and the atmosphere hazy, so that we could not see far. The shoals were ahead of us, and we had only two fathoms, and even less, of water. The captain and helmsman were confused, and hardly knew where they were. This happened two or three times. In order to avoid the shoals, we had to keep to the east. We were fearful we should strike upon them, and it was therefore best to look out and keep free of them. About three o'clock we caught sight of the main land of Cape Cod, to which we sailed northerly. We arrived inside the cape about six o'clock, with a tolerable breeze from the west, and at the same time saw vessels to the leeward of us which had an east wind, from which circumstance we supposed we were in a whirlwind. These two contrary winds striking against each other, the sky became dark, and they whirled by each other, sometimes the one, and sometimes the other being strongest, compelling us to lower the sails several times. I have never seen such a twisting and turning round in the air as at this time, the clouds being driven against each other, and close to the earth. At last it became calm and began to rain very hard, and to thunder and lighten heavily. We drifted along the whole night in a calm, advancing only twelve or sixteen miles.

23d, Sunday. A breeze blew up from the northeast. It was fortunate for us that we arrived inside of Cape Cod yesterday evening, before this unfavorable weather, as we should otherwise have been compelled to put back to Rhode Island. We could now still proceed; and we laid our course northwest to Boston. We arrived at the entrance of the harbor at noon, where we found a considerable rolling sea caused by the ebb tide and wind being against each other. There are about thirty islands here, not large ones, through which we sailed, and reached Boston at four o'clock in the afternoon, our captain running with his yacht quite up to his house in the Milk-ditch.[1]

The Lord be praised, who has continued in such a fatherly manner to conduct us, and given us so many proofs of His care over us; words are wanting to express ourselves properly, more than occasions for them, which we have had abundantly.

We permitted those most in haste to go ashore before us, and then went ourselves. The skipper received us politely at his house, and so did his wife; but as it was Sunday, which it seems is somewhat strictly observed by these people, there was not much for us to do today. Our captain, however, took us to his sister's where we were welcome, and from there to his father's, an old corpulent man, where there was a repetition of the worship, which took place in the kitchen while they were turning the spit, and busy preparing a good supper. We arrived while they were engaged in the service, but he did not once look up. When he had finished, they turned round their backs, and kneeled on chairs or benches. The prayer was said loud enough to be heard three houses off, and also long enough, if that made it good. This done, he wished us and his son welcome, and insisted on our supping with him, which we did.

---

[1] This seems to mean the creek which made in from the cove at the foot of Milk Street.

There were nine or ten persons at the table. It being in the evening, and we strangers, Mr. Padechal requested us to lodge with him this night, as we did, intending in the morning to look out for accommodations. We were taken to a fine large chamber, but we were hardly in bed before we were shockingly bitten. I did not know the cause, but not being able to sleep, I became aware it was bed-bugs, in such great numbers as was inconceivable. My comrade, who was very sleepy, fell asleep at first. He tumbled about very much; but I did not sleep any the whole night. In the morning we saw how it was, and were astonished we should find such a room with such a lady.

But before we part from the East River, we must briefly describe it. We have already remarked that it is incorrect to call this stream a river, as both ends of it run into the sea. It is nothing but salt water, an arm of the sea, embracing Long Island. It begins at the Little Bay of the North River, before the city of New York, pouring its waters with those of the North River into the sea, between Sandy Hook and Coney Island. In its mouth before the city, and between the city and Red Hook, on Long Island, lies Noten Island [1] opposite the fort, the first place the Hollanders ever occupied in this bay. It is now only a farm with a house and a place upon it where the governor keeps a parcel of sheep. From the city, or from this island, the river runs easterly to Correlaers Hoeck and the Wale Bocht, where it is so narrow they can readily hear one another calling across it. A little west of Correlaers Hoeck, a reef of rocks stretches out towards the Wale Bocht, half way over, on which at low tide there is only three or four feet of water, more or less. The river then runs up northerly to Hellgate, where there is an island, in front of which on the south side are two rocks, covered at high water, and close to the island, besides others which can be easily seen. Hellgate is nothing more than a bend of the river, which, coming up north, turns thence straight to the east. It is narrow here, and in the middle of the bend or elbow lie several large rocks. On either side it is wider, consequently the current is much stronger in the narrow part; and as it is a bend the water is checked, and made to eddy, and then, striking these rocks, it must make its way to one side or the other, or to both; but it

[1] Governor's Island.

cannot make its way to both, because it is a crooked bay, and
therefore it pursues its course until it is stopped on the opposite side of the bay, to which it is driven, so much the more
because it encounters these rocks on the way.   Now between
the rocks there is no current, and behind them it is still; and
as the current for the most part is forced from one side, it
finds liberty behind these rocks, where it makes a whirlpool.
You must therefore be careful not to approach this whirlpool,
especially with small vessels, as you will be in danger of being
drawn under.   It makes such a whirlpit and whistling that
you can hear it for a quarter of an hour's distance, but this is
when the tide is ebbing, and only, and mostly, when it is running the strongest.   The river continues from thence easterly,
forming several islands, generally on the left-hand side, although there are some in a large bay on the right.   When you
have passed the large bay of Flushing, which is about eight
miles from Hellgate, or rather, as soon as you get round the
point, and begin to see an opening, you must keep well to the
northeast, in order to sail clear of a long ledge of rocks, some
of which stick out of the water like the Lizard in the Channel
near Falmouth.   After you have passed this you sail easterly
along the shore without anything in the way.   There are
islands here and there, near the land, but they are not large.
The end of Long Island, which is one hundred and forty-four
miles long, runs off low and sandy.   Continuing east you pass
Plum Island, which is about four miles in length.   Behind the
bay of Long Island called the Cromme Gouwe[1] there are several small islands, Gardiner's Island and others.   At the east
point of Plum Island there is a reef, or some small rocks, but
keeping on to the eastward, you sail far enough from them.
From Plum Island to Adriaen Blocx Island [2] the course is east
a distance of twenty or twenty-two miles.   This island is eight
miles long.   Thence to Maertens Wingaert the distance is
fifty-two to fifty-six miles further east, and Blockx Island is
hardly out of sight when you see Maertens Wingaert.   Between
Plum Island and Blockx Island you leave Fisher's Island to
the north, nearest Plum Island; and between Blockx Island

[1] "The crooked bay," i. e., Peconic Bay.
[2] Block Island, discovered by Adrian Block.   The journalist is wrong as to
Rhode Island not lying within the coast.

and Maertens Wingaert you leave on the coast Rhode Island,
which does not lie within the coast, as the chart indicates, but
outside, and lies nearest Maertens Wingaert. With Maertens
Wingaert begin the Elizabeth Islands, which consist of six or
seven islands lying in a row, close to each other, towards the
coast. The width between Maertens Wingaert and the Elizabeth Islands is eight miles. There is a fine sound or strait for
sailing between them, although Maertens Wingaert is somewhat longer. This island is about twenty-eight miles in length
towards the east. A little within the east point of it a reef of
rocks stretches out three miles from the shore, so that it is best
to keep nearest the Elizabeth Islands, although there is room
enough between Maertens Wingaert and the reef to sail
through with large ships, as there is three and two and a half
fathoms of water at low tide. At the westerly point of the
Elizabeth Islands there are several rocks, one large and several
small ones, called after their fashion, the Sow and Pigs. There
is a beautiful bay, and anchorage ground on the east end of
Maertens Wingaert.[1] From this point of Maertens Wingaert
the course is east-southeast about twenty miles, to Nantocket
upon the west point of which there is a good bay with anchorage ground. The land is low and sandy; it is fourteen or
sixteen miles long. There are several shoals outside in the
sea, and also inside between the island and the main land, but
they do not run out beyond the east point. When you have
the east point to the west-southwest of you, steer straight north
to Cape Cod, about twenty-eight miles; but you must here
time the tides, which run strong east and west; the flood to
the west, and the ebb to the east. The flood tide pulls to the
shoals, and the ebb tide on the contrary sets eastwardly to the
sea. Cape Cod is a clean coast, where there are no islands,
rocks or banks, and therefore all such laid down on the charts
of the great reef of Malebarre and otherwise are false. Indeed,
within four, eight and twelve miles, there is sixty to sixty-five
fathoms of water. This cape or coast is about twenty-eight
miles long due north; and from thence to Cape Ann it is also
due north, but to Boston it is northwest. There are many
small islands before Boston, well on to fifty, I believe, between
which you sail on to the city. A high one, or the highest, is

[1] Vineyard Haven.

the first that you meet. It is twelve miles from the city, and has a light-house[1] upon it which you can see from a great distance, for it is in other respects naked and bare. In sailing by this island, you keep it on the west side; on the other side there is an island with many rocks upon and around it, and when you pass by it you must be careful, as a shoal pushes out from it, which you must sail round. You have then an island in front, in the shape of a battery, which also you leave on the larboard, and then you come in sight of the island upon which the fort stands, and where the flag is flown when ships are entering.[2] That, too, lies to the larboard, and you pass close enough to it for them to hail the ship, what you are, from whence you came, and where you are bound, etc. When you are there you see the city lying directly before you; and so you sail into the bay before the town, and cast anchor. There is a high hill in the city,[3] also with a light-house upon it, by which you can hold your course in entering.

24th, Monday. We walked with our captain into the town, for his house stood a little one side of it, and the first house he took us to was a tavern. From there, he conducted us to the governor, who dwelt in only a common house, and that not the most costly. He is an old man, quiet and grave.[4] He was dressed in black silk, but not sumptuously. Paddechal explained the reasons of our visit. The governor inquired who we were, and where from, and where we were going. Paddechal told him we were Hollanders, and had come on with him from New York, in order to depart from here for England. He asked further our names, which we wrote down for him. He then presented us a small cup of wine, and with that we finished. We went then to the house of one John Tayller, or merchant

[1] It can hardly have been more than a beacon. The first lighthouse was built in pursuance of an act of 1715, the preamble of which begins, "Whereas the want of a lighthouse at the entrance of the harbour of Boston hath been a great discouragement to navigation," etc. The new lighthouse was to be erected "on the southermost point of Great Brewster, called Beacon Island."

[2] George's Island; next, Castle Island, with the "castle" first built in 1635.

[3] Beacon Hill.

[4] Simon Bradstreet, elected in May, 1679, was governor of Massachusetts till 1686—the last governor under the old charter. He had come out in 1630, and was now seventy years old.

tailor,[1] to whom William van Cleyf had recommended us; but we did not find him. We wanted to obtain a place where we could be at home, and especially to ascertain if there were any Dutchmen. They told us of a silversmith who was a Dutchman, and at whose house the Dutch usually went to lodge. We went in search of him, but he was not at home. At noon we found this merchant tailor, who appeared to be a good sort of a person. He spoke tolerably good French, and informed us there was a ship up for England immediately, and another in about three weeks. The first was too soon for us, and we therefore thought it best to wait for the other. We also found the silversmith, who bade us welcome. His name was Willem Ros, from Wesel. He had married an Englishwoman, and carried on his business here. He told us we might come and lodge with him, if we wished, which we determined to do; for to lie again in our last night's nest was not agreeable to us. We exchanged some of our money, and obtained six shillings and six-pence each for our ducatoons, and ten shillings each for the ducats. We went accordingly to lodge at the goldsmith's, whom my comrade knew well, though he did not recollect my comrade.[2] We were better off at his house, for although his wife was an Englishwoman, she was quite a good housekeeper.

25th, *Tuesday*. We went in search of Mr. Paddechal this morning and paid him for our passage here, twenty shillings New England currency, for each of us. We wanted to obtain our goods, but they were all too busy then, and promised they would send them to us in the city the next day. We inquired after Mr. John Pigon, to whom Mr. Robert Sanders, of Albany, promised to send Wouter the Indian, with a letter, but he had received neither the letter nor the Indian; so that we must offer up our poor Indian to the pleasure of the Lord. We also went to look after the ship, in which we were going to leave for London. We understood the name of the captain was Jan Foy. The ship was called the *Dolphin*, and mounted sixteen guns.[3] Several passengers were engaged. There was a sur-

---

[1] Original, "Jan Tayller of [Dutch for *or*] Marchand Tayller." No John Taylor of Boston answering to the description has been identified.

[2] Sluyter was from Wesel, on the Rhine. Though it was a German town, many of its inhabitants were Dutch (like Peter Minuit) and Walloon.

[3] Captain John Foy appears in the records of the court of assistants, as still master of the *Dolphin*, in 1691.

geon in the service of the ship from Rotterdam, named Johan
Owins, who had been to Surinam[1] and afterwards to the island
of Fayal,[2] from whence he had come here, and now wished to
go home.   There was also a sailor on board the ship who spoke
Dutch, or was a Dutchman.   The carpenter was a Norwegian
who lived at Flushing.

26*th, Wednesday.*   We strove hard to get our goods home,
for we were fearful, inasmuch as our trunk was on deck, and
it had rained, and a sea now and then had washed over it,
that it might be wet and ruined; but we did not succeed, and
Paddechal in this exhibited again his inconsiderateness, and
little regard for his promise.   We resolved to take it out the
next day, go as it would.

27*th, Thursday.*   We went to the Exchange in order to
find the merchant tailor, and also the skipper, which we did.
We agreed for our passage at the usual price of six pounds
sterling for each person, with the choice of paying here or in
England; but as we would have less loss on our money here,
we determined to pay here.   After 'change was over there was
preaching,[3] to which we had intended to go; but as we had
got our goods home, after much trouble, and found several
articles wet and liable to be spoiled, we had to stay and dry
them.

28*th, Friday.*   One of the best ministers in the place being
very sick, a day of fasting and prayer was observed in a church
near by our house.   We went into the church, where, in the
first place, a minister made a prayer in the pulpit, of full two
hours in length; after which an old minister delivered a sermon
an hour long, and after that a prayer was made, and some verses
sung out of the Psalms.   In the afternoon, three or four hours
were consumed with nothing except prayers, three ministers
relieving each other alternately; when one was tired, another
went up into the pulpit.[4]   There was no more devotion than
in other churches, and even less than at New York; no respect,

---

[1] A Dutch settlement in Guiana, owned at this time by the province of
Zeeland; the present Dutch Guiana.

[2] In the Azores.

[3] The Thursday Lecture.

[4] This fast is not noted in the elaborate list in Mr. Love's *Fast and Thanks-
giving Days of New England.*   The Old South Church had a fast on June 29,
O. S., but this was June 28, N. S.

no reverence; in a word, nothing but the name of Independents; and that was all.

29*th, Saturday.* To-day a captain arrived from New York, named Lucas, who had sailed from there last Friday. He said no ships had arrived there from Europe, and that matters remained as we left them. There was a report that another governor was coming to New York, and it was said he was a man who was much liked in Boston; that many complaints had been made against the other one, such as oppressing the people, imposing high duties when his instructions provided they should not be more than two per cent., I believe, rendering a false account, in which he had charged a dock as having been made at a cost of twenty-eight pounds sterling which had not cost a cent, as the citizens had constructed it themselves, etc.[1] This will perhaps cause some change in these parts and relieve the people. Lucas brought with him the sister and brother-in-law of Ephraim's wife, recently married, but we had never spoken to them.[2]

30*th, Sunday.* We went to church, but there was only one minister in the pulpit, who made a prayer an hour long, and preached the same length of time, when some verses were sung. We expected something particular in the afternoon, but there was nothing more than usual.

JULY 1*st, Monday.* We wrote to De la Grange, at New York, concerning our letters from Europe, and also to Robert Sanders, at Albany, in relation to Wouter.

2*d, Tuesday.* We had a conversation with the captain at the Exchange. He intended to sail round Ireland, which suited us very well, for although it was said the Hollanders were at peace with the Turks, there were many English vessels taken by them daily, and under such circumstances we ran some danger of being plundered, fighting with them, and perhaps being carried into Barbary. It was therefore better to

[1] There was an official inquiry into these charges. See accusation and defense in *N. Y. Col. Doc.*, III. 302, 308.

[2] The bridegroom was Captain Theunis de Key (b. 1659), son of Jacob Theuniszen van Tuyl of New York. The bride was Helena van Brugh, half-sister of Elizabeth Rodenburg, being the daughter of the latter's mother Catharina Roelofs by her second husband, Johannes Pieterszen van Brugh of Haarlem and later of New York.

go around, although it would be late. We went on board the
ship with the captain, in order to look through her. She
pleased us very much, as she was larger than the *Charles*, in
which we came over. We bespoke a berth in the gunner's
room, on the starboard side. The ship was said to be a good
sailer, and the captain to be one of the most discreet navigators
of this country. All that was agreeable to us. In the evening
Ephraim's wife's sister and her husband called upon us, but
they were not much in a state to be spoken to, in regard to
what was most necessary for them, nor was there much opportunity.

3d, *Wednesday*. Our captain said he would leave a week
from to-day. Nothing further occurred.

4th, *Thursday*. Nothing transpired.

5th, *Friday*. In the afternoon Thomas [Theunis] De Key
and his wife, half-sister of Elizabeth Roodenburgh, came to
visit us, but we conversed little about religious matters, following the providence of the Lord.

6th, *Saturday*. Nothing occurred.

7th, *Sunday*. We heard preaching in three churches, by
persons who seemed to possess zeal, but no just knowledge
of Christianity. The auditors were very worldly and inatten-
tive. The best of the ministers whom we have yet heard is a
very old man, named Mr. John Eliot,[1] who has charge of the
instruction of the Indians in the Christian religion. He has
translated the Bible into their language. After we had already
made inquiries of the booksellers for this Bible, and there was
none to be obtained in Boston, and they told us if one was to
be had, it would be from Mr. Eliot, we determined to go on
Monday to the village where he resided, and was the minister,
called Rocsberry [Roxbury]. Our landlord had promised to
take us, but was not able to do so, in consequence of his having

---

[1] Rev. John Eliot (1604–1690), the Apostle to the Indians, came over to
Massachusetts in 1631 and in 1632 was ordained as "teacher" of the church of
Roxbury. He soon engaged in efforts to Christianize the Indians, and in 1646
began to preach to them in their own tongue. He formed a community and church
of "praying Indians" at Natick, and others elsewhere. His translation of the
Bible into the dialect of the Massachusetts Indians was completed in 1658.
The first edition of the New Testament, printed at Cambridge, was issued in
1661, the whole Bible (Old Testament of 1663, New Testament of 1661 imprint,
and metrical version of the Psalms) in 1663.

too much business. We therefore thought we would go alone and do what we wanted.

JULY 8*th, Monday.* We went accordingly, about six o'clock in the morning, to Rocxberry, which is three-quarters of an hour from the city, in order that we might get home early, inasmuch as our captain had informed us, he would come in the afternoon for our money, and in order that Mr. Eliot might not be gone from home. On arriving at his house, he was not there, and we therefore went to look around the village and the vicinity. We found it justly called Rocxberry, for it was very rocky, and had hills entirely of rocks. Returning to his house we spoke to him, and he received us politely. As he could speak neither Dutch nor French, and we spoke but little English, we were unable to converse very well; however, partly in Latin, partly in English, we managed to understand each other. He was seventy-seven years old,[1] and had been forty-eight years in these parts. He had learned very well the language of the Indians, who lived about there. We asked him for an Indian Bible. He said in the late Indian war, all the Bibles and Testaments were carried away, and burnt or destroyed, so that he had not been able to save any for himself; but a new edition was in press, which he hoped would be much better than the first one, though that was not to be despised. We inquired whether any part of the old and new edition could be obtained by purchase, and whether there was any grammar of their language in English. Thereupon he went and brought us one of the Old Testaments in the Indian language, and also almost the whole of the New Testament, made up with some sheets of the new edition of the New Testament, so that we had the Old and New Testaments complete.[2]

---

[1] Eliot was not quite seventy-six.

[2] The first edition of the whole Bible seems to have been 1040 copies, of the separate New Testament, 500. Many copies were lost or destroyed in the Indian war of 1675–1676; but 16 copies now existing of the New Testament, and 39 of the Bible, in this first edition, are listed in Mr. Wilberforce Eames's bibliography. In 1677 Eliot began to prepare a revised edition of the whole work. It was published in 1685. The printing of the New Testament portion was begun in 1680 and finished in the autumn or winter of 1681; the printing of the Old Testament was not begun until 1682.

Wonderful to relate, the identical copy of the Old Testament (edition of 1663, and metrical Psalms) which Eliot presented to Danckaerts and Sluyter is

He also brought us two or three small specimens of the grammar. We asked him what we should pay him for them; but he desired nothing. Thereupon we presented him our *Declaration* in Latin,[1] and informed him about the persons and conditions of the church whose declaration it was, and about Madam Schurman[2] and others, with which he was delighted, and could not restrain himself from praising God the Lord,

still in existence, in the library of the Zeeland Academy of Sciences at Middelburg in the Netherlands. It lacks the title-page, but in its place contains the following manuscript note. See the *Proceedings* of the Massachusetts Historical Society, XIII. 307–310, and the Dutch pamphlet there named.

"All the Bibles of the Christian Indians were burned or destroyed by these heathen savages. This one alone was saved; and from it a new edition, with improvements, and an entirely new translation of the New Testament, was undertaken. I saw at Roccsberri, about an hour's ride from Boston, this Old Testament printed, and some sheets of the New. The printing-office was at Cambridge, three hours' ride from Boston, where also there was a college of students, whether of savages or of other nations. The Psalms of David are added in the same metre.

"At Roccsberri dwelt Mr. Hailot, a very godly preacher there. He was at this time about seventy years old. His son was a preacher at Boston. This good old man was one of the first Independent preachers to settle in these parts, seeking freedom. He was the principal translator and director of the printing of both the first and second editions of this Indian Bible. Out of special zeal and love he gave me this copy of the first edition, for which I was, and shall continue, grateful to him. This was in June, 1680.

"Jasper Danckaerts."

[1] The Labadists' declaration of their orthodoxy and of their reasons for separating themselves from the national (Dutch Reformed) church was first issued in French, in 1669. Two editions of a Dutch translation were published: the first, "translated from the French by N. N.," at Amsterdam in 1671; the second, "translated from the French by P. Sluiter," at Herford in 1672, both by the same printer. Of the former, there is a copy in the library of Haverford College; of the latter, in the New York Public Library. Two editions in German are also known (Herford, 1671, 1672). The Latin, here referred to, is entitled "Protestatio Sincera Purae et Verae Reformatae Doctrinae Generalisque Orthodoxiae Johannis de Labadie," and is to be found in the book *Veritas sui Vindex, seu Solemnis Fidei Declaratio Joh. de Labadie, Petri Yvon, Petri du Lignon, Pastorum,* etc. [the Dutch and German have also the names of "Henry and Peter Sluiter, preachers," on the title-page] (Herford, 1672).

[2] Anna Maria van Schurman (1607–1678), a woman of prodigious learning, held in the highest esteem by literary contemporaries in Holland as well as other lands. She renounced her literary associations to affiliate herself with Jean de Labadie and his followers, shared their fortunes at Amsterdam, Herford, Altona, and Wieuwerd, where William Penn visited her in 1677; and died among them at Wieuwerd in 1678.

that had raised up men, and reformers, and begun the reformation in Holland. He deplored the decline of the church in New England, and especially in Boston, so that he did not know what would be the final result. We inquired how it stood with the Indians, and whether any good fruit had followed his work. Yes, much, he said, if we meant true conversion of the heart; for they had in various countries, instances of conversion, as they called it, and had seen it amounted to nothing at all; that they must not endeavor, like scribes and Pharisees, to make Jewish proselytes, but true Christians. He could thank God, he continued, and God be praised for it, there were Indians whom he knew, who were truly converted of heart to God, and whose profession, he believed, was sincere. It seemed as if he were disposed to know us further, and we therefore said to him, if he had any desire to write to our sort of people, he could use the names which stood on the title-page of the *Declaration*, and that we hoped to come and converse with him again. He accompanied us as far as the jurisdiction of Roxbury extended, where we parted from him.

9th, Tuesday. We started out to go to Cambridge, lying to the northeast of Boston, in order to see their college and printing office. We left about six o'clock in the morning, and were set across the river at Charlestown. We followed a road which we supposed was the right one, but went full half an hour out of the way, and would have gone still further, had not a negro who met us, and of whom we inquired, disabused us of our mistake. We went back to the right road, which is a very pleasant one. We reached Cambridge about eight o'clock. It is not a large village, and the houses stand very much apart. The college building is the most conspicuous among them. We went to it, expecting to see something unusual, as it is the only college, or would-be academy of the Protestants in all America, but we found ourselves mistaken. In approaching the house we neither heard nor saw anything mentionable; but, going to the other side of the building, we heard noise enough in an upper room to lead my comrade to say, "I believe they are engaged in disputation." We entered and went up stairs, when a person met us, and requested us to walk in, which we did. We found there eight or ten young fellows, sitting around, smoking tobacco, with the smoke of which the

room was so full, that you could hardly see; and the whole
house smelt so strong of it that when I was going up stairs I
said, "It certainly must be also a tavern." [1] We excused ourselves, that we could speak English only a little, but understood Dutch or French well, which they did not. However,
we spoke as well as we could. We inquired how many professors there were, and they replied not one, that there was not
enough money to support one. We asked how many students
there were. They said at first, thirty, and then came down
to twenty; I afterwards understood there are probably not
ten. They knew hardly a word of Latin, not one of them, so
that my comrade could not converse with them. They took
us to the library where there was nothing particular. We
looked over it a little. They presented us with a glass of wine.
This is all we ascertained there. The minister of the place
goes there morning and evening to make prayer, and has
charge over them; besides him, the students are under tutors
or masters.[2] Our visit was soon over, and we left them to go
and look at the land about there. We found the place beauti-
fully situated on a large plain, more than eight miles square,
with a fine stream in the middle of it, capable of bearing heavily
laden vessels. As regards the fertility of the soil, we consider
the poorest in New York superior to the best here. As we
were tired, we took a mouthful to eat, and left. We passed by
the printing office, but there was nobody in it; the paper sash
however being broken, we looked in, and saw two presses with

[1] The first building of Harvard College, the building "thought by some to
be too gorgeous for a Wilderness, and yet too mean in others apprehensions for a
Colledg" (Johnson, *Wonder-Working Providence*, p. 201), had partly tumbled down
in 1677. The building now visited was the "New College," the second Harvard
Hall, built with difficulty 1672–1682 and destroyed by fire in 1764. Edward
Randolph, in a report of October 12, 1676, writes: "New-colledge, built at the
publick charge, is a fair pile of brick building covered with tiles, by reason of the
late Indian warre not yet finished. It contains 20 chambers for students, two in
a chamber; a large hall which serves for a chappel; over that a convenient
library." A picture of the building may be seen in the *Proceedings* of the Massachusetts Historical Society, XVIII. 318.

[2] Rev. Urian Oakes, minister of Cambridge, was at this time acting president, and was installed as president in the next month. There were apparently
seventeen students in the college at this time who subsequently graduated, and
perhaps a few others. The library no doubt contained more than a thousand,
perhaps more than fifteen hundred books.

six or eight cases of type. There is not much work done there. Our printing office is well worth two of it, and even more.[1] We went back to Charlestown, where, after waiting a little, we crossed over about three o'clock. On our way home our skipper, John Foy, met us; we spoke to him, and in our respective names, paid him the money for our passage, six pounds each. He wished to give us a bill of it, but we told him it was unnecessary, as we were people of good confidence. I spoke to my comrade, and we went out with him, and presented him with a glass of wine. His mate came to him there, who looked more like a merchant than a seaman, a young man and no sailor. We inquired how long our departure would be delayed, and, as we understood him, it would be the last of the coming week. That was annoying to us. Indeed, we have found the English the same everywhere, doing nothing but lying and cheating, if it but serves their interest. Being in the house again, Ephraim's brother-in-law, Mr. De Key, and his wife made us a visit.

10th, Wednesday. We heard that our captain expected to be ready the first of the week.

11th, Thursday. Nothing occurred.

12th, Friday. We went in the afternoon to Mr. John Teller's, to ascertain whether he had any good wine, and to purchase some for our voyage, and also some brandy. On arriving at his house, we found him a little cool; indeed, not as he was formerly. We inquired for what we wanted, and he said he had good Madeira wine, but he believed he had no brandy, though he thought he could assist us in procuring it. We also inquired how we could obtain the history and laws of this place. At last it came out. He said we must be pleased to excuse him if he did not give us admission to his house; he durst not do it, in consequence of there being a certain evil

---

[1] The allusion is to the printing-office at Wieuwerd, which Dittelbach, *Verval en Val der Labadisten* (Amsterdam, 1692), p. 50, says was a very costly one. The Labadists had everywhere maintained their own printer, Loureins Autein going with them in that capacity from Amsterdam to Herford. As to the building occupied by the famous Cambridge press, Randolph mentions "a small brick building called the Indian colledge, where some few Indans did study, but now it is a printing house." Printing here was this year at a low ebb; nothing is known to have been printed but the second edition of Eliot's Indian New Testament.

report in the city concerning us; they had been to warn him
not to have too much communication with us, if he wished
to avoid censure; they said we certainly were Jesuits, who
had come here for no good, for we were quiet and modest,
and an entirely different sort of people from themselves; that
we could speak several languages, were cunning and subtle of
mind and judgment, had come there without carrying on any
traffic or any other business, except only to see the place and
country; that this seemed fabulous as it was unusual in these
parts; certainly it could be for no good purpose. As regards
the voyage to Europe, we could have made it as well from New
York as from Boston, as opportunities were offered there.
This suspicion seemed to have gained more strength because
the fire at Boston over a year ago was caused by a Frenchman.
Although he had been arrested, they could not prove it against
him; but in the course of the investigation, they discovered
he had been counterfeiting coin and had profited thereby,
which was a crime as infamous as the other.   He had no trade
or profession; he was condemned; both of his ears were cut
off; and he was ordered to leave the country.[1] Mr. Tailler
feared the more for himself, particularly because almost all
strangers were addressed to him, as we were, in consequence
of his speaking several languages, French, some Dutch, Spanish,
Portuguese, Italian, etc., and could aid them.   There had also
some time ago a Jesuit arrived here from Canada, who came to
him disguised, in relation to which there was much murmuring,
and they wished to punish this Jesuit, not because he was a
Jesuit, but because he came in disguise, which is generally bad
and especially for such as are the pests of the world, and are
justly feared, which just hate we very unjustly, but as the
ordinary lot of God's children, had to share. We were compelled to speak French, because we could not speak English,
and these people did not understand Dutch. There were some
persons in New York who could speak nothing but French, and
very little English.   The French was common enough in these

---

[1] The case is that of Peter Lorphelin, accused in connection with the great
fire of August 8-9, 1679, computed to have resulted in a loss of two hundred
thousand pounds. Found guilty of clipping coin, he was punished as above;
Records of the Court of Assistants, I. 145.   No real evidence seems to have connected him with the fire.

parts, but it seemed that we were different from them.   Of all this we disabused Mr. Tailler, assuring him we were as great enemies of that brood as any persons could be, and were, on the contrary, good Protestants or Reformed, born and educated in that faith; that we spoke only Dutch and French, except my companion, who could also speak Latin, and had not come here to trade, but to examine the country, and perhaps some morning or evening the opportunity might arrive for us to come over with our families, when affairs in Europe, and especially in Holland, might be settled, as the times there had been bad enough; that if they would be pleased to listen to Mr. Eliot, the minister at Roxbury, he could give them other testimony concerning us, as we had particularly conversed with him.   This seemed in some measure to satisfy him.   I think this bad report was caused by some persons who came from New York, truly worldly men, whom we had not sought when we were there, nor they us, and who, although they knew better, or at least ought to have known better, yet out of hatred to the truth, and love of sin, said of us what they conceived, and their corruption inclined them to say.   But the Lord who alone knows us rightly will forgive them, and make Himself known to them if it pleases Him, and then they will know us.

13th, Saturday.   As we had promised Mr. Eliot to call upon him again, we went to Roxbury this morning.   We found him at home, but he excused himself that he had not much time, and had a great deal to do.   He called his son, who was there, and who also appeared to be a minister,[1] to speak with us; but we excused ourselves, and said we would not hinder him and would rather leave.   However, several questions and reasons passed between us in relation to the Confession which we had given him, and which he praised highly, and in relation to the professors of it, both pastors and people, in regard to which we satisfied him; but the son, who was neither as good nor as learned as his father, had more disposition or inclination to ridicule and dispute, than to edify and be edified.   We told him what was good for him, and we regretted we could not talk more particularly to him.   But the father remarked that if the professors were truly what they

[1] Doubtless Benjamin Eliot, youngest son of the Apostle, who assisted his father in his labors as pastor and as translator.

declared in the Confession, he could not sufficiently thank God for what He had done. We assured him it was so, and took our leave. He requested us to stop and dine with him, but we excused ourselves.

14th, Sunday. We went to church, but heard a most miserable sermon by a young person, a candidate.

15th, Monday. The burgesses drilled and exercised in the presence of the governor. There were eight companies on foot, and one on horseback, all which divided themselves into two troops or squadrons, and operated against each other in a sham battle, which was well performed.[1] It took place on a large plain on the side of the city. It did not however terminate so well, but that a commander on horseback was wounded on the side of his face near the eye, by the shot of a fusil, as it is usually the case that some accident happens on such occasions. It was so in New York at the last parade, when two young men on horseback coming towards each other as hard as they could, to discharge their pistols, dashed against each other, and fell instantly with their horses. It was supposed they were both killed, and also their horses, for there were no signs of life in them; but they were bled immediately, and after two or three hours they began to recover, and in two days were able to go out again. One of the horses died. We went to see John Teller, and paid him for the wine and brandy. He seemed to have more confidence in us. We gave him to read, as further proofs, the letters which Mr. Ephraim Hermans and Mr. John Moll had written to us from the South River, both of whom he knew. He told us the Reformed of Rochelle had sent some deputies to the colony of Boston and the Independent church there to request the liberty to come over and live in a place near them, or among them, and in their country, which was granted them; and that they returned home three months ago.[2]

16th, Tuesday. We packed our goods in readiness to leave.
17th, Wednesday. We placed our goods on board ship.

[1] Detailed orders for this general training and sham-fight, as executed in 1686 by eight companies of foot and four troops of horse, may be seen in the *Proceedings* of the Massachusetts Historical Society, XXXIII. 328–330.

[2] A dozen Huguenots came to Boston the next year, and in 1686 a settlement of them was formed at Oxford, Massachusetts.

18*th, Thursday*. We took leave of Mr. Teller, thanking him for his attention and kindness, and presented him with a copy of our *Cantiques Sacrés*,[1] for which he was thankful. We would cheerfully have given him the *Maximes*[2] also, but our goods were packed on board the ship, and we could not get at them. He was now of a better mind and well satisfied, returning us our letters with thanks. While we were sitting at table this noon, it thundered very hard, whereupon one of the daughters of the woman of the house where we were staying commenced to scream and cry. We asked her if she were afraid of the thunder, upon which her mother inquired of us, if we were not. We said no, but the word had scarcely escaped our lips before there came a frightful clap, which seemed to cleave the heart from the body, and entirely changed our ideas. My comrade, Mr. Vorsman, turned as pale as a white sheet, and could hardly speak. I was fearful he had met with some mishap, but he recovered himself. It was said there had scarcely ever been heard there such thunder. One man was killed, and two others not far from being so. These three persons were running in a field, and two of them seeing and hearing the weather lay down flat on the ground under a tree; the third man played stout and brave, jeering at the others who called to him to come with them. Soon the lightning struck him dead to the earth, and separated the other two from each other. There was also a hard rock, not far from our lodgings, split through.

19*th, Friday, and* 20*th, Saturday*. Nothing occurred.

21*st, Sunday*. Coming out of the church, Mr. Teller spoke to us, and invited us to dine with him, but we thanked him.

22*d, Monday*. We took our leave, and went on board the ship, which was all ready to sail, except that they were waiting for the captain.

23*d, Tuesday*. After some delay the captain came on board with the rest of the passengers, accompanied by many of their friends. Weighed anchor at three o'clock in the after-

[1] Labadie's *Cantiques Sacrés* are to be found in *Fragmens de Quelques Poësies et Sentimens d'Esprit de M. Labadie* (Amsterdam, 1678), but it would seem that they must also have been issued separately.

[2] Labadie, *Abrégé du Véritable Christianisme Théorique et Pratique, ou Recueil de Maximes Chrestiennes* (Amsterdam, 1670).

noon, it being almost low water, and set sail with a southwest
and south-southwest wind. In passing the fort we fired the
salvo, which it answered; the pilot and the company then left
us and we put to sea. But before going further to sea we must
give a brief description of New England, and the city of Boston
in particular.

When New Netherland was first discovered by the Hollanders, the evidence is that New England was not known; because the Dutch East India Company then sought a passage by
the west, through which to sail to Japan and China; and if
New England had been then discovered, they would not have
sought a passage there, knowing it to be the main land; just
as when New Netherland and New England did become known,
such a passage was sought no longer through them, but farther
to the north through Davis and Hudson straits. The Hollanders, when they discovered New Netherland, embraced under
that name and title all the coast from Virginia or Cape Hin-
loopen eastwardly to Cape Cod, as it was then and there
discovered by them and designated by Dutch names, as sufficiently appears by the charts. The English afterwards discovered New England and settled there.[1] They increased so
in consequence of the great liberties and favorable privileges
which the king granted to the Independents, that they went
to live not only west of Cape Cod and Rhode Island, but also
on Long Island and other places, and even took possession of
the whole of the Fresh River,[2] which the Hollanders there were
not able to prevent, in consequence of their small force in New
Netherland, and the scanty population. The English went
more readily to the west, because the land was much better
there, and more accessible to vessels, and the climate was
milder; and also because they could trade more conveniently
with the Hollanders, and be supplied by them with provisions.
New England is now described as extending from the Fresh
River to Cape Cod and thence to Kennebec, comprising three
provinces or colonies: Fresh River or Connecticut, Rhode
Island and the other islands to Cape Cod, and Boston, which
stretches from thence north. They are subject to no one, but

---

[1] This is to ignore the voyages of Gosnold, Pring, Weymouth, etc., and the
settlement at Fort St. George in 1607.

[2] The Connecticut.

acknowledge the king of England for their lord,[1] and therefore
no ships enter unless they have English passports or commis-
sions.   They have free trade with all countries; but the return cargoes from there to Europe go to England, except those
which go secretly to Holland.   There is no toll or duty paid
upon merchandise exported or imported, nor is there any im-
post or tax paid upon land.   Each province chooses its own
governor from the magistracy, and the magistrates are chosen
from the principal inhabitants, merchants or planters.   They
are all Independents in matters of religion, if it can be called
religion; many of them perhaps more for the purposes of enjoying the benefit of its privileges than for any regard to truth
and godliness.   I observed that while the English flag or color
has a red ground with a small white field in the uppermost
corner, where there is a red cross, they have here dispensed
with this cross in their colors, and preserved the rest.[2]   They
baptize no children except those of the members of the congregation.   All their religion consists in observing Sunday, by
not working or going into the taverns on that day; but the
houses are worse than the taverns.   No stranger or traveller
can therefore be entertained on a Sunday, which begins at
sunset on Saturday, and continues until the same time on
Sunday.   At these two hours you see all their countenances
change.   Saturday evening the constable goes round into all
the taverns of the city for the purpose of stopping all noise and
debauchery, which frequently causes him to stop his search,
before his search causes the debauchery to stop.   There is a
penalty for cursing and swearing, such as they please to im-
pose, the witnesses thereof being at liberty to insist upon it.
Nevertheless you discover little difference between this and
other places.   Drinking and fighting occur there not less than

---

[1] The reading is *eer*, but *heer* was of course intended.   The control by the
English king was much more real than is here indicated.   The next sentence
alludes to the Navigation Acts and their evasion.   As to customs, Edward Randolph had in 1678 been appointed collector for New England, and had begun his
conflict with the Massachusetts authorities, but with little success thus far.
Land-taxes did in fact exist.

[2] On Endicott's cutting of the cross from the flag, in 1634, see Winthrop's
Journal, in this series, I. 137, 174, 182.   Since the decision then reached (1636),
the cross had been left out of all ensigns in Massachusetts except that on Castle
Island.

elsewhere; and as to truth and true godliness, you must not expect more of them than of others. When we were there, four ministers' sons were learning the silversmith's trade.

The soil is not as fertile as in the west. Many persons leave there to go to the Delaware and New Jersey. They manure their lands with heads of fish. They gain their living mostly or very much by fish, which they salt and dry for selling; and by raising horses, oxen, and cows, as well as hogs and sheep, which they sell alive, or slaughtered and salted, in the Caribbean Islands and other places. They are not as good farmers as the Hollanders about New York.

As to Boston particularly, it lies in latitude 42° 20′ on a very fine bay. The city is quite large, constituting about twelve companies. It has three churches, or meeting houses, as they call them.[1] All the houses are made of thin, small cedar shingles, nailed against frames, and then filled in with brick and other stuff; and so are their churches. For this reason these towns are so liable to fires, as have already happened several times; and the wonder to me is, that the whole city has not been burnt down, so light and dry are the materials. There is a large dock in front of it constructed of wooden piers, where the large ships go to be careened and rigged; the smaller vessels all come up to the city. On the left-hand side across the river lies Charlestown, a considerable place, where there is some shipping. Upon the point of the bay, on the left hand, there is a block-house, along which a piece of water runs, called the Milk Ditch.[2] The whole place has been an island, but it is now joined to the main land by a low road to Roxbury. In front of the town there are many small islands, between which you pass in sailing in and out. On one of the middlemost stands the fort, where the ships show their passports. At low tide the water in the channel between the islands is three and a half and four fathoms deep, in its shallowest part. You sail from the city southeasterly to the fort, by passing Governor's Island on the larboard, and having passed the fort, you keep

[1] The meeting-houses of the First Church, North Church, and South Church (built 1640, 1650, 1672).

[2] The battery at the foot of Fort Hill, north of which a cove and creek then ran to the foot of Milk Street. The narrow isthmus to Roxbury existed when the first settlers came.

close to the south, then southeast, and gradually more to the east to the sea. On reaching the sea we set our course due east, with the wind south-southeast, and made good progress.

24th, Wednesday. The wind and our course continued the same; but it is to be observed, the compass here is a point and a half northwesting. We spoke an English ship bound to Virginia. We found our latitude [42°] 40' north, and the distance we had sailed 96 miles.

25th, Thursday. The wind became more southerly, but we held our course the same as before, or east by south. Latitude 42° 68'. Distance reckoned to be 136 miles. The English ship which had remained in company until now, left us. It began to blow so hard in the evening that we had to reef the topsails and take in the mainsail, and proceed with the mizzensail and foresail.

26th, Friday. The wind was due south, although it had been a little more westerly during the night. We observed the latitude 42° 51'; reckoned the distance run 96 miles.

We had stipulated, when we engaged our passage, to eat in the cabin, but when we got to sea we did not do so. There were ten passengers besides us two, and among them two females. These ten had jointly bought a large quantity of provisions and groceries, and placed them in the cabin, they having such power over the captain. We were therefore compelled to remain outside, although we remonstrated. We saw afterwards that it was the Lord's doings, who would not that we should be in nearer communion with such wicked persons. We then arranged to eat with the mate and another passenger above on the half deck. We four brought together what provisions we had, and were well satisfied with each other. We had to-day a good topsail breeze and fine weather.

27th, Saturday. It was rainy during the night; and although our bunk was in the gunner's room, it leaked in there very much. At sunrise it cleared up a little. We could not obtain any observation, but supposed the latitude was 43°. The course was east-southeast, the distance run 100 miles. As it was Saturday evening a hog was killed, there being seven or eight on board the ship.

28th, Sunday. The weather was fine, with a westerly wind, but not an entirely clear atmosphere.

Among the passengers in the cabin was a minister, an Independent, who had formerly been in the East Indies, at Bantam on the island of Java. He had been visiting his friends in New England, but undoubtedly could not obtain any situation among them, and was returning to England in order to sail if he could in the first ships back to the Indies. This poor minister, every morning and evening, made a prayer, read some chapters out of the Old and New Testaments, and sang a psalm, all after the manner of the Independents. On Sundays he preached both in the morning and afternoon, and we attended in order to avoid scandal and dissipate as much as possible the breath of calumny.

We could not obtain any altitude to-day, in consequence of the haze. Our course had been almost the whole night southeast by east and the course was therefore east by south; the distance was upwards of eighty miles. At noon it became calm, afterwards rainy, and in the evening the wind changed to the northwest, but continued still.[1] . . .

[AUGUST, 1680] 17th, Saturday. I slept very little last night in consequence of the noise. We had sailed during the night a little to the east, because our captain was afraid of falling on the island of Bus,[2] as he was not much west of it, though according to our reckoning he was to the east of it. We found our latitude was 57° 30', and therefore hoped to pass Bus and the rock Rockol.[3] We sailed on several courses, but the one maintained was northeast by north. The distance sailed was 100 miles . . .

18th Sunday. We took an observation. Latitude 58° 30'. It was very cold here and the days long. The wind continued northeast and north-northeast, with hard weather, which

---

[1] Several pages are here omitted, narrating nineteen days of voyaging, but containing nothing of importance or of interest. The *Dolphin's* course was over the Newfoundland banks, and then around the north of Scotland into the North Sea.

[2] Buss Island has a curious history. It was reported as discovered in 1578, and again in 1668 and in 1671. An elaborate map of it was then published, and for a hundred years it appeared on charts of the North Atlantic as a considerable island, about lat. 58° N., long. 28° W. from Greenwich. But it has no existence and, though volcanic subsidence is possible, it probably never did exist.

[3] Rockall, a lofty and rocky islet in the North Atlantic, lat. 57° 36' N., long. 13° 41' W.

caused us to take in our sails, and about ten o'clock in the evening to tack about. I remained on deck myself, in order to keep a lookout for the great rock Rockol.

19*th*, *Monday*. We obtained an observation at 57° 51', and we still more believed we were before the rock Rockol, which lies in 57° 40': but we put our hope and trust in God, committing ourselves into His hands.

20*th*, *Tuesday*. It became gradually more still, and at last we could sail east-northeast, and northeast. We had sailed 72 miles. We could not take an observation.

21*st*, *Wednesday*. The wind was northwest, and our course east and east by north, with little headway. We found the latitude 58° 10'; the course held was east by north; the distance 40 miles. We, therefore, supposed we were between Rockol and St. Kilda.[1] Towards evening the wind shot from the north-northwest, so that we could sail east-northeast, and afterwards northeast by east; but there was a rolling sea, and, therefore, we could not go ahead much because it came from the front. The wind however improved.

22*d*, *Thursday*. The wind was west-northwest, and the course northeast by east, with the sea continuing to roll against us in front. We found ourselves at noon in 59° 5', at which we rejoiced, because we had to enter the North Sea between the 59th and 60th degree. The distance sailed was 88 miles upon several courses. At noon the course was set northeast by east in order to sail above the island of little Barro.[2] There was a small purse made up by the passengers, each one contributing what he pleased, for the person who should first discover land. We gave two shillings each. The minister would not give anything. It seems that meanness is a peculiarity of this class of people. This was done in order that the sailors might look out more zealously for land, and so we might not fall upon land unexpectedly. The purse was nailed to the mast, so that, being always in sight, it might be a constant incentive, and whoever might first see land might take it off. We were becalmed the whole night.

[1] A remote island of the outer Hebrides, the westernmost of the group.

[2] Apparently this does not mean the island of the Hebrides now called Barra, but that called Bernera, west of Lewis—Barra Major on some contemporary maps.

23d, *Friday*. It was calm, beautiful weather. They thought they saw land, so the sailors said, and that it was Barro, but I could observe nothing. We also had greener water, and therefore supposed we were on soundings. The deep lead was thrown, but at 200 fathoms it came short. The latitude was 59° 34′, the wind northeast, and we sailed east, for we were almost in the latitude of the south point of Shetland. We saw, several times, quantities of spermaceti drifting, a yellowish fat, which lies in the water, all together, but solid like the green scum which floats in ditches. We also saw rockweed floating; and a small land bird came on board the ship, from which we concluded we were approaching land. The wind was more free, and after running out and in it remained north-northeast. It blew so hard that the topsails had to be reefed at first, and then taken in. We sailed sometimes east, then east by north and east by south, and again east.

24th, *Saturday*. It blew very hard from the north-north-east accompanied by rain, and we therefore could not ascertain the latitude but reckoned we were in 59° 20′. The course was held half way between east and south, which brought us near the before mentioned rocks. It became calm at night.

25th, *Sunday*. It continued calm until noon. We obtained the latitude, 59° 30′. Our progress was 40 miles, and the course a little more north than east. At noon the wind was south and south-southeast, with a fresh breeze. We saw this morning a flock of land birds, like finches; also pigeons and small gulls, which keep themselves on the shore. Towards evening it was very foggy. We sailed during the night east-southeast.

26th, *Monday*. It was tolerably good weather, but it soon came up thick and rainy with a strong wind. We continued sailing east by south. Calculated the distance 56 miles. We kept a good look-out, for my reckoning upon the one chart was out and differed from the other 32 miles. The Lord protects us from disaster, and will guide us further, as we fully trust in Him.

27th, *Tuesday*. We had not had during the whole voyage such hard weather as during this night. The wind was southeast and south-southeast, with a thick mist and rain, which at last made us lie by, with only the mizzen sail, in a hard short sea which tossed and pitched us. We saw all day many land

and sea birds which caused us to look out carefully for land. The distance made was 84 miles. At evening the wind was south-southwest, whereby we sailed or drifted east by south and south-southeast until day.

28th, Wednesday. It was better weather, and we again began to sail. The wind was southwest. The lower sails were well reefed, but we shipped several heavy seas. The sea rolled the whole day. It was lucky for a sailor that the Lord preserved him from being washed overboard by an over-breaking sea; it was a narrow escape, but in floating off he caught a rope or something, to which he clung and was saved. We saw much sea-weed, and whole flocks of rock and land birds, and also a species of ducks and geese, besides another kind of bird. Fish lines were made ready, but we could catch nothing. The latitude was 59° 51', which was a good height and encouraged us. We sailed still east-southeast on a maintained east course.

29th, Thursday. While we were at prayer this morning, "Land! Land!" was called out; and although these prayers were so drowsy and miserable, especially for us, who were opposed to their doctrines, I had to restrain and mortify myself by not going up on deck, as several did, and almost all wished to do. It was the gunner who first discovered land, and took from the mast the little purse, in which he found 28 shillings and 6 pence sterling, that is, fifteen guilders and fourteen stivers, a good day's wages. The land we saw was the Orkney Islands, 28 to 32 miles south-southeast of us, which we sketched as well as we could. About two hours afterwards we saw very high land in front of us to the leeward, which we supposed at first was Fairhill,[1] an easy mistake to make, as we had made our latitude 59° 48', but we soon saw other land in front on the starboard, and we now discovered that the land to the larboard was the rock Falo, and that on the starboard was Fairhill, which agreed very well with our latitude. I sat on the main yard to observe how the land rose up, and while there saw a vessel or a sail, which soon caused great consternation on board of our ship, and still more when I said there were two

---

[1] Fair Isle is a lonely island midway between the Orkney and Shetland islands. Sailing between these groups, the voyagers saw first Orkney, then Foula Island (here Falo), then Fair Isle. The manuscript contains at this point profile sketches of the islands of Fairhill and Foula.

of them. They were afraid they were Turks; and so much
did this idea blind them that eyes, understanding, and reason
had no office to perform.   These small vessels were certainly
large ships and Turks.   Everything was put out of the way;
many did not know what they were doing from fear, which increased greatly, when they saw one of the vessels coming towards us before the wind.   It was all hurly-burly, and every
one was ordered immediately to quarters. I was very busy, our
place being on the quarter-deck where there were four guns,
which I pushed into the port holes.   These were loaded and
we were soon ready for fight.   In the meanwhile, the vessel
coming nearer, the minister, who should have encouraged
the others, ran below into the powder room, all trembling and
shaking.   He inquired if that was far enough below water,
and if he could be shot there.   Another person from the East
Indies was with him.   The surgeon had all things ready for the
battle, but unfortunately I looked out and saw it was a Dutch
smack with a small topsail, flying the Prince's flag.   But they
silenced me; Turk it was, and Turk it should remain, and I
must go back to my quarters.   At last she came alongside,
and they hailed her, but could not understand what was replied.   I was then called upon to speak to them, and I went
on the stern and saw that it was as I had said.   I inquired
where they were from, and what they were doing there.   They
answered, they were from Amsterdam; were cruising in search
of two East Indiamen which the Chamber of Amsterdam[1] had
missed, and they wanted to know whether we had seen anything of them.   We informed them we had seen no ships since
we were on the banks of Newfoundland, and we were from New
England, bound to London.   We asked if there were any
danger from the Turks.   None at all, they said, which gave
courage to our captain and others, as well as the minister, who
had emerged from the powder room, where he had hidden
himself.   We also inquired how affairs stood with England,
Holland, and France.   They answered, well, as far as they
knew.   Having obtained this information, I told our captain
such good news was worth a salute, and he fired a six-pounder
shotted.   The Dutch captain asked for a little tobacco in ex-

[1] The Chamber of Amsterdam was one of the local component boards of the
Dutch East India Company.

change for pickled herrings; but many excuses were offered, and he got none. He said the other vessel was a Hollander from Iceland, and we had nothing to fear; that almost all the ships which we might see in the North Sea were ships from Holland; a remark which annoyed our captain and the others very much; and not being able to stand it, they tacked about ship and wore off, leaving the cruiser and passing outside, or between Fairhill and the Orkneys.

30th, Friday. We had lain over again at midnight, with a south-southwest wind. At daybreak it was entirely calm. I was called out of my berth to go to the captain, in order to discriminate the land, distinguishing Fairhill and the Orkneys. He exhibited great ignorance and fear, for we had seen the land well the day before, and the cruiser had fully informed us; he knew well enough how we had sailed during the night, and with what progress, and that we all agreed with the foregoing height of the pole. We took several crayon sketches of Fairhill and the other lands, the more because they are not shown from that side in the Zeespiegel of Lichtende Colom.[1] We found the latitude to-day to be 59° 40'. Many birds came round the ship, and some sparrow hawks and small blue hawks, which we caught with our hands. We stretched over again to the Orkneys, in order to be clear of Fairhill; the wind being southeast and southeast by east, we had foggy and misty weather.

31st, Saturday. We saw the Orkneys this morning, although we had shifted eight miles during the night. We stretched away from them again and discovered a strong current, which the nearer Scotland and the Orkneys it was the stronger it was. It runs mostly east and east-southeast, and west and west-northwest. The latitude obtained was 59° 26'. At evening we found ourselves about 28 or 32 miles from Fairhill north-northeast. This is a beautiful round hill, as its name in English denotes. We held our course with several tacks, over and back, to reach the North Sea. We saw several ships but could not get near enough to speak to them.

September 1st, Sunday. The weather was misty; the wind as before, calm. Could not obtain the latitude, but we

---

[1] "Sea Mirror or Shining Column," an atlas of marine charts published by Peter Goos of Amsterdam in various editions, in 1654 and later years.

reckoned we had sailed about forty miles, east by south. We saw some herring-busses.

2d, *Monday*. The wind continued southeast and south-southeast. The weather was good but calm and misty. We calculated the latitude 58° 40'. We kept beating from and to the shore.

3d, *Tuesday*. It was still drizzling and calm. We saw several vessels in which we would gladly have been, in order to see if there were no opportunity of going in them to Holland, whither they seemed to be sailing, or at least to obtain some refreshment of fish or something else; but the captain would not consent. At noon we turned towards the shore and sailed mostly south.

4th, *Wednesday*. The wind southeast and south-southeast, with dead water as if we were sailing in a river. We had been near the shore all night, on various courses, of one, two, and three points difference. We took a good observation, namely, 58° 8'; the distance sailed was sixty miles, the course held south-southwest. At noon the water was greener, and we therefore supposed we were in deeper water. We saw this morning the four *ockers*,[1] before mentioned behind us, but we were soon afterwards out of sight of them.

5th, *Thursday*. Our course was east by north and east-northeast, now a little in, and then again out. The wind was mostly south-southwest. We found the latitude 58° 34', so much were we set north. We had not gone ahead far, as there was not much wind, and the sea rolled directly against us. We reckoned the distance to be at night forty miles. But it was entirely calm, and the wind subsided with mist and rain. We drifted thus all night. The deep lead was thrown at midnight, and eighty fathoms of water were found. We endeavored to catch some fish, but did not succeed. We caught several sparrow hawks and small blue hawks.

6th, *Friday*. We had made little progress. The wind was northwest. There was a thick mist with drizzling rain. Our course until noon was east-southeast; the latitude was 59°; the distance 104 miles. We spoke an *ocker*, and inquired where we were. He said he was lying on the reef to fish, about 136 miles, he supposed, from Newcastle in Scotland,[2] southwest of

---

[1] Dutch fishing-boats.

[2] England, rather. There is no such reef or shallow as is described below.

him, which agreed well with our calculation. Had 50 fathoms of water. This reef shoots out from the coast of Jutland and runs into the middle of the North Sea, northwardly around the Shetland Islands, and from thence almost to Rockol, but it lies nearer to the Scottish coast than to the coast of Norway, and a little more so than is represented on the chart. We caught many birds and also swallows.

7th, Saturday. It had been very calm through the night; but the wind shifted to the south, and we therefore had to change our course continually; at last it was south-southeast, and we could not sail higher than west by north. We found the latitude 56° 24', but could not judge well because the sun was obscured. The reckoning was 55° 55'; the course was south by west; the distance 56 miles. We here came into a whole school of tunnies which afforded us great amusement. We also saw several ships ahead of us and heard much firing of guns

8th, Sunday. Calm and rainy weather. We had made, this whole night and from noon yesterday, not more than 28 or 32 miles progress. The course was south-southeast sailing over against the wind, in order to come upon the Doggerbank.[1] Saw several vessels, one of which ran before us, over to New-castle. Reckoned at noon to-day we were 40 miles from the Doggerbank.

9th, Monday. In the morning watch, threw the deep lead in 25 fathoms, sandy bottom, green, white and red. About ten o'clock we had 20 fathoms with the same ground. The atmosphere was thick and hazy. The latitude we supposed was 55° 19'. We were now certainly on the Doggerbank. We caught many young *spier hayties*, which the English call *dogs*, and because large numbers of these fish always keep there, the bank, which is very large and almost makes the figure of a fishing boat, is called the Doggerbank. At four o'clock we had 18 fathoms, and in the evening 17. The course still south-southeast, and the wind northeast, breezy and calm, inter-mingled. In the night the deep lead was thrown several times, and we found 19, 18, 15 and 14 fathoms of water.

10th, Tuesday. The wind blew from almost all points; at ten o'clock it was northeast and east-northeast, with 12, 11,

---

[1] The Dogger Bank is a great shoal in the North Sea, lying between northern England and Denmark.

10, 9½ fathoms of water. The latitude was 54° 44′. We saw
several large ships and heard heavy firing of guns which made
our captain and others very serious, for we heard 40 or 50 shots.
Seeing a ship behind us, we let the sails run and waited for her.
On her approaching us, we found she was a Dutch flute;[1] and
when we spoke her, they said they were from Muscovy, bound
for Amsterdam. We wished with our whole hearts we were on
board of her with our goods, for we should then sooner have
been home. There was a rolling sea, so that there was no
prospect of being put aboard of her; besides, the captain
would not have been willing. They could not tell us much
news. We asked where they reckoned they were, and they
said not far from where we knew, that they were on the Doggerbank. In the evening we found the water deeper than 20
fathoms, and afterwards 25, at midnight 30, and in the day
watch 45, with a bottom of fine sand.

11th, *Wednesday*. In the forenoon, found the water more
shallow, 25, 23 and 20 fathoms, and we therefore believed we
had passed from the Doggerbank to the Welle,[2] another bank
so called. We obtained a good observation, and the latitude
was 54° net; the ship's altitude 5′ being deducted, left 53° 55′,
which agreed very well with our chart, with the depth, and our
reckoning. The distance was put at 40 miles. We saw many
ships around us, but could speak none. It continued calm
until evening, when we found 20 and afterwards 17 fathom
water, over a coarse red and white sandy bottom, mixed with
small stones. The course was south-southeast.

12th, *Thursday*. The latitude 53° 45′, that is, the height
of our eyes above the water being deducted; the distance 24
miles; the course south-southeast, a little southerly. We
reckoned we were at the middle of the Welle bank. We
longed for a good wind, and we were only sixty miles from
Yarmouth and 100 or 104 from Harwich. We fished a little,
but only caught two or three small codfish, and hauled up
with the hook a great quantity of stone and sea weed. In the
first watch the wind was north and northeast, with slack water
in 15, 14, 17, 19 and 20 fathoms. The captain therefore sailed

[1] See p. 21, note 1.
[2] The Well Bank lies south of the Dogger Bank, and off the mouth of the
Humber.

southeast and southeast by south, through fear of the Leme-
noirs[1] and other Yarmouth shoals.

13th, *Friday*. It blew a stiff topsail breeze. We had 17
and 18 fathoms of water, which looked quite white, and made
me think we were near the White Water, another bank so named
on which there is 17 and 16 fathoms. We sailed south-southwest. We waited for a herring-buss coming towards us, and
spoke to her. She was from Rotterdam, had been at sea
a long time, and had seen no land. They told us they were
between Wells and the White Water, nearer the latter, and
that South Foreland was south-southwest of us. They could
tell us nothing more. We wished we were in the buss, for then
we might have been in the Maes that evening, as she had a
good wind. The latitude was 52° 50′. We sailed southwest
in 23 fathoms of water, with a bottom of fine sand a little red-
dish and mixed with black. In sailing towards the shore we
had 18 fathoms; when about three, or half past three o'clock
in the afternoon they cried out, Land! and proceeding further
on, we saw the grove near Yarmouth, and shortly afterwards
Yarmouth steeple, southwest by west and west-southwest from
us. We sailed more southerly and discovered the whole coast.
We came to anchor about seven o'clock in 16 fathoms.

14th, *Saturday*. It had been good weather through the
night, and we had rested well. We saw when the sun rose,
which shone against the coast and was entirely clear, how the
coast ran. The land is not so high as it is west of the Thames
to Land's End. There are many villages. Yarmouth looked
like a pleasant little place, as it lay north-northwest of us. We
saw many ships sailing one way and the other. Having waited
for the ebb to run out we got under sail about eight o'clock.
We sailed by Sowls,[2] and came to anchor again about three
o'clock in the afternoon. The passengers had everything ready
to go ashore, and so overland to London. There was a signal
made with the flag from our ship, and a shot fired for a pilot
or some one else to come on board. Towards evening a small
boat came with five men, but no pilot. The flood making

---

[1] The Leman Bank lies some forty miles northeast of Yarmouth, and south
of the Well Bank; the White Water, next mentioned, lies east of the latter,
toward the Frisian coast.

[2] Southwold, on the Suffolk coast.

about nine or ten o'clock in the evening, and running along the whole Scottish and English coast, from the Orkneys to the Thames, we sailed on again until we came to another village where our passengers went ashore. It was about midnight. The weather was fine and the moon shone bright; we fired five or six guns. The minister was sad and complained that it was Sunday, or Saturday evening, and he dared not go ashore, lest he should break the Sabbath; but finally he let his wishes override his scruples, and went off with the passengers. We obtained a pilot and some refreshments, and then sailed on till we came before Dunwich,[1] the oldest place in England, and once the mightiest in commerce. We came again to anchor in order to wait for the tide. The wind continued west-southwest.

15th, Sunday. The wind mostly as before. We were under sail about ten o'clock, with the flood tide, and tacked along the land in seven fathoms of water to the point of Aldborough,[2] to reach which we made five or six short tacks. Running close to the shore, we came among a fleet of, I think, full 200 coal ships, all beating up the river, which made it difficult to avoid each other. We passed through the King's Channel. I have never seen so many sunken ships as there were in the mouth of the Thames, full eight or ten in different places, from various causes. The tide being spent we came to anchor before a village called St. Peter.

16th, Monday. The wind being mostly north, the weather was cold and piercing. The whole fleet was under sail, with the flood tide, and we along with them. They had talked loudly in Boston of the sailing qualities of our ship, but almost the whole coal fleet sailed ahead of us.

18th, Wednesday. The wind remained still, with mist. We saw it would be some days yet before the ship would reach the city, and therefore determined to go up in a wherry, that is a row-boat, from Gravesend. As soon as one came along-

---

[1] Dunwich, now mostly under the waters of the North Sea, was once an important place, and one of considerable antiquity. The bishopric of the East Saxons was established there in A. D. 630; indeed, the town dates from Roman times (Sitomagus).

[2] Still on the Suffolk coast. The King's Channel, mentioned below, was the chief entrance into the estuary of the Thames from the northeast.

side we went aboard, and passed by Gravesend and other villages. It was nine o'clock in the evening when we landed at
St. Catharines,[1] and went to a tavern called the Dutch Smack,
but they would not receive us. We then went to the Inlander,
the landlord of which was a Fleming, and a Papist, but not the
worst one. We paid for the boat three English shillings in all.
We three, namely, Vorsman, Jan Owins, the surgeon of our
ship, a Rotterdammer, and myself, supped together; this was
the first time we had slept in a bed in a long time.

19th, Thursday. We went through the city, the newly
built portion[2] as well as the other, but we found it very different from what we had imagined. We went to the Exchange
and conversed with our captain and the other passengers. We
endeavored to find the first vessel going to Holland. They
told us there were two smacks or galiots lying ready, and would
leave on Monday, for which we prepared ourselves.

20th, Friday. We went to Withal [Whitehall], where the
king resides, and where we supposed we should see something
special in the buildings, but in this we were mistaken. There
are better places in London; the best house there was the ban-
queting house, which does not surpass some merchants' houses
in Amsterdam. We strolled into St. James's Park, which is
nothing but a large inclosed meadow, with some canals and
ditches dug through it, in one portion of which are ducks swim-
ming, and willow trees planted. The guard on horseback
coming ahead, we heard the king[3] was in the park. We went
in, but did not see him; but walking through we saw his curiosities of birds which he kept there in cages slightly enough
closed, such as eagles, cranes, a very large owl, a toucan, birds
which we call *hoontjen* in Friesland, *virviteaus*, doves, starlings,
and others of little importance. He had received from the
Indies, by the last ships, two ostriches or cassowaries which
were shut up and much prized, though they are very common
in Holland. We came to his horse stable; there was only one
horse in it, and that was so lean it shamed every one, as also
did the small size of the stable, which stood near that of the
Duke of Monmouth, where there were six tolerable good Frisic

---

[1] Just east of the Tower of London, where now are the St. Katharine Docks.
[2] Meaning the part newly built since the Great Fire of 1666.
[3] Charles II.

horses, with a saddle horse or two. Our stables[1] look more
kingly than these. We were about leaving the place when we
heard them cry out, "To arms! to arms!" to a troop of soldiers
standing there, and looking around, we saw at a distance the
king coming, accompanied by six or eight noblemen, from whom
you could distinguish him only from his having his hat on his
head, while they had theirs off. He saluted all who saluted
him, as he passed along, which he also did to us. I will not
speak of his person as he has been sufficiently described by pen
and burin. Nor will I speak of the condition of London. The
long and short of it is, that city is larger than Amsterdam, but
does not approach it, or any other city in Holland, either in
neatness or in the regularity of the buildings, even those
erected since the great fire. What are worthy of mention is a
certain column, very high and well constructed, erected on
the spot where the great fire broke out in 1666, and the Tower,
not prettily built, but very old, constructed by the Romans
in the time of Julius Cæsar.[2] Whitehall and Westminster,
and all within them, are not worth going to see.

   21st, Saturday. Our ship having arrived before the city
yesterday, we went on board to bring away our goods, as also
did the surgeon. We took leave of the captain, mate, and
carpenter, who was a young man and a Norwegian, stupid, but
not the most evilly disposed. He had our love, and I had occasionally conversed with him when we were on the watch together at night, and sometimes made an impression upon him.
He lived at Flushing, and wished, he said, that he could go
and live with me even for nothing. He desired me not to forget
him. I must also say this of the captain, that he was well
known in London, and in all Boston, as a pious, good, and discreet man; but I was astonished when I saw and heard the
following circumstance. A poor servant, who had served his
time out in New England, came to him in Boston and asked if
he could go over with him; he would do his best in working
like any other sailor for his passage, as he well understood ship-
work. The captain told him he might go with him. When

---

[1] At Wieuwert.
[2] The Tower of London has no such antiquity. The oldest part dates from
William the Conqueror. The monument commemorating the Great Fire, erected
by Sir Christopher Wren, still stands in Fish Street Hill, near London Bridge.

we were at sea, this person was sick several days, and when he recovered did as well as he could, but, it is true, he did not do all that an experienced sailor could have done. When we arrived in the North Sea the captain made a memorandum by which this poor fellow promised to pay half the passage money, that is, thirty guilders, when he arrived in London. He called him, and read it to him, and told him, because he could not work like a good sailor, he must sign that writing, and if he did not do so, he would sell him again when he reached London, which he assured him would be done. The man began to complain and cry, saying he had not so promised, but he would work like any other, and do as well as he could. But notwithstanding his crying and objecting he had to sign the paper, or be sold. In this appeared the piety and sense of justice of our captain, though perhaps the other was not entirely without blame, though he had had blows enough. It seems he had some friends in London who paid the amount.

I must here mention another word about Boston, which is, that I have never been in a place where more was said about witchcraft and witches. From time to time persons had been put in prison, and executed; and a woman was in prison and condemned to die, when we left there.[1] Very strange things were told of her, but I will not repeat them here.

22d, Sunday. I went into the Dutch church, where a young man who was a Cocceian preached.[2] In the afternoon we went to the French church, and in going there passed by a large gate, through which many people were entering into a great hall. We looked in, and when we saw they were Quakers, walked quickly away, and went into the French church, whose congregation is much larger, and its church much smaller than the Dutch church—so small indeed, that they could not all

---

[1] On May 20, 1680, Elizabeth Morse, wife of William Morse, of Newbury, was indicted and tried in Boston, for practising witchcraft upon her own husband. She was convicted and sentenced to be hanged; and was in prison at Boston, at the time our journalist was there, awaiting her execution. It is, undoubtedly, her case to which he refers. She was, however, released in 1681.

[2] In 1550 Edward VI. gave the church of the Augustinians (Austin Friars) to the Dutch Protestants in London, and the neighboring church of St. Anthony's Hospital in Threadneedle Street to the Walloons. Both were destroyed in the Great Fire, but had now been rebuilt. The Dutch church had two ministers. The habit of interchange between the two churches, mentioned below, prevailed in Pepys's time, and was still maintained as late as 1775.

get in. When therefore the Lord's Supper was administered, they used the Dutch church, and the Dutch preached then in the French church, as they are not far apart. But as the French church was especially for the French, we went out, my comrade for the purpose of inquiring after Mr. Owins, and I to go to the Dutch church again, where another Cocceian preached well enough. I saw there the envoy from Holland, a Zeelander, whom I knew, with his family;[1] but he did not know me.

23d, *Monday*. It was said we were to leave to-day, but we saw it would not be the case. The captain, with whom we were to go, was one Douwe Hobbes of Makkum, who brings birds over from Friesland every year for the king. There was a boat lying there ready to leave for Rotterdam, but it seems they intended to go in company.

24th, *Tuesday*. No departure to-day either. While we were at the Exchange, there was a great crowd of people in the street. We saw and heard two trumpeters, followed by a company of cavalry dressed in red, then a chariot drawn by six horses, in which was the Duke of York. Then came some chariots of the nobility, and the Prince Palatine,[2] with several chariots, and two trumpeters in the rear.

25th, *Wednesday*. Could not sail yet, but the Rotterdammer sailed with thirty passengers, with little or no freight. In going down she broke the bowsprit of our ship. Mr. Ouwen left us in her, after we had taken leave of him.

26th, *Thursday*. Heard early this morning our ship was going down the river, for she lay opposite our room; we immediately hurried ourselves. It was very uncivil in the mate, for the captain was still in the city, and would go to Gravesend. We took a wherry and went after her, as she had not gone far in consequence of the mist and lightness of the wind. We drifted to-day scarcely outside of the ships.

[1] Dirk van Leiden van Leeuwen (1618–1682), burgomaster of Leyden, but born at Briel, in Zeeland.

[2] This was the electoral prince Karl (1651–1685), afterward (August, 1680–1685) the elector Karl II., son of Karl Ludwig, grandson of Frederick V. and Elizabeth, and great-grandson of James I. of England. He had been sent to England by his father in a vain endeavor to persuade the latter's cousin, Charles II., to relieve the Palatinate by taking action against Louis XIV. An entertaining account, by his tutor, of their visit in 1670 to his aunt at Herford and to the Labadists, may be found in Miss Una Birch's *Anna Maria van Schurman* (London, 1909), pp. 168 *et seq.*

27th, Friday. It was misty and calm. We therefore did not go as far as the current would have carried us. We had to come to anchor in consequence of the mist, in order not to drift against the ships, or upon the shoal.

28th, Saturday. We drifted and clawed along until we came to anchor before Gravesend, as the Rotterdammer did an hour or two afterwards. Owins, who was not very well accommodated, called out to us as we passed, and asked if we would not go ashore with him. We declined, for we could not have wished to have been better accommodated, as we two had a large, fine cabin to ourselves.

29th, Sunday. When we took our goods out of the ship at London, we let our trunks be examined, but there was nothing inspected. We gave the inspectors a penny and they were satisfied. Our skipper arrived now at Gravesend in the night, and had everything made ready for the inspectors. We had ourselves ready for their arrival. They came on board about eight o'clock, but they looked once only in the hatches without asking anything, and went away again. We went ashore in the forenoon and dined there. We had been to London, and the captain said we should eat the ship's ordinary fare, which seemed now to us princely fare. However, as he was most of the time drunk when on shore, he had given it no consideration. We went through Gravesend to look at it, but it does not signify much—it is more foul and dirty in name than in fact. We also went out into the country a little, which pleased us best. I have never seen anywhere so many blackberries, which were now ripe. The ebb tide having come, we got under sail yet before evening, the wind being good, but it did not continue so long. Opposite Gravesend there is a strong castle well fortified, and another one of less importance on the lower side. Whenever ships pass up or down, they must strike [the flag] here in going between the two fortifications.[1] We arrived at evening before the river of Chatham, where we anchored.

30th, Monday. The wind was easterly and light. We scratched along as far as to get in the King's Channel, as also did the Rotterdammer, which sailed down with us.

---

[1] Tilbury Fort on the north side of the Thames, opposite Gravesend, and probably Shorne Battery on the south side. The "river of Chatham" is of course the Medway, where Admiral de Ruyter in 1660 had burned King Charles's ships.

OCTOBER 1*st*, *Tuesday.*   The wind as before; we therefore tacked with the tide before the Naze,[1] intending to run into Harwich, both for the purpose of waiting for a good wind, and to buy a store of provision which the skipper through his drunkenness had forgotten.   The Rotterdammer, which had not kept along the shore with us, but had continued through the King's Channel, finding no good harbor there, returned again to Chatham, in order, as the wind continued south southeast, to go out along the south shore, and thus we separated.

2*d*, *Wednesday.*   The wind still easterly.   We therefore made several tacks, and ran into Harwich; a miserably poor little fort stands on the east point of the bay, yet you must strike your flag as you sail by it.   The bay is large and suitable to harbor a great number of ships.   The town is on the west side, passing which, a small river runs up into the land. We anchored about ten o'clock in the morning.   We went ashore and dined, and I then, in company with some others, walked out of town; but my comrade returned, having concluded to cross over in the packet boat, and went to inquire about it.   When I returned he told me it would leave that evening, and would save much time.   He spoke to our skipper, who was not willing to release us without our paying him the whole passage money, namely two ducatoons apiece.   Many words passed and hard enough they were on both sides, in which the skipper was very impertinent, yet not altogether in the wrong.   We went aboard, and his passion having subsided, we satisfied him with two ducats,[2] and took our goods to the packet boat.   We went ashore to enter our names, according to the custom; my comrade giving his acknowledged name, I was compelled to do the same.   We paid twelve shillings and sixpence each.   We went into another room to take fresh leave of our captain and mate, when there came a scoundrel to take down our names and examine our goods, as he said, and we were compelled to give the same names again, in order that they might agree with those given before; but he was a swindler and obtained from each of us another shilling, for he did not go on board to examine, although he could perhaps do so; we went quickly on board to look after our property.   It was

---

[1] The easternmost point of the Essex coast, just south of Harwich.
[2] Say four dollars instead of five.

about nine o'clock at night when we started; but as it was so calm we came outside without casting anchor, having a full moon and delightful weather. A sand reef stretches out into the sea from the before-mentioned little fort, inside of which the water is the deepest, being three and four fathoms at low water. It is shallowest in the middle, and level towards the west shore, having two fathoms of water or less. There are two lights in the town, which you bring in range, in order to sail in or out. The highest light stands most inside, and when that comes west of the lowest you are west of the gate or channel; and when it is east, you are east of the channel, and are on, or east of the reef.

3d, Thursday. The wind east-southeast, and we therefore sailed along the shore past Orfordness[1] into the sea. The course thence to the Maes is east by south, but we sailed for the most part east, and sometimes east by north. I thought our Friesland smack was at sea before evening, for the wind was better for her than for us, as the course from Orfordness to the Texel is east-northeast, which was a due side wind. It was also better for the Rotterdammer.

4th, Friday. The wind east-southeast and east by south, but still. We continued our course easterly, and sometimes a little more northerly. We threw the deep lead and had 18 fathoms of water. The latitude at noon was 52° 25'. I warned them that we were too low, and would come before Schevelingh.[2] This packet was so full of fleas that it was impossible for me to sleep. Every passenger who desired a berth had to pay five shillings for it, but we did not. There was such a hard rain in the night, accompanied by thunder and lightning, that we could not keep dry in the vessel below, for it leaked there as if it were open, or not much better. We had an English minister on board, who had been called to the English church at Rotterdam. He lay and prayed, and groaned, as hard and loud as if he would die of fear.[3] The wind shifting to the southwest we held it close.

---

[1] A point on the Suffolk coast, some dozen miles northeast of Harwich.

[2] Now Scheveningen, a famous watering-place near the Hague.

[3] The Rev. John Spademan, of Swayton, in Lincolnshire, was called to the English Presbyterian church at Rotterdam, as successor to Mr. Maden, who died in June, 1680.

5th, Saturday. When day came, and it had cleared up somewhat, we saw at nine o'clock the tower of Schevelingh directly east, or in front of us, and half an hour afterwards that of Gravesend [1] to the leeward, whereupon we were compelled to beat, in order to bring into the Maes, which we continued to do the whole day till midnight, before we reached Briel. Coming to the pier there, most of the passengers left for Maassluis, so as not to wait, but we could not do so on account of our goods.

6th, Sunday. As soon as it was day we put our goods on board the Rotterdam ferry-boat, which was to leave about nine o'clock. In the meanwhile we went to look about the place, and in the church, where a Cocceian preaches. After breakfast we went on board, but it was ten o'clock before we got off. We had to beat as far as Schiedam, where some royal yachts were lying, which had sailed with us from Gravesend, and had brought over the Prince Palatine, who had gone on to the Hague.[2] We were delayed somewhat here, in consequence of transferring some persons into another boat. We reached Rotterdam about two o'clock, and were informed that no boat carrying goods left for Amsterdam on Sundays; but that one left Delft at six o'clock, and we had time enough to go there. We left our goods on board the canal-boat for Delft, and started at three o'clock for that city, where we arrived at five, and learned that we had been misinformed, and that the boat from Delft to Amsterdam left daily at four o'clock. We had to go and lodge in a tavern for twenty-four hours. We went to church.

7th, Monday. In order not to be all day at Delft, we walked on to the Hague, and passed by the house of Sister d'Owerk.[3] I asked my comrade whether I should not inquire

---

[1] Gravesande lay some distance to the north of the mouth of the Maas, Briel at the south side of its main mouth, Maasluis a few miles up the river, on its northern bank.

[2] See p. 291, note 2.

[3] Mr. Murphy says, "my sister d'Owerk." But the French phrase here used, "ma seur d'Owerk," means sister in the religious sense. The lady designated is one of whom Penn speaks in his account of his tour in Germany and Holland in 1677. Reaching the Hague, "The first thing we did there, was to enquire out the Lady Overkirk, a Person of a Retired and Religious Character, separated from the publick worship of that Country" . . . "Sister of the Somer-

after our friends, and if perchance any of them were at the
Hague; but he would not consent. We returned to Delft at
two o'clock, and after dinner left at four for Amsterdam.

8th, Tuesday. Having passed through the night as best
we could, we arrived at five o'clock in the morning before the
gate of Amsterdam, which was opened at six, and we were
admitted. We went close by the house of M. Bardewits,[1]
where I was again inclined to go in, but my comrade not approving of it at the Hague, I abandoned the idea. We put up
at the inn where we lodged before our departure, and had our
goods brought there, paying five shillings freight for our goods
alone. We separated in order to do our business as speedily
as possible. I went to deliver all the letters, and my comrade
to sell the amber. We met on the Exchange at noon. When
I had delivered my letters, I went to the boat for Sneek,[2] to
inquire how it was at the House,[3] and when she would sail.
They would leave on Thursday evening; and all went well at
the House as far as they knew. My comrade, who had also
made inquiries, brought the same word. He told me also how
he had succeeded with the amber; that it was all spurious, and
was worth nothing. He therefore had determined to send it
back again just as we had received it. We went in the afternoon to perform some errands for the woman with whom we
had lodged at New York, delivering two beaver skins to her
husband's daughter.[4] And with this we consumed the day.

9th, Wednesday. This was a day of public prayer. We
had nothing more to do except to buy a large Bible for Mr.
Ephraim Hermans, according to our promise, with his spermaceti, which we did. It cost us twenty-eight guilders, because it was the last one of Ravesteyn's edition.[5] There was

dykes." *Works* (ed. 1726), I. 108, 107. By birth she was Isabella van Sommelsdyk. Her husband, Hendrik van Nassau, lord of Ouwerkerk, was captain of the
body-guard of William III., later in England his master of the horse, and for
thirty years his faithful follower and intimate.

[1] See p. 7, note 3.   [2] In Friesland, near Wieuwerd.
[3] The house of the Labadists at Wieuwerd.
[4] See p. 190, for this daughter of Jacob Hellekers by his first wife.
[5] The heirs of Paulus van Ravesteyn of Amsterdam had published in
1670 an octavo edition of the States-General ("authorized") Dutch version
of the Bible. In 1680 another, Remonstrant, version was published in the
same city.

a new edition in press at the Fish Market, at the place where we bought this one, upon the point of the gate as you go to the Post Office. We put it on board of the ship of which Jan Gorter was captain and which would leave in a month's time, and addressed it to Mr. Arnout de la Grange, to whom we also sent the amber with directions what to do with them. My comrade wrote to Ephraim, and also to Annetie Versluis.

10th, Thursday. We had our goods in good time in the boat. My comrade had also a basket with distilling glasses (retorts) in it, which he had bought. I went to Joannis van Ceulen, mathematician, who had made a new sea-atlas, a copy of which he had sent to the king of England, and also to the king of France.[1] It is a beautiful work; but he was surprised, after having corrected it so much as he had, that I should point out to him several errors. I endeavored to obtain a chart of Maryland, from Augustine Herman's draught, but could not find it here; nor could I in England.[2] At four o'clock we went on board of the boat. The wind was light and contrary, so we only drifted along. It was good weather. Our hearts gave thanks to God when we reflected through what ways He had conducted us, and how fatherly He had preserved us, and brought us here. There sprang up a breeze in the night, so that,

11th, Friday, in the morning, we passed by Urck,[3] and arrived at the Lemmer, where our goods were examined; but we had nothing to pay, and went on. It was so calm, with the wind contrary, that it was midnight before we arrived at Sneek. It was very dark and rainy, and we were fearful we could not find the way, else we should have gone to the House in the night.

12th, Saturday. Having given directions to our skipper, how he should send our goods after us, and having paid him, we went to speak to the boatman, who was to take the goods. It was about seven or half-past seven o'clock when we left Sneek on foot. After going some distance on our way, we passed through Bosum; and about ten o'clock reached our

---

[1] Grand Nouvel Atlas de la Mer (Amsterdam, 1680), by Johannes van Keulen.

[2] See p. 114, note 2.

[3] A small island in the Zuyder Zee. Lemmer is a village on the Friesland shore, from which one would go up by canal to Sneek, and so on to Wieuwerd.

house, where all arms and hearts were open to receive us, which they did with affection and tenderness, in the love of the Lord, who had been with those who had remained at home, and us who had travelled, all now brought together, and united by His mercy.   To Him be the power, and wisdom, and honor, and glory to all eternity.   Amen.

INDEX

INDEX

Aarsen, Francis, lord of Sommelsdyk, see Sommelsdyk, Cornelis van.

Abram, boatswain, 39.

Achter Kol, 91 n., 92, 93, 149, 160, 172, 178; proclamation against, 182; discharge of, 224; Gov. Carteret escorted to, 239, 243; authority over, 241.

Adams, Richard, 117, 117 n., 122; visit with, 123.

Africa, corsairs from, 38 n.

Albany, 169, 171; proposed visit to, 185, 188; arrival at, 198, 212; described, 216–217; beer of, 221; river navigable to, 225. *See also* Fort Orange.

Album Studiosorum Academiae Lugduno-Batavae, 168 n.

Aldborough, 287.

Alkmaar, 17, 17 n.

Alrichs, Peter, 104, 110, 144; information concerning, 104 n., 146–147; passport given by, 116; inquiry made by, 142; plantation of, 148, 148 n., 150.

Altona, in Holstein, 7, 97; Labadists at, xxiii, 7 n., 97 n.

Amazon River, 37.

Amboy, 162.

Amsterdam, packet, 4; arrival at, 5, 296; rule concerning pilots of ships of, 16, 295; ships from, 21.

Andersson, Måns, 116, 116 n.

Andros, Gov. Sir Edmund, 45 n.; recommendation of, 58 n.; appointment by, 106 n.; visits with, 167, 185, 187–188, 230–231; proclamation by, 182, 182 n.; leave taken of, 238; relations with Carteret, 239–244, 244 n.; government of, 248–249.

Ann, Cape, 258.

Antonis Neus (Anthony's Nose), headland, 225.

Apoquemene, 127, 130.

Appoquinimink, Creek 110, 110 n.

Aquackanonck (Passaic), 85 n., 86, 169, 170, 171; description of, 175; falls of, 176.

Arensius, Rev. Bernhardus, Lutheran minister, 217 n.

Armuyden, 45.

Arundell, Lord, defence under, 24 n.

Arundell of Trerice, Richard, Lord, governor of Pendennis castle, 29 n.

Autein, Loureins, Labadists' printer, 268 n.

Azores, islands, 38.

Bahamas, channel of, 37.

Baltimore, Lord (Cecilius Calvert, second lord), 132 n.; negotiations with, xix.

Baltimore, Lord (Charles Calvert, third lord), 132 n.

Baltimore, Lord (George Calvert), grant to, 132, 132 n.

Baltimore County Land Records, xx n.

Barbadoes, 28; run from, 52; oysters for, 54; ribbons for, 62; ship from, 231; trade with, 244–246; ship for, 253.

Bardewisch, *or* Bardowitz, merchant, conventicle of, 7, 7 n., 296.

Barents, *or* Barn, Islands, 64, 64 n.

Barkelo, Herrman van, description by, 113 n.

Barro, island, 278, 278 n., 279.

Bayard, Petrus, conveyance to, xx, 141 n.; convert to Labadism, xxiv; naturalization of, xxviii; visit from, 237; biographical information, 237 n.

Bayard, Thomas F., xx.

Beachy Head, 20.

Beacon Hill, 259.

Beaver, ship, 169, 169 n., 171, 190.

Beeren, *or* Barren Island, 51, 51 n.

Beerent, a guide, 149, 161, 162.

Bergen, 82, 82 n., 84, 84 n., 85, 165.

Berkeley, John, Lord, 66 n.; grant to, 154, 154 n.

Berkeley, Sir William, recall and death of, 132 n.–133 n.

Berkum, H. van, *De Labadie en de Labadisten,* xxiii n.

301